D1601142

THEORIES OF READING
IN DIALOGUE

An Interdisciplinary Study

Thomas W. McCormick

UNIVERSITY
PRESS OF
AMERICA

Lanham • New York • London

Copyright © **1988** by

University Press of America, ® **Inc.**

4720 Boston Way
Lanham, MD 20706

3 Henrietta Street
London WC2E 8LU England

British Cataloging in Publication Information Available

Library of Congress Cataloging-in-Publication Data

McCormick, Thomas W., 1949–
Theories of reading in dialogue : an interdisciplinary study /
Thomas W. McCormick.
p. cm.
Bibliography: p.
Includes index.
1. Reading—Philosophy. 2. Reading, Psychology of.
3. Phenomenological psychology. 4. Reading comprehension—
Philosophy. I. Title.
LB1050.2.M37   1988
428.4'01—dc 19   88–20821 CIP
ISBN 0–8191–7168–9 (alk. paper)
ISBN 0–8191–7169–7 (pbk. : alk. paper)

All University Press of America books are produced on acid-free paper.
The paper used in this publication meets the minimum requirements of
American National Standard for Information Sciences—Permanence of Paper
for Printed Library Materials, ANSI Z39.48–1984.

ACKNOWLEDGMENTS

I wish to express my sincere gratitude to the members of my doctoral committee, Doctors Tom Crowell, George Huttar, Lenore Langsdorf, Robert Reddick, and Harry Reeder, for their help and guidance in completing the initial form of this project. Each contributed in different and special ways to improve the quality (the quantity is my fault!) of my 1985 dissertation, of which this book is a revision.

The International Linguistic Center (Dallas, Texas) of the Summer Institute of Linguistics graciously allowed me to use their computers and LaserJet printer during the final stages of preparing this manuscript for the University Press of America. I am especially grateful for the support and assistance of Dr. Eugene Loos, Dr. Tom Crowell, and Jim Eliason.

Finally, my friends are to be thanked for their support and their prayers--especially Loren and Denise Laugtug, Steve and Kathy Bredehoeft, Jim and Barb Boelkins, Charles and Vicki Smith, and my best friend, Penny.

Tom McCormick
June 4, 1988

TABLE OF CONTENTS

PART I

CHAPTER 1: AN INTRODUCTION TO THEORIES OF READING

CHAPTER 2: AN INTRODUCTION TO PHENOMENOLOGICAL THEORIES OF READING

PART II

CHAPTER 7: A FURTHER DIALOGUE ON ISSUES OF COMPREHENSION

CHAPTER 8: CRITIQUE IN READING

CHAPTER 9: The role of play in reading

PART III

CHAPTER 10: The practice of literacy instruction

INTRODUCTION

A recent computer search was conducted in an effort to find information by or about the three phenomenologists of reading to be considered in this book. The search was done through ERIC--the Educational Resources Information Center--which indexes approximately a quarter millon documents and 800 journals related to "programs, research and development efforts, and related information that can be used in developing more effective educational programs" (The national institute of education n.d.:2). The results: Paul Ricoeur, zero entries; Wolfgang Iser, zero entries; and Georges Poulet, two entries--one in Spanish, and one in German. When the scope of the search was expanded to other authors in related areas (notably, philosophy and literary criticism), who have written significant works on the topic of reading, the results were scarely different: Jacques Derrida;, zero entries; Jonathan Culler, zero entries; Roland Barthes, one entry; Norman Holland, one entry; David Bleich, one entry; and Stanley Fish, three entries.

On the other hand, there is almost no reference in the above-mentioned authors to the host of reading researchers who fill the files of ERIC.[1]

Whatever the reason may be for this failure to interact, such a failure appears to me lamentable indeed. My purpose in this book, therefore is to develop reading theory by bringing these two perspectives on the subject of reading into dialogue. It is hoped that this work will, to some extent, contribute to the "call for theory" which Sticht, et al. issue (1974:6). The problem, as they see it, is that the number of empirical studies has grown larger and larger, and the number of models or partial models continues to proliferate,[2] but the "empirical data are not adequately organized" (Sticht, et al. 1974:7) due to a lack of theory. Similarly, Kintsch (1976:10), who highlights the impact of theory on practise:

---

[1] Iser's (1978) references to Frank Smith's *Understanding Reading* (1971, first edition) is a notable exception, though his quoting of Smith is occasionally out of context. For example, Iser (1978:119) quotes Smith's discussion of the role of distinctive features in letter identification to support his exposition of the reader's "synthetizing [sic] activity" at the macro-level of textual structures. That the micro-processes involved in letter identification might be the same as (or analogous to) the macro-processes of text processing is itself a highly significant point; but Iser does not explicitly thematize it as such. This example well illustrates the different interests of the two classes of researchers sketched above, the potential for a fruitful dialogue, and the undeveloped form of the very few points of contact which do exist.

[2] Geyer (1971) reports more than 40 such models; Gibson and Levin (1975:12), at least 30. Today there are even more.

ix

I conclude . . . that practise in reading instruction
is largely intuitive, relying upon "experience" and
program evaluation studies, and only to a small
extent upon basic research findings. The reason
for this undesirable state of affairs is, in my
opinion, the lack of theory.

Chapters 1-2 (Part I) introduce the partners of the dialogue. I will
call the first group "the reading researchers" or "the reading specialists."
This group is made up of educational psychologists, cognitive psychologists,
instructional psychologists, linguists, and psycholinguists. The second group
consists of three phenomenologists of reading. These three are Paul
Ricoeur, Wolfgang Iser, and Georges Poulet.

Because there is very little evidence that either side is significantly
aware of the other, Part I presents a brief but thorough introduction to
both sides. It is hoped that after reading Part I the interested reader will
not only have sufficient background for the discussions of Part II (chapters
4-9), but will also recognize the difficulty which has kept these two "camps"
relatively ignorant of one another. It is also hoped that by presenting these
two perspectives with their different interests and methodologies back-to-
back, the reader will realize that, in fact, these two groups do have much in
common and have much to contribute to one another.

Chapters 3-9 (Part II) will bring these two perspectives into
interaction with one another, first in general terms, and second, with regard
to four questions which emerge as significant issues in reading theory.
These four questions are (1) What is meaning?, (2) What is
comprehension?, (3) What is the role of critique in reading?, and (4) What
is the role of play in reading? In response to each of these questions I will
explore the resources of the different perspectives. In the process, central
aspects of the theories of the reading specialists will be subjected to
philosophical scrutiny, and in most cases, found wanting. Similarly, I will
also show the need for further development in the phenomenological
theories of reading. Some of this needed development is pursued in Part
II.

Chapter 10 (Part III) concludes this study with an application and
summary of the theoretical points gleaned from Part II.

It is hoped that not only will this study advance reading theory (and
practice), but also that it might stimulate further recognition of the value of
these researchers, further dialogue, and further discoveries about that very
significant human activity, reading.[3]

---

[3] This book is a revised version of my 1985 dissertation submitted to the Humanities
Department of the University of Texas at Arlington.

CHAPTER 1

An Introduction to Theories of Reading

Though there are many models of reading, reading theorists classify them into three types. These three are usually termed (1) bottom-up theories, emphasizing the written text, (2) top-down theories, which emphasize the contribution of the reader, and (3) interactive theories, which recognize both bottom-up and top-down processes interacting simultaneously throughout the reading process. In these characterizations it may be helpful to think of the "top" as the reader, and the "bottom" as the written text. The basic controversy among these theories concerns the location of the source of control in the reading act: Is it the text, or the reader, which controls the reading process, or both? This three-fold characterization of reading theories will serve as my basic organizational strategy which recurs frequently throughout the discussions of Part II.

1.1   Bottom-up theories

The bottom-up approach to reading theory and practice is perhaps the "common sense" or naive understanding of reading. Though I say "naive" I do not mean to discredit the insights of this theory which has been held by very respectable scholars. The fundamental insight is that reading is a process of responding to a printed text and essentially consists in decoding the graphic symbols to arrive at the meaning. As Durkin (1980:7-8) puts it, in this model ". . . words are processed individually and sequentially and meaning derives directly from them." Alternate names given in the literature for this model are "text-driven" (e.g. Durkin 1980), "data-driven" (e.g. R. Anderson 1977), and outside-in (Smith 1982). Here we look first at the theories of the linguists Leonard Bloomfield (e.g. 1942a, b) and Charles C. Fries (e.g. 1962), and then at the theory of Philip B. Gough (e.g. 1976).

1.1.1   The reading theory of Leonard Bloomfield

Bloomfield became interested in reading instruction in the 1930s when his son was about to begin school (Moe 1976:240; cf. Bloomfield and Barnhart 1961:3, 9). In 1938, he handed a copy of his reading system to Clarence Barnhart who would later see this reading system through to publication after Bloomfield's death. "Bloomfield" says Barnhart, "told me that he had devised the system because the methods used in the schools were non-scientific in nature and ignored the fundamental principles of the scientific study of language developed during the last 150 years" (Bloomfield and Barnhart 1961:9). As a "linguistic system," Bloomfield's approach "separates the problem of the study of word-form from the study of word-meaning" (Bloomfield and Barnhart 1961:9). Bloomfield reasoned that since a child enters school with a basic command of his spoken language, the basic task of learning to read is the learning of "the printed equivalents for his oral vocabulary" (Chall 1967:24). Bloomfield himself

1

describes reading, in what Barnhart takes as "his definition" (Bloomfield and Barnhart 1961:10), as follows:

> In order to read alphabetic writing one must have an ingrained habit of producing the phonemes of one's language when one sees the written marks which conventionally represent these phonemes. A well-trained reader, of course, for the most part reads silently, but we shall do better for the present to ignore this fact, as we know that the child learns first to read aloud.
>
> The accomplished reader of English, then, has an overpracticed and ingrained habit of uttering one phoneme of the English language when he sees the letter *p*, another phoneme when he sees the letter *i*, another when he sees the letter *n*, still another when he sees the letter *m*, still another when he sees the letter *d*, and so on. In this way, he utters the conventionally accepted word when he sees a combination of letters like *pin, nip, pit, tip, nit, dip, dim, mid.* What is more, all readers will agree as to the sounds they utter when they see unconventional combinations, such as *pid, nin, pim, mip, nid, nim, mim.* It is this habit which we must set up in the child who is to acquire the art of reading. If we pursue any other course, we are merely delaying him until he acquires this habit in spite of our bad guidance (Bloomfield and Barnhart 1961:10, 26).

The first task of reading, then, is learning the code or the alphabetic principle by which "written marks . . . conventionally represent . . . phonemes" (Bloomfield and Barnhart 1961:26). The meaning of the text is expected to come naturally as the code is broken based on the reader's prior knowledge of words, their meanings, and the syntactical patterns of his language. Clearly there is an implicit understanding here of the relation between speech and writing which Bloomfield makes explicit in his "Linguistics and Reading" articles (1942, 1970) and also in his introductory essay to *Let's Read* (1961:19-42).

Bloomfield clearly favored the priority of speech over writing. For him, "Writing is merely an attempt, more or less systematic, at making permanent visual records of language utterance" (Bloomfield 1942; 1970:385); and again, "Writing is merely a device for recording speech" (Bloomfield and Barnhart 1961:20). Speech is considered an ancient phenomenon and writing, in comparison, "something artificial and relatively modern" (Bloomfield and Barnhart 1961:20). Writing is closely related to "drawing pictures to represent a message" and in fact "seems in every instance to have grown out of *picturing*" (Bloomfield 1970:385). The

important implication which Bloomfield draws is that since "picturing . . . is
. . . not based upon language at all" (since one who knows the conventions
of the drawing can understand the picture even if he does not understand
the language), the "art of writing is not a part of language" (Bloomfield
1942; 1970:384). Based on such a view of written discourse, it is quite
understandable that Bloomfield would conceive of reading as decoding
writing into speech.

1.1.2   The reading theory of Charles C. Fries

Charles Fries, in agreement with Bloomfield, defines reading as
essentially a decoding process. Fries was certainly aware of what was in his
time termed a "broader concept of reading." That conception included
"the cultivation of a whole array of techniques involved in understanding,
thinking, reflecting, imagining, judging, evaluating, analyzing, . . . reasoning,
and in making emotional and social judgment" (Fries 1962:118). However,
he considered such activities as the "use of reading" and not as constituting
"the reading process" (Fries 1962:118). This distinction rests on the fact
that

> Every one of the abilities listed may be developed
> and has been achieved by persons who could not
> read (Fries 1962:118).

As with Bloomfield, this approach "assumes the primacy of language
and talk" (Fries 1962:xi). Consequently, writing is

> . . . the substituting of patterns of graphic shapes
> to represent the language signals of a code for the
> patterns of sound waves that have been learned as
> representing the same language signals;

> . . . and reading is the responding . . . to the
> language signals represented by patterns of
> graphic shape as fully as he has already learned to
> respond to the same language signals of his code
> represented by patterns of auditory shapes (Fries
> 1962:119).

The "only essential difference," then, between reading and listening is "the
means of connection to the human nervous system" (Fries 1962:119):   in
the former case, the stimulation of the nerves in the eye; and in the latter,
the stimulation of the nerves in the ear (Fries 1962:119).[1] Fries, though, is
quick to clarify his position by noting that merely pronouncing words--
"word calling" (Fries 1962:120)--is neither reading nor talking. Instead, the

---

[1] However, in distinction from Bloomfield, the decoding of visual/graphic shapes need not
be mediated by the sounds.   In fact, the graphic shapes substitute for the sound waves,
and therefore seem to replace them.

response to the graphic sign must also "[elicit] a meaning response" (Fries 1962:120) if it is in fact reading.

This relation of "meaning" to "decoding" calls for further clarification in the reading theory of Fries. In reply to Jeanne Chall--who evidently had inquired of Fries as to the proper classification of his approach according to a decoding/meaning dichotomy--Fries writes (in a letter to Chall dated July 8, 1966, quoted in Chall 1967:343):

> Our approach is certainly *not* a phonic approach.
> It is *not* an approach that gives primary emphasis
> to decoding . . . we would have to insist that our
> type of approach gives primary emphasis to
> reading for *meanings*.

> Notice also that we have said "reading for
> meanings" for we are concerned from the very
> beginning with not only situation meanings, but
> with the lexical meanings of the words, the
> structural meanings of the sentences, and the
> cumulative meanings of the succession of
> sentences as connected by sequence signals into a
> unit . . . .

> If you have to classify it, put it first with
> "reading for meanings," with special emphasis on
> the word *reading* and on the plural of *meanings*.

However, Chall and almost[2] all others continue to classify the Fries program as one which emphasizes "decoding" rather than "meaning" (cf. for example Chall 1967:29, 31, 343; Moe 1976:241; Dechant 1976:47-49; Gibson and Levin 1975:284). Let us examine Fries' model of reading to see why this evaluation continues in spite of his protests.

Fries presents his view of reading most clearly in chapter four of *Linguistics and Reading* entitled "The Nature of the Reading Process." There he divides the process of learning to read into three stages. In considering Fries' view of reading it is necessary to distinguish between the reading process itself and the process of learning to read. From a consideration of the stages of learning to read, we will glean what Fries says about the process of reading itself. The first stage of learning to read is the "transfer" stage "during which the child is learning to transfer from the auditory signs for language signals, which he has already learned, to a set of visual signs for the same signals" (Fries 1962:132). During this stage the reader learns to "respond quickly to the patterns of graphic shapes and the correlating portions of the language signal they represent . . ." (Fries

---

[2] The only possible exception I am aware of is C.C. Fries' son P.H. Fries; cf. chapter 4.1.

1962:120). Though there are two stages yet to describe, Fries already identifies this first "transfer" stage with reading proper. Says he,

> The process of learning to read . . . is *the process of transfer* from the auditory signs . . . to the new visual signs . . . . Learning to read, therefore, means developing a *considerable range of habitual responses* to a specific set of patterns of graphic shapes (Fries 1962:120-121).

Reading, then, is at least a set of habitual responses (to graphic shapes). This is the characteristic "decoding" emphasis by which others classify his approach.

Because ". . . [most] written material contains less of the language signals than does talk" (Fries 1962:130), and since reading means responding to the "graphic shapes as fully as he has already learned to respond to . . . auditory shapes" (Fries 1962:119), the reader must supply ". . . the portions of the oral signals that are not represented in the graphic signs" (Fries 1962:130). The second stage of learning to read is the "productive" stage (Chall 1967:31), and it is here that the missing signals are supplied. I propose that it is with this stage that much of the disagreement between Fries and his critics is generated. Thus the second stage will receive close attention.

With the second stage the responses to the visual patterns become "automatic" (Fries 1962:132) or "unconscious" (Chall 1967:31) and "the cumulative comprehension of the meanings signalled enable the reader to supply those portions of the signals which are not in the graphic representations themselves" (Fries 1962:132). The point of special interest here is the inference that Fries considers the student already a "reader" prior to this stage--I take "the reader" in the preceding quote to be a proper designation for the one learning to read *prior to* his supplying what is "not in the graphic representations themselves." Thus Fries continues to emphasize that "Learning to read, therefore, means developing a *considerable range of habitual responses* to a specific set of patterns of graphic shapes" (Fries 1962:121).

It must be admitted, however, that there is an ambiguity in Fries' use of the terms "reading" and "reader," especially with regard to this second stage of learning to read. There is, then, also the related confusion about what reading itself is. On the one hand, it seems reading need not involve decoding to sound since in reading the graphic shapes *substitute for* the visual. Fries even emphasizes that in listening and reading "The message is the same; the language code is the same; the language signals are the same . . ." (Fries 1962:119; repeated by Fries for emphasis 1962:132). On the other hand, writing contains fewer signals than the oral, and it is ". . . the portions of the oral signals . . . not represented in the graphic signs" (Fries 1962:130) which reading must supply. How can precisely those "portions of the oral signals" be supplied if there is not

5

some necessary decoding to the oral required in reading? It is possible, I suppose, for signals which are not themselves oral to be supplied, and just those signals which would be present if the message were oral, and are not present because the message is not oral. But (1) this makes the oral the standard; (2) given a unique message, how would a reader know what signals would be present if the message were oral unless there were some oral actualization, at least in the imagination;[3] and (3) Fries does use the terminology "the portions of the *oral signals*" (Fries 1962:130; emphasis added). Each point supports the claims of Fries' critics that his position is decoding in emphasis.

A related confusion (if not an inconsistency) is how "the *same* signals" (Fries 1962:119; emphasis added) in talking/listening, writing/reading can differ, with the written being fewer than the oral (Fries 1962:130ff).

Further, because the written form has fewer signals than the oral, it is difficult to see (as Fries claims) that reading is simply a matter of learning new habitual responses (to the visual rather than to auditory signals) of the same kind involved in listening. The problem is compounded (for Fries' view) by the fact that ". . . the cultivation of a whole array of techniques involved in understanding, thinking, reflecting, imagining, . . . [etc.]" (Fries 1962:118) is seemingly relegated to uses of reading, rather than to the learning of reading proper. It would seem, though, that many of these skills are needed in reading to a greater extent than otherwise employed in oral language comprehension, and even more pointedly, different skills are needed in reading due to the differences between oral and written language which Fries notes.

Finally, it can be readily admitted that with Fries' description of reading as supplying missing signals, as active responding (Fries 1962:131), and "carrying forward . . . a complete cumulative comprehension" (Fries 1962:131), a top-down emphasis is present. But it must also be admitted that this top-down emphasis is present in a rather undeveloped, highly constrained, and often confusing (if not inconsistent) form. Because of these unclarities, it is not difficult for me to see why so many classify Fries as decoding in emphasis: That which is most clearly and explicitly developed is reading as "a passive process of receiving meanings" (Fries 1962:130f) by means of habitual responses. To be fair to both sides, I conclude that (1) Fries is bottom-up in emphasis, but that (2) he is not exclusively bottom-up in emphasis.

The third stage completes the process of learning to read. It is the "imaginative" stage (Chall 1967:31) when "reading is used . . . in the acquiring and developing of experience--when reading stimulates the vivid imaginative realization of vicarious experience" (Fries 1962:132). Though

---

[3] But "imaginative realization of vicarious experience" (Fries 1962:132) is a third stage "use of reading."

6

Fries does consider this a stage in the process of learning to read, note that here "reading is used" and that he has already distinguished "uses of reading" from "the reading process" (Fries 1962:118).

1.1.3 The reading theory of Philip B. Gough

Philip Gough originally presented his paper "One Second of Reading" in 1971 at a conference on "The Relationships between Speech and Learning to Read."[4] Since then this paper has been much anthologized and discussed. No doubt the reason is that in the face of a climate of opinion holding overwhelmingly to a contrary view, Gough had cogently reasserted the older and discredited "bottom-up" model of reading.

Gough "posits a strictly serial process: letter-by-letter visual analysis, leading to positive recognition of every word through phonemic encoding" (Wildman and Kling 1978-79:154). In this model, lexical, syntactic and semantic rules are applied to the phonemic output which itself has been decoded from the print. The essential points of the model are that these processes all occur unidirectionally and in very short time intervals; e.g. letters are processed at the rate of 10 msec. each. As Gough says,

> In the model I have outlined, the Reader is not a guesser. From the outside, he appears to go from print to meaning as if by magic. But I have contended that this is an illusion, that he really plods through the sentence, letter by letter, word by word (1972:354).[5]

Though the different theorists differ in detail, there is a more or less coherent perspective which can be distilled with regard to the "bottom-up"

---

[4] The entire conference proceedings are found in Kavanagh and Mattingly 1972, and Gough's paper is on pages 331-358.

[5] The LaBerge-Samuels model rests on a similar basis. Though they stress the role of attention at the various stages of both learning and processing, and emphasize the development of automaticity in associating various units processed (e.g. the phonological with the semantic), they still "view reading acquisition as a series of skills, regardless of how it appears to the fluent reader" (LaBerge and Samuels 1976:574).

In this judgment of LaBerge and Samuels' work as bottom-up, Rumelhart 1977, Wildman and Kling 1978-79, and Durkin 1980 agree. Lovett (1981:10), however, considers this model to be interactive. Such a disagreement makes the further point that the classification of reading theorists is a matter about which there is sometimes significant disagreement and discussion. The most controversial judgments which I have made are with regard to Fries and Goodman. Some would classify Fries as top-down or interactive and Goodman as transactive.

models of reading. This perspective is summarized by R. Anderson (1977:5) as follows:

> There is a series of discrete processing stages each corresponding to a level of linguistic analysis. Analysis proceeds from the most primitive low-order level to the most complex high-order level. As a first step, feature analyzers are brought to bear to discriminate horizontal, vertical, and oblique line segments; open and closed loops; intersection with a horizontal plane; and so on. From these, letters are identified. Strings of letters are analyzed into clusters with morphophonemic significance. Words are recognized. Strings of words are parsed into phrase constituents. Word meanings are retrieved from the subjective lexicon. Eventually a semantic interpretation of a sentence is produced. Sentence meaning is conceived to be the deterministic product of the lower-order levels of analysis and, presumably, the meaning of a text is a concatenation of the meanings of its component sentences.

In what follows, this "bottom-up" model is first contradicted by the "top-down" theorists, then re-integrated into the theory of reading by those supporting an interactive theory. In anticipation of this latter view, I concur with R. Anderson (1977:7) that with regard to the comprehension, learning, and recall of texts, it is "to assert the obvious, [that] the processes involved in analyzing the print itself are also crucial."

1.2   Top-down theories of reading

The second class of reading theories which I review here typically has been called "top-down." Alternative names for this model found in the literature are the "hypothesis test" model (Wildman and Kling 1978-79:155-159), the "concept-driven" model (Durkin 1980:7; R. Anderson 1977:5), and the "inside-out" model (Smith 1982:193; 1979:31).

> The essence of these models is that analysis of the sensory signal begins centrally, rather than peripherally, with the derivation by the listener/reader of a hypothesis regarding the information in the sensory buffer. From this hypothesis, the listener/reader generates a list of distinctive sensory features that such information would have if it was present.
>
> These features are then compared to the externally generated features, resulting in a match

(perception and comprehension) or a mismatch (generation of new hypotheses until a match is obtained) (Wildman and Kling 1978-89:155).

The text is not read "squiggle by squiggle," but rather the reader samples the text to either "confirm or reject hypotheses about its content" (R. Anderson 1977:5). At the "top" here are the conceptual hypotheses which are generated by the reader based on his knowledge of both the world and language (Durkin 1980:7); at the "bottom" is the print of the written text.

The two recognized proponents of this approach are Frank Smith, a journalist turned reading researcher, and Kenneth S. Goodman, a reading specialist presently at the University of Arizona. Here I focus on the work of Frank Smith since he announces himself an advocate of this approach while Goodman, contrary to what most critics say about him, classifies himself in the third category of theories, the interactive theories (cf. e.g. Goodman 1981:477; 1979b:658f; 1973:15).[6] I will, however, draw on Goodman occasionally to clarify points from Smith's presentation and to document his points of agreement with Smith (Smith considers himself in basic agreement with Goodman; cf. Smith 1982:232).

1.2.1   The top-down reading theory of Frank Smith

Our first concern in presenting Smith's top-down model will be to compare it to the bottom-up models presented in the previous section. First I show the points of agreement; then points of disagreement.

1.2.1.1 Areas of agreement with bottom-up theorists

The only point of agreement of any significance which I can find is that access to the print is a necessary part of reading. Indeed this is a most basic agreement; perhaps trivial, but a point that does need to be made since some critics have misunderstood Smith because of his strong emphasis on the contribution of the reader. However, Smith (1982:193) says

> . . . no top-downer would want to claim that reading is not an interaction with the text in any case. Just because meaning has to be brought by the reader does not mean that *any* meaning will do.

Indeed, "Access to visual information is a necessary part of reading but it is not sufficient" (Smith 1982:10). As already intimated in the opening paragraphs of this section, Smith does give a priority to the "nonvisual information" which the reader already possesses. But here, in order to emphasize his agreement with the bottom-up approach, we note that for Smith "Reading always involves a combination of visual and nonvisual

---

[6] Smith too conceives of reading as "interactive" as we shall see below, cf. Smith (1982:11).

information. It is an interaction between a reader and a text" (Smith 1982:11; emphasis omitted); and one aspect of this "nonvisual information" is knowing how to read in the sense of recognizing print (Smith 1982:10). Beyond this, and even within what has already been said, there are distinct differences between Smith and what was presented in the first section. Three main areas of disagreement will be noted in what follows: (1) Reading is not decoding written language to spoken language; (2) Reading does not involve the processing of each letter and each word; and (3) Reading is a matter of bringing meaning to print, not extracting meaning from print.

1.2.1.2 Areas of disagreement with bottom-up theorists

Contrary to the bottom-up theorists, Smith rejects the notion that a reader must first decode written language to speech for comprehension to occur. Says Smith,

> It is not necessary to "say" what a written word is before we can comprehend its meaning. We no more need to say a written word is "cat" in order to understand it then we need to say that a particular animal is a cat in order to recognize it (1982:136).

Here his point is that we can learn to recognize words just as we learn to recognize any other of the thousands of objects in our world; not through the mediation of spoken language, but directly from its meaning (in a sense we will clarify later). Smith, however, goes on to make his point even stronger:

> . . . it is neither necessary *nor possible* for writing to be comprehended in this way [by a process of "decoding" written symbols into speech]. Instead written language must be directly attacked for meaning (1975:184; emphasis added).

Here his argument is that though it is possible to "decode to sound," this process "is only possible through the intermediary of meaning" (Smith 1975:180).

> In other words, it is only by understanding what you read that you can read aloud or to yourself ....
> The sound must come last and can be dispensed with altogether (Smith 1975:180).

Smith supports this claim with four observations about the differences between spoken and written language which are worth rehearsing here. First, we do get a type of meaning from the visual properties of print and not from sound. Otherwise, how could we know that there is improper spelling in such a sentence as *"The none tolled hymn*

10

. . ." (Smith 1975:181)? If meaning were accessible only through the sounds of the words, there would be no basis for saying that misspelling exists here. Nor is there any basis upon which to account for the difference in ease of reading between the misspelled and the properly spelled versions of such a sentence. Second, some words, such as "read" and "winds" are differentiated in speech, but not in writing. Our articulation of such sentences as

He winds his watch while the children read.

I read *yesterday that the winds would be strong*
(Smith 1975:181).

depends then on the meaning which precedes their spoken counterparts.[7] Third, meaning in speech is often conveyed by intonation; but in writing, the meaning must be understood before the proper intonation can be produced. And, fourth,

> It is not true that we need the alphabet to help us remember the names or meanings of all the written words we recognize. We can all recognize and recall many thousands of words in our spoken language vocabulary, and many thousands of different faces and animals and plants and objects in our visual world, without any such clues. Why should this fantastic memorizing capacity suddenly fail in the case of reading (Smith 1978:182)?

Smith, then, concludes

> . . . that any written language is read as Chinese is read--directly for meaning--and the fact that some written languages are also more or less related to the sound system of a spoken language is quite coincidental as far as the reader is concerned" (1982:154).

Does Smith then have any use for phonics--the sounding out of words by letter-sound correspondences which are taught? Yes, "Phonics will in fact prove of use--provided you have a rough idea of what a word is in the first place" (Smith 1978:57). This "use" is the elimination of alternatives (Smith 1982:136-144). For instance, if you know (or guess) that "horse" is some kind of animal, then phonics can help to eliminate "cat," "dog," "pig," etc.; but attempting to choose the proper pronunciation of

---

[7] Though in this case a knowledge of syntax can be appealed to to disambiguate the pronunciations, Smith elsewhere shows that syntax can itself sometimes be ambiguous, with the only recourse for disambiguation being meaning. For example, is the following sentence active or passive: "Father was seated by the bishop" (Smith 1978:74)?

"ho" from the "11 possible answers" in English will be a difficult, if not futile exercise (Smith 1982:139). Again Smith emphasizes that such a strategy as "sounding it out" is in fact dependent on meaning in the first place. Says he, "Children learn phonics through reading, they do not learn to read through phonics" (1975:184). He illustrates this by noting that phonics only works if the meaning of the word is already known in advance (1978:57; 1982:139). Further, Smith notes that the use of phonics is neither the only, nor is it the best strategy for word identification. The usual strategy of a fluent reader when confronted with an unknown word is first to skip it and count on redundancies to supply the meaning; second, to guess at the meaning from context; third, to use analogy with known words; and fourth, to use phonics. A fifth strategy, which Smith thinks is likely the most natural for the new reader, can also be employed: Ask someone else what the word is. Thus Smith concludes that phonics does have a use, but notes that it is only one of the possible strategies, which, however, is neither the best nor the most natural. Finally, he notes that even the use of phonics is dependent on prior meaning.

The second major area of disagreement between Smith's view and that of the bottom-up theorists is that reading is "not a consequence of reading words and letters" (Smith 1978:123). According to Goodman (1976c:59) the notion that

> . . . being careful to perceive, recognize, and
> process each letter or each word is necessary to
> successful reading . . . [is an] atheoretical
> commonsense [notion that is] totally inappropriate
> to understanding the reading process.

However, both Smith and Goodman acknowledge that "fluent readers can . . . identify letters, identify words and comprehend meanings" (Smith 1978:123; cf. Goodman 1973:21). Their point, though, is that "these are independent aspects of reading; they [the fluent readers] cannot and do not accomplish them at the same time" (Smith 1978:123); and further, that reading for meaning is not only "the best strategy," but an alternative which is not dependent on word and letter identification (Smith 1978:123). In fact, Smith claims that "normal reading *demands* comprehension prior to and even without the identification of words" (Smith 1978:119). This claim is supported by several experimental facts. First, if letters are arranged into meaningful words, twice as many can be recognized in the same time as a nonmeaningful sequence of letters. Second, if a reader is "making sense" of a passage, less than one half of the "distinctive features" of letters are actually needed and used (Smith 1978:119f). Indeed the "bottleneck" between the eyes and the brain is so narrow that "at least three-quarters of the visual information available in text must actually be ignored" (Smith 1982:12). Third, the brain, which "determines what we see and how we see it" (Smith 1982:25), does not see everything in front of the eyes, nor can it see anything immediately in front of the eyes, nor does it

12

receive information from the eyes continuously (Smith 1982:25).[8] Coupled with the normal reading times of experimental subjects, these facts lead to the conclusion that reading must be selective and dependent on nonvisual information: The brain simply does not have the time to process all the information in front of the eyes. This disagreement with the bottom-up theorists, then, is based in and supported by experimental psycholinguistics.[9]

The third area of disagreement between Smith and bottom-up theorists has already been implicit in the preceding presentation. To make it explicit: Meaning is brought to print, not derived from print. Clearly, for Smith, ". . . what transpires behind the reader's eyes, in the reader's brain, makes a far greater contribution to reading than the print in front of the reader's face" (Smith 1982:4). Both Smith and Goodman quote with approval the psychologist Paul Kolers, "Reading is only incidentally visual" (Smith 1982:12; Goodman 1969:17). "Even when the text is quite new and unfamiliar" (Smith 1982:9), the "nonvisual information" is more important, constituting "the core of reading" (Smith 1982:12).

These three areas of disagreement effectively demonstrate that a substantially different theory of reading is presented by Smith than by those represented in the previous section. Though this comparison between Smith and "bottom-up" theorists has offered an introduction to Smith's view and a sketch of his theory, we now need to go beyond such a fragmentary sketch to a positive presentation of the theoretical framework which supports Smith's position.

1.2.1.3 A positive presentation of Smith's position

Smith operates from two theoretical orientations: information-processing psychology and psycho-linguistics.

> The underlying theoretical perspective of information-processing psychology is that the primary function and activity of the human brain--at least with respect to its commerce with the outside world--is actively to seek, select, acquire,

---

[8] Cf. Smith (1982:26-36) for the physiological basis of these statements.

[9] Smith is well aware that we may think we see words when we read, and readily admits that we obviously *"look at* words" (Smith 1978:118). This "looking at," however, is "in the same sense that we look at the paper they are printed on, . . . we need be no more *aware* of the words than we are of the paper if we are concerned with meaning" (Smith 1978:118). Quite emphatically, then, *"When we identify meaning in text--it is not necessary to identify individual words"* (Smith 1978:117). Obviously the reader does need to look at the print and it is the print which plays the decisive role in the acquisition of specific meaning. Smith's point, though, is that it is not words as words which serve this role. Rather, "We can make sense of text directly from the distinctive features of the print. . ." (Smith 1978:117). (Soon I will explain just what Smith means by "distinctive features.")

outside world--is actively to seek, select, acquire, organize, store and, at appropriate times, retrieve and utilize information about the world (Smith 1975:2).

Psycholinguistics, for Smith,

> . . . is an interdisciplinary field of study where psychology and linguistics intersect. It is concerned with how individuals learn, use and comprehend language (1975:3).

These two disciplines, then, form the background and framework for Smith's theory of reading.

Though Smith is hesitant to give a definition of reading, he is nonetheless quite clear as to its basis. Says he, "Reading is seen as . . . based on *comprehension* . . ." (1982:3). Further, "To understand comprehension theoretically is of crucial importance in the study of reading, for teachers as well as for researchers" (Smith 1982:15).

Smith says,

> I shall refer to comprehension in reading as a matter of "making sense" of text, of relating written language to what we know already and to what we want to know (1982:15).

And yet comprehension in reading is not unique; it is simply a species of all comprehension, specially adapted to the peculiarity of printed matter (Smith 1982:161). Thus I discuss comprehension in general first; then return later to comprehension in reading.

Smith's view of comprehension

Comprehension in general *"means relating new experience to the already known"* (Smith 1978:10). It is "not a quantity of anything and therefore cannot be measured"; it is "a state" (Smith 1978:15). It is "not the opposite of ignorance," but "the opposite of confusion" (Smith 1978:15). Simply put, "We comprehend the situation that we are in if we are not confused by it "1978:15).

Note now the interlocking concepts which form the basis of Smith's views. Comprehension is the lack of confusion; lack of confusion is "a condition where no uncertainty exists" (Smith 1978:15); *"information"* is that which *"reduces uncertainty by the elimination of alternatives"* (Smith 1978:14), and

14

*Comprehension is the condition of having cognitive
questions answered, the absence of uncertainty . . .*
Comprehension exists, in other words, when there
is no residual uncertainty (Smith 1975:34).

Central to this approach is that only that which answers the questions being
asked counts as information. The visual information from the text is
certainly needed for reading but it is "just the beginning" (Smith 1982:22);
in a sense "reading is what you do with visual information" (Smith
1982:22). The information is "the basis upon which a meaning is
interpreted; an experience constructed or the exploration of an idea
launched" (Smith 1982:23). However, even the reception of visual
information is filtered by the brain of the perceiver which makes a far
greater contribution to reading than the print itself (Smith 1982:4). In
short, reading--from reception of visual information to comprehension--is
"purposeful, selective, [and] *anticipatory"* (Smith 1982:3). Consequently,
comprehension is "relative to the knowledge and purpose of the individual
receiving it" (Smith 1982:16) and "specific . . . to the precise nature of the
individual's uncertainty" (Smith 1975:34). It is at this point that the
information-processing model intersects with psycho-linguistics.

Smith's model of comprehension, then, goes "behind the reader's
eyes" (Smith 1982:4), to the "cognitive structures in our heads" (Smith
1975:10f). The "already known" to which new experience is related is
contained, says Smith, in our heads as a theory of the world. Smith wants
to suggest "that the theory of the world that we have in our heads is in fact
exactly like a theory in science; it has the same kind of composition and
serves precisely the same function" (Smith 1978:11). Three specific
functions are noted (Smith 1978:11f):

1. It provides a useful summary of everything learned.

2. It influences how we perceive and interpret new data.

3. It is a fruitful source of useful hypotheses about the future.

Contrary to scientific theories, though, the theory of the world in our
head is "implicit knowledge." It serves as the basis of our comprehension
by generating questions, predictions, and plans based on what is already
known. However,

. . . the questions we ask in reading are almost invariably implicit;
we are not generally aware of the questions that we ask or even that we
are asking them (Smith 1978:126).

Our theory, then, precedes our actual experience, which in turn
either confirms our predictions, or forces an alteration in our theory. And
"making sense" of the world, i.e. comprehending, is accomplished "by
interpreting our interactions with the world in the light of our theory"
(Smith 1982:54). In short, predictions are the questions we ask the world,

15

based on our theory, and comprehension is receiving the answers to these questions (Smith 1982:68; 1978:85).

The question might then arise, what motivates this process of theory construction and modification? Smith's answer is direct: The ability to construct a theory of the world is "innate" (Smith 1978:88) and the ability to predict and learn is "a natural process, . . . a natural part of being alive and growing up" (Smith 1978:87). Such is the good news: Reading is a natural process which in many ways does not need to be learned; rather, the job of the teacher (largely) is not to interfere with it.[10]

Before looking more directly at reading, there is one final aspect of Smith's theory of comprehension which must be discussed. This amounts to a close-up view of "the theory . . . in our heads."

There is a structure to this theory which consists of three basic components (1975:12ff; 1982:54ff): (1) categories, (2) rules for category membership, and (3) interrelations among the categories. For Smith, "To categorize means to treat some objects or events as the same, yet as different from other objects or events." Further, this is an "innate propensity" (Smith 1982:56). Second, category membership is determined by sets of rules which are "systems of . . . *distinctive features*" (Smith 1975:13), i.e. those particular features which objects or events must have (one set of features), and not have (another set of features) to entitle admittance to each category in question. In short, the sets of distinctive features uniquely define each category. Third, the theory in our heads is structured by various relations among the categories, such as class inclusion, property relations, and functional relations (Smith 1975:13f). With these structures in mind, we are ready to look directly at the theory of reading based on this general view of comprehension.

Smith's theory of reading

We have already said that for Smith comprehension is *the* basis of reading. In particular, two basic comprehension skills are needed. These are, first, "the prediction of meaning and the sampling of surface structure to eliminate uncertainty" (Smith 1975:185); and, second, "the ability to make the most economical use possible of visual information" (Smith 1975:185).Prediction, we have seen, is the basis of comprehension: "Comprehension depends upon prediction"(Smith 1978:78); ". . . it is the basis of our comprehension of the world" (Smith 1982:60). Prediction prefigures the questions to which comprehension is the answer. With regard to reading, we select alternatives by prediction. Various alternative meanings are eliminated and various alternatives remain. Prediction, then, minimizes uncertainty in advance and thus "relieves the visual system and memory of overload in reading" (Smith 1982:68). This is the first skill needed in reading, and again, it is a "natural process."

---

[10] This point is explicitly developed in Smith 1979, 1981, and in Smith and Goodman 1971.

After prediction, the reader selects

> . . . among our remaining alternatives by *sampling* the surface structure, looking for limited "matches," or correspondences, with our expectations. Rather than decode surface structure exhaustively, we bring meaning, or a limited set of alternative meanings, to it (Smith 1975:94).

Just as in recognition of other perceptual objects, we do not need to process all the information available, so too in reading, we select only those distinctive features which are necessary for the purposes at hand.

> *When we identify meaning in text--it is not necessary to identify individual words.* We can make sense of text directly from the distinctive features of print (Smith 1978:117).

Here we rejoin our earlier discussion of Smith's disagreements with the bottom-up theorists, and especially, those in the second major area: Reading is "not a consequence of reading words and letters" (Smith 1978:123). Smith says:

> To summarize, neither individual words, their order, nor even grammar itself, can be appealed to as the source of meaning in language and thus of comprehension in reading. Nor is it possible to decode from the meaningless surface structure of writing into the sounds of speech in order to find a back route into meaning. Instead some comprehension of the whole is required before one can say how individual words should sound, or deduce their meaning in particular utterances, and even assert their grammatical function. I am not saying that any utterance can be taken to mean anything; with most utterances only one interpretation is intended and usually there is little argument about the interpretation that should be made. But this agreement does not explain how decisions about meaning are reached and how the essential ambiguity of surface structure is overcome (Smith 1978:75).

In short, then, while admitting the necessity for the reading of print and the attendant visual information, Frank Smith focuses on and emphasizes the contribution of the reader to the comprehension which is the goal of reading.

17

1.3   Interaction models of reading

The third class of reading model attempts to combine the valid insights of the two previous classes--bottom-up and top-down--into one coherent model. These models are called "interactive." In such models, "top-down and bottom-up processes operate simultaneously at all different levels of analysis, they work to pull the various fragments of knowledge and information into a coherent whole" (Adams and Collins 1977:40). Since this is how Goodman has always understood his view of reading (Goodman 1979b:659), and because Goodman's self judgment is clearly sustained, I include his theory here (even though many others consider his view to be "top-down"). Second, a brief introduction to schema theory is given. Schema theory will be a major topic in chapters 5 and 6.

1.3.1   Preliminary considerations

Two preliminary considerations precede this more detailed presentation of interactive models. First, I present the usual critiques which are offered of the bottom-up and the top-down theories. This will be useful because, in general, the interactive theorists acknowledge the validity of both sides of these criticisms, and yet also recognize that neither critique is completely destructive of its object. Second, the question of whether these two models simply address two different situations--the bottom-up, that of the beginning reader, and the top-down that of the fluent reader--must be discussed.

1.3.1.1 Bottom-up and top-down theories critiqued

Critique of the bottom-up models

Brewer 1972, in criticizing Gough's paper, presents what are the usual contemporary objections to the bottom-up model. These points of disagreement are as follows. First,

> The biggest disagreement is that Gough allows no interaction of higher-level processes on the lower-level processes. But a number of studies show that letter-recognition time is faster for words than non-words; that more text is seen per a given exposure duration if material is in words or sentences; that readers often actually see words which are not present when confronted with typographical errors (Brewer 1972:361f).

In the literature, this objection is often termed the problem of "linearity," which results in "cognition [being] effectively isolated from perception" (Lovett 1981:3).

Second, and similarly, Gough does not allow his lexical search process to be affected by previously processed information. But says

Brewer, citing examples, ". . . it is clear that at the level of awareness both preceding and following information contribute to the reading given a particular lexical item" (Brewer 1972:363). Consider, for example, "The painter said the new paint was lighter, but his assistant had trouble picking it up" (Brewer 1972:363).

Third, the time figures for the brain-eye processing of visual information are challenged, an argument which interacts with the points above; e.g. fixation time of the eye on the print depends on the difficulty of material. Again the influence of higher-level processes must be assumed.

Fourth, some studies show that since letters are "decoded" directly to meaning, reading exists without a letter-to-sound transfer. Exclusive letter-to-sound transfer implies the deaf could not learn to read; but they do.

In addition to these objections, which arose at the conference where Gough originally presented his paper, further evidence has accumulated against such a rigid bottom-up model. Negatively the main line of this development has challenged the validity of the arguments used to support the existence of the grapheme to phoneme correspondence rules by which the transfers from letters to sounds are supposedly made (cf. Henderson 1982, chapter 5; Gough 1985). Positively, the main line of this development has been to confirm that prior knowledge is crucial for comprehending prose. The evidence has indeed been overwhelming and has been brought to bear at all recognized levels of processing: letter-word recognition, syntactic, semantic, and text interpretation.[11]

Further, it has been widely recognized that "Gough was unable to offer any clear suggestion as to how it [the comprehension device] might achieve its purpose . . ." (Mitchell 1982:133; cf. also Lovett 1981:3). Gough, in fact, recognized this himself, calling his model's semantic interpreter "Merlin" to "draw attention to its almost magical properties" (Mitchell 1982:133).

In addition, the bottom-up models give little or no attention to the problems of integrating sentences and propositions (Mitchell 1982:133).

Further still, Gough has no contribution to make to the understanding of the acquisition process. He simply says, "How the child solves the decoding process is a mystery, but many do" (Gough 1972:353).

Finally, Lovett points out that though Gough insists that "the Reader is not a guesser" (Gough 1972:354), he does allow that when the

---

[11] Cf. e.g. Adams and Collins 1977; Anderson, et al. 1977; Pichert and Anderson 1977; Marshall 1981; Lovett 1981; Chitra and Steffensen 1980; Adams and Bruce 1980; Rumelhart 1975, 1977, 1980; Durkin 1980; Henderson 1982, especially pp. 202ff and 323ff; Gough 1985; and the literature cited therein.

reader's comprehension is disrupted by pauses and he cannot identify a word, he must guess (Lovett 1981:18).

Gough himself has not been insensitive to these criticisms. In fact, in a recent "Postscript" to his original "One second of reading" article, Gough (1985:687) begins by saying, "This model is wrong." However, he goes on to say "I take this to be a mark of virtue," claiming that ". . . much, if not most, of what we know about word recognition has been learned in the effort to refute it" (Gough 1985:687).[12]

Critique of the top-down models

The major criticism of the top-down models is that they fail to generate testable hypotheses (Lovett 1981:4). Instead of promoting research the claims are "pronounced somewhat dogmatically" (Lovett 1981:4). For instance, "There was little serious attempt to reconcile these proposals [the major claims of the top-down approach, e.g. that only units of meaning enter the reader's memory system] with what is known of the parameters of our perceptual and memory system" (Lovett 1981:4).

There have also been, however, objections to more specific claims. For example, Smith claims that meaning must be known before a sentence can be uttered. But nonsense can be uttered (e.g. "The Jabberwocky") when there is no prior meaning associated with the words to be known. Further, Smith seems to use "a very broad and loose definition of reading" (Sticht, et al. 1974:64) such that errors at the word level do not prohibit reading as long as meaning (i.e. some meaning) is retained. The authors just cited object that this does not do justice to reading as a communication activity which must take the textual sense into more careful account. Further still, Smith (1973:77) claims: "Individual words do not carry any information about how they should be articulated." "But clearly . . . [such words as PERmit and perMIT] give *some* information about how they should be articulated even in a list" (Sticht, et al. 1974:64). Finally, Smith's interpretation of the physiological evidence (e.g. his figures about the rate of words/second in eye fixations) as applied to reading is disputed (Sticht, et al. 1974:65).

These, then, are the main criticisms of the top-down and the bottom-up models found in the literature. We turn now to consider the claim that the two models simply focus on different stages of reading development.

---

[12] In particular, Gough is willing to concede (1) that the "serial assumption ['that we read words letter-by-letter from left to right'] is false" (Gough 1985:687), and that (2) not all of word recognition is mediated by phonological recoding (Gough 1985:687). He still claims, however, that (1) the letter mediates word recognition, and (2) that "most words . . . are recognized through phonological recoding" (Gough 1985:687).

1.3.1.2 Models of reading and stages of reading

Writing in 1981, Lovett can still say (not without justification),

> Despite the profound differences which characterize their descriptions of skilled reading, virtually all adult models embrace the same implicit assumptions in their approach to the early stages of the process. From the analysis-by-synthesis advocates (e.g. Smith 1971, 1973) to the linear stage proponents (e.g. Gough 1972), the almost universal assumption is that beginning reading is a strictly linear or bottom-up process--that access to higher order, more "cognitive" influences awaits the automatization of basic decoding skills and is, therefore, the sole preserve of the fluent reader . . . .this approach . . . carries with it the presupposition of a basic discontinuity between the early process and ultimate fluency (Lovett 1981:24).

However, Lovett goes on to note that ". . . there is recent evidence to suggest that early reading is not the totally bottom-up process it is assumed to be" (Lovett 1981:24). Citing several studies (Doehring 1976; Siler 1974; Weber 1970; Biemiller 1970) she concludes, "These data support the hypothesis that higher order constraints influence the act of reading very early in the course of its development" (Lovett 1981:24).

Then, reporting on her own study which was designed specifically to test the discontinuity assumption (cf. Lovett 1979), Lovett (1981:26) again concludes,

> . . . these data underline the extent to which early reading behavior is directed by higher order cognitive and linguistic constraints and illustrate just how "top-down" the normal process is for these Grade 1 and 2 children.

In particular, Lovett detected in the young children ". . . the same principles of informational selectivity and processing economy that guide the skilled reader . . ." (Lovett 1981:28).

Ehri (1978:17) summarizes the relevant conclusions regarding the beginning reader as follows:

> It appears that initially the identities imposed upon a new word are primarily syntactic and semantic rather than phonological, that these cues are amalgamated with only some graphic symbols in the word, and that only gradually the full

21

printed form becomes associated with the abstract form stored in the lexicon.

And in a more recent study, Ehri and Wilce 1985 conclude that in fact visual information is more prominent for early readers than sound.

Consequently, our conclusion is that the assumption of a discontinuity between beginning and fluent readers (an assumption which divides the requisite skills in terms of bottom-up and top-down, respectively) is not an adequate account. Rather, all reading behavior (and especially early reading behavior, since this has been the point of greatest dispute) must be defined interactively.[13]

1.3.2 The reading theory of Kenneth S. Goodman

As already noted, the views of Goodman are often understood as quite close to those of Frank Smith. Thus he is the prime candidate for

---

[13] Before leaving this discussion of fluency, some readers may be interested in what is currently understood by "fluency." Marshall (1981:43f) presents the following generalizations about "the truly fluent reader" (references in the following have been omitted):

1. "The truly fluent reader remembers meaning rather than exact wording of a discourse . . .

2. "The truly fluent reader remembers familiar information better than unfamiliar. Information is considered familiar if it is presented to the reader prior to reading . . . , if the reader has experienced it previously . . . , if it produces concrete images in the readers" minds, . . . or if it is repeated frequently in the discourse . . .

3. "The truly fluent reader can understand complex discourse even though reading speed decreases as complexity increases . . .

4. "The truly fluent reader knows enough about the variety of discourse structures that poorly structured discourse can be read without loss of comprehension . . . , although reading time is greater . . .

5. "The truly fluent reader remembers superordinate ideas more frequently than subordinate ideas . . . regardless of the surface order of the information . . .

6. "The truly fluent reader remembers subordinate major ideas more frequently than subordinate minor ideas . . .

7. "The truly fluent reader remembers different information when reading for different purposes . . .

8. "The truly fluent reader makes inferences that tend to integrate information . . .

22

the transition from the top-down models of the previous section to the interactive models.

Says Goodman,

> [My model] assumes the goal of reading is constructing meaning in response to text . . . It requires interactive use of grapho-phonic, syntactic, and semantic cues to construct meaning. My model is thus interactive (1981:477);

and further,

> An interactive model is one which uses print as input and has meaning as output. But the reader provides input, too, and the reader, interacting with text, is selective in using just as little of the cues from text as necessary to construct meaning (Goodman 1981:477).

Though Goodman does emphasize the role of the text more than Smith, he is still quite opposed to that view of reading (typical of the bottom-up models) which insists that reading "involves exact, detailed, sequential perception and identification of letters, words, spelling patterns and large language units" (Goodman 1976a:497; cf. also Goodman 1976c:59). On the other hand, Goodman agrees with Smith that ". . . the entire reading process should be geared to the reconstruction of the message" (Goodman 1969:15). And, as with Smith, comprehension--which is the "constructing [of] meaning" (Goodman 1979b:658)--is central. The entire reading process is seen by Goodman as a "getting to meaning": "Reading is not reading unless there is some degree of comprehension . . ." (Goodman 1973:26). Perhaps the best way to understand how Goodman holds these two points of view together is to understand that at the core of his theory is this commitment:

> . . . language processes must be studied in the context of their use. If they are dissected, stopped or unnaturally constrained then the relative significance of constituents to wholes is altered (Goodman 1979b:658).

The context of reading includes both a reader who seeks "to comprehend the writer's meaning" (Goodman 1976c:58) and a printed text composed of grapho-phonic, syntactic, and semantic cues to that meaning sought (Goodman 1979b:658). Both, and more importantly, the interaction of the two, are essentially involved. Reading, then, is defined by Goodman as

> . . . *a complex process by which a reader reconstructs, to some degree, a message encoded by a writer in graphic language* (1976b:472).

23

With this preliminary orientation I now discuss Goodman's theory of reading as it is centered around the five key terms which he has used to describe reading: *"interactive, psycholinguistic, active, constructive, tentative"* (1979b:659).

We have already noted the sense of "interactive" which Goodman uses: The reader's input to meaning is as significant as the textual input. Says Goodman, "I believe that what the reader brings to the text is as important as what the author did in understanding the meaning a given reader constructs" (1979b:660).

Perhaps more than anyone else Goodman has introduced the term "psycholinguistic" into discussions of reading. Since his 1967 article, "Reading: A Psycholinguistic Guessing Game" (cf. Goodman 1976a), the term has been a commonplace throughout the literature on reading. The term "psycholinguistic" as used by Goodman is meant to capture both sides of the interactive process: the subject side, "psycho-"; and the textual side, "-linguistic." And yet, a unified process is in view in which subject and object are not so simply divided and defined. The reader possesses linguistic competence (Goodman 1976b:488f) which is used "to predict syntactic patterns and leap toward a sense of the text" (Goodman 1979b:658). In fact, reading is described as a linking together of "optical, perceptual, syntactic and semantic cycles" (Goodman 1979b:658), all of which are utilized *by the reader* in the service of "the main preoccupation [of] . . . constructing meaning" (Goodman 1979b:658).

The use of "active" in the description of reading emphasizes that the reader has a central contribution to make. *The reader* "uses the strategies of sampling, predicting, confirming, and correcting" (Goodman 1979b:658) which depend on the linguistic-textual cues. *The reader* seeks for meaning and the comprehension achieved is "always the combined result of what the reader understood prior to reading and the effectiveness of comprehending" (Goodman 1979b:658). In brief, the comprehension which is achieved, is achieved only because "the reader is concerned for meaning" (Goodman 1976c:64) and "brings to his reading the sum total of his experience and his language and thought development" (Goodman 1976a:501; cf. also 1973:15).

Reading is "constructive" because there is

> Nothing intrinsic in the writing system or its symbols [which] has meaning. There is nothing in the shape or sequence of any letters or grouping of letters which in itself is meaning (Goodman 1976b:472).

Rather, "Meaning is in the mind of the writer and the mind of the reader" (Goodman 1976b:472); and thus, it is the reader who reconstructs a message in interaction with written language (Goodman 1973:15). Further, the meaning of the text is not given all at once, but part at a time; and most significantly, "we only 'know' the parts when we've created meaning for the whole" (Goodman 1979b:659). Thus, the whole, which can only be constructed from the parts of the text by the reader's contributions, is the prerequisite for the proper knowledge of the parts. Consequently, all the "intermediate aspect[s] of reading" are incomplete and "tentative" (Goodman 1979b:660).

We have just seen the main source of the tentativeness of reading: the part-whole relations within the text and within the processes of meaning construction by a reader "condemned" to reading in sequential time. Goodman, though, says more about this process, which goes to the heart of his conception of reading:

> Reading is a selective process. It involves partial use of available minimal language cues selected from perceptual input on the basis of the reader's expectation. As this partial information is processed, tentative decisions are made to be confirmed, rejected, or refined as reading progresses . . . . More simply stated, reading is a psycholinguistic guessing game (Goodman 1976a:498).

Here three further notions--expectation, selectivity and guessing--amplify Goodman's key term "tentative." The message which the reader produces is only "partly dependent on what the writer intended, but also very much dependent on what the reader brings to the particular text" (Goodman 1976c:58). Here again the syntactic, semantic, and graphophonic strategies are used, but it is essential to Goodman's view that these strategies are used in the first place to guide the process which selects graphic cues.

> The ability to anticipate that which has not been seen, of course, is vital in reading, just as the ability to anticipate what has not yet been heard is vital in listening (Goodman 1976a:498).

Because reading proceeds in cycles of guessed and anticipated meaning, and confirmation and modification of the predictions, the reading is "always tentative to some degree" (Goodman 1979b:660). "In fact, reading is a rapid series of guesses, tentative information processing" (Goodman 1973:19).

In conclusion, I give Goodman's presentation (1967:507f) of his model of reading from his 1967 article, which he still (1979a:659) considers the best summary of his views:

"1. The reader scans along a line of print from left to right and down the page, line by line

"2. He fixes at a point to permit eye focus. Some print will be central and in focus, some will be peripheral; perhaps his perceptual field is a flattened circle

"3. Now begins the selection process. He picks up graphic cues, guided by constraints set up through prior choices, his language knowledge, his cognitive styles, and strategies he has learned

"4. He forms a perceptual image using these cues and his anticipated cues. This image then is partly what he sees and partly what he expected to see

"5. Now he searches his memory for related syntactic, semantic, and phonological cues. This may lead to selection of more graphic cues and to reforming the perceptual image

"6. At this point, he makes a guess or tentative choice consistent with graphic cues. Semantic analysis leads to partial decoding as far as possible. This meaning is stored in short-term memory as he proceeds

"7. If no guess is possible, he checks the recalled perceptual input and tries again. If a guess is still not possible, he takes another look at the text to gather more graphic cues

"8. If he can make a decodable choice, he tests it for semantic and grammatical acceptability in the context developed by prior choices and decoding

"9. If the tentative choice is not acceptable semantically or syntactically, then he regresses, scanning from right to left along the line and up the page to locate a point of semantic or syntactic inconsistency. When such a point is found, he starts over at that point. If no inconsistency can be identified, he reads on seeking some cue which will make it possible to reconcile the anomalous situation

"10. If the choice is acceptable, decoding is extended, meaning is assimilated with prior meaning, and prior meaning is accommodated, if necessary. Expectations are formed about input and meaning that lie ahead.

"11. Then the cycle continues."

With regard to this model, Goodman; makes two further points: First, the steps do not necessarily take place in the sequential form outlined (Goodman 1976a:507); and second, though the outline is complex, he claims that, in fact, it is not complex enough to account for the actual behavior of readers (Goodman 1976a:508).

26

1.3.3 Schema theories of reading

Schema theory is "basically a theory about knowledge" (Rumelhart 1980:34), how it is represented and how it is used. All knowledge, according to schema theory, is packaged into units which are the schemas.[14] "A schema, then, is a data structure for presenting the generic concepts stored in memory" (Rumelhart 1980:34). It contains "the network of interrelations that is believed to normally hold among the constituents of the concept in question" (Rumelhart 1980:34; cf. also van Dijk 1977:21), as well as "information about how this knowledge is to be used" (Rumelhart 1980:34). The knowledge contained in schemas is "our conventional knowledge of the world" (van Dijk 1977:18), and it extends at the upper levels to ideologies and at the lower levels to patterns of excitations associated with letter-recognition. In short, "our schemata *are* our knowledge. All of our generic knowledge is embedded in schemata" (Rumelhart 1980:41).

Rumelhart (1980:40f) summarizes the major features of schemas by listing six characteristics, which are given here with brief explanations when deemed helpful.

1. Schemas have variables, i.e. they have slots which are to be filled by the particulars of the situation. Each particular filled schema is an "instantiation" of the generic schema.

2. Schemas can be embedded one within another. For instance, many people have a schema for going to the doctor and within that schema is a subschema for behavior in the waiting room (cf. Haberlandt and Bingham (1982:32ff)).

3. Schemas represent knowledge at all levels of abstraction (from ideologies/cultures to letter recognition).

4. Schemas represent knowledge rather than definitions, a point we return to below.

5. Schemas are active processes containing pointers to other schemas relevant to interpretation (Haberlandt and Bingham 1982: 36).

6. Schemas are recognition devices whose processing is aimed at the evaluation of their goodness of fit to the data being processed.

Because schemas are forms of knowledge which all people have, including of course readers, schema theories of reading could be seen as a particular variety of top-down theories. The proponents of schema

---

[14] The plural of "schema" is variously "schemata" and "schemas" in the literature. I will user "schemas" consistently throughout, except when "schemata" occurs in quoted material.

theories of reading, however, also recognize that the "text is obviously part of the meaning-creation process" (Spiro 1980:250). As Durkin (1980:6) puts it, reading comprehension (the heart of reading; cf. chapters 5-7) is "filling the slots in the appropriate schemata in such a way as to *jointly satisfy* the constraints of the message *and* the schemata" (emphasis added). Thus, both the text and the reader share the control of the reading process in this conception of reading. In the words of Adams and Collins (1977:1), in an article entitled "A schema-theoretic view of reading," the goal of schema theory is "to specify the interface between the reader and the text." Both bottom-up and top-down processes are conceived of in terms of schemas. Incoming data evokes low level schemas in accordance with the "best fit" (Adams and Collins 1977) while a simultaneous top-down search for data to fit higher order, partially filled schemas is also pursued. In short, reading in the schema-theoretic account is interactive (cf. e.g. Adams 1980:24).

In summary, then, reading is understood as the

> ... activation, focusing, maintaining, and refining of ideas [i.e. our knowledge as schemas] toward developing interpretations (models) that are plausible, interconnected, and complete (Tierney and Pearson 1981:11).[15]

Schema theories of reading represent the forefront of reading research today. The schema is the most sophisticated and promising theoretical construction offered by the reading researchers to explain the reading process, in particular, reading comprehension. As such, schema theories receive further attention and critique in Part II below.

---

[15] The "ideas" referred to here do indeed include "concepts" in the more or less common sense of the term (cf. Rumelhart 1980:34; Armbruster 1976:13; Adams and Bruce 1980), but the focus of the contribution of schema theory has been on higher level cognitive structures. These "higher levels" involve types of background knowledge which go beyond conceptual knowledge per se. This background knowledge is primarily cultural (Joag-dev and Steffensen 1980:20). It includes the illocutionary and perlocutionary functions of language (the locutionary function is the conceptual level; Adams and Bruce 1980), as well as a knowledge of social structures--such as beliefs, and beliefs about beliefs--which are likely to be operative in social interactions, as for example relations to a doctor, or behavior in a restaurant (Adams and Bruce 1980; Bruce 1980). Story knowledge is another kind of cultural background knowledge which is of special interest for reading (cf. Adams and Bruce 1980). For example, the knowledge of what characters and animals might be expected to do in a story, e.g. talk or not. Further, the knowledge of genre types and the implied reading strategies are included in story knowledge (Adams and Bruce 1980:25ff).

1.3.4 A general critique of interactive models

Having previously presented the standard critiques of the bottom-up and top-down theories, it would be leaving a false impression if the standard objections to the interaction theories were not also given. The most general criticism is that, at present, the model is not sufficiently detailed, on the one hand (cf. e.g. Lovett 1981:7; Mitchell 1982:136), and, on the other, it is too particular, thus lacking a comprehensive general theory (e.g. Harker, et al. 1982:167). In short, the theory is in its infancy, an admission its proponents are quick to make. More specifically, the model is criticized for not delineating the "constraints on the number and type of processes which can simultaneously occur in parallel" (Lovett 1981:7). If the information processing capacity of the reader is not to be assumed infinite, such constraints are required. And even if an infinite capacity is assumed, some account of the actual processing of readers (which is clearly not infinite) must be given. Related to this is the recognition that insufficient attention has been given to the basis on which various kinds of hypotheses are generated and to the varying influences of each knowledge source, differing strategies, and various reading conditions (Mitchell 1982:136). Fundamental to the last concern is that of Harker, et al. (1982:167): There is no general account of how schemas are acquired and how a piece of discourse is recognized as an instantiation of a schema. Finally, Smith (1983:67) claims that this is so due to the commitment of many schema theorists to "lean on an extremely narrow conception of comprehension that characterizes computer-based models of language." We will examine this situation in greater detail in chapter 5.

Because the interaction model of reading attempts to take into account the strong points of both the bottom-up and the top-down models, and tries to avoid the criticisms leveled against each, it should be clear that interaction theories offer the most promising approach to the theory of reading today. Further, the criticisms which it has received (as above) are due to either its incompleteness (due to its relative infancy), or to an undue, and unnecessary, reliance on a "narrow conception of comprehension" rather than upon any fundamental flaw in theoretical or experimental design. These reasons for preferring interaction theories of reading to the other models available can be persuasive enough for those working in this kind of reading research. They can, though, be even more thoroughly grounded in the philosophical sense. Such will be our task in Part II. First, though, three phenomenological (in the philosophical sense to be clarified later) theories of reading are presented in the following chapter. The interesting, and significant, point to notice in these phenomenological theories is how closely they resemble the interaction theories.

29

CHAPTER 2

AN INTRODUCTION TO PHENOMENOLOGICAL THEORIES OF READING

Twentieth century western philosophy since the 1950's has taken a definite linguistic turn. Martin Heidegger and Hans-Georg Gadamer in Germany; the structuralists and Paul Ricoeur in France; and Ludwig Wittgenstein, John Austin, and John Searle in the Anglo-American tradition are the main indications of this new interest in language. More recently this interest has focused on questions of discourse and such related concerns as the processes of reading and interpretation.

This new attention to discourse, text, and interpretation is not without interest to those of us concerned with reading, for the question of reading is intimately involved in these current discussions. Here we discuss reading as understood by two contemporary philosophers--Paul Ricoeur and Wolfgang Iser--and one literary critic, Georges Poulet. All three operate in the general philosophical climate of phenomenology. All three have taught in both Europe and the United States. Ricoeur, however, has developed perhaps the most thorough theory of language and text on the contemporary scene. Thus I present his theory of text and interpretation first, but only insofar as it reflects directly on his theory of reading. Then the reading theories of Iser and Poulet are presented.

2.1   Paul Ricoeur's theory of reading

Reading, for Riceour, is related to writing in a manner analogous to the hearer-speaker relation. And yet the dialogical situation of the speaker-hearer is so radically disrupted by the text as written that dialogue can no longer serve as the model for the writing-reading relation (Ricoeur 1976:25f; 1981a:146). Rather, this latter relation must be reconceived based upon the status of a text as written discourse. What this status is, how it disrupts the dialogue situation, and what this implies for a proper conception of reading is now our concern.

2.1.1   Written discourse and distanciation

The text as written discourse makes explicit a condition of communication which is not otherwise so clearly displayed: all discourse is a dialectic of event and meaning (Ricoeur 1976:8-12, 25). As event, discourse is a temporal phenomenon, "an existence in duration and succession" (Ricoeur 1976:9). Discourse as event occurs in the present and then, as event, discourse vanishes. Our daily conversations attest to this transitory quality of discourse. It is true, though, that with the passing of the event, we are left with a residue. This residue Ricoeur says is the meaning, "the propositional content" (Ricoeur 1976:10) which abides. It can, in fact, be not only understood, but also identified and reidentified in future actualizations (1976:19-22; 90). In dialogue, event--the saying--and meaning--the said--are intertwined and co-present to one another. But in written discourse this is not so: meaning has been fixed and remains, separated or distanced from the event of production which has passed away.   Discourse as written then is incomplete discourse for it waits to be reactualized as event.   This reactualization is precisely the task of reading. Before discussing reading per se however, there are yet five more disruptions--Ricoeur calls them distanciations--which writing introduces to discourse, each of which conditions his conception of reading.

The second distanciation (the first is the distanciation of event from meaning) is due to the fact that "writing renders the text autonomous with respect to the intention of the author" (Ricoeur 1981a:139).   While in spoken discourse the subjective intention of the speaker and the verbal meaning of the proposition overlap and usually coincide, writing disrupts this relation.   Consequently, the "textual meaning and the psychological meaning have different destinies" (Ricoeur 1981a:139), or in short, the text and therefore interpretation (and reading as we will see later) are "de-psychologized" (Ricoeur 1976:30).   This is not to say that authorial meaning loses all significance but that "authorial meaning becomes properly a dimension of the text to the extent that the author is not available for questioning" (Ricoeur 1976:30; cf. 1981a:146f).[1]   Because of this distance from the author's intention, the relation between reading and writing is more complex than the face-to-face relation of a dialogue.   This greater complexity will unfold in what follows.

Third, what is true of the transcendence of the psychological conditions of production is also true of the sociological conditions.   As with other works of art, the literary work is opened to unlimited "readings" in different socio-cultural conditions.[2]

> In short, the text must be able, from the sociological as well as the psychological point of view, to "decontextualize" itself in such a way that it can be "recontextualized" in a new situation--as accomplished precisely by the act of reading (Ricoeur 1981a:139).

I will return to this role of reading later.

Fourth, not only the production of discourse, but "the opposite end of the communication chain" (Ricoeur 1976:31), the relation to the hearer, is also disrupted by writing.   In the dialogue situation the addressee is known in advance; a written text is addressed instead "to an unknown reader and potentially to whoever knows how to read" (Ricoeur 1976:31).

---

[1] And even when the author is available, his statements of interpretation are not granted a normative status. See further discussion of the "intentional fallacy" in Ricoeur 1976:30.

[2] Later I will challenge the (possible) implication here that literary works of art are different in this regard from non-literary works.

Says Ricoeur, "It is part of the meaning of a text to be open to an indefinite number of readers and, therefore, of interpretations" (Ricoeur 1976:31f).[3] While the previous two points focused on the right of the text, its semantic autonomy, this point focuses on the right of the reader to interpretation. These two "rights" converge to generate the whole dynamic of interpretation which significantly shapes Ricoeur's concept of reading.

Fifth, writing introduces into discourse a disruption of reference. Says Ricoeur, "All references in the dialogical situation . . . are situational" (Ricoeur 1976:35). The "here and now" is the final reference in dialogue: a common situation is created by the speakers, and reference by gesture or linguistic speech, e.g., demonstratives, "locks into that situation" (Van den Hengel 1982:40). With writing, though, ostensive reference is suspended and the message, at the expense of the reference, can be emphasized for its own sake. Because of this suspension of ordinary reference, this "new sort of distanciation . . . could be called a distanciation of the real from itself" (Ricoeur 1981a:142). But suspension is not abolition, and a text, because it can suspend ordinary reference, can liberate a new "power of reference to aspects of our being in the world that cannot be said in a direct descriptive way" (Ricoeur 1976:37). This new reference, though, is "discontinuous with that of everyday language" (Ricoeur 1981a:142). Writing, then, because of these disruptions to the dialogical situation, "reveals this destination of discourse as projecting a world" (Ricoeur 1976:37; cf. also 84).[4] This destiny is that of "enlarging our concept of the world" (Ricoeur 1976:37), and as we shall soon see (cf. section 2.1.3 *The sixth distanciation*), of ourselves as well. The sixth distanciation involves the distancing of the reader from himself in reading. However, since this disruption is based in the reader's interaction with the written text during the act of reading, I first consider the implications of the above five distanciations for the reading process before returning to the sixth distanciation.

2.1.2 Reading and appropriation

Thus far writing has been seen to introduce disruption into the dialogical situation of discourse. Ricoeur admits that these five distanciations--event from meaning, authorial intention from textual meaning, the text from the sociological conditions of production, the "speaker" from the addressee, and the ostensive reference from secondary reference--constitute the text as "alien," or other. Thus distanciation ". . . transforms all spatial and temporal distance into cultural estrangement"

---

[3] The term "text," for Ricoeur, refers in the first instance to written material. Other usages are employed, but by way of analogy with written texts as the prototype (cf. e.g. Ricoeur 1981a:197ff).

[4] In chapter 8 I will challenge the notion that only writing "reveals this destination." Whether writing reveals this destination most clearly will, however, remain an open question.

(Ricoeur 1976:43). However, he also insists that "distanciation is the condition of understanding" (1981a:144), which is the goal of all discourse, whether spoken or written: "the understanding of a text [culminates] in self understanding" (Ricoeur 1981a:158).

How then can this "estrangement" be overcome? What is the solution which bridges the necessary distance on the one hand, and the sought-for understanding on the other? Ricouer's answer is to the point:

> Reading is the *pharmakon*, the "remedy," by which the meaning of the text is "rescued" from the estrangement of distanciation and put in a new proximity which suppresses and preserves the cultural distance and includes the otherness within the ownness (Ricoeur 1976:43; cf. also Ricoeur 1981a:164).

Herein lies the culmination of Ricoeur's contribution to a theory of reading: appropriation. Appropriation is the dialectical counterpart to distanciation; the making " 'one's own' what was 'alien' " (Ricouer 1976:43; cf. also Ricoeur 1981a:159). The means of appropriation is reading.

However, to appreciate Ricoeur's concept of reading, it is important to note how it is that distanciation is the condition of appropriation. To do so we retrace the significance of the five distanciations previously discussed. Remember first that writing has divorced meaning from event (distanciation 1). Reading therefore must reconstitute this meaning as discourse, that is, as meaning and event. Reading must become "like speech . . . a concrete act which is related to the text as speech is related to discourse" (Ricoeur 1981a:159). How this is accomplished is conditioned by the semantic autonomy of the text (distanciations 2 and 3). What is presented to a reader is not the voice of a speaker in dialogue, but a text-- a work of literary composition in a particular genre and with an individual style (Ricoeur 1981a:145ff; Van den Hengel 1982:42-44). Thus in order for the text to "speak" the reader must submit to, or decode, the codifications which have been fixed by writing (distanciation 4). This process of submission Ricoeur calls "explanation" and ties it directly to the distanciation which conditions understanding. The "possibility of an explanatory attitude in regard to the text" is conditioned by "the constitution of the text as text" (Ricoeur 1981a:153); and as we have seen, it is precisely "the positive and productive function of distanciation" (Ricoeur 1981a:131) which serves to characterize and constitute the text as text.[5] Before understanding and in order to understand, the reader must

---

[5] The term "explanation" is not commonly used by other reading theorists. We will see, however, that there are considerable conceptual similarities with what is commonly called "decoding" in other reading theories. Ricoeur uses the term "explanation" (*erklaren*) because it is in common use in the hermeneutic traditions with which he is in dialogue. Ricoeur credits Dilthey with introducing this term into hermeneutical discussion by

prolong the suspension of the referential relation to the world and to the "speaking subject" (i.e. the implied author; distanciation 5) and situate himself in " 'the place of the text'," "a place which is a non-place," an inside without an outside (Ricoeur 1981a:153). Specifically this means submitting to the structures of word formation, sense, grammaticality, narrativity, etc. which are inherent in the text. Before having an outside reference to the world and to others, the text is a system of internal relations, a structure; in other words, initially the semiological dimension of the text dominates its semantic dimension (Ricoeur 1981a:159). The understanding of the reader then is mediated by explanation which is an action *of* the text, *within* the text, rather than a subjective process of the reader *on* the text (Ricoeur 1981a:162-164).⁶ "The text seeks to place us in its meaning . . ." (Ricoeur 1981a:161).

This is an "intra-textual concept of interpretation" (Ricoeur 1981a:162) in which the reader places himself in the position of the exegete (Ricoeur 1981a:162,164). Thus to read is to interpret (Ricoeur 1981a:174) which means "to place himself in the meaning [i.e. the sense, 164] indicated by the relation of interpretation which the text itself supports" (Ricoeur 1981a:162). Using the interpretation of metaphor as "a paradigm for the explanation of a literary work" (Ricoeur 1981a:174), Ricoeur says of this "intra-textual" moment:

> The decisive moment of explanation is the construction of a network of interactions which constitutes the context as actual and unique. In so doing, we direct our attention towards the semantic event which is produced at the point of intersection between several semantic fields. The construction is the means by which all of the words taken together make sense (Ricoeur 1981a:174).

Here the important points are first, "the construction rests upon 'clues' contained in the text itself" (Ricoeur 1981a:175), and second, the best reading "takes account of the greatest number of facts furnished by the text itself" (Ricouer 1981a:175). Both points derive from the character of a text: the first, because a text is *written* and thus must be brought to "speak" for itself by the reader; the second because the text is a *work*, a

---

contrasting "explanation" as the method of the natural sciences, with "interpretation" as appropriate to the historian and later all the human sciences. Ricoeur's strategy is to reestablish "explanation" on the basis of (structural) linguistics conceived of as a "human science," and thus to integrate "explanation" as a dialectical moment within the hermeneutical process (cf. Ricoeur 1981a:145-184; 1976:71-95).

⁶ This is not to imply that the reader is totally uninvolved. Rather, the action of the text on itself becomes action, i.e. "event," only because of the reader. The role of the reader, then, is parallel to that of the exegete for whom "to interpret is to place himself within the sense indicated by the relation of interpretaion supported by the text" (Ricoeur 1981a:164).

> . . . singular totality . . . a kind of individual
> [whose] singularity can be regained . . . only by
> progressively rectifying generic concepts which
> concern the class of texts, the literary genre and
> the various structures which intersect in this
> singular text (Ricoeur 1981a:175).

2.1.3 The sixth distanciation

The necessity of this objective process of explanation brings with it a
sixth and final distanciation. This final distanciation will prepare us for our
further treatment of *how* reading as appropriation proceeds. Because the
language system or code--language as *langue*[7]--which the reader confronts in
a text is atemporal and universal, the distanciation inherent in the text
interferes with the constitution of the reader as subject. This distances the
reader from himself (cf. Ricoeur 1981a:113; 94; 144) in the following way.
Just as *langue* is independent of the individual subjectivity of the reader, so
too the decoding-explanatory-critical procedures needed to decipher *langue*
"depersonalize" the reader in order to achieve conformity with this object
of attention. The space the reader must enter is a purely semantic, non-
psychological space (Ricoeur 1976:76), quite different from the space of
daily life. As Ricoeur puts it, "This process of dispossession [of the
narcisstic ego] is the work of the sort of universality and atemporality
implied by the explanatory procedures" (Ricoeur 1981a:192; cf. also 94).

However, not only must the reader submit to this depsychologization imposed by the distanciations of the text (Ricoeur
1981a:164); he must overcome it by appropriation. The model used by
Riceour for this distanciation-appropriation dialectic is "play," since it is
precisely "in play that subjectivity forgets itself" (Ricoeur 1981a:186).

> Play is not determined by the consciousness which
> plays; play has its own way of being. Play is an
> experience which transforms those who participate
> in it. It seems that the subject of aesthetic
> experience is not the player himself, but rather
> what "takes place" in play . . . . What is essential
> is the "to and fro" . . . of play . . . . Play is
> something other than the activity of a subject.
> The to and fro of play occurs as if by itself, that is
> without effort or applied intention (Ricoeur
> 1981a:186).

Play then is the "how" of appropriation and with this "how" comes our
final concern, the "what" of appropriation. As mentioned before, reading

---

[7] The term comes from the usage of Ferdinand de Saussure refers to the system of signs
which constitute language. It is distinguished from *parole* which is language as actualized,
i.e. speech. This distinction is discussed further in chapter 4.

is not complete until discourse has been reconstituted as event. In terms previously introduced, this event quality of discourse involves the recontextualization of the meaning of the text: The reference to the world which had been suspended must be reintroduced, now guided by and formulated by the text as structure.

Herein lies the great power of texts: Various worlds and modes of being in the world can be proposed in the mode of play and the constitution (recontextualization) of these worlds as meaningful brings with it a contemporaneous constitution of the self in relation to these worlds.[8]

Not only reference but with it the self of the reader was first of all suspended by the distanciations appropriate to discourse as text. Both are together reconstituted in reading. Reading, then, is the remedy perfectly fit to overcome the distanciations inherent in discourse as text. And yet that which is "made one's own" by reading is strictly conditioned by the prior alienation. As Ricouer says:

> . . . what is "made our own" is not something mental, not the intention of another subject, nor some design supposedly hidden behind the text; rather, it is the projection of a world, the proposal of a mode of being-in-the-world, which the text discloses in front of itself by means of its non-ostensive references. Far from saying that a subject, who already masters his own being-in-the-world, projects the *a priori* of his own understanding and interpolates this *a priori* in the text, I shall say that appropriation is the process by which the revelation of new modes of being . . . *gives* the subject new capacities for knowing himself. If the reference of a text is the projection of a world, then it is not in the first instance the reader who projects himself. The reader is rather broadened in his capacity to project himself by receiving a new mode of being from the text itself (Ricoeur 1981a:192).

---

[8] Elsewhere Ricoeur develops his understanding of (1) what this mutual formation of self- and world-understanding involves (e.g. Ricoeur 1981a:53-62; 178; 192f; in short, the realm of being is more fundamental than knowing, and understanding is best understood as fundamentally a matter of being), and (2) how this "reconstruction" occurs (Ricoeur 1981a: 171-181). It is of interest that he too gives a major role to "guessing" as do Goodman (1976) and Smith (1971:98f; 1978b:85ff). These topics will be discussed in greater detail in chapter 6. What is of special interest in Ricoeur's approach is the sensitivity to lived experience of both an epistemological and, more importantly, an ontological sort. At this point in the theory, many anthropological insights regarding world view, etc., interlock with this theory of reading.

Briefly put,

> It is the text, with its universal power of unveiling
> [a world and new modes of being] which gives a
> *self* to the *ego* (Ricoeur 1981a:193).

This relation of text as structure to appropriation, and especially the role of reading in the relation, however, deserves further attention. Reading will be conceived of as a dialectic. This dialectic reflects and is motivated by the dialectics which (1) are inherent to all language; (2) are especially highlighted by written discourse; and (3) ground Ricoeur's whole hermeneutical project. To review, these dialectics are, first, that of event and meaning (Ricoeur 1976:8-12), and second, within meaning, the dialectic of sense and reference (Ricoeur 1976:19-22). Coordinate with these dialectics are, on the one hand, the explanatory procedures associated with meaning as sense and the distanciations inherent to a text, and, on the other hand, interpretation understood as self-understanding associated with meaning as reference and the event of appropriation. Consequently, just as language is "the incessant conversion of one into the other in discourse" (Ricoeur 1978:116), so too explanation and interpretation each "refer back by means of its own peculiar features, to the other" (Ricoeur 1981a:160), each calling for its complement in the other (Ricoeur 1981a:185). For our purpose, the striking feature of this basic dialectic is the central role given to reading. For Ricoeur, "It is at the very heart of reading that explanation and interpretation are indefinitely opposed and reconciled" (Ricoeur 1981a:164); and again, ". . . reading is the dialectic of these two attitudes" (Ricoeur 1981a:152).

Consequently two ways of reading are offered (Ricoeur 1981a:158). It is with a sketch of these two ways that I will summarize and conclude this presentation of Ricoeur's theory of reading.

> The first way of reading is exemplified today by
> the various structural schools of literary criticism.
> Their approach is not only possible, but legitimate.
> It proceeds from the acknowledgement of what I
> have called the suspension or suppression of the
> ostensive reference. The text intercepts the
> "worldly" dimension of the discourse--the relation
> to a world which could be shown--in the same way
> as it disrupts the connection of the discourse to
> the subjective intention of the author. To read, in
> this way, means to prolong the suspension of the
> ostensive reference and to transfer oneself into
> the "place" where the text stands, within the
> "enclosure" of this worldless place. According to
> this choice, the text no longer has an exterior, it
> only has an interior. To repeat, the constitution of
> the text as a text and of the system of texts as
> literature justifies this conversion of the literary

object into a closed system of signs, analogous to the kind of closed system that phonology discovered underlying all discourse, and which de Saussure called *la langue*. Literature, according to this working hypothesis, becomes an *analogon* of *la langue* (Ricoeur 1981a:216).

In the second way of reading we ". . . lift the suspense [of the text's reference to a surrounding world and to the audience] and fulfill the text in present speech. It is this second attitude which is the real aim of reading" (Ricoeur 1981a:158). In this second way, "we create a new ostensive reference thanks to the kind of 'execution' that the act of reading implies" (Ricoeur 1976:81). Ricoeur's favorite model for this "execution" is the performance of a musical score guided by the sameness of the music, yet unique in its actualization (Ricoeur 1976:59, 75; 1981a:159, 174). This "enactment" of the text (Ricoeur 1981a:159) signals the fulfillment of the discourse of the text, the culmination of reading "in a concrete act which is related to the text as speech is related to discourse, namely as event and instance of discourse" (Ricoeur 1981a:159). Here the properly semantic dimension of the text, as distinguished from its semiological dimension, is realized in the reading subject (Ricoeur 1981a:159).

No doubt this presentation of "the two ways of reading" remains at this point merely suggestive. I will, however, postpone further discussion until Part II where Ricoeur's theory is examined in relation to other reading theories.

2.2   Wolfgang Iser's theory of reading

Wolfgang Iser's concern in *The Act of Reading* is to develop "a theory of literary communication" on the "ground-plan" of the reading process (Iser 1978:ix). Since "a literary text can only produce a response when it is read . . . reading is therefore the focal point of this study" (Iser 1978:ix). His basic thesis is that both a subjective contribution by the reader and a context are necessary for a text to be meaningful (Iser 1978:19). However, a literary work cannot be reduced to either the subjectivity of the reader or the text itself (Iser 1978:21). Rather, the reader and the text form two poles, the interaction of which actualizes, situates, and constitutes the work as work, virtual in character and dynamic in its virtuality (Iser 1978:21). This virtuality is an immediate consequence of the fact that neither pole can be reduced to the other. Interaction is thus central, and the book unfolds as a search for the basic conditions of this interaction. An "implied reader" is posited as a transcendental[9] model, the purpose of which is to offer "a means of describing the process whereby textual structures are transmuted through ideational activities into personal experiences" (Iser 1978:38).

---

[9] Transcendental in this context means a description of the conditions for the possibility of something, here reading.

There is no doubt that in Iser's model of reading there is a priority given to the text itself. The "verbal aspect [of the text] guides the reaction [of the reader] and prevents it from being arbitrary" (Iser 1978:21). The text imitates "this 'transfer' of text to reader" (Iser 1978:107); it "set[s] in motion . . . acts of comprehension" (Iser 1978:108). Yet "any successful transfer . . . depends on the extent to which this text can activate the individual reader's faculties of perceiving and processing" (Iser 1978:107). The necessity for this "creative side of reading" testifies to the "very lack of control" exerted by the text (Iser 1978:108). In short, "the reader 'receives' . . . [the message] by composing it" (Iser 1978:21); thus, both "poles" of the reading process are necessary.

Iser's starting point is "the fact that the linguistic signs and structures of the text exhaust their function in triggering developing acts of comprehension" (Iser 1978:107f). No doubt this "triggering" is already reading, yet "the reader's enjoyment begins when he himself becomes productive, i.e. when the text allows him to bring his own faculties into play" (Iser 1978:108). This productive stage of reading--that of "the developing acts of comprehension"--is Iser's special concern, and its necessity is underlined by "the fact that the whole text can never be perceived at any one time" (Iser 1978:108); instead it "can only be imagined by way of different consecutive phases of reading" (Iser 1978:109). This is the basic fact which distinguishes the " 'object' of the text" from "empirically existing objects" and consequently the role of the reader from that of an observer (Iser 1978:109). The subject-object relation of observation is replaced by "a moving viewpoint which travels along inside that which it has to apprehend. This mode of grasping an object is unique to literature" (Iser 1978:109).

Each consecutive phase of reading must be synthesized with the others and thus the " 'object' of the text" is arrived at slowly, constituted by that process called reading. At each point in this process, however, "The reader's wandering viewpoint is, at one and the same time, caught up in and transcended by the object it is to apprehend" (Iser 1978:109). It is caught up in the object because the object is constituted by the syntheses which the reader himself produces; and most importantly, these acts of synthesis transfer the text into the consciousness of the reader. The reader's viewpoint is transcended by the object because every aspect of the object and every synthesis remains incomplete--at no point can the synthesis claim to be representative of the object *in toto* (Iser 1978:109). Iser goes on to develop the processes involved in the functioning of this "wandering viewpoint." These processes, which we now consider in order, are first, the dialectic of protension and retention; second, image-building; and finally, the role of blanks and negation.

2.2.1 The dialectic of protension and retention

For Iser, the dialectic of protension and retention is generated at the sentence level of discourse. Each sentence has a correlate[10] which finally is a "portrayed world" (Iser 1978:110). Though each sentence as semantic pointer implies an expectation--Iser's "protension" (following Husserl 1964)--the various sentences do not automatically fulfill one another's expectations. Rather the intentional correlates of succeeding sentences interplay and cause a continual modification of the previous expectations which are themselves retained in memory. "Thus every moment of reading is a dialectic of protension and retention . . ." (Iser 1978:112), and the reader's position is at the point of intersection between retention and protension (Iser 1978:111). Five points follow from this basic conception of reading as dialectic.

First, the obstacles to a continuous, uninterrupted flow of thinking are to be taken, not as unwanted vexations, but rather as "paradigmatic of the many processes of focusing and refocusing that take place during the reading of a literary text" (Iser 1978:113). "Surprising twists and turns" should be expected and accepted as stimulation to the creative activity of the reader (Iser 1978:112). For after all, it is not the text which formulates the expectations nor the modifications nor the connectibility of memories, but the reader. Thus the "unexpected" is simply a sign calling for the greater involvement of the reader with the matter of the text.

Second, the basis of this involvement in the text is the process of building consistency. The reader, in order to cope with the increasing complexity generated by the dialectic between memory and new expectation, groups the material being presented by the text into gestalts. The basis of the choosing of gestalts is the consistency of the interpretation implied. This principle of consistency Iser seems to accept as a universal operation, citing psycholinguistic experiments and aesthetic research for support (Iser 1978:119). However, though the implication is that it is necessary for the reader to proceed this way, it is also admitted that gestalts are only relatively closed units, and that modifications and rearrangements may also be necessary as the elements excluded by the selection process inherent in gestalt formation reassert themselves, challenging the validity of the previous closures.

Third, "Through gestalt-forming, we actually participate in the text, and this means that we are caught up in the very thing we are producing" (Iser 1978:127). In short, the dialectic of protension and retention makes text into an event. Because the gestalts formed by the reader are tentative, "we [as readers] react to what we ourselves have produced" (Iser 1978:128f). In fact, the text "owes its presence in our minds to our own reactions and it is these that make us animate the meaning of the text as a

---

[10] More precisely, an "intentional correlate." What this means for the phenomenologists, including Iser, will be further explained in chapter 3.

reality" (Iser 1978:129). The gestalts enable "the reader actually to become aware of the inadequacy of the gestalts he has produced, so that he may detach himself from his own participation in the text and see himself being guided from without" (Iser 1978:134). Thus the reader "is [both] involved, and he watches himself being involved" (Iser 1978:134). The very involvement, or "entanglement" (Iser 1978:129) with the text which is occasioned by the efforts to balance the gestalts both renders the text "a presence for us" (Iser 1978:131) and provides the condition by which reading becomes an experience. When the gestalts do not balance, the various criteria of orientation used for the formation of these gestalts are pushed back into the past: Their validity for the now present is suspended (Iser 1978:132). Our own store of experience, by means of which we have tried to balance or make sense of the textual presentation, is restructured by the unfamiliarity of the text. "The old conditions the new, and the new selectively restructures the old" (Iser 1978:132). Iser stresses the importance of this interaction between the old and the new, for it is only by this process that, as Ricoeur says, the reader is given a new capacity for knowing himself. In Iser's words, "The resultant restructuring of stored experience makes the reader aware not only of the experience but also the means whereby it develops" (Iser 1978:134).

The fifth correlate of the dialectic of protension and retention is that the evocation of expectations does not normally follow a strict time sequence. The perspectives evoked by any particular sentence may not be, and usually are not, their immediate predecessors. Thus the wandering viewpoint builds up gestalts and integrates linguistic signs with the associated contexts of both present and recalled fact. Though the linguistic sign may stimulate, and even evoke, the recall, the "extent and the nature of this recalled context are beyond the control of the linguistic sign" (Iser 1978:116). Further, "it is possible that aspects may now [i.e. in recall] become visible that had not been so when the fact had settled in the memory" (Iser 1978:116). The point here is again Iser's basic thesis: ". . . the textual sign and the reader's conscious mind merge in a productive act that cannot be reduced to either of its component parts" (Iser 1978:116).

2.2.2 Image-building

The second main process involved in reading as understood by Iser is image-building. Though the reader begins with the schemas of the text, the meaning of the text must be assembled by the reader. The components of this assembly are both given by the text and contributed by the reader. "It is as if the schema were a hollow form into which the reader is invited to pour his own store of knowledge" (Iser 1978:143). The image is the basic element of the mental activity of the reader by which trial combinations are compiled from the given data. Mikel Dufrenne maintains that this compilation also involves the mobilization of "modes of implicit knowledge" which follow "the course of a previous experience undergone by the body" (1973:348). By means of the image the consciousness of the reader opens itself to the meaning of the text as object by prefiguring this meaning on the basis of both the given of the text and

42

what is not given by the text but is contributed by the past lived experience of the reader. Because the level of contribution of this implicit knowledge is that of lived experience, Iser terms this process "passive synthesis."[11]

By passive synthesis several aspects of meaning are meant. First, passive syntheses are not judgements because (1) "neither assessment nor predication makes itself explicit in the link-up of facts" (Iser 1978:139) and (2) passive synthesis is dependent on and takes place along the time axis of reading while judgements are "independent of time" (Iser 1978:150). Second, passive synthesis "takes place below the threshold of consciousness" (Iser 1978:139). There is a sense here of an automatic acceptance and composition of the ingredients of meaning, but this must be modified by the next point. Third, the reader is definitely "involved in composing images out of the multifarious aspects of the text by unfolding them into a sequence of ideation and by integrating the resulting products along the time axis of reading" (Iser 1978:150). It is to this involvement of the reader in the image-building process that occurs within passive synthesis that we now turn our attention.

The image-building process is very significant for the experience of the reader. By it he is drawn away from the "real world" by the elimination of "the subject-object division essential for all perception" (Iser 1978:140). This division is eliminated because the reader is absorbed into the image which he himself produces: The mental imagery which accompanies and mediates the emergence of the aesthetic object--the meaning of the text--is itself the production of the reader.

> The non-given or the absent enters into his
> presence, and he enters into theirs. But if we are
> absorbed into an image, we are no longer present
> in a reality--instead we are experiencing what can
> only be described as an irrealization in the sense
> that we are preoccupied with something that takes
> us out of our own given reality (Iser 1978:140).

This irrealization of reality has consequences for the reader's subsequent relation to both his "own given reality" and to his own constitution as subject.

Irrealization is primarily familiar to us as we encounter its "escapist" effect in literature. The temporary isolation from the "real world" induced by reading often results in a kind of awakening when the reading process is terminated. According to Iser, this "does not mean that we now return to it [the "real world"] with new directions" (Iser 1978:140). Rather, this "real world" appears observable for a time because the subject-object division suspended by reading is necessarily reinstituted (for it is the basis

---

[11] Iser follows Husserl here too; cf. Husserl 1931, 1952, 1960, 1973.

for all perception) and is thus accentuated by the termination of the reading process.

> Suddenly we find ourselves detached from our world, to which we are inextricably tied, and able to perceive it as an object. And if this detachment is only momentary, it may enable us to apply the knowledge we have gained by figuring out the multiple references of the linguistic signs, so that we can view our own world as a thing "freshly understood" (Iser 1978:140).

The reader's constitution of the meaning of the text implies not only the emergence of a totality from the interacting textual perspectives, thus drawing him toward irrealization; "but also, through formulating this totality, it enables us to formulate ourselves and thus discover an inner world of which we had hitherto not been conscious" (Iser 1978:158).

Because the subject-object division has been removed by the image-building process of reading, "the reader becomes occupied by the author's thoughts" (Iser 1978:155). This results in a division within the subject himself; he leaves his own disposition, or habitual nature, by bringing "into his own foreground something which he is not" (Iser 1978:155). Of course the reader's own orientation does not disappear completely, but it does recede into the background. This division within the subject not only allows the reader to be present to the text, but brings about a tension, the resolution of which not only involves the reader more deeply with the text but also with himself as well. According to Iser, the spontaneity of the reader is mobilized as the new present experience of reading must be incorporated into the habitual orientation of the self which had been relegated to background. Herein lies the transforming power of reading: The presentness of the image built by reading and the past of habitual orientations interact "to formulate something in us" (Iser 1978:158). Iser, following W.D. Harding (Harding 1968:313ff), terms this "something" the formulation of wishes or the definition of desires. He credits this power of formulation to neither our own past nor our conscious orientation; rather, "the conditioning influence must be the alien thoughts" which we think from the text (Iser 1978:158). However it must be remembered that the subjectivity of the reader can never be excluded from this process; thus the text is the condition which "enables us to formulate ourselves and thus discover an inner world of which we had hitherto not been conscious" (Iser 1978:158).

Throughout Iser's considerations of irrealization and its consequences, the elimination of the subject-object division affected by image-building is basic. It behooves us then to clarify further the basic features of image-building.

The basic features of the image-building process, says Iser, are "theme and significance, which require stabilization through fields of reference" (Iser 1978:147). I first consider "theme," which develops the interaction of reader and text.

Because the meaning of the text is not fully represented by any one of the different perspectives presented, but rather emerges from their continuous interaction, "a constantly shifting constellation of views" (Iser 1978:96) is offered to the reader. Since the reader cannot embrace all the perspectives at once, there is always one view with which the reader is involved. This view is called by Iser the "theme" (Iser 1978:97). The previous perspectives and themes, however, are still present, but as a "horizon" which conditions the reader's attitude toward the present theme. Three effects follow from this theme-horizon structure which itself "constitutes the basic rule for the combination of textual strategies" (Iser 1978:97).

First, it bridges the gap between text and reader.

> The structure of theme and horizon constitutes the vital link between text and reader because it actively involves the reader in the process of synthesizing an assembly of constantly shifting viewpoints, which not only modify one another but also influence past and future synthesis (Iser 1978:97).

Second,

> . . . the structure of theme and horizon transforms every perspective segment of the text into a two-way glass, in the sense that each segment appears against the others and is therefore not only itself but also a reflection and an illuminator of those others (Iser 1978:97).

The interaction of perspectives then not only expands and changes each perspective due to its relation to the others, but results in the relativization of each perspective and the consequent emergence of the meaning of the text as a viewpoint which transcends every other particular perspective. This transcendental viewpoint is compiled from the perspectives represented in the text, yet these perspectives are themselves set up for observation from the position of the aesthetic object as transcendental. Inasmuch as the positions presented in the text are actual selections from the social or literary world outside the text, the reader will see these norms in a new light as he reacts to the world incorporated in the text.

Third, the implication of the preceding point is that the meaning of the text is *not* built up from some kind of simple combination of the perspectives presented in the text. Rather the perspectives in the text are mutually transformed; the meaning

. . . is the formulation of that which has not yet been formulated and as such it offers the reader a transcendental vantage point from which he can see through all the positions that have been formulated (Iser 1978:99).

Theme, then, and its correlate, horizon, form a very significant aspect of the reading process. As we noted previously, it is one of the basic features of the image-building process. The second basic feature is termed by Iser "significance" (Iser 1978:147). As we will see, theme and significance are tied closely together.

As the attention of the reader shifts from theme to theme, and as the themes interact with and transform one another, a unified theme of the text is built up. And yet, says Iser,

. . . the theme is not an end in itself, but a sign for something else, it produces an "empty" reference, and the filling-in of this reference is what constitutes the significance (Iser 1978:147).

Though the building of the theme is also dependent upon the synthesizing faculties of the reader (Iser 1978:150, 151), the role of the reader is especially underlined by the category of significance. While "meaning is the referential totality which is implied by the aspects contained in the text and which must be assembled in the course of reading" (Iser 1978:151),[12] "significance is the reader's absorption of the meaning into his own experience . . . the active taking-over of the meaning by the reader" (Iser 1978:151). In this way the reader is essential to the fulfillment of reading. As Iser puts it,

Thus the meaning of the literary text can only be fulfilled in the reading subject and does not exist independently of him . . . (Iser 1978:150).

In summary then, the reading subject integrates the various textual perspectives. Imagination renders the meaning of the text present as image--sometimes pictorial, sometimes semantic (Iser 1978:147). The "synthetizing faculties" of the reader are placed at the disposal of the unfamiliar reality of the text.

Consequently, as readers we "produce the meaning of that reality, and in so doing enter into a situation which we could not have created out of ourselves" (Iser 1978:150). Further, the constitution of this meaning goes hand in hand with its apprehension: so unique is the perception of

---

[12] Meaning is otherwise termed (by Iser) "the theme" (Iser 1978:147), "the imaginary object" (Iser 1978:148), "the aesthetic object" (Iser 1978:98), and "the transcendental viewpoint" (Iser 1978:98).

the aesthetic object (Iser 1978:149)! The "full significance" of the process of passive synthesis, however, lies in the fact that the reader himself is constituted as subject in this process of the constitution of meaning (Iser 1978:150).

2.2.3 Blanks and negation

The third main "process" involved in reading--after the dialectic of protension-retention and image-building--is the role of blanks and negation. We have already seen both the necessity for the reader to synthesize the various textual perspectives into a unified theme or meaning and the priority given to the text--"what is not formulated [in the text, but is formulated by the reader] does arise out of what *is* formulated" (Iser 1978:147). The question before us now is: what modes does the written *text* employ "in order to bring about and simultaneously guide the conceivability of the unwritten" (Iser 1978:147)? Iser's answer is "blanks and negation." A blank is a potential connection between textual perspectives which "designates a vacancy in the overall system of the text" (Iser 1978:182). Blanks are "the unseen joints of the text" which break up the connectability of the text (Iser 1978:189). Negation, on the other hand, invokes familiar or determinate elements only to cancel them out, thus guiding the reader to modify his attitudes toward the familiar by adopting "a position *in* relation to the text" (Iser 1978:169). We now examine in more detail, and in order, these two basic structures of textual indeterminacy.

Blanks are structured within the text in order to stimulate or induce operations of "ideation to be performed by the reader on terms set by the text" (Iser 1978:169). To the extent that the text presents the unfamiliar, the unforeseeability of the textual sequence is signalled by blanks. But blanks arise in other ways too. First, it is not possible to say everything about a topic; what is not said is a textual blank (Iser 1978:180). Second, because there is neither a face-to-face situation nor a common regulative context or frame of reference (as there is in the situation of dialogue), there is a gap between the text and the reader. This fundamental gap (Iser also calls it a "blank," 1978:167) also gives rise to gaps within the text as the reader processes the text while being guided by the text. Thus, blanks arise from the unique character of the text-reader relation and the resultant reading process.

This unseen structure *regulates* the connectability of the perspectives but it does not *formulate* the connection--that is the role of the reader. Iser notes three functions of the blank.

The first is the promotion of connections between segments of the text. Whenever two or more positions are related and influence one another, then a referential field is always formed. This is the first structural quality of the blank--"it makes possible the organization of a referential field of interacting projections" (Iser 1978:197).

47

Second, after organizing a referential field, "it is as if the blank in the field of the reader's viewpoint has changed its position" (Iser 1978:198). Now the blank "enables the reader to produce a determinate relationship between them [the connected segments]" (Iser 1978:198). This relationship is the recognition of "affinities and difference and . . . the pattern underlying the connections" (Iser 1978:197f).

The third and "most decisive function of the blank" (Iser 1978:198) is the formation of the *structure* of the referential field which guides the build-up of the aesthetic object. This function is dependent on the previously formed referential field and further clarifies the theme-horizon structure previously discussed. Remember that the viewpoint which is focused upon is the theme and the preceding themes become horizon. When a previous theme loses its thematic relevance it is "turned into a marginal, thematically vacant position" (Iser 1978:198). The important point here is that the reader occupies these blanks, which Iser calls vacancies, as the standpoint from which he views the theme. But in being a standpoint, the vacancies modify and are modified by the theme of focus, until ultimately the various textual perspectives are transformed "into the aesthetic object of the text" (Iser 1978:198).

Two further points regarding the blank are worthy of note. First, the structured operations which the blanks initiate guide the path which the wandering viewpoint follows. As connections are made, promoted by the blank, it is as if the blank shifts to propose new possible connections. In fact the shifting blank is responsible for the sequence of colliding images which condition each other and out of which the aesthetic object emerges (Iser 1978:203). Second, the promotion of reader-executed connections is the very means by which reader participation is induced. This execution "transmits the reciprocal interaction of textual positions into consciousness" (Iser 1978:203) and inextricably "entangles" the reader with the work.

Together with the blank, negation constitutes the main mode by which the aesthetic object is structured. The text operates by negation when it invalidates a familiar norm. This creates a new, and initially ambiguous, relation between the reader and the familiar world. The past norm is negated, but the present is not yet formulated. Negation places the reader between "no longer" and "not yet" (Iser 1978:213).

Three features of negation are presented by Iser. First, negation makes comprehension possible by tracing out what is not given, allowing the mental images of the reader to penetrate the text, and thus enabling the unformulated to be communicated. Second, negation points out a deficiency in familiar knowledge, and sets the reader to resolve the problems of understanding caused by this deficiency by finding the hidden cause.

Negativity, then, embraces both the question [posed by the text] and the answer, and is the condition that enables the reader to construct the meaning of the text on a question-and-answer basis (Iser 1978:228).

Third, negation allows and enables the unfamiliar to be manifest under the same conditions as the familiar, and thus marks out a relation to what is in dispute (Iser 1978:229). The world of the text appears in a state of alienation, but because it appears under the condition of the familiar, the presence of a potential meaning is implied (Iser 1978:229).

The functioning of the blanks and negation help to balance out the fundamental "imbalance" (Iser 1978:167)[13] between text and reader by initiating an interaction in which the reader fills the hollows of the text with his own mental images. As Iser puts it,

The intimate connection between the two functions is the basic condition that gives rise to the interaction between text and reader. They are the hollow form into which the meaning is to be poured, and as such they bring about the process, unique to literature, whereby knowledge is offered or invoked by the text in such a way that it can undergo a guided transformation in and through the reader's mind. It is through the blanks that the negations take on their productive force: the old negated meaning returns to the conscious mind when a new one is superimposed onto it; this new meaning is unformulated, and for precisely this reason needs the old, as this has been changed by the negation back into material for interpretation, out of which the new meaning is to be fashioned (Iser 1978:216f).

2.3 Georges Poulet's theory of reading

The guiding principle for Georges Poulet's phenomenology of reading is the relation between subject and object. Initially, "books are objects" (Poulet 1969:53), material and immobile; the reader is the subject. But reading is an act which brings surprising modifications to this initial situation. It is these modifications which are of special interest to Poulet.

---

[13] The text is dependent on the reader for its "speech" in a manner in which neither partner of a dialogue is dependent on the other; further, the reader must be guided by the text while always being confronted by the indeterminancies generated by "the gap" of the unique text-reader relation.

49

For Poulet, though "Books are objects," even in their pre-being-read state they "are not just objects among others" (Poulet 1969:53). Instead, they are like

> . . . animals for sale, kept in little cages, and so obviously hoping for a buyer . . . . They wait. Are they aware that an act of man might suddenly transform their existence? They appear to be lit up with that hope. Read me, they seem to say (Poulet 1969:53).

And when the book is read? When a book is read it "is no longer a material reality. It has become a series of words, of images, of ideas which in their turn begin to exist" (Poulet 1969:54). The book as paper and ink is of course still there, but "at the same time it is there no longer, it is nowhere" (Poulet 1969:54). A new existence has begun which is neither "in the paper" nor "in external space." The "place" of this new existence is "my [the reader's] innermost self" (Poulet 1969:54). This then is the surprising modification which the book as object undergoes in the act of reading. A no less surprising modification occurs in the reader and further modifies the book as content. It is to this subjective modification which we now turn our attention.

In the act of reading, a most remarkable transformation is effected in the reader himself. As Poulet puts it:

> I am someone who happens to have objects of his own thought, thoughts which are part of a book I am reading, and which are therefore the cogitations of another. They are the thoughts of another, and yet it is I who am their subject. The situation is even more astonishing than the one noted above [the disappearance of physical objects, even the book as physical object]. I am thinking the thoughts of another. Of course, there would be no cause for astonishment if I were thinking it as the thoughts of another. But I think it as my very own (Poulet 1969:55).

In short, in the act of reading, "My consciousness behaves as though it were the consciousness of another" (Poulet 1969:56). Poulet's experience, which he explores phenomenologically in his essay "Phenomenology of Reading," is simply that reading alienates him from himself: Another "I" replaces his own; the subject of the thoughts he thinks is an alien subject (Poulet 1969:56f). Says he, "When I am absorbed in reading, a second self takes over, a self which thinks and feels for me" (Poulet 1969:57).

So astonishing and powerful is this subjective transformation in reading that it serves then as the central element in Poulet's "definition" of reading. "Reading, then," he says,

. . . is the act in which the subjective principle which I call "I" is modified in such a way that I no longer have the right, strictly speaking, to consider it as my "I." I am on loan to another, and this other thinks, feels, suffers, and acts within me. . . . Now it is important to note that this possession of myself by another takes place not only on the level of objective thought, that is with regard to images, sensations, ideas which reading affords me, but also on the level of my very subjectivity (Poulet 1969:57);

and again,

Reading is just that: a way of giving way not only to a host of alien words, images, ideas but also to the very alien principle which utters them and shelters them (Poulet 1969:57).

The question to which Poulet (1969:57) then turns is: "Who is the usurper who occupies the forefront? What is this mind who all alone by himself fills my consciousness and who, when I say "I," is indeed that "I"?" In a manner quite in keeping with that of Ricoeur, Poulet dismisses the possibility that the subject revealed through reading is that of the author (Poulet 1969:58). Rather, at the moment of absorption in reading what matters is

. . . to live, from the inside, in a certain identity with the work and the work alone. It could hardly be otherwise. Nothing external to the work could possibly share the extraordinary claim which the work now exerts on me. It is there within me, not to send me back, outside itself, to its author, nor to his other writings, but on the contrary to keep my attention rivetted on itself. It is the work which traces in me the very boundaries within which this consciousness will define itself. It is the work which forces on me a series of mental objects and creates in me a network of words, beyond which, for the time being, there will be no room for other mental objects or for other words. And it is the work, finally, which, not satisfied thus with defining the content of my consciousness, takes hold of it, appropriates it, and makes of it that "I" which, from one end of my reading to the other, presides over the unfolding of the work, of the single work which I am reading (Poulet 1969:58-59).

Though the work as work is given the place of prominence with "its own inner meaning" and "its formal perfection" being exalted over the acknowledged importance of "a mass of biographical, bibliographical, textual, and general information" (Poulet 1969:58), still there is a "subjective principle which animates" the work (Poulet 1969:58), a "consciousness inherent in the work [which] is active and potent" (Poulet 1969:59). That into which the book as object is transformed by reading

> . . . is no longer just an object, or even simply a living thing. I am aware of a rational being, of a consciousness; the consciousness of another, no different from the one I automatically assume in every human being I encounter, except that in this case the consciousness is open to me, welcomes me, lets me look deep inside itself, and even allows me, with unheard-of-license, to think what it thinks and feel what it feels (Poulet 1969:54).

And again,

> ". . . by the act of reading, a work of literature becomes (at the expense of the reader whose own life it suspends) a sort of human being, . . . it is a mind conscious of itself and constituting itself in me as the subject of its own objects" (Poulet 1969:59).

And yet, remember that this "other" is not the author per se.

Poulet never does answer his own question of just who this "usurper" is. However, he does affirm a "transcendence of mind" which haunts all critical efforts at elucidation of works and is "constrained to acknowledge that all subjective activity present in a literary work is not entirely explained by its relationship with forms and objects within the work" (Poulet 1969:68). Poulet goes on to explain:

> There is in the work a mental activity profoundly engaged in objective forms; and there is, at another level, forsaking all forms, a subject which reveals itself to itself (and to me) in its transcendence over all which is reflected in it. At this point, no object can express it, no structure can any longer define it; it is exposed in its ineffability and in its fundamental indeterminacy (Poulet 1969:68).

Poulet offers only two possibilities for this transcendent "whatever it may be" (Poulet 1969:68): either an invisible life of the individual artist independent of the work; or, "as Valery thinks, an anonymous and abstract consciousness presiding, in its aloofness, over the operations of all more

52

concrete consciousness" (Poulet 1969:68). We will take up this question again in Part II. For now, though, let us descend again from these almost mystical heights to consider what Poulet says about the act of reading which links the two transformations--of the object and the subject.

The "precise moment" (Poulet 1969:54) at which the book as object is transformed is when the reader sees ". . . surging out of the object I hold open before me [the book] a quantity of signification which my mind grasps" (Poulet 1969:54). This perception of "significations which have made themselves at home there [i.e in my mind]" (Poulet 1969:54) is also the evidence that "my consciousness behaves as though it were the consciousness of another" (Poulet 1969:56). Thus mental awareness of significations is the key to Poulet's conception of the act of reading. By "significations" he means "images, ideas, words, objects of my thought" (Poulet 1969:54), and though he admits not knowing *how* these transformations come about (Poulet 1969:54), Poulet does give a phenomenological description of *what* happens. The point of special interest to him is that the objects of thought which the book reveals are "dependent on my [the reader's] consciousness" (Poulet 1969:55). They are "purely mental entities" which "relinquish their existence as real objects" (Poulet 1969:55). Thus by reading, the reader is delivered over (by himself as reader) to "fictitious" or unreal beings, beings which are dependent on language and the reader's consciousness. Says Poulet: "I become a prey of language," and "Language surrounds me with its unreality" (Poulet 1969:55). The advantage of this "transmutation through language of reality into a fictional equivalent" (Poulet 1969:55) is that first, the fictional reality is "indefinitely more elastic than the world of objective reality" (Poulet 1969:55); and second (and most important), because the objects of the mind are mental objects, "I am persuaded . . . that I am freed from my usual sense of incompatibility between consciousness and its objects" (Poulet 1969:55). There are indeed objects of which the mind is conscious, but they are "subjectified objects" (Poulet 1969:55). Presumably, then, there are advantages which the reader enjoys on his "return to the world of objective reality"; but Poulet does not even mention what these might be, unless it is a greater sense of belonging or compatibility with oneself in the world and any consequent enrichment of life. Perhaps this breakdown of the barrier between the reader and the book as an object in the world is a model and foretaste of the falling away of the barriers which alienate. What Poulet says of the relation of a reader to a book--"You are inside it; it is inside you there is no longer either outside or inside" (Poulet 1969:54)--may in some appropriately modified sense be the goal for literacy with regard to the relation between reader and Reality (however that may be defined).

This now completes the survey of reading theories, those of both the reading specialists and the phenomenologists. My task now will be to orient these two "camps" with respect to one another and to promote dialogue between them.

CHAPTER 3

READING THEORIES AND THE HISTORY OF WESTERN PHILOSOPHY

3.1   A preliminary orientation

This chapter will orient the reading theories of the two preceding chapters with reference to one another. My general approach recognizes trends within the theories of the reading specialists which associate the poles of these theories with general philosophical movements. In particular, the bottom-up theories are seen as variations of philosophical empiricism, while the top-down theories reflect philosophical rationalism. Further, the interactive theories are rough phenomenological. No strict identification between the (generally) psychological theories of the reading specialists and these philosophical movements is claimed; only a rough correlation. Making such a correlation, however, is offered as a preliminary footbridge between these two partners of our dialogue. This bridge will not bear a lot of heavy traffic, but it does establish a real link, and does allow enough commerce so that a more substantial structure can be built later. Such construction is the task which follows in chapters 4-9.

3.2   Empiricism and rationalism: an introduction

Both empiricism and rationalism are approaches to the theory of knowledge. The major question to which they seek answers are, What do we know?, How do we know?, and perhaps the best reference point for a consideration of the distinction between empiricism and rationalism, What is the origin of knowledge? (cf. Copelston 1958:16). For the empiricist, "we have no ideas at all other than those derived from experience which comes to us via our senses" (Brown 1969:60). Our factual knowledge is, according to the empiricist view, ultimately based on perception and is built up by means of induction. The mind is conceived of as fundamentally receptive. In Locke's famous phrase, it is a *tabula rasa*, a blank slate, which "received all its impressions *from outside*" (Brown 1969:62; emphasis added). Locke, Berkeley, and Hume are the major representatives of empiricism in the history of Western philosophy.

Philosophical rationalism, on the other hand, emphasizes reason, rather than experience, as "the source and norm of knowledge" (Thilly 1964:252). As Leibnitz (1896:70) said: ". . . all the thoughts and acts of the soul come from its own depths, with no possibility of their being given to it by the senses."

The rationalist claims some kind of innate or *a priori* truths. Such truths are either "present in the mind at or before birth" or are at least "inborn dispositions of the mind to form conceptions under certain circumstances" (Nelson 1967:197). The term "innate" emphasizes the inherent, "built-in" character of these ideas. They are given as part of what it is to be human. The term "*a priori*" emphasizes that such ideas are

55

not derived from experience; they are nonempirical (Hamlyn 1967:140). Usually the concept of innateness entails the notion of the a priori in at least two senses: (1) innate ideas are chronologically before sensory experience; and (2)

> . . . they are not composed from or testable in sensory experience but since they provide the basis for all scientific knowledge, they are also *a priori* in the logical or epistemological senses (Nelson 1967:197).

The ideal of the rationalist system of truth is deduction starting from self-evident principles. The entire project of knowledge, then, is seen as "the self-unfolding of the reason itself" (Copelston 1958:17).

Descartes is the leading figure of rationalism, together with Spinoza and Leibnitz. Though rationalism attempts to eliminate merely subjective factors from the knowing process (following the mathematical model as its ideal), in another sense it marks a radical turn to subjectivity as the basis of sure knowledge. Descartes' famous *cogito ergo sum* ("I think, therefore I am") indicates this subjective foundation for sure knowledge. Though Descartes thought he could eliminate all other possible foundations for knowledge by doubting their existence, he could not eliminate the certainty that the one who doubted did in fact exist as a personal subject, even in the midst of his most intense (methodological) doubts. Thus, for Descartes, the thinking (doubting) subject provided a stable, sure starting point for further deductions.[1]

It is this primary attention of the rationalists to the contributions of the subject and the empiricists' attention to the objects of experience which tends to identify the former with top-down and the latter with bottom-up theories of reading. There is, however, a further complication introduced by the general psychological orientation of the reading theories. This complication will be discussed in section 3.5 below.

3.3   Empiricism and bottom-up theories

In chapter 1 I characterized the primary distinction between the bottom-up and the top-down theories of reading in terms of different answers to the question of control in reading. For the bottom-up theories, the text or the print controls or "drives" the reading process. The reader is constrained by that which is outside of himself, i.e. the text. This is much like empiricism with its emphasis on the mind receiving "all its impressions from the outside" (Brown 1969:62).

---

[1] I am following the line of argument presented by Hintikka 1967, Reeder 1978, and others, that Descartes' famous *"Cogito, ergo sum"* rests upon (among other premises) the performative aspect of thought. As such it is more than an objective truth; it is essentially a subjective experience.

As with the empiricist, the focus of the bottom-up theories is on sense experience. That which is unique to reading, as opposed to the oral use of language, is "the means of connection to the human nervous system" (Fries 1962:119), in particular, the stimulation of the nerves in the eye. So strong is this stimulus-response emphasis in Bloomfield and Fries, that they both are often associated with behaviorism, a clearly empiricistic psychology.[2]

Further, the empiricist preference for the principle of induction, building from the particular (i.e. sense data) to the general (i.e. ideas, meaning), is almost exactly reproduced by the bottom-up theories. Recall that bottom-up theories begin with the most primitive (written) linguistic level (the features of letters) and proceed unidirectionally to build to the most complex, higher-order levels. Sentence meaning is then "conceived to be the *deterministic* product of the lower-order levels of analysis" (R. Anderson 1977:5; emphasis added).

It is true that in the bottom-up account of reading there is the recognition of the importance of prior meaning; in particular, the prior meaning of oral language use is the basis for meaning in reading. Such prior knowledge, however, attains neither the status nor the function of *a priori* innate knowledge as represented in both philosophical rationalism and top-down theories of reading.

3.4 Rationalism and top-down theories

Three major rationalist emphases are present in top-down theories of reading. First, there is the central and foundational attention to the subject. The priority for Smith, for example, is the information which the reader already possesses. Contrary to the empiricists and the bottom-up theorists, the information which Smith emphasizes is nonvisual, the meaning the reader brings to the text "prior to and even without the identification of words" (Smith 1978:119). Though the top-down theorists are not concerned with exactly the same questions as the rationalists, there is no doubt that both start with the subject as the key to their theoretical systems.

Second, for Smith as for the rationalists, the attainment of certainty is fundamental to comprehension; and that certainty is radically dependent on the subject. Certainty for Smith is synonymous with comprehension and is a state of having one's questions answered. For Descartes, certainty is a state which cannot be doubted, and thus is comprehended as the bedrock basis for further deductions. Though there are significant differences in these two views, both aim for and make central certainty as experienced by the subject in relation to himself.

---

[2] This association is considered in greater detail in the next chapter with regard to theories of meaning.

The third similarity between the rationalists and the top-down theorists is the frank acknowledgment of "innateness" by both. Smith joins the rationalist side of the debate regarding the fundamental origin of knowledge. Says he, the ability of the reader to predict and learn, that is, to make the essential contribution to the reading process, is "a natural process . . . a natural part of being alive and growing up" (Smith 1978:87). He even terms this ability "innate" (Smith 1978:88; cf. also Smith 1982:56).

These three parallels, then, warrant at least a preliminary association between philosophical rationalism and the top-down theories of reading.

3.5   Phenomenology introduced

According to Wild (1962:7), ". . . phenomenology originated with the profound and creative criticism of British Empiricism that was inaugurated by Brentano and Husserl at the very end of the nineteenth century." The phenomenological slogan has been "Back to the things themselves," and thus phenomenology has been termed a "radical empiricism" (Edie 1962:19, 28; Wild 1962:7). Phenomenology clearly recognizes that "there are some factors in the material [objects being studied] which direct [the contributions of the receiver] . . . into channels not of his choosing" (Spiegelberg 1965:131).

And yet, phenomenology is clearly not just another brand of traditional empiricism. Phenomenology rejects, for example, as "unfounded and unclarified metaphysical presuppositions" (Edie 1962:19) such traditional doctrines of empiricism as

> . . . its latent body-mind dualism, its empty-mind
> ("container") theory of consciousness, its
> conceptions of the subject as the passive receptor
> of discrete, simple, atomic impressions from the
> "outside world," etc. (Edie 1962:19).

So profound has been the phenomenological criticism of empiricism, that in his efforts to get "back to the things themselves," Husserl, the recognized founder of phenomenology, turned to Descartes, the rationalist, "as the greatest model of such a radical return to what is given beyond the shadow of a doubt" (Spiegelberg 1965:133).

As with the rationalists, Husserl returned to subjectivity to establish and elaborate the foundations of the certainty which he sought. In this sense Descartes is recognized as the forerunner of phenomenology (Edie 1965:20ff). And yet phenomenology also goes beyond traditional rationalism.

Phenomenology, then,

> . . . is neither a science of objects [empiricism] nor
> a science of the subject [rationalism]; it is a
> science of *experience*. It does not concentrate
> exclusively on either the objects of experience or
> on the subject of experience, but on the point of
> contact where being [the objects] and
> consciousness [the subject] meet (Edie 1962:19).

At the radical level of the point of contact between the subject and objects
which phenomenology seeks to attain "empiricism and rationalism are no
longer exclusive of one another" (Thevenaz 1962:52). As Husserl puts it, in
the phenomenological attitude, "the distinction between 'springing forth
from without' and 'what is added to it by the mind [Geist]' disappears."[3]
Put in these terms, it is easy to see that phenomenology attempts to
surpass, or penetrate beneath, the subject-object distinction which has
generated both the rational/empirical and the top-down/bottom-up
distinctions.

What, then, is the program of phenomenology? What does it try to
do, and how does it do it?

Thevenaz (1962:37) prepares us for some disappointment and
frustration with regard to such questions:

> This question [What is phenomenology?] is as
> irritating for the layman who hearing the word
> would like to know at least roughly what it means,
> as it is for the historian of philosophy or the
> philosophical specialist who has the feeling of
> pursuing an elusive doctrine, never clearly defined
> during the fifty years of its rich evolution . . . .

As Edie (1962:29) puts it, it is "still impossible to define the
phenomenological method in a simple manner." Obviously, I will not make
that my aim here.

But I can say enough for my purposes. Again according to
Thevenaz (1962:39), phenomenology is both "methodical and groping."
Though the subject-object distinction in its traditional sense is surpassed by
phenomenology,

---

[3] Husserl, Manuscript B III 10, p. 14 (1921) as quoted in Landgrebe (1981:45).

What remains is the distinction of that which is
most basic and genetically primitive and yet akin
to the ego, that which is contingent, and the lawful
formation of reproduction, association,
apperception, and other constitutive
accomplishments whereby the lawfulness of these
formations is not accidental but essential (Husserl,
as quoted in Landgrebe, 1981:45).

Phenomenology, then, studies particular human experiences and gropes
toward unveiling and explicating this "essential lawfulness of each form of
experience" (Biemel 1977:292). Reading is, of course, one such "form of
experience."

The method of phenomenology's "methodical groping" is called the
phenomenological reductions. Without going into detail (cf. e.g.
Spiegelberg 1962:133ff; Ricoeur 1967:87-89, 146-148, etc.; Reeder n.d.:9ff,
54ff), the reductions are philosophical procedures or mental practices,
which are supposed to provide philosophical access "to a position which
will still be neither objectivist (or naturalist), nor metaphysical, nor . . .
psychologistic or subjectivist" (Thevenaz 1962:46). In short, the reductions
are to bring to light (and provide a means for studying) that point of
contact between consciousness and the world which I referred to earlier.
Phenomenology calls this "point of contact" the intentionality of
consciousness, meaning by that consciousness's essential characteristic of
always being *of . . . [something]*. Consciousness is always directed to its
objects, and participates in the constitution of all appearances to
consciousness. Thus, while empiricism reduces consciousness to the object-
pole and rationalism reduces consciousness to the ego-pole, phenomenology
insists that both object and ego poles are always given together and must
be studied as such. Thus both Descartes' idea of a consciousness closed in
on itself, thus attaining certainty, and the empiricist idea of the subject as
merely a passive receptor of sense data are rejected in favor of a different
starting point.

I am avoiding a fuller treatment of the phenomenological reduction
not only because of the complexity of the topic, but primarily because
Husserl's conception of it has not withstood the further developments
within the phenomenological tradition. In particular Ricoeur's
reinterpretation of the reduction will be discussed shortly. But first an
introduction to Husserl's perspective on psychology.

Husserl first confronted the necessity for a philosophical reflection
on psychology with regard to questions about the foundations of
mathematics and logic. The then wide-spread view, which Husserl himself
at one time embraced, regarded psychology as the necessary and sufficient
foundation of logic. This approach was an attempt to convert all objects
into psychological experiences (cf. Spiegelberg 1965:93ff). Husserl objected
that man's psychological states are unstable and thus do not provide the
secure foundation needed to account for the stability of logical objects as

we all experience them. Rather, logical structures exhibit an independence from the experiencing subject. They are "completely autonomous of, in the sense of not being man-made, and so are not ontologically dependent upon 'the knowing subject' " (Langsdorf and Reeder n.d.:11). Such objects Husserl called "ideal," later extending this conception to characterize all meaning (cf. chapter 4). Though the "particular mode of existence [of ideal objects] always remained undetermined" (Spiegelberg 1965:106), Husserl pointed out that "there is *no evidence* for claiming that the objects of knowledge are caused by man" (Langsdorf and Reeder n.d.:11).

The phenomenological experience of ideal objects, then, disallows grounding experience in psychology alone. However, rather than opposing psychology Husserl sought both to ground empirical psychology in a deeper phenomenological account of all human experience (including science) and to establish a distinctly phenomenological psychology as the "unveiling of the *a priori* structures of the life of the mind . . . something without which there can be no life of the mind" (Biemel 1977:289).

That which prevents psychology from providing an adequate account of human experience, is "its blindness with regard to intentionality" (Gurwitsch 1974:78). So fundamental is intentionality that any attempt to account for human experience without reckoning with both its poles is doomed to failure. Phenomenology, then, claims to elucidate "the fundamental structures of conscious experience which constitute the very conditions of the possibility of any conscious experience whatsoever" (Edie 1962:20). In this sense, phenomenology is ". . . a transcendentalism of a very special sort" (Edie 1962:28).

Husserl's claim is that transcendental subjectivity is the direction in which philosophy should look in order to complete its task of elucidating the foundations of human experience, thus providing a basis for science, including psychology. This "transcendentalism" is special because it is qualified by the discovery of intentionality: ". . . the transcendental is . . . another name for the constituting intentionality of consciousness" (Thevenaz 1962:48). This "constituting," however, is *both* active *and* passive. With the introduction of the concept of passive constitution, Husserl's transcendentalism "distinguishes itself from traditional transcendental philosophies, which since Kant, have considered all syntheses as the 'spontaneity of an *act* of understanding' " (Landgrebe 1981:50; emphasis added). But the acknowledgement of both passivity and activity is another way of insisting on both poles of intentionality.

The notion of "transcendental subjectivity" in Husserl lacks precision, and thus there is still no general consensus about what it means (cf. Landgrebe 1981:50ff). Consequently, because the reductions were to lay bare this transcendental subjectivity, they also lack precision. In short, the fate of Husserl's conception of the phenomenological reductions is the same as that of "transcendental subjectivity." Be that as it may, we too will confront this area of thought in our study of reading, especially in chapters 7-9. The point to note here, though, is that Husserl claims that psychology is unable to adequately deal with "transcendental subjectivity," however that may be understood. We will see this claim borne out in our own investigations.

3.6 Ricoeur's place in the phenomenological tradition

Ricoeur has followed closely, and participated in, the phenomenological movement. He is recognized as "clearly the best French interpreter of Husserl" (Spiegelberg 1965:565), and

> . . . the French philosopher best qualified to bridge the remaining gap between German and French phenomenology, and to preserve the continuity of the phenomenological tradition in a creative fashion (Spiegelberg 1965:578).

He is, however, "anything but Husserl's most orthodox French disciple" (Spiegelberg 1965:565).[4]

Ricoeur is critical of Husserl's phenomenology in ways which have a direct bearing on a theory of reading. In general, Ricoeur replaces Husserl's commitment to transcendental subjectivity as the ultimate foundation--as reflected, for example, in his notion of transcendental subjectivity--with a theory of the text and the subject's relation to it as reader. This general change of perspective can be expressed in particulars which are introduced here, but developed in following chapters.

First, the ideal of scientificity is challenged. Here Ricoeur follows Heidegger's further radicalization and enlargement of Husserl's conception of intentionality:

> . . . not only the mind of man is intentionally related to the world (which would actually be a reintroduction of an implicit body-mind dualism); it is man himself, as a concrete, living, experiencing, thinking, perceiving, imagining, willing, loving, hating, communicating being who is intentional of the world (Edie 1962:27).

Heidegger is not satisfied that consciousness, even transcendental consciousness, is an adequate foundation. Husserl's foundation is "still too 'idealist,' too 'subjectivist' in his [Heidegger's] eyes" (Thevenaz 1962:57). Rather,

---

4 Ricoeur is being considered here because his relation to the phenomenological tradition is extensive. Iser and Poulet, on the other hand, have made particular contributions to the phenomenology of reading, but have not interacted with the tradition to the extent that Ricoeur has.

He bases himself on a more clearly ontological
structure beneath the level of consciousness . . .
from which alone one is able to understand the
possibility and meaning of a consciousness or of a
transcendental ego (Thevenaz 1962:57).

For Heidegger, then, Being is the correlate or object of human
intentionality. This is beginning "from above" (Thevenaz 1962:60) indeed,
in a sense not dreamed of by the psychologically oriented top-down reading
theorists.

And yet, Being for Heidegger is not a clear concept. As Thevenaz
(1962:60) puts it:

Being [is] conceived as a kind of obscure and
hidden power, that consents to manifest itself, . . .
that condescends thus to give itself to man, like a
kind of grace, to come out of itself, to express
itself, to make itself meaningful.

In the later Heidegger, language (and in particular, the words of the poet)
tends to replace the Being of the earlier Heidegger as the center of
attention.

Without following Heidegger in every detail, Ricoeur does
acknowledge this "ontological shift." He recognizes that human knowing is
"always preceded by a relation which supports it" (Ricoeur 1981a:105), a
relation which is precisely *not* a relation to an object. The ontological
condition of understanding (i.e. taking Being into account as fundamental)
precedes any subject-object distinction. Thus, the psychological categories
of the subject and the whole human project of knowledge are founded on
and are functions of a more profound relation of man's belonging to Being.
Husserl's ideal of scientificity (and that of the reading theorists) does not
adequately reckon with this dimension.

Second, "Ricoeur objects to Husserl's 'logicist prejudice,' which gives
the theoretical acts of consciousness priority over the affective and
volitional acts" (Spiegelberg 1965:565). As in the preceding point, it is man
as a whole, and not just as mind, which is intentionally related to the world.
Ricoeur claims that the phenomenological evidence does not allow the
conclusion that the non-theoretical acts are only founded on the theoretical.
This point too will be relevant for reading theory (cf. chapter 7).

Third, Ricoeur does not think that Husserl has adequately accounted
for the passivity of consciousness's acts of constitution. Ricoeur claims that
the phenomenological reduction ultimately concerns "the reference of a
consciousness to a transcendence" (Ricoeur 1967:9). But Husserl wanted
to bracket, or suspend, any attachment to or belief in, the whole domain of
transcendence. Husserl did tend toward the recognition of this
nonreducible "pre-given passive universal" (Ricoeur 1967:12) in his

63

attention to "the life-world." But such a tendency failed to do full justice to the ontological concerns of Heidegger and Ricoeur (cf. point one above).[5]

Finally, Ricoeur reconceives of the phenomenological reduction in linguistic terms in such a way as to make the doing of the reduction virtually synonymous with reading. The "reduction" of the world and the natural relation to it occurs as the distanciations of the text and reading function to dispossess the reader of his world and himself (cf. e.g. Ricoeur 1974:91f; 1981a:131ff; 182ff). This reconception of the reductions is part of Ricoeur's greater attention to language, which also distinguishes him from Husserl. In particular, Ricoeur has sought to integrate insights from French structuralism.

These departures of Ricoeur from traditional Husserlian phenomenology are immensely interesting to philosophers, especially those of the phenomenological tradition. They are also potentially just as interesting to reading theorists. "Potentially," I say, because many find Ricoeur's thought inaccessible. I will attempt to actualize some of this potential in the following chapters.

3.7 Phenomenology and interaction theories of reading

At this point it should be very clear that the phenomenological perspective has much in common with the interaction view of reading. Both acknowledge that the subject and the object of perception are bound up together and that each must and can be properly considered only in relation to the other. Further, both poles of experience--i.e. the ego and the object (to use phenomenological terms)--provide input to the constitution of the experience. With regard to reading, this implies that both the text and the reader must be fully acknowledged; but further, such acknowledgment will be adequate only if the text and the reader are considered as bound up together in an interactive relationship.

There are, though, significant differences between phenomenology and the interactive reading theories. These differences are adequately summarized in terms of the distinctions between (1) philosophy as a foundational enterprise versus psychology, and (2) epistemology (the theory

---

[5] Though Ricoeur himself is still vague on the role and character of what he means by transcendence, and how to integrate this concern into phenomenology, I will develop this issue in several places in the following chapters. In light of this further discussion later, it is of interest that Thevenaz (1962:61) considers Heidegger's Being to be "no longer a transcendental foundation . . . ; it tends to become once more simply transcendent." And again, "Heidegger comes back, in a roundabout way and against his express intentions, to the classical conception of metaphysical ontology. . . . what could this foundation be except transcendence in a metaphysical sense?" (Thevenaz 1962:65).

of knowledge and knowing) versus ontology (the inclusion of the theory of Being as fundamental). I have already sketched these differences above. The remaining chapters of Part II will develop these differences, supplying more detailed discussions centered around the key concepts of meaning and comprehension.

CHAPTER 4

STUDIES OF MEANING IN READING THEORIES

That meaning is of central importance to reading theory is obvious to all. There is not a single reading theorist who does not acknowledge the importance of meaning in reading. The reason is obvious: Comprehension, the agreed upon goal of reading (cf. chapters 5 and 6), *is* "comprehension of meaning." Simply put, "The meaning of an expression in a language is what a competent speaker of the language *understands* by that expression" (Platts 1979:43; emphases added). Consequently, it is no surprise that Lovett says, ". . . reading theorists must address the issue of meaning . . ." (Lovett 1981:11). And yet, this acknowledgement comes in the context of the frank recognition that "Nowhere is our ignorance more blatant . . . than in the area of semantic processing" (Lovett 1981:11).

That the question of meaning is "a particularly formidable task" (Lovett 1981:11) is not a new acknowledgement; nor is the recognition of ignorance. Bloomfield (1933:140) said,

The statement of meanings is therefore the weak point in language-study, and will remain so until human knowledge advances very far beyond its present state.

No doubt there have been advances in the study of meaning since Bloomfield's time, and yet, "The literature on this subject contains a bewildering diversity of approaches, conceptions, and theories . . ." (Alston 1964:11). Meaning remains "one of the most ambiguous and most controversial terms in the theory of language" (Ullmann 1962:54). And more recently, Putnam (1978:81):

The amazing thing about the theory of meaning is how long the subject has been in the grip of philosophical misconceptions, and how strong these misconceptions are.[1]

No less is this the case with regard to meaning in reading theories. We will, in fact, find (in what follows) that the meaning of meaning shifts from theory to theory, each one with philosophical difficulties.

It is generally accepted that there are two basic theories of meaning espoused among reading theorists. Not surprisingly, these two approaches line up with the categorization of reading theories in general. What Bloome 1983 calls the "conventional theory" is basically bottom-up: Meaning is in the print; the reader decodes the print to meaning in order

---

[1] Ogden and Richards (1923:186f), for instance, noted over 20 definitions of meaning. Today there exist even more.

to derive the author's meaning. The alternative theory of meaning Bloome terms the "constructivist theory." This theory recognizes the role of the reader who participates in the construction of meaning in interaction with the text. Here the top-down influence of the reader in interaction with the text is recognized as integral to meaning. Having said this, though, it is still not at all clear what meaning is for the reading theorists.

The purpose of this chapter is to explore more thoroughly the conceptions of meaning in reading theories. Representatives from the three categories of reading theories (bottom-up, top-down, and interactive) will be critiqued with regard to their theories of meaning. Then a phenomenological theory of meaning will be presented and brought to bear on the question of meaning in reading.

4.1 The theory of meaning of Bloomfield and Fries

Bloomfield and Fries have written on the topic of meaning more explicitly than any other bottom-up theorists.[2] It is to their theory that we now turn our attention.

This theory of meaning is generally judged to be a behaviorist theory (e.g. Alston 1964, 1967; Langsdorf 1980).[3] The focus of such a theory is on "publicly observable aspects of the communication situation" (Alston 1964:25). As Bloomfield put it,

> We have defined the *meaning* of a linguistic form as the situation in which the speaker utters it and the response which it calls forth in the hearer (1933:139);

and again,

---

[2] Gough, for instance, makes no claim to understanding the arrival of meaning in the reading process, calling the semantic processor "Merlin" to highlight its magical and mysterious quality.

[3] Both Bloomfield and Fries, however, preferred the term "physicalism" to "behaviorism" (Fries 1962:233, note 13). To designate the theory of meaning of these two men as "behaviorist" is not, however, to say that either one was a thoroughgoing behaviorist. Fries, for example, was not anti-mentalistic nor mechanistic in his view of man or the universe (P.H. Fries 1985a). But having said that, it still seems to be the case that both Fries' and Bloomfield's theories are subject to the usual criticisms leveled against behaviorist accounts of meaning. If this judgment is in error (as P.H. Fries 1985b thinks), then I think that is so due to (1) a behaviorist-type *emphasis* in both Fries and Bloomfield, (2) the lack of extended treatment of the topic of meaning, (3) inattention to some of the issues of contemporary concern (not a culpable fault), and (4) some confusing formulations, much as noted with respect to Fries in chapter 1. Parenthetically, in this day of reader-response criticism, it is interesting to note Fries' emphasis on listener/reader reaction. Bloomfield, on the other hand, emphasizes the initial situation.

We can define the meaning of a speech-form
accurately when this meaning has to do with some
matter of which we possess scientific knowledge
(1933:139).

And for Fries, the stimulus-response language of behaviorism becomes
prominent:

Lexical meaning consists of the recurrent "sames"
of the stimulus-response features that regularly
accompany recurrent "sames" of the arrangements
of contrastive features that constitute the word-
patterns (Fries 1962:111);

and similarly for "grammatical meanings" (Fries 1962:111f), and "social-
cultural meaning" (Fries 1962:112).

The main difficulty with the behaviorist theory of meaning is ". . .
correlating the multiplicity, and perhaps even the infinity, of situations to
the uniformity which we experience and expect when using meanings"
(Langsdorf 1980:106). As Alston (1964:26) points out, the behaviorist
theory predicts common features or functions discernible in both the
situations and the responses of the utterance of any particular expression in
a given sense. This commonality, however, ". . . seems not to be the case"
(Alston 1964:26), not even in the simple descriptive cases (Alston
1964:26f), and especially not in the cases where the reference is to states of
affairs remote from the context of utterance (Alston 1964:27; cf. Ullmann
1962:59). Rather, as Wittgenstein and others point out, the commonality
between the same terms used in different situations is of the nature of
"family resemblances" rather than common features. Consider, for
example, the meaning of "run" in "run on a bank," "run in a stocking," and
"run around a track." Though common features can be found, two
difficulties remain for the behaviorist account of meaning. First, it seems
impossible to locate in a consistent and persuasive manner those features
(held in common by the various senses) in either the situation or the
psychological responses of the language users. Second, the common
features found--e.g. rapid movement (actual or assumed), in the "run"
example--do not account for all the meaning in the actual use of "run" in
the examples above. For example, the sense of a "tear" in the stocking is
not conveyed by the common feature "rapid movement."

Two further difficulties with the behaviorist theory are noted by
Ullmann 1962. First, if meaning is located in the situations of utterance
and response, then no account is available of the effect of language on the
situations (Ullman 1962:59). This point will become a major concern in
chapter 8. Second, and a related point: meaning is located outside of
language, and language is then understood as meaningless, simply a code of
symbols (as in Fries 1962:100). But clearly meaning is expressed and
communicated *in and through* language.

Finally, in anticipation of an alternative model to be presented later in this chapter, I point out here that the behaviorist model is tied closely, even inherently, to the communication situation. I postpone, however, the critique of this issue until later.

Though there are these serious, and in my judgment fatal, difficulties with the behaviorist theory of meaning, there are aspects of meaning which this theory has taken note of, which must be included in any adequate account of meaning. The emphasis on "the observable," whether stimuli or responses, does show clearly that language use is embedded in the public domain. So strong is this aspect in Bloomfield, that Ullmann (1962:60) considers his theory to be primarily referential, and concludes that "The failure of the Bloomfield experiment clearly shows that one cannot have a referential definition of meaning without positing a middle term between the name and the referent" (Ullmann 1962:60). What Ullmann is pointing out here with regard to theories of meaning is the same point which is the major critique of bottom-up reading theories in general: there must be an acknowledgment of the contribution of the subject to meaning.

This, then, leads us quite naturally to a consideration of meaning in the top-down reading theory of Frank Smith.

4.2   The theory of meaning of Frank Smith

Only a brief review of our summary of Smith's reading theory is needed to highlight the significance of meaning in this theory. Meaning is, in fact, central. Says Smith, ". . . my aim . . . is to show that readers must bring meaning *to* print rather than expect to receive meaning *from* it" (1978:50; similarly Smith 1982:76, 160, 193). What, then, is meaning for Smith?

Most simply, the meaning of a text is some kind of relation to what is already known (cf. e.g. Smith 1978:10; 1982:15). The kind of relation is one of a matching or correspondence which relates textual[4] answers to the questions posed by the predictions which are themselves motivated by what the reader knows and/or wants to know (cf. e.g. Smith 1978:78; 1982:60).

Though simply put, the preceding account is vague for several reasons. First, this account of meaning is abstracted from what is said specifically about "comprehension" and not about "meaning" per se.[5] This

---

[4] Smith (1982:23) does acknowledge the necessity of interpretation.

[5] "Comprehension" is generally taken to be the human experience of understanding. That which is understood is the "meaning." The two are of course closely correlated as subject (comprehension) and object pole (meaning) of a single experience. There are, though, characteristics of the experience of meaning (i.e. comprehension) which validate the present use of the two terms as distinguishable. These characteristics are presented explicitly at the end of section 4.3 below.

approach is to some extent justified because of the close relation between comprehension and meaning. Especially is this the case in Smith's theory, which not only relates these two concepts--and in an important sense conflates them (see below)--but also says much about comprehension directly, and little about meaning. However, it does not yield precise conceptions of meaning.

A more basic source of vagueness, though, is that no account of the status of the already known is included. In what follows I present (what I take to be) Smith's remedy to these two objections. The evaluation of these remedies, however, will reveal fundamental difficulties with Smith's theory of meaning (each of which also contributes to an irremediable vagueness).

The closest Smith comes to telling us directly *what* meaning is, is really an answer to *where* it is:

> . . . meaning does not lie in the realm of language at all, but in the underlying thought processes of the language user (1975:84).

> Meaning [is] . . . in the minds of the users of language . . . (1982:70).

> As long as meaning is not detached from the producer's purpose or intention, there is very little chance of semantic or philosophical confusion (1977:642).

The conclusion, then, is that meaning is a psychological state. The difficulty with this psychological approach is, as Langsdorf has pointed out, that it ". . . cannot account for the uniformity of meaning which is evident in our experience" (1980:105). Both the behavioral theory of meaning and the mental state theory are subject to the same critique: They tie meaning too exclusively to that which is variable (whether the external situation or the internal mental situation) and thus do not have an adequate basis to account for the stability of meanings (e.g. the stability of the concept "two"). Another side of this same criticism is that meanings then become ". . . private and peculiar to the biography of each mind, [a fact which] contradicts the character of meanings as available for validation [e.g. through dialogue] " (Langsdorf 1980:105). The lack of clarity in Smith's theory of meaning can be noted in this context as a confusion between "comprehension" and "meaning": Both have been reduced to psychological states. It is, though, still possible to distinguish "comprehension" and "meaning" in Smith's theory, a fact which unfortunately does not remedy the present confusion. The basis of this distinction is Smith's "theory of the world in the head" to which we now turn our attention.

71

The "already known" which serves as the basis of comprehension is, presumably, the meaning which the reader brings to the text, and comprehension is its employment in concrete acts of knowing. This "already known" is treated by Smith in substantial detail (cf. chapter 1) in terms of "the theory of the world in our heads" (e.g. Smith 1982:54ff). The first point to note, though, is that this theory is "in our heads" and thus does not escape the concerns of the previous point. Smith's focus is on *cognitive* structures as his explication of his "theory" (in the head) makes plain. The theory is composed of (1) categories or systems of distinctive features, (2) rules for assigning objects to the categories, and (3) interrelations among the categories, such as class inclusion and functional relations (Smith 1975:11ff).

Smith, however, is not thoroughly consistent in treating the theory of the world in our heads in cognitive terms, a point which will prove to his advantage in later discussions. Says he, "Theories in the head are 'implicit knowledge' " (1975:43; cf. also 1982:65). Smith traces his notion of "implicit" to the work of Michael Polanyi, specifically to the concept of the tacit dimension (Smith 1975:43). This is especially interesting since "the tacit" in Polanyi is regularly explicated in terms of the "inarticulate" (e.g. Polanyi 1958:86f), the "ineffable" (Polanyi 1958:87-91), the "indeterminate" (Polanyi 1958:86-8 7, 104, 150), and the "unspecifiable" (Polanyi 1958:62-63, 398).[6]

Thus Smith's "theory in our heads" contains "our *skills* by which we interact with the world" (Smith 1982:60), "all our feelings, values, and intentions" (Smith 1982:60), and is ". . . not only the source of our beliefs and expectations, our hopes and fears, but also of our motivations and abilities" (Smith 1975:37). These "contents" of the theory, though, seem to escape the category of "cognitive," especially when the latter is articulated in terms of systems of distinctive features. As Polanyi (1958:62f) notes:

> [Mental effort includes] . . . the usual process of unconscious trial and error by which we *feel our way* to success and may continue to improve on our success without specifiably knowing how we do it--for we never meet the causes of our success as identifiable things which can be described in terms of classes of which such things are members;

> Each single step in acquiring this domain [of knowledge, manners, laws, many different arts] was due to an effort which went beyond the hitherto assured capacity of some person making it . . . . It relied on an act of groping which

---

[6] Of further interest to our present concern (Smith's theory of meaning) is the fact that these discussions of Polayni are in the context of discussions of meaning (Polayni 1958:63, 150) and comprehension (Polayni 1958:398).

originally passed the understanding of its agent and of which he has ever since remained only subsidiary aware . . . .

It is difficult to see how Smith's cognitive categories and rules--which are not innate, but which are constructed by the individual (Smith 1978:88)--can account for this process of knowing since, according to Polanyi, this process (1) never meets identifiable (in terms of distinctive features) things; while the functioning of Smith's categories and rules depends on identifiability in terms of distinctive features; (2) exceeds the capacities of understanding (in terms of the specifiably known); while Smith's categories are specifically the "specifiably known"; and (3) ". . . is an action, but one that has always an element of *passivity* in it" (Polanyi 1958:63); while Smith's account of reading strongly emphasizes only the active contribution of the reader.[7]

Smith, however, seems to be aware of this discrepancy in his theory for he makes a fundamental shift in a recent essay. In "A metaphor for literacy--creating worlds or shunting information" (Smith 1983:117-134), Smith breaks with the primacy granted to the "information-processing psychology" in his earlier work (e.g. Smith 1975:2). The earlier dependence on this model--which highlights the cognitive as an information structure--is clearly one source for the difficulties just discussed. In this essay Smith argues that:

1. "Very little of what the brain contains is information" (Smith 1983:119-122)

2. "Very little of the brain's commerce with the world [including other people] is the exchange of information" (Smith 1983:122-124)

3. "Learning is rarely a matter of acquiring information" (Smith 1983:124-125)

4. "The brain is not very good at acquiring information;" it is not the most "natural" thing for the brain to do (Smith 1983:125-126)

5. "Language is not a particularly efficient means of communicating information;" it is not the most "natural" thing for language to do (Smith 1983:126-127).

Smith's alternative in this essay is that ". . . the primary, fundamental, and continual activity of the brain is nothing less than the creation of worlds" (Smith 1982:118). Here the metaphor ". . . pictures the brain as an artist, as a creator of experience for itself and for others, rather than as a dealer in information" (Smith 1982:119). Though this new

---

[7] Similiar critiques of science as based finally in elements which evade the usual account of scientific knowledge as objective are found in Kuhn 1970, Cassirer 1946, Weimer 1979, and others.

development in Smith is exceedingly interesting, especially in the light of the role of "the world" in the phenomenological theories to be discussed later, problems remain unresolved in Smith's approach.

First, if Smith were to identify meaning with that to which an expression refers in the world created by the reader (in interaction with the text) or with the *relation* between the expression and its referent, he still would not have an adequate account of meaning.[8] Two fundamental difficulties confront such a referential theory of meaning, the last of which makes it unlikely that Smith would follow this line of reasoning. First, there is a proper distinction between meaning and reference, since two different expressions can refer to the same individual: for example, "Sir Walter Scott" and "the author of Waverly," or "the morning star" and "the evening star" (to pick two famous examples). It should be clear that the members of each pair do not mean the same thing, but do refer to the same thing. Reference, then, is not a sufficient basis for meaning. Second, to base meaning on reference is to reduce meaning to some other phenomenon, in this case an object "in the world." If Smith were speaking of a world "out there," his top-down emphasis on the reader's contribution to meaning would be compromised. However, his "world" is in fact a (theory of a) world in our *heads*, the reference to which would not surpass the psychological states of the subject, nor escape the earlier critique of such theories.[9]

The second difficulty with Smith's recent view of reading as the creation of worlds lies with the concept "create." Smith's notion of meaning (and comprehension) as based on a relation to the familiar, already known is rendered increasingly problematic as "create" is taken to mean ". . . to cause to come into existence, to generate possibilities of experience" (Smith 1983:119). How the radically new comes to be, and to be understood, on the basis of the already known is not discussed by Smith; and yet, the new-old relation is at the heart of his theory. Consequently, the concept "meaning" becomes even less explicable.

Third, Smith's emphasis on creativity further aggravates the coherence of his views with those of Polanyi (with whom he seems to

---

[8] It is, however, not at all clear that Smith does so identify meaning. Neither is it clear that he does not, especially since the correspondence or matching relation between the "to be understood" and the "already known" seems so central to his understanding of meaning in his earlier (i.e. pre-1983) work. Perhaps the most charitable judgment is simply that Smith's account of meaning is not sufficiently developed.

[9] A third standard objection to referential theories of meaning is that it does not seem to be true that all meaningful expressions do in fact refer (cf. Alston 1964:14ff). The usual objection is stated at the word level, both with regard to functors (e.g. conjunctions and prepositions) and isolated content words (e.g. pencil). Though I have not found Smith to be explicit on this point, Goodman (with whom Smith is usually in agreement) avoids this objection by claiming that meaning is a clause-level phenomenon (Goodman 1976c:61).

intend to agree), specifically with regard to the element of "passivity" which Polanyi identified in all acts of knowing. While Smith asserts that the reader is "a creator of experience for itself and for others" (1983:119), Polanyi notes that the knowing person recognizes that ". . . he has not *made them* [the relations of meaning] but *discovered them*" (1958:63).

We are not finished with the discussion of creativity in reading and the problems it poses for reading theories. It will recur elsewhere in this chapter and the next three. Our point here, though, is to note that Smith's account of meaning is inadequate as it stands. And yet he has identified two factors which must be both distinguished and included in an adequate account of meaning: the cognitive and that which escapes explication in terms of cognitive structures.[10] Further, Smith has recognized that "Subjects are intrinsic to the presence of meaning" (Langsdorf 1980:106). Since meaning exists only insofar as subjects are active in conferring or constructing meaning, this aspect of Smith's contribution must be retained. In this regard, however, his location of meaning as "in the mind" must be rejected for the reasons given.

Finally, again in anticipation of a later discussion, I note that for Smith too (as for the behaviorists) the discernment of meaning in reading is conceived of as attached to the writer's intention and thus is rooted in the interpersonal relation between the reader and the writer (Smith 1977:642; 1982:76; also Goodman 1976c:58). In short, a conversational schema is basic to Smith's conception of reading.

4.3   Interaction theories of meaning

The interaction theories which I choose to discuss with regard to meaning are the schema theories.[11] Schema theory, says Rumelhart, is "basically a theory about knowledge" (1980:34). In fact, he goes on to say that ". . . our schemata *are* our knowledge. All of our generic knowledge is embedded in schemata" (Rumelhart 1980:41). Thus, being basically epistemological, schema theories have much to do with meaning.

To review briefly, schemas are "cognitive templates" (Armbruster 1976:13), "mental structures" (Anderson, et al. 1977:2), "data structures" (Rumelhart and Ortony 1977:101) which represent general knowledge by means of slots or placeholders which are filled by the data from the particular cases encountered in experience. Because they represent what is already known (Adams and Bruce 1980; Durkin 1980; R. Anderson 1977),

---

[10] Though "the cognitive" is recognized here as integral to a theory of meaning, Smith's use of "distinctive features" to characterize the formation and operation of the cognitive categories will be challenged in the next chapter where an alternative is proposed.

[11] My reasoning is that schema theories are the focus of most of the contemporary research in interactive reading theories, and thus, being the most developed, provide us with the most explicit notions relating to the discussion of meaning.

they are a priori in character representing the basis of the top-down processes.[12] Schemas are "the key units of the comprehension process," with "comprehension . . . considered to consist of selecting schemata and variable bindings that will 'account for' the material to be comprehended, and then verifying that those schemata do indeed account for it" (Rumelhart and Ortony 1977:111). In short, comprehension is filling the slots of schemas, and meaning, in general, is that which is understood; i.e. the filled schemas.

The schema-theoretic account of meaning has three major weaknesses. First, inasmuch as schemas are psychological or cognitive structures, they fall prey to the weaknesses of psychological theories of meaning. The primary weakness--that there is no basis for an account of the identity and stability of meanings--is reflected throughout the writings of schema theorists. The emphasis on the top-down contribution of the reader highlights the variability to be expected from individual to individual, even to the extent of characterizing this contribution as "creation" (e.g. Adams and Bruce 1980:37; Collins, et al. 1977:1; Spiro 1979:2). There is, though, a milder form of the conception of the reader's contribution, and that is that ". . . personal history, knowledge, and belief influences the interpretations [that are given texts]" (R. Anderson, et al. 1976a:17). Because these influences are pervasive--"Every act of comprehension involves one's knowledge of the world as well" (R. Anderson, et al. 1976:4)--meanings cannot be stable. The fact that there is stability is accounted for by the fact that the schemas "incorporate general knowledge" (R. Anderson 1977:2) which is shared by and is common to the members of a certain group or culture. The basis of stability, then, is group psychology or sociology, which is inadequate to account for the high degree of similarity, if not identity, of meanings cross-culturally (e.g. numbers, or logical structures).[13]

A second weakness of schema theories is that they are close enough in form to what can be referred to as the picture theory of meaning to be subject to the critique of this latter theory. The picture theory of meaning holds that "a meaning is given to the mind by a sort of mental picture" (Reeder 1980:160). In other words, the meanings of words are mental pictures or images; in short, an inner, private psychological state of the

---

[12] The weak sense of *a priori* is used here; i.e. though the schemas precede the experience which they are used to comprehend, no comment is made (with the "weak" usage) regarding the innate or acquired status of these schemas. The strong sense of a priori claims an innate status which is, in some sense, prior to all experience.

[13] It is true that different cultures have different ways of counting and arguing. I know of no evidence, however, which contradicts the stated conclusion. That is, regardless of cultural differences, the number 2 is a stable concept (whether or not the concept is lexicalized) and *modus tollens* is a valid logical structure (whether or not it is *used* as in and of itself persuasive).

language user.[14] Similarly, a proposition is taken to be "a picture of reality," a verbal representation of "the situation that it represents" (Wittgenstein 1961, 4.021; similarly 4.01(2), 4.031(1), 4.0311, etc.). In a manner quite reminiscent of such "pictures of reality," schema theory depends on the construction of a "scenario" (e.g. R.C. Anderson, et al. 1976a; Collins, et al. 1977; Tierney and Pearson 1981) within whichthe situation described might plausibly occur. These "scenarios" are, in schema-theoretic language, the filled schemas. Given this language usage, the type of examples regularly employed in the literature--restaurants, parties, descriptions of houses, etc.-- and the highly imagistic "slots" which are filled in these scenes, it seems fair to conclude that "the schema" is "a sort of mental picture."[15]

There are four recognized weaknesses of the mental picture theory of meaning with which schema theories must reckon. Reeder summarizes these as follows (1980b:161-162):[16]

1. "Mental pictures are not always present when meaning is present" (Reeder 1980b:161). A sign can be used with or without imagery, and meaning persists even when images vanish.

This objection cuts most deeply against a purely schema-theoretic account of meaning. What picture, or schema, for instance, is essential to the concept of the number 2, or robbery, or the buying of a house? Though there can be a variety of pictures appropriate to any of these, none of them are essential, and the concept involved persists independently.

2. "Pictures require interpretation: The same mental image may be used (meant) in different ways (with different meanings)" (Reeder 1980a:161).

---

[14] Cf. Reeder 1984b:18, 25, 104; Specht 1969:115-119; Pitcher 1964:75-104, 201-213.

[15] To be fair, though, it must also be acknowledged that this is by no means a position held to explicitly by even one schema theorist; nor is it as pervasive at every level of schema theory (e.g. three levels of schemas are noted by Adams and Bruce 1980-- conceptual, social, and story knowledge--with the first being the least susceptible to the picture theory characterization (however, under "story knowledge," the "image" (Adams and Bruce 1980:25) plays a crucial role)); nor do all schema theorists hold to the same conception of schemas--Iran-Nejad 1980, for example, conceives of a schema as a highly dynamic, transient, functional gestalt, more a process than a structure. (He does, though, hold a minority opinion at this point.) This divergence of opinion, however, does not threaten my characterization of schema theories as, in general, implying an at least incipient picture theory of meaning. Due to the lack of development of the concept of meaning in these theories, we can only say "incipient" and hope that the critique offered here may help to both prod further development and steer that development away from recognized pitfalls.

[16] Reeder supports these arguments with references from the works of Wittgenstein and Husserl.

2. "Pictures require interpretation: The same mental image may be used (meant) in different ways (with different meanings)" (Reeder 1980a:161).

Though schema theorists acknowledge this fact (due to the theory's emphasis on the necessity of interpretation (e.g. Reynolds 1981; Pichert and Anderson 1976; R.C. Anderson, et al. 1976a; R.C. Anderson, et al. 1977), because interpretation is itself grounded in schemas (which, of themselves, need interpretation; cf. next point), this account of meanng is finally ungrounded. Thus R.C. Anderson, et al. (1976a:18) acknowledge that schema-theoretical account of reading is "an incomplete explanation."[17]

3. "From a mental picture alone it is not possible to conclude anything about a meaning which it may accompany" (Reeder 1980b:161).

The meaning to be associated with a picture or schema is due to the active meaning-conferring involvement of the subject, not to the picture or schema itself, a point to be noted below (in favor of schema theory). Here the point is that the schemas themselves, as cognitive structures, cannot account for the meanings which they convey (or "embody") through instantiation.

4. "The notion of one picture standing of itself for many things is untenable" (Reeder 1980b:162).

The point here is that though there might be general schemas, these are understood as schemas only when the means of instantiation of particular samples is also understood.[18] This "means of instantiation" is termed "matching" or "correspondence" in schema theories. It is the means of filling a particular schema, of relating the *general* schema and the *specifics* of a particular experience. The role of "matching" is central in points 2, 3, and 4 above and is another weak point in schema theory to which we now turn our attention.

The third major weakness of the schema account of meaning has to do with the explication of the link between the general schema and its application. In general, the emergence of meaning in a particular case is understood as due to the matching of the given constraints of a text with the available schemas with their waiting slots. In general very little is said about the how of this process and the impression is often left that this

---

[17] The point, in fact, is the basis of Iran-Nejad's 1980 criticism of the conception of schemas as structures rather than processes, or transient constellations of shared elements.

A similar problem with regard to the schema-theoretic notion of comprehension is noted in chapter 5.

[18] Again Iran-Nejad 1980 is on the forefront of the development of this point in insisting that schemas are functional processes rather than structures.

matching is a quasi-mechanical process. This impression is due to the rigidity in the conception of the schema as structure, and an early (in the history of the theory's development) overdependence on what Smith (1983:67) calls "computer-based models of language." Though there are variables and a general openness inherent to schemas, this openness is usually presented as a rather well-defined "waiting . . . to be filled" (Durkin 1980:6).

There has, though, been a great deal of uneasiness with this rigid notion of the schema as structure. The purpose of schema theory in the first place was to give an account of the contribution of the reader to the meaning of the text. Though its attention to the cognitive structures of that contribution has tended to obscure the reader's (as reader, rather than as a set of cognitive structures) own contribution, evidence of this contribution is also very much a part of schema theory. What Husserl says with regard to images is also applicable to instantiations of general schemas:

> Resemblance between two objects, however precise, does not make the one to be the image [or the instantiation] of the other. Only a presenting ego's power to use a similar as an image-representative of a similar makes the image [or instantiation] *be* an image [or instantiation] (1970:594).

The point is that the ego must confer meaning on an instance of resemblance; in fact, the ego must construct or create the resemblance as resemblance in the first place.

That the ego is active in schema instantiation is definitely a central part of schema theory (e.g. Adams and Bruce 1980; Bruce and Rubin 1980; Kane and Anderson 1977; Adams and Collins 1977; Collins, et al. 1977; etc.). However, though this aspect is often acknowledged, and variously termed "construction," or "creation," or "inference," very little is said about its actual functioning. Indeed Trabasso 1980 is quite honest to admit that for the schema-type theories the processes involved remain, at heart, "a mystery."[19]

In spite of these weaknesses of a schema-theoretic account of meaning, and in some cases, even because of them, schema theories do hold several potential advantages. First, the debate within schema theories as to whether the schema is a structure or a function holds the potential for avoiding the critique of the picture theory of meaning, which does have a justified application to schema theory in its present form. As Reeder 1980

---

[19] Collins, et al. 1980 do study eight problem-solving strategies which can be used in this "construction," but still the application of these strategies in any particular case is mysterious. Quite possibly to admit "mystery" is the best anyone can do. (Spiro 1980 conjectures the same.) Further discussion of this point will recur in the next two chapters.

points out, the Wittgensteinian rejection of the mental picture theory of meaning does argue against psychological entities (including schemas) as the basis of meaning, but does not bear against the notion of "structure" which Husserl develops. This non-psychological, non-metaphysical, epistemological structure will be presented in the next section under the term *"ideal objects."* The point here is that schema theory's recognition of the role of structure, and a structure which obtains beyond the individual psyche (it contains "general knowledge"), holds the potential for reformulation so as to avoid some of the above critique.

On the other hand, the focus on the schema as a "rule" or a "dynamic function" highlights in a needed way that meaning is not purely structural in the impersonal sense, but as Langsdorf (1980:106) puts it, "[meanings] are only present insofar as subjects function so as to confer meanings; for unlike natural phenomena, meanings are not experienced as 'just there'." The problem which remains for schema theory, though, is how to reconcile these two notions, the structural and the functional.

The second potential advantage of schema theory is an expansion of the above point. In agreement with the top-down theorists, schema theory recognizes that no account of meaning is adequate which does not acknowledge the role of the reader. And, more specifically, not just the reader in general, but the particular perspective the particular reader takes on a text. As Pichert and Anderson (1976:2) put it, ". . . imposing a schema on a text simply means viewing the text from a certain perspective." The conclusion, then, with regard to textual structure is that ". . . structure is not an invariant property of text, but rather that it depends upon perspective" (Pichert and Anderson 1976:6). We will return to this point later. Here the contribution of schema theory is to note explicitly that the particular perspective of the reader "imposes" structure. Or to anticipate the phenomenological account, the "mode of attending" to the text must be considered in any account of the "object" in question.

Third, though there is vagueness in the schema account at this point, these theories do well to recognize the importance of "matching" or "correspondence" in the generation of meaning.[20]

Fourth, though no account of meaning can rest securely on the psychological basis alone, no account is complete without this aspect. As Kockelmans says,

> . . . not only could psychology profit from further
> contact with philosophy, but philosophy, in turn,
> can profit from a closer association with
> psychology (1967:351).

---

[20] This judgment is premature here, but will follow from the discussions in chapters 5, 6, and 7 to follow, being treated most directly in chapter 7, and again in chapter 9.

Finally, there is in schema theory, even at the point at which it is most vulnerable to the critique of the picture theory of meaning--the picture-like quality of schemas--two aspects of meaning which must not be denied. First, meaning does have reference to the "real world." In short, that which is meaningful does have reference to our lives as lived day-by-day. In the next section, we will seek a solution to the problem of how to avoid a reference theory of meaning while still acknowledging the obvious importance of reference to meaning. Second, it is not to be denied that ". . . meaning can only be grasped as an image" (Iser 1978:9), and that the images we possess during reading are of a "peculiar hybrid character: at one moment they are pictorial, and at another they are semantic" (Iser 1978:147). Ricoeur also gives much attention to this point, even designating this unity of the quasi-sensory and the semantic "the schema" (1975a:213).[21]

Having now completed a survey of the theories of meaning in the major reading theories, I conclude that the neglect of meaning as a thematized topic by these theorists is a major shortcoming. Though they all recognize that meaning is crucial and use the term freely, there remains almost no explicit treatment of the subject. Rather, (mostly) implicit theories of meaning are used uncritically, and, as we have seen, bring with them fundamental philosophical difficulties. It is at this point that the phenomenologists have, perhaps, the most to contribute to the opening up of new areas of reading research. However, before turning to these philosophical theories of meaning, I quote from Mohanty (1977:27) four facts about meaning which must be accounted for by any satisfactory theory of meaning:

> A satisfactory theory of meaning, then, should take cognizance of the following facts: (1) meanings are characterized by a sort of identity and contextual independence, and they can be shared and communicated intersubjectively so that it is legitimate to say of them that they are objective; (2) on the other hand, they stand internally related to the mental life (thought, feeling, and intentions) of the persons participating in them; (3) in spite of their sort of identity, which suggests they do not belong to the real order of temporally individuated events, they nevertheless serve as mediums of reference to things, events, persons, places, and processes in the world; and (4) they are incarnate in physical expressions, words, and sentences, which from one point of view are conventional signs and thus

---

[21] I return to this promising intimation in chapter 7, discussed there in conjunction with the third advantage of schema theory mentioned above, i.e. the role of "matching" or resemblance.

extrinsic to the meanings and yet, from another point of view, are united with the meanings they signify in such a manner that both form a most remarkable sort of wholeness.

According to our preceding analyses, we see (roughly speaking) that the behaviorist account fails on points 1 and 2, and succeeds on points 3 and 4; while the top-down approach of Smith and the interactive-schema theories fail on point 1 and succeeds on 2, 3, and 4. In spite of the successes, though, all these theories are severely hampered by their lack of development and their vagueness.

The phenomenological account of meaning which follows aims to meet the four facts which Mohanty mentions. Ricoeur's theory will serve as our touchstone and framework as a representative of phenomenology,[22] though I will refer to Iser throughout this presentation also, noting areas of agreement and disagreement with Ricoeur.

4.4   Ricoeur's theory of meaning

Before discussing Ricoeur's theory of meaning directly (section 4.2) and then implications for reading theory in two important areas (section 5), I present his model of language which serves as the background against which "meaning" is to be understood.

4.4.1   Ricoeur's model of language

Ricoeur's model of language is not unitary. Rather he believes in "two kinds of linguistics--semiotics and semantics" (Ricoeur 1976:8). The first is based on the sign, conceived of in the tradition of Saussure as the unity of the signifier--e.g. a sound, a written pattern, or any physical medium--and the signified--the differential value in a system. The second finds its characteristic unit in the sentence. These two kinds of linguistics are, for him, two distinct sciences:

> Moreover, these two sciences are not just distinct, but also reflect a hierarchical order. The object of semiotics--the sign--is merely virtual [i.e. it is not a real or actual object, but only appears as an object as the result of an abstraction performed on the actual]. Only the sentence is actual as the very event of speaking. This is why there is no way of passing from [i.e. within] the same methodology to a more complex entity. The sentence is not a larger or more complex word, it is a new entity. It

---

[22] I am not unaware that Ricoeur's account is better termed a hermeneutic phenomenology and as such differs in important ways with the theory of Husserl; cf. chapter 3, section 5.

may be decomposed into words, but the words are something other than short sentences. A sentence is a whole irreducible to the sum of its parts. It is made up of words, but it is not a derivative function of its words. A sentence is made up of signs, but is not itself a sign (Ricoeur 1976:7).

This distinction is, for Ricoeur, "the key to the whole problem of language" (Ricoeur 1976:8).

It is important to point out that for Ricoeur, discourse, his term for language as used or actualized, has "the ontological priority" (Ricoeur 1976:9) over language as system. The reason is simple:

The system in fact does not exist. It only has a virtual existence. Only the message gives actuality to language, and discourse grounds the very existence of language since only the discrete and each time unique acts of discourse actualize the code (Ricoeur 1976:9).

Ricoeur's basic interest is not the linguistics of the sign but the linguistics of the sentence. In his terms, his interest is in discourse or the theory of texts, specifically in the interpretation of texts. This interest leads him to further characterize the two objects of the two linguistics in distinction from each other and thus to further clarify his model of language. Four distinctions will be noted.

"Discourse," he says, "is given as an event: something happens when someone speaks (Ricoeur 1981a:133). Discourse, then, is "realized temporally and in the present" (Ricoeur 1981a:133); the system of language or the code is "virtual and outside of time" (Ricoeur 1981a:133) or rather, is "in time as a set of contemporaneous elements" (Ricoeur 1976:3).

Second, discourse is "linked to the person who speaks" (Ricoeur 1981a:133), it is "intentional; it is meant by someone" (Ricoeur 1976:3); while the code or language as system has no subject, "the question 'who speaks?' does not apply at this level" (Ricoeur 1981a:133). Closely related to the preceding point, discourse is ". . . arbitrary and contingent, while a code is systematic and compulsory for a given speaking community" (Ricoeur 1976:3).

Thirdly, language as discourse and system differ: "discourse is always about something" (Ricoeur 1981a:133), it " refers to a world which it claims to describe, express or represent" (Ricoeur 1981a:133); the signs of language, though, "refer only to other signs in the interior of the same system" (Ricoeur 1981a:133). In short, the system of signs has no outside, only an inside.

83

Fourth, and finally, discourse also has "another person, an interlocutor to whom it is addressed" (Ricoeur 1981a:133); "language," on the other hand, is "only a prior condition of communication" (Ricoeur 1981a:133). In these four ways, then, discourse as event distinguishes itself from the system of signs which have constituted the primary object for linguistics, at least since Saussure. In summary, discourse has time, a subject with freedom, a world, and an addressee.

Discourse, however, is not only event; it is also meaning. Says Ricoeur,

> Just as language, by being actualized in discourse, surpasses itself as system and realises itself as event, so too discourse, by entering the process of understanding, surpasses itself as event and becomes meaning (Ricoeur 1981a:134).

This basic "tension" (Ricoeur 1981a:134) or "dialectic" (Ricoeur 1981a:132; also 1976:8ff) between event and meaning, then constitutes language as discourse, Ricoeur's primary concern, and the background for our consideration of meaning. Two final points will conclude this presentation of Ricoeur's model of language: First, the notion of structure in discourse, and finally, the role of dialogue in this model.

Ricoeur does grant structure to discourse, but not a structure in the analytical sense of structuralism, i.e. as "a combinatory power based on the previous oppositions of discrete units" (Ricoeur 1976:11). Rather, there is only one kind of linguistic unit which constitutes the subject matter of the linguistics of discourse: the proposition.

> Consequently, there is no unit of a higher order that could provide a generic class for the sentence conceived as a species. It is possible to connect propositions according to an order of concatenation, but not to integrate them (Ricoeur 1976:10).[23]

Since there is just one kind of unit, it cannot be defined by its opposition to other units. But it still has structure. Its structure, though, is synthetic, i.e. it is constituted by the ". . . intertwining and interplay of the functions of identification [the function of the noun] and predication [the function of the verb] in one and the same sentence" (Ricoeur 1976:11). The subject picks out a unique identity and the predicate ". . . designates a kind of quality, a class of things, a type of relation, or a type of action" (Ricoeur 1976:11).

---

[23] This claim needs to be evaluated in the light of much contemporary work in linguistics, usually termed discourse or text grammar.

The interaction of these two distinct functions provides discourse with its structure.[24]

Finally, Ricoeur seems to agree with Heidegger in rejecting communication to others, and thus the dialogical situation, as the primary function and situation of language (Ricoeur 1981a:58). Rather, Ricoeur accepts " 'pointing out', 'showing', 'manifesting' " (Ricoeur 1981a:58) as the supreme function of language. However, he is not consistent here for he frequently asserts that ". . . the first and fundamental feature of discourse . . . [is] that it is constituted by a series of sentences whereby someone says something to someone about something" (Ricoeur 1981a:138; cf. also 152, 157, 159, etc.); thus tying himself again to the communication situation.[25]

Iser presents a more consistent relation to the communication situation under the term "implied reader." The implied reader is

> . . . a transcendental model which makes it
> possible for the structured effects of literary texts
> to be described. It denotes the role of the reader,
> which is definable in terms of textual structure and
> structural acts (Iser 1978:38).

"Transcendental" here carries the philosophic sense of designating "the conditions of possibility for." Thus even though distanciation is also, for Iser, inherent to the text-reader relation (e.g. Iser 1978:166) and a necessary condition of comprehension (e.g. Iser 1978:189), a communication-like situation is posited as the transcendental, though not the real, condition of reading. Ricoeur, in effect, operates on the same basis, though he is so intent upon recognizing and emphasizing the integral quality of distanciation, that he does not develop the transcendental perspective as explicitly as does Iser. The six distanciations of Ricoeur as discussed in chapter 2 and Iser's "transcendental perspective," then, should be taken as mutually qualifying. For example, Ricoeur's "intention of the text" (Ricoeur 1981a:161) is dependent on such a notion as Iser's "implied reader," for only subjects have "intention." Similarly, Iser's "implied reader" is at best "like" a real reader in a manner analogous to how the event of reading is only "like speech" (Ricoeur 1981a:159). At most, the transcendental "implied reader" and the real speaker are subcategories of a broader conception of subjectivity; they are not equivalent. More precisely, "the transcendental" is the condition of possibility of "the real," and its mode of being is akin to the ideality of meaning. As Iser (1978:34) puts it:

> The concept of the implied reader is therefore a
> textual structure anticipating the presence of a

---

[24] Iser's more developed notion of structure will be presented in section 5.1.

[25] I return to a further discussion of this question of the role of the communication situation in language use in chapter 8.

recipient without necessarily defining him . . . .
Thus the concept of the implied reader designates
a network of response-inviting structures, which
impel the reader to grasp the text.

In short, the implied reader is the particular role which the real reader is invited to play (Iser 1978:34).[26]

4.4.2 Ricoeur's theory of meaning

Just as discourse is constituted by the dialectic of event and meaning, so too, meaning is conceived of by Ricoeur as a dialectic. This dialectic, which Ricoeur considers to be "fundamental" (Ricoeur 1976:21) and "original" (Ricoeur 1976:20), is the dialectic of sense and reference. Based upon this dialectic Ricoeur gives his most concrete definition of semantics:

The most concrete definition of semantics, then, is
the theory that related the inner or immanent
constitution of the sense to the outer or
transcendent intention of the reference (1976:21f).

Consequently, we will examine what Ricoeur means by "sense" and "reference," and finally, the relation between them which is termed a "dialectic."

4.4.2.1 Meaning as sense

Sense, in Ricoeur's view, is closely related to language as system (*la langue*) as discussed in the preceding section. *Langue*, we must remember, is the collective codes which are systematic and compulsory for a particular language community. Ricoeur, though, departs from this traditional view, in part, when, after establishing the almost synonymous relation of sense-*langue*-ideality, he says that "The sense of the work is its internal organization . . ." (1981a:93). Here he is following the structuralist extension of the original *langue/parole* distinction in which "Literature . . . becomes an analogon of *la langue*" (Ricoeur 1981a:216), with oppositional structures as the central object of analysis (1981a:215ff).

---

[26] The chief criticism of Iser's approach is that

The reading subject . . . is not a specific, historically situated
individual but a transhistorical mind whose activities are, at
least formally, everywhere the same (Suleiman 1980:25).

However, because Iser expounds this notion in terms of structure--i.e. textual structure and the structure of reading acts--I will continue our discussion of this point again in section 5.1 below where structure is discussed directly.

Further, as intimated above, sense is also closely related to the fundamental phenomenological notion of ideality. For example, Ricoeur refers to the "ideal structure of sense" (1976:20) and ". . . the sense which is its [the proposition's] ideal object" (1981a:111). What then is ideality?

Meaning, says Ricoeur,

> . . . is not an idea which someone has in mind; it is not a mental content but an ideal object which can be identified and reidentified, by different individuals in different periods, as being one and the same object. By "ideality," they [Frege and Husserl] understood that the meaning of a proposition is neither a physical nor a mental reality (1981a:184).

Here, then, we see the fundamental move of phenomenology which breaks with a psychological basis for meaning. Defined negatively first,

> Meaning [in this sense] is neither the object referred to nor representation of the object, nor a mental picture, nor even an intuition of the object (Mohanty 1977:22).

Positively, the conception of the ideality of meaning is meant to account for "an essential moment of our experience of meanings" (Mohanty 1977:27). Three aspects of this experience are outlined by Mohanty (1977:27):

> . . . first, discourse--and especially, logical discourse--requires that meanings retain an identity in the midst of varying contexts; second, meanings can be communicated by one person to another, and in that sense can be shared; third, in different speech acts and in different contexts, the same speaker or different speakers can always return to the same meaning. The concept of ideality attempts to capture this "objectivity" of meaning--its identity, communicability, and repeatability.

The point is that, though meanings are only realized in the consciousness of a living subject, meanings so constituted present their own evidence to consciousness that their status is "independent" (Kockelmans 1967:90) [obtains "independently" say Langsdorf and Reeder (n.d.)] of any actualization.

The mode of being of these ideal objects is understood in the phenomenological tradition as "pure possibility" (Husserl 1970:71), what Kockelmans calls "being-in-itself" (1967:90), going on to assert that

87

"Psychological considerations can never totally account radically for these ideal beings" (1967:90).[27]

4.4.2.2 Meaning as reference

Sense, then, is that which ". . . correlates the identification function [the function of the 'noun'] and the predicative function [the function of the 'verb'] within the sentence" (Ricoeur 1976:20); it is *immanent* to the discourse, and objective in the sense of ideal" (Ricoeur 1976:20; emphasis added); in short, it is the " 'what' of discourse" (Ricoeur 1976:19). But sense does not exhaust either the meaning of meaning, or the meaning of discourse. Meaning is also the "about what" of discourse, that about which the discourse speaks. Meaning, in this sense, is termed by Ricoeur "reference." Reference is not immanent to discourse, but transcends language itself to "connect up" with the world. The reference of discourse, says Ricoeur, is

> . . . the truth value of the proposition, its claim to reach reality. Reference thus distinguishes discourse from language (*langue*); the latter has no relation with reality, its words returning to other words in the endless circle of the dictionary. Only discourse, we shall say, intends things, applies itself to reality, expresses the world (Ricoeur 1981a:140).

In short, "It is another name for discourse's claim to be true" (Ricoeur 1976:20).

Reference, however, like sense, is also "objective" in that (1) it is what the sentence or text does rather than what a speaker does (i.e. there is a proper distinction between utterance meaning and utterer's meaning; cf. Ricoeur 1976:19), and (2) it is based on and mediated by the ideality of sense. I consider these two points in order. The first point will lead us into a consideration of the role of the author's intention and the related implied communication model, as well as its alternative. Our second point must consider the relation between sense and reference.

Already we have seen that Ricoeur draws clear distinctions between spoken and written discourse (cf. chapter 2) and that this distinction makes a difference with regard to the role of the author's intention in reading and

---

[27] For further development of this point, cf. Mohanty 1964, 1974, 1977.

Iser also seems to affirm the ideality of meaning (1978:151), but does not clearly distinguish between sense and reference, when he "defines" meaning in terms of reference (1978:151). He does, though, have much to say about the structure of he text (e.g. Iser 1978:53ff, 180ff); cf. section 5.1 below.

interpretation (cf. chapter 2). To expand on this latter point, there occurs in a written text a definite break with the author's intention:

> With written discourse, the author's intentions and the meaning of the text cease to coincide (Ricoeur 1981a:200).

And again,

> For the text is an autonomous space of meaning which is no longer animated by the intention of the author . . . (Ricoeur 1981a:174; also 112, 132, 139, 192, 200, 218).

In one word, this relation between authorial intent and textual meaning is one of *distance*: There is no necessary coincidence. Since the author's intention is no longer directly available, the reader has access only to the text and the meaning is achieved by reading. As Ricoeur says,

> Sometimes I like to say that to read a book is to consider its author as already dead and the book as posthumous. For it is when the author is dead that the relation to the book becomes complete and, as it were, intact. The author can no longer respond; it only remains to read his work (Ricoeur 1981a:147).

Consequently, because there is no speaker available who is referring in his speaking, the reference of the text is first of all what the text does in the reading of it. In this sense, then, reference is "objective": It is generated by the text, in a manner which we will consider in more detail later (cf. chapter 7).

What, then, does this say about the communication model of dialogue which, on the one hand, serves as the basis for so many reading theories, but which, on the other hand, is so radically disrupted by the distanciations introduced by the writing-reading situation?

Though Ricoeur can go so far as to say, "Nothing is less intersubjective or dialogical than the encounter with a text . . ." (Ricoeur 1981a:191), he does submit that "reading becomes like speech" (Ricoeur 1981a:159) and "releases something like an event in the present time" (Ricoeur 1981a:185). Thus the very element which has "died" in writing-- the event--is restored by reading. Further an intention is restored by reading, but it is first of all "the intention of the text" (Ricoeur 1981a:161). Ricoeur does, then, go a fair distance in the direction of restoring the reading of a text to the dialogue model. But he also insists that ". . .

the text" (Ricoeur 1981a:111), and "the world" of the text (Ricoeur 1981a:202). The consideration of this latter notion will lead us further into Ricoeur's unique contribution to the notion of reference, and to the beginnings of a clarification of his alternative to the communication model.[29]

The reference of a text, its claim to be about something, Ricoeur says, ". . . reaches the world not only at the level of manipulable objects, but at the level [of] *Lebenswelt* . . ." (Ricoeur 1981a:141). *Lebenswelt*, or literally the lived-world, is a level of human experience. It is contrasted with a "nature objectified and mathematicized by Galilean and Newtonian science" (Ricoeur 1981a:119), and is typified by ". . . the artistic, historical and lingual experience which precedes and supports these objectifications and explanations" (Ricoeur 1981a:119). Ricoeur is concerned, though, that the *Lebenswelt* not be ". . . confused with some sort of ineffable immediacy" and not be ". . . identified with the vital and emotional envelope of human experience" (Ricoeur 1981a:119). Rather, *Lebenswelt* is to be ". . . construed as designating the reservoir of meaning, the surplus of sense in living experience, which renders the objectifying and explanatory attitude possible" (Ricoeur 1981a:119).

This functioning of reference to reach the *Lebenswelt* is not, however, always easy to notice. It is "fiction and poetry," Ricoeur (1981a:141) says, which displays this feature most clearly. The ability of language to refer to this fundamental level of human experience is a great achievement which must be fully accounted for in a philosophical theory of language and interpretation. How, then, does Ricoeur account for it?

Here again the distinction between oral and written discourse is decisive for Ricoeur. In oral discourse the problem of reference--what are you talking about?--is ". . . ultimately resolved by the ostensive function of discourse" (Ricoeur 1981a:141). When a question of mutual understanding arises, the answer is

> . . . determined by the ability to point to a reality
> common to the interlocutors. If we cannot point
> to the thing about which we speak, at least we can
> situate it in relation to the unique spatio-temporal
> network which is shared by the interlocutors
> (Ricoeur 1981a:141).

In short, "It is the 'here' and 'now', determined by the situation of discourse, which provides the ultimate reference of all discourse" (Ricoeur 1981a:141). However, with writing there is no longer a common situation

---

[29] A fuller development of "the world" and its philosophical grounding is presented in chapter 6, section 3 where it is more naturally considered in the context of the discussion of understanding, the context in which it was first developed by Heidegger, whom Ricoeur follows on this point.

90

... determined by the ability to point to a reality
common to the interlocutors. If we cannot point
to the thing about which we speak, at least we can
situate it in relation to the unique spatio-temporal
network which is shared by the interlocutors
(Ricoeur 1981a:141).

In short, "It is the 'here' and 'now', determined by the situation of
discourse, which provides the ultimate reference of all discourse" (Ricoeur
1981a:141). However, with writing there is no longer a common situation
between writer and reader, nor is the "ostensive character of reference"
(Ricoeur 1981a:141) maintained. In fictional literature this abolition of
ostensive reference is extended to the seeming destruction of the world:
There is nothing actual to which it refers. This destruction of the primary
reference, though, ". . . is the condition of possibility for the freeing of a
second order reference" (Ricoeur 1981a:141), and it is this reference which
refers at the level of *Lebenswelt*.

The text, then, is the very place where the world appears. Ricoeur
prefers to say that the world appears *"in front of* the text" (1981a:141). His
main concern here is two-fold: (1) to emphasize that the meaning of the
text is *not* "concealed *behind* the text" (Ricoeur 1981a:141); and (2) to
underline the fact that we grasp not a psychological intention, but a world.
Finally, Ricoeur says this world is "a *proposed world* which I could inhabit
and wherein I could project one of my ownmost possibilities" (Ricoeur
1981a:142).[30] In this way, by conceiving of reference in correlation with the
world of the text, Ricoeur both avoids the communication-dialogue model
of reading and presents his alternative model.[31]

4.4.2.3 The relation between sense and reference

With Ricoeur's language of the relation of reference to proposed or
possible worlds, we are returned to a consideration of sense, whose mode
of being is that of "pure possibility," and its relation to reference. This is
our second point with regard to the "objectivity" of reference, and our final
point of this section: Reference is mediated by the ideality of sense.

Ricoeur often talks as if sense precedes reference. Note for
instance:

---

[30] Ricoeur's notion of "world," however, must be distinguished from Smith's "world in our
head." This point is further developed in chapter 6.

[31] Similarly Iser, who even "defines" meaning in terms of reference: "Meaning is the
referential totality which is implied by the aspects contained in the text and which must be
assembled in the course of reading" (1978:151). The "aspects contained in the text" are
the structures of the text discussed in section 5.1 below.

> The speaker refers to something on the basis of, or through, the ideal structure of the sense (Ricoeur 1976:20).

and,

> To understand a text is to follow its movement from sense to reference, from what it says, to what it talks about (Ricoeur 1981a:218; cf. also 1976:92).[32]

This, however, is not the final word. Ricoeur, in fact, reverses this priority very decisively when he says:

> If language were not fundamentally referential, would or could it be meaningful? How could we know that a sign stands for something, if it did not receive its directions towards something for which it stands from its use in discourse? Finally, semiotics appears as a mere abstraction of semantics. And the semiotic definition of the sign as an inner difference between signifier and signified presupposes its semantic definition as reference to the thing for which it stands.

> It is because there is first something to say, because we have an experience to bring to language, that conversely, language is not only directed toward ideal meanings, but also refers to what is (Ricoeur 1976:21; similarly 1975a:217).

This priority of life and experience[33] in linguistic studies is, in Ricoeur's language, "the ontological condition of reference" (Ricoeur 1976:21). Further, this "ontological condition" is ". . . reflected in language as . . . the postulate according to which we presuppose the existence of singular things which we identify" (Ricoeur 1976:21).

---

[32] Similarly Iser 1978 emphasizes throughout that texts are systems (e.g. 71f), and that they "initiate" (27) the process of meaning which is fundamentally referential (151). Taken together, these points support the kind of sense-reference construction which Ricoeur develops, though without being as explicit as Ricoeur. Iser, though, is thoroughly interactional, stressing both top-down (e.g. 53, 124, 135, 153, 167, 224) and bottom-up (e.g. 120, 152, 157, 169) processes.

[33] That is, the pre-linguistic situation of belonging, embedded in *Lebenswelt*; cf. chapter 6, section 3.

some sense--of what we refer to),[35] and both presuppositions rest on the human experience of being in the world and thus having something to say. On the other hand, when presented with a text to be read, we must consider the sign-words first of all (Ricoeur 1975a:92), and consequently we can proceed to the reference only by understanding the sense. Because the meaning of the text is ". . . no longer animated by the intention of its author" (Ricoeur 1981a:174), the otherwise spontaneous movement from sense to reference is slowed, and can even be suppressed (Ricoeur 1975a:92f), as the reader must reconstruct the sense of the text. As the meaning as sense is constructed by the reader, the ideality of sense--its being as "pure possibility"--as it were, penetrates the reference to which it is "regularly connected" (Ricoeur 1975a:217). This reference is then projected by the reading as a possible world.

This mutual dependence of sense and reference on each other, together with their proper distinction from one another, is what Ricoeur means by the dialectic of meaning (Ricoeur 1976:19-22).

Before plunging deeper into some of the issues raised in the preceeding discussions, let's pause to evaluate this phenomenological theory of meaning in the light of Mohanty's four criteria presented at the end of section 3.

The phenomenological theory of meaning is formulated so as to satisfy the "facts" of the experience of meaning, or so its proponents claim. Reviewing the four "facts" as previously outlined by Mohanty, I find that the phenomenological theory does indeed provide an adequate account of these "facts". First, the notion of ideality is formulated specifically to capture the identity and contextual independence of meanings. Second, because ideality is essentially epistemological, meaning is necessarily related to the subject who is designated "meaning-conferring." Third, as we have seen, the ideality of sense is the mediator of reference; and fourth, this sense is expressed in ordinary discourse, both spoken and written. Thus on all four counts the phenomenological theory of meaning is judged to be successful.

---

[35] Even the lack of reference of an expression or fictional entities does not weaken this claim. Says Ricouer (1975a:217): ". . . not to have a reference is another trait of reference that confirms that the question of reference [and existence, 1976:21] is always opened by that of sense."

4.5   Further discussions

Here we take up two issues calling for further development from the preceding discussion. The first is the question of the structure of a text conceived of as "in-the-text." The second is a development of the idea of reference in literary works. Finally, we note that these two issues are not unrelated, but that the full exploitation of this relation will depend on an expanded and enriched version of an interactive theory of reading.

4.5.1   Is there structure in the text?

The belief that there is structure in the text is closely tied to the bottom-up view of reading as the decoding or extracting of meaning from the print. The meaning to be derived, in this scheme, is assumed to be the author's meaning, and decoding transfers this meaning to the mind of the reader. So common has this view been that Bloome 1983 calls it the conventional theory of reading; and so influential is it that even theorists otherwise committed to an interaction theory seem to espouse it. Thus Meyer 1981 speaks of "structure embedded in the text" (1981:30), and "the author's structure in the text" (1981:35). Similarly, Goodman (e.g. 1976c:58) speaks of "the writer's meaning," and Smith (1977:642) of "the producer's purpose or intention." This talk of authorial intent now seems naive in the light of Ricoeur's critique. Surely there is intent involved, for meaning is not "just there," but in reading authorial intent is itself a construction of the reader's reading of the text, and is not otherwise (i.e. independently) available. In short, the meaning of the text is the basis of claims about authorial intent and not vice versa. But what is meaning, and what is its relation to structure, and of both to "the text"?

For the phenomenologist, meaning (in the ideal sense) is a structure, a *"legitimating structure"* (Reeder 1980:159) which, because of its sameness, makes knowledge possible. It obtains independently of any given instance of it, and yet manifests its independence only in and through the constructive engagement of human consciousness. Further, meaning so conceived is neither "in" the text as a spatio-physical object, nor "in" the consciousness of the reader, at least as far as its "native home" is concerned. This is the point of terming meaning "ideal." As Golden (1983:144) puts it,

> Phenomenological theory proposes that meaning
> of the literary work lies at the intersection
> between reader and text. This point of
> convergence, however, can never be precisely
> pinpointed because it can neither be reduced to
> the reality of the text nor to the subjectivity of the
> reader . . . .

Similarly, Iser locates meaning at the point of interaction, which is "[not] actually represented in the text, let alone set out in words" (Iser 1978:35). Thus, "It is, then, an integral quality of literary texts that they produce

94

something which they themselves are not" (Iser 1978:27).[36] Thus a way of summarizing that meaning is (1) dependent on the engagement of consciousness with its object, and (2) not "native" to either pole of this relation.

Further, this account does justice to "the facts" as reported by the reading researchers: On the one hand, there is *a* meaning to a text which is structured; and on the other hand, this meaning is dependent upon the "event-like" engagement of the reader, and thus can vary from reader to reader. Before speaking to the harmonization of these seemingly divergent views, more must be said about each alternative.

The assumption throughout most studies of discourse structure (e.g. Meyer 1983; van Dijk 1981, 1982; Kintsch 1977; Frederickson 1975a,b; Rumelhart 1975, 1977b; etc.) is that there is a meaning, that is, one correct reading of a text and that this meaning is properly seen from "the point of view of the author" (Meyer 1983:11). Though difficulties are acknowledged in finding this meaning, the assumption is that "with practice" (Meyer 1983:11), even "considerable training" (Meyer 1983:35), the analyses of a text will be univocal.

Ricoeur and Iser also identify, not the author's intention, but a structure "in the text." This is one dimension of their "bottom-up" emphasis. Ricoeur designates a text as a work, which means (among other things) that it is characterized by "organisation and structure" (Ricoeur 1981a:138). Thus discourse is "a structured work" (Ricoeur 1981a:138), such that

> The [subject] matter of the text is to its structure
> as, in the proposition, the reference is to its sense
> (Ricoeur 1981a:111).

Similarly, Iser (1978) speaks of "textual structure" (35) which initiates (27), brings about (35), influences (153), prestructures (26), and conditions (153) the meaning which the reader assembles. Here the text is a system of signs (79) which are interconnected "prior to the stimulation of the individual reader's disposition" (120), thus controlling the arbitrariness of meaning construction (120).

This assumption of either meaning or structure as "in the text" likely stems from the experience of meaning as ideal, as Ricoeur's correlation of structure with sense (as quoted in the preceding paragraph; cf. also Ricoeur (1976:20), "the ideal structure of sense") and his further designation of sense as "ideal" (cf. section 4.1) would suggest. That is, since the meaning

---

[36] If it is thought that there is a defensible case that literary texts are significantly different on this point than "ordinary" text, cf. Fish, "How ordinary is ordinary language?" (1980:97ff; cf. also 268ff).

we do arrive at presents itself to us as existing independently from us, it is a short step to the positing of a meaning and a structure of the text.

The difficulty which these theorists confront, though, issues directly from their interactive conceptions of reading. As Meyer (1983:12) points out,

> The structure of the information read from a text may appear different to readers with different prior knowledge and purpose.

This is basic interactive theory (and has been for years; e.g. Goodman 1969; Rumelhart 1975; similarly Smith 1971); and yet writing in 1983, Meyer can still say, with reference to the role of schemas in text structure,

> None of the three approaches [Meyer, Frederikson, Kintsch] has systematically examined prior knowledge frames or schemata and their contribution to the text comprehended in the reader's mind, although all have recognized a need to pursue this issue (Meyer 1983:12).

Though this seems lamentable from Meyer's perspective, and thus constitutes a challenge and call to further research, from another perspective this delay of a systematic examination may indeed be fortunate. Some (e.g. Fish 1980; Derrida 1972, 1981; DeMan 1979; Crosman 1980) are thoroughly convinced that there is not one inherent structure in a text and thus any research efforts to find it will be in vain. This point is illustrated very effectively, for example,[37] by Fish 1980 and Crosman 1980 through various studies of the history of literary criticism. Even opposite meanings of the same passage can be and have been advanced by very reputable scholars. If this view is taken to its extreme, the text is a highly unstable object at every level of its linguistic structure. Says Derrida,

> . . . every element [of the text]--phoneme or grapheme--is constituted from the trace it bears in itself of the other elements in the chain or the system. This linking . . . , this tissue, is the *text*, which is only produced in the transformation of another text. Nothing, either in the elements or in the system, is ever or anywhere simply present or absent. Throughout there are only differences and traces of traces (Derrida 1972:38, as translated and quoted by Suleiman 1980:41).

Derrida's point is that "differences" are "within each element of the text and constitutive of the text *as* text" (Suleiman 1980:41): So thorough is the

---

[37] The growing body of "deconstructive criticism" further illustrates this point.

impossibility of a definitive reading of a text! There simply is not, in Derrida's view, "an autonomous, identifiable, and unique entity: the *text* itself" (Suleiman 1980:40).[38]

Further, so essential is the active engagement of the reader in the production of meaning, that Fish (for one) thinks that "What does the text do (to you)?" is a better question to ask than "What does the text mean?" In fact, the meaning of the text *is* what the text does! Fish (1980:28), then, introduces

> . . . the idea of *meaning as an event*, something that is happening not visible to the naked eye but which can be made visible (or at least palpable) by the regular introduction of a "searching question" (what does this do?).[39]

Though these views of Fish, Derrida, etc. are extreme in that they give almost no credit to bottom-up processes, even Ricoeur and Iser--who as we have seen, do grant the text a controlling role--acknowledge the necessary, even determinative, role of the reader. Iser (1978) emphasizes that the totality which a text assumes is "not formulated," (35)"[not] actually represented in the text, let alone set out in words" (35), but must be assembled (35), performed (27), built (118ff) by the reader. Here the gaps or indeterminacies of the text rule, for: (1) there are many different possibilities for the reader to choose from; and (2) ". . . there is no frame of reference to offer criteria of right or wrong" (Iser 1978:230).[40] Similarly, Ricoeur (1981a:174) speaks of a discursive moment of construction or restructuration which is "on the side of the reader" (cf. Ricoeur 1975a:195f).

The point, then, is that there is as strong evidence on the side of there not being one, fixed structure-meaning (inherent) in a text (and whatever structure-meaning is found being radically conditioned by the act of reading), as there is for the existence of that (ideal) structure-meaning which exists independently of the reader. This "independence," because it is independent of the reader, thereby creates the presumption

---

[38] We will return to a brief critique of Derrida in what follows and in chapter 9.

[39] Similarly Iser says, "The constitution of meaning, therefore, gains its full significance when something *happens* to the reader" (1978:152; cf. 152-159, 125-134).

[40] And yet Iser does assume that there is a "basis for comparing and assessing interpretations" (1978:118). Chapter 8 will take up the question of the role of "critique" in reading.

that its "location" must be in the text, the only other "commonsense," concrete place it could be.[41]

Fortunately, from my perspective, not only are these views not irreconcilable, but the phenomenological theory of meaning outlined already provides the needed framework for such a reconciliation. Three arguments support this claim.

First of all, to say that there is more than one reading of a text is not to say that there is no meaning-structure to the text. Whatever meaning there is an ideal structure, which, to the degree that meaning arose from a reading of the text, does have traces (at least) to be *found* "in the text." The further question then is whether such a reading is the best (or better) reading, and criteria for such a decision (e.g. Is that "trace" actually there, or is there another perspective on the same "data" which better accounts for what you thought you saw?) need to be determined (though it must be admitted that any criterion and any application of it, is itself an interpretation and as such open to discussion and evaluation (on what basis? etc.)).

Second, structure itself need not be conceived of as a single-level, univocal phenomenon. If, for example, meaning-structure were conceived of by analogy with syntactic structure in relational grammar,[42] then a network of relations might obtain which could even appear contradictory on a surface reading.[43]

---

[41] That there are surface-structure linguistic (discourse) features objectively in the text, does not in itself warrant the conclusion that the structure of the discourse is itself *in* the text. It is true that any legitimate reading of a text must take account of the surface-structure linguistic features; but it is not true that these features, in and of themselves, constrain one and only one structure, and therefore, one and only one reading or interpretation of the text. As Fish 1980 (and others) have shown, what is taken as a linguistic structure in the first place is itself a product of an interpretation which has been generated by non-textual as well as textual factors. Inasmuch as there may be more than one reading of a text, there will also be more than one (linguistic) structure.

[42] Cf. Perlmutter 1983; Perlmutter and Rosen 1984. At present, though, relational grammar has not developed beyond a treatment of clauses, and thus this analogy is merely suggestive. Its success at this level, though, does warrant further serious consideration. However, increasingly, there are alternative interpretations for the data which relational grammar has so eloquently (and formally) explained. Thus the "merely suggestive" above is further underlined.

[43] Finally, I suspect that one's views on the question of the relation between diverse interpretations and their possible harmony is grounded in one's metaphysical preference with regard to the ancient philosophical question of the relation between "the one" and "the many." Though the arguments have raged now in favor of the one, now in favor of the many, an either-or alternative is not required on this question. As Van Til (1975:25) has said, "Using the language of the One-and-Many question we contend that in God the

Third, though the phenomenological account is criticized for being elusive and contradictory with regard to the question of how much freedom the reader has, versus how much control the text has (Suleiman 1980:24), the phenomenologist simply responds that he is just reporting the lived-evidence for the phenomena in question (in this case the acts of reading). There is, though, further philosophical grounding of this approach, which finally is an ontology of man.[44] Nonetheless, this ontology is frankly paradoxical: Man's projection of his own possibilities is also already and always a projection within a prior "being thrown." Similarly, the question of man's [here, the reader's] freedom is answered on the basis of this same paradoxical structure, which Ricoeur expounds in terms of a dialectical unity of the voluntary and the involuntary (cf. e.g. 1966). This is not the place to delve into these issues. Instead I simply express for the phenomenological tradition the typical appeal: Is this an adequate and insightful account of your own reading experience and the accounts of others? Phenomenological evidence, though private in origin, is open to public discussion and validation (Reeder 1984).

In conclusion, the question of the existence of structure in the text is finally a question of (1) the structure of meaning, and (2) the meaning (and structure) of structure. The first point is answered by the ideality of meaning; the second is left with the suggestion of a reconsideration of structure along the lines of syntactic structure in relational grammar.[45] And both points are further clarified by the consideration of "fundamental ontology" as sketched by the third argument above (and further developed in chapter 6).

4.5.2: A further discussion of the idea of reference

Just as discourse is the dialectic of event and meaning, and meaning the dialectic of sense and reference, so too, reference is a dialectic. This point has not yet been made, but is essential to a fuller discussion of the reading process, especially with regard to the constitution of the reader, and the restoration of something like the communication situation. The structure of meaning, and specifically the dialectic of reference, will serve as the basis of our further consideration of this restoration which itself is more appropriately taken up in our later discussions of comprehension

---

one and the many are equally ultimate. Similarly, Balthazar (1965:105): "Here [i.e. with the Trinity] is the original and native place of the 'identity' of identity and nonidentity ...." Thus, the orthodox Christian doctrine of the Trinity is offered as the solution to the one/many, identity/difference problem. This is the alternative I prefer to believe, and it is a question of belief for each of us, regardless of the view espoused. More will be said on this topic in chapters 8 and 9.

[44] This position is taken up explicitly and further developed in chapter 6.

[45] Ricoeur himself looks to the Chomskian school (to which, broadly speaking, relational grammar belongs) for a "new conception of structure" (1974:89f).

(chapter 7 and 8). The same area of concern is taken up here, but from the perspective of meaning, particularly the dialectical pole of reference.

"Reference," says Ricoeur, "is itself a dialectical phenomenon" (1975a:75). We have already seen that reference is a "transcending motion towards an extra-linguistic 'outside' " (Ricoeur 1975a:92). This, though, is but one pole of the dialectic of reference. Ricoeur goes on to note that

> To the extent that discourse refers to a situation, to an experience, to reality, to the world, in sum to the extra-linguistic, it also refers to its own speaker by means of procedures that belong essentially to discourse and not to language (1975a:75).

These procedures are (1) the personal pronouns, which refer, and thus have meaning in the fullest sense, only when used by a speaker (and "author"),[46] (2) the tenses of verbs which are "anchored in the present" (Ricoeur 1975a:75) as the moment when the discourse is uttered, thus orienting the discourse in time and (3) the demonstratives (e.g. "this" and "that") which situate the discourse in space with reference to the speaker.[47] Thus discourse always refers both to a world, and to a speaker.

These two references, though, do not exhaust the functioning of reference. "In fact," says Ricoeur, "we should speak of a triple reference, for discourse refers as much to the one to whom it is addressed as to its own speaker" (1981a:168). As we have noted, though, writing disrupts this "addressed to someone" characteristic of dialogue communication and creates its own audience from "whoever knows how to read" (Ricoeur 1981a:202).

These three references--to a world, a speaker, and an audience-- then, constitute the functioning of reference in discourse. Though writing, or the text as text, disrupts the otherwise spontaneous functioning of reference, the text, because it is an instance of discourse, ". . . is not without reference . . ." (Ricoeur 1981a:148); and we assume this means

---

[46] The use of "author" here is meant to indicate that there is no simple correspondence between the actual author and the one to whom the personal pronouns refer in the reading of the text. First of all, authors are, in general, under no obligation to present their own point of view when using personal pronouns. Further, because reading involves interpretation, the "author" of the reader's reading is always an interpretive construct just as the meaning of the text is. These two reasons preclude the simple correspondence indicated.

[47] Though Ricoeur aligns these three with "the three fundamental behaviours of man speaking and acting through discourse" (1975a:75), elsewhere (1981a:168) he admits to other possibilities. Ricoeur is silent, though, as to whether these other possibilities would also align with the three previous categories.

reference in its three-fold nature. The interesting point for our study is that, for Ricoeur, ". . . the task of reading . . . will be precisely to fulfill the [three-fold] reference" (Ricoeur 1981a:148).[48] How this task is conceived of by Ricoeur (and the other phenomenologists) has already been sketched in chapter 2 and will be further studied in following chapters. Comprehension, as discussed there, will follow the lines of meaning as outlined here. Before pursuing that inquiry, though, we consider comprehension as conceived of by the reading researchers so that the interaction between the differing perspectives might be more thorough and penetrating.

---

[48] Similarly Iser, "As the theme is not an end in itself, but a sign for something else, it produces an "empty" reference, and the filling-in of this reference is what constitutes the significance" (1978:147).

CHAPTER 5

COMPREHENSION IN READING THEORIES

I seriously doubt whether any reading theorist disputes Brown's statement that "The goal of reading is to achieve understanding of the text" (1980:454); or Beck's that ". . . comprehension . . . is, of course, the *sine qua non* of reading" (1981:78). As a recent textbook in reading education puts it, comprehension is "the core of reading" (Mangieri, Baker, and Walker 1982:63ff). A serious weakness in most of these theories, though, is the lack of theoretical grounding and clarity regarding the concept of understanding, which is alternatively termed comprehension. As Wilson (1983:382) put it, "No one really knows what comprehension is." The purpose of this chapter is to examine various aspects of the concept of understanding (or comprehension) as found in the relevant literature.

The various views of meaning just discussed (chapter 4) bear directly on their corresponding views of comprehension and register their differences there, for all acknowledge that comprehension is comprehension of meaning. In short, the two terms--meaning and comprehension--are reciprocally defined.[1]

Chapters 5-7 discuss the question of comprehension. Chapter 5 is composed of two sections. In section 1, comprehension theories from the three main classes of reading theories will be reintroduced (cf. chapter 1 for more detail). Going beyond a mere reintroduction, though, are (1) an expanded account of schema theories, and (2) the introduction of van Dijk's (et al.) text grammar. These two "exceptions" serve as the basis for section 2 which examines these two approaches to comprehension in greater detail. The first--schema theory--is interactive; and the second--van Dijk's text grammar--is arguably bottom-up in emphasis. Rather than devote a separate section to a separate top-down theory, it is more convenient to consider the theory of Frank Smith bit by bit as related issues arise in other contexts. Some of this piecemeal evaluation will occur in this chapter, but more in the next. Chapter 6 presents the phenomenological theories of comprehension and begins the dialogue between the phenomenologists and the reading specialists. Chapter 7 picks up the main points of interest from chapter 6 and develops the dialogue further.

---

[1] Beck (1977b:116) goes so far as to say, ". . . I will use the terms meaning and *comprehension* synonymously."

103

5.1 A reintroduction of reading theories of comprehension

5.1.1 Bottom-up theories of comprehension reintroduced

For the bottom-up theorists,

> . . . apart from decoding skills, reading comprehension is dependent upon linguistic, conceptual, cognitive, and general knowledge abilities that are similar to those required for aural language comprehension (Beck 1981:78-79).

Both the status and the character of this "reading comprehension," however, is severely compromised in the standard bottom-up theories.

With regard to its status, recall that for Fries such skills as "understanding, thinking, reflecting, imagining, judging, evaluating, analyzing, . . . reasoning, and . . . making emotional and social judgments" (Fries 1962:118) are ". . . all matters of the uses of language and are not limited to the uses of reading" (Fries 1962:118). As such, comprehension per se does not constitute the reading process (Fries 1962:118). On the other hand, mere "word calling" (Fries 1962:120)--the pronouncing of sounds from text without meaning--is not reading. As Fries puts it,

> To be "reading," the response to the graphic signs must also have all the features of some language signal operating in a language code, eliciting a meaning response (Fries 1962:120).

Though Fries recognizes that comprehension cannot be excluded from reading, he does, in effect, so exclude it. Reading proper is *the process of transfer* from the auditory signs for language signals . . . to the new visual signs for the same signals" (Fries 1962:120); that is, the visual replaces the auditory as "the means of connection to the human nervous system" (Fries 1962:119). Once that connection is made, then all the other language processing skills proceed "as usual" (i.e. as in the verbal-aural case). One such "ability" (Fries 1962:118) is comprehending. Consequently, Fries has rendered the status of comprehension in reading ambiguous at best--is comprehension part of reading or isn't it?--and exiled it from reading proper, at worst.

Because of this peripheral status of comprehension, very little (almost nothing!) is said by the bottom-up theorists about what comprehension is and what role it plays in reading. This lack of attention to the character of comprehension is epitomized by the work of Gough. As Lovett (1981:3) puts it,

> Gough made no pretense of understanding the semantic memory and comprehension requirements of skilled reading: the model's

104

semantic interpreter was labeled "Merlin" and its depository the "PWSGWTAU"-- or the "Place Where Sentences Go When They Are Understood"!

In short, for Gough, comprehension is thoroughly mysterious, if not "magical" (Mitchell 1982:133).[2]

In sum, these bottom-up theories offer very little with regard to the notion of comprehension. There is, though, another class of text-based theories which do offer a substantial contribution to our understanding of understanding. These are the text or discourse grammars of which van Dijk is a fair representative.[3]

For van Dijk, central to discourse comprehension is the "formation of macro-structures" (van Dijk 1977:29f). Macro-structures are, in effect, summaries (van Dijk 1977:28) which are formed in the process of reading a text by means of four macro-rules which will be introduced and explained later. These macro-rules operate on text propositions and are considered to be more or less unconscious in the reader. The macro-structures produced by the macro-rules are, however, not identical with the schemas previously mentioned. Rather, they are ". . . closely related but entirely different" (van Dijk 1977:22). Says van Dijk,

> Frames [Schemas] . . . are conventional and general. Most members of a society or culture have approximately the same set of frames. Macro-structures do not have this character. Instead, they are ad hoc information, i.e., the particular global content of a particular discourse (van Dijk 1977:22).

The important point here, whose significance emerges in section 2.2, is that macro-structures are construed as "a representation of the meaning of the text" (Morgan and Sellner 1980:195); i.e., they are produced by "a linguistic operation performed on texts to recover content" (Morgan and Sellner 1980:195). In short, macro-structures are structures of the text.

Kintsch, who follows van Dijk closely, uses the ability to summarize-- via macro-structures--as the key to determining how well subjects comprehend stories (cf. 1977; Kintsch and van Dijk 1975).

---

[2] In the judgment of Mitchell, the LaBerge-Samuels model is similarly deficient: "In its present (1974) version, the model says very little about comprehension and nothing about the control of eye movement" (1982:134). With this judgment I concur.

[3] It must be acknowledged, though, that van Dijk (et al.) are more accurately classified as interactive with a text-based emphasis.

In short, for some theorists, to comprehend is to summarize by means of macro-structure formation. These claims will be examined in more detail in section 2 below.

5.1.2 Top-down theories of comprehension reintroduced

For Frank Smith, who has the most thoroughly worked out top-down approach, comprehension is the major category of his system. To review briefly (cf. chapter 1 for the details), "Reading is seen as . . . based on *comprehension*" (Smith 1982:3). While the decoding of the visual information (i.e. the print) is reading proper for the bottom-up view, the use of the print is "just the beginning" for Smith (Smith 1982:22): ". . . reading is what you do with visual information" (Smith 1982:22); reading is "only incidentally visual" (Smith 1982:12).

Smith, though, is in agreement with the bottom-up view on the following point: Reading comprehension is a special case of comprehension in general. And, more than any other reading theorist, Smith has written directly on the topic of comprehension.

In general, comprehension is regarded as a state, or a condition "where no uncertainty exists," that is "when we have no unanswered questions" (Smith 1982:15). Comprehension in reading, then, is ". . .a matter of 'making sense' of text, of relating written language to what we know already and to what we want to know" (Smith 1982:15).

Implicit in such statements is Smith's very strong conviction that comprehension is "relative to the knowledge and purposes of the individual receiving it" (Smith 1982:16). This is the top-down emphasis, and it is this strong element of subjectivity and relativity which brings the strongest protests from Smith's opponents. Taken to its logical extreme, Smith's view implies that someone who has no unanswered questions about a topic can be said to comprehend a book about that topic on almost any reading of it, in fact, even before reading the book, as long as no new questions are raised by the book itself. But how, on Smith's view, can new questions be raised--at least comprehensible questions--if comprehension depends in the first place "on what the individual already knows and needs or wants to know" (Smith 1982:16)? If, for example, I neither already know, nor need or want to know anything about some obscure area of medical research (no matter how important!), can I be said to comprehend this area? In such a state, I am neither confused nor uncertain, and so according to Smith, I ought to be comprehending. But am I not rather simply ignorant?

Now of course such an extreme is (I trust) absurd, and Smith is not intending to allow such a reading of his view. He explicitly says, for instance, that reading is an "interaction between a reader and a text" (Smith 1982:11; emphasis omitted), and that "there is a reciprocal relation between the two" (Smith 1982:10). Further, "I am not saying that any utterance can be taken to mean anything . . ." (Smith 1978:75). And yet, so insistent is he that "the reader must clearly exercise control" (Smith

1982:3) in the reading process, and is not "under the control of the text" (Smith 1982:2), that I think Smith's opponents have rightly detected a fundamental tension and inconsistency in his theory.

The preceding, though, is only meant to reintroduce Smith's thoughts on comprehension. Further discussion of his views will recur throughout the remainder of this chapter and the next.

5.1.3 Interactive theories of comprehension reintroduced

Beck (1981:79) summarizes well the sense of comprehension as understood by interactive theorists:

> The notion that the meaning of a text is constructed as opposed to being extracted from the textual materials serves to point out that comprehension is an interactive process between previously acquired knowledge and the content of what is read.

Though all interactive theories recognize the essential role of prior knowledge, most such contemporary theories have given considerable attention to the form or organization fo this prior knowledge. These are the "schema theories."[4]

The granddaddy of much of contemporary cognitive psychology and the "patron saint" of schema theories--F.C. Bartlett--concluded that "comprehension consists of an 'effort after meaning' " (Spiro 1980:247). Spiro quotes Bartlett as writing, "Speaking very broadly, such effort is simply the attempt to connect something that is given with something other than itself" (Spiro 1908:247 from Bartlett 1932:227). Bartlett developed his views in terms of schemas, thus pioneering the notion which has become foundational in many recent theories of comprehension.

Rumelhart, for instance, says

> . . . the process of understanding discourse is the process of finding a configuration of schemata that offers an adequate account of the passage in question (Rumelhart 1980:47).

Similarly, Winograd summarizes schema (frame, script) theories as follows:

---

[4] I am using this term "schema" loosely here to include the role of "frames," "scripts," etc.

There is a common primary focus in all of these
theories. They emphasize that the understanding
of an utterance is largely a process of fitting it into
larger schemas, known to speaker and hearer as
part of their previous knowledge about the world
they inhabit (Winograd 1977:76).

The important emphases in these theories with regard to
comprehension are (1) the reader makes an active contribution to reading,
usually termed the "construction" of meaning (Beck 1981:79; R. Anderson
1977:5; Tierney and Pearson 1981:11) or even "creation" (Collins, et al.
1977:1; Spiro 1979:2; Adams and Bruce 1980:37); (2) the world, or more
precisely, world knowledge plays a very significant role in the reader's
activity; (3) the interaction between the reader and the world (-knowledge)
aims toward the creation/construction of "a complex scenario (or model)
within which the events described might plausibly occur" (Collins, et al.
1977:1); (4) this activity is the *progressive* refinement of a model or scenario
(Tierney and Pearson 1981:11); and (5) the guiding principle in this
progress toward "plausibility" is the notion of coherence (R. Anderson
1977:5), understood as the fitting or matching of "the text against the
reader's world" (Tierney and Pearson 1981:11) in a manner which is
complete and interconnected.

The further exploration of schema theories which promises so much
for contemporary theories of reading comprehension will follow shortly
(Section 2.1 below).

In summary, then, there seem to be two major kinds of "definitions"
of reading comprehension, and a third which synthesizes the two. The first
recognizes the contribution of the reader via schemas. Such theories we
might term top-down theories. The second emphasizes the linguistic
operations motivated by the text itself. These are the bottom-up theories.
Actually, each of these types, at least in the theories we are examining,
includes elements of the other. Thus all these theories are "interactive,"
including both bottom-up and top-down processes in interaction, though
with varying emphases on one or the other kind of process. No one denies
that reading comprehension requires word recognition or identification and
syntactic processing (bottom-up concerns); and no one disputes that the
reader must bring some prior knowledge to the comprehension task (a top-
down concern).

In what follows, I first examine schema theories of comprehension
(a top-down emphasis), and second, the summarization view of van Dijk, et
al. (an interactive theory with a bottom-up emphasis).

5.2   Schema theories of comprehension

Even a cursory overview of the literature in cognitive psychology,
reading theory, and artificial intelligence research shows that schemas have
been and continue to be very powerful theoretically and useful practically.

108

Here I review some of the strengths of schema theory which contribute to a theory of discourse comprehension.

5.2.1 The strengths of schema theories

First, schema theory makes a very clear claim about what comprehension is--it is the filling of schemas, the matching of information from the text with slots in the schemas. This "definition" is compatible with a rather common sense of the term comprehension, what Frank Smith calls "making sense of the world [by] relating new experience to the already known" (Smith 1975:10; emphasis deleted). Most people would agree, I imagine, that we usually know what to do in a situation by relating new experience to the familiar and already known. Discourse understanding, then, means activating and filling the appropriate schema, from print recognition through and to whatever level of processing we want or need.

Second, schema theory can account for both the similarities and the differences in comprehension which occur in text comprehension (cf. e.g. Spiro and Tirre 1979; Spiro 1979; Dunn et al. 1979; etc.). Reading is not passive, but active and motivated by the expectations and desires of the individual. Thus the purposes of the reader as well as the peculiarities of his/her own schemas with their varying slots, default values, recognition of fit, and evaluation of goodness of fit, account for the differences. The similarities in comprehension derive from the similarities among schemas which are themselves derived from personal experience which is thoroughly social and thus in many, if not most, respects similar. In short, the individual has a major role in comprehension, and thus comprehension is as similar and different as individuals are. An "adequate account" of the text-data, then, depends on individual purposes. As Brown (1980:a454) puts it:

> . . . understanding is not an all or nothing phenomena, it must be judged against the criteria set by the reader as a goal of the activity.

Third, schema theory recognizes both top-down and bottom-up processing in comprehension (Rumelhart 1980:41f; Collins, Brown, and Larkin 1980:387ff). Such a theory is required by the experiential evidence accumulated in reading research (cf. e.g. Adams 1980 for an overview). Further, such dual-simultaneous processing seems to be required by the common experience of reading as the "progressive refinement from an initial (and partial) model to more and more refined models of the text" (Collins, Brown, and Larkin 1980:387).

Fourth, schema theory is in keeping with the latest research regarding category structure (cf. Mervis 1980 for an overview). Briefly, this research contradicts the traditional theory which is perhaps most characteristically summarized by the tenet that "A category is defined by a set of criterial attributes" (Mervis 1980:282; she also gives four other tenets). Rather, categories seem to be structured as sets of "family resemblances," organized around the best example. The best examples are those "family members" which share the largest number of attributes widely shared with other family members and which have the fewest attributes shared with similar but different categories. Here, then, the best example is much like the schema. While the traditional theory of categorization would take comprehension to be the matching and manipulating of "criterial attributes," comprehension for the best example theory is a matter of degrees of resemblance. Consequently there are fuzzy boundaries and differences of opinion, much the same as those noted with regard to individual differences (point two above). In this regard, schema theory is compatible with experimental results (Mervis 1980), and common experience.

Since Frank Smith's account of reading depends on the recognition of "distinctive features" in the sampling of print, it is subject to reevaluation based on the critique of Mervis (1980), et al. This, however, may work to his advantage since his point is that, due to the time constraints in actual reading experiments, the reader does not have the time that is required for the letter-by-letter reading posited by some theorists (e.g. Gough; cf. chapter 1). The sampling of some, rather than all, of the distinctive features of print is Smith's proposed solution to the facts of reading time constraints. The judgment of "degrees of resemblance," however, may in fact take less time than the sampling of distinctive features and thus favor Smith's proposal. On the other hand, the discernment of "degrees of resemblance" may well require some notion of the sampling of "distinctive features."

Fifth, schema theory can account for a great deal of learning. For schema theory, learning is the process(es) by which new schemas are developed. There are three processes posited to account for learning (Rumelhart 1980:52-54). The first is "accretion" (Rumelhart 1980:52f) or fact learning, the retrieval of stored information about a text or event. The second is "tuning" (Rumelhart 1980:52ff), by which existing schemas evolve or change to be more "in tune" with new experience. The third process is the most problematic. Rumelhart calls it "restructuring" (Rumelhart 1980:52). It is the process by which new schemas are created. There are two basic ways new schemas can be formed in this theory. First, by analogy: ". . . a new concept is like an old one except for a few differences" (Rumelhart 1980:54) which are substituted into a copy of the old schema.[5] Second, new schemas can be induced from the experience of the repetition of certain spatio-temporal configurations. Though this last point is especially problematic, and will serve as the first weakness noted in the theory, it must be granted that the other processes do account for a great deal of learning behavior.

Before turning to a consideration of weaknesses in the theory, a final implicit strength is noted. This concept of comprehension by means

---

[5] Here "concept" seems to be used by Rumelhart as interchangeable with "schema."

of schemas implies a subject, the one who comprehends and who in some sense transcends and controls the process. The control is not absolute, though, since the schemas are presented to the subject with a high degree of givenness by experience which itself is influenced by the social fabric of culture as well as by invariants in nature, even perhaps, the nature of the subject, a question not taken up by this theory. However, though there is a degree of givenness to the schemas, the subject is active in the recognition of the fit (of "fillers" from experience to the slots of the schemas), in the evaluation of the goodness of the fit, and constantly throughout the learning process. In short, the process in not mechanical.[6] For those who value the freedom of the human subject in the process of production and interpretation of discourse, this is a welcome aspect of schema theory.

5.2.2 Weaknesses of schema theories

The following weaknesses in schema theory are presented with the aim of improving the theory, which obviously presents many valuable contributions to a theory of comprehension. Proposals for modifications of the theory are given, when possible, following each point.

First, though, reading comprehension is given the "clear" definition of "the process of choosing and verifying conceptual schemata to account for the text to be understood . . ." (Meyer 1981:31), the "how" of the choosing and verifying, and the meaning of "to account for" are left without either adequate exposition or theoretical grounding.

Second, Rumelhart himself recognizes the problem which the creation of new schemas poses for schema theory:

> Schema induction does cause some difficulty for the notion of schemata as I have outlined them. In order for schema induction to work properly, we much posit some aspect of the system sensitive to the recurrence of configurations of schemata that do not, at the time they occur, match any existing [for the particular reader] schemata. Such a system is not a natural part of a schema-based system (Rumelhart 1980:54).[7]

---

[6] It can not be doubted, however, that there are also machine-like elements in the typical schema theory conception of the schema. For a presentation of this point, cf. Beers 1987, sections 5.2.2 (especially note #11) and 7.2.1 below. However, the above noted elements of reader participation generally highlighted by schema theory preclude too severe a judgement against schema theory at this point. Perhaps the best conclusion is that further clarification and development is required, some of which follows in subsequent chapters. Cf. also Beers 1987 for further suggestions.

[7] Rumelhart's language in this quote is not as clear as it might be. How, for instance, can a "configuration of schemata" occur when they are not "existing *schemata*"? Perhaps it

111

The problem Rumelhart acknowledges is that recognition in schema theory is in terms of fitting preexistent schemas. How, then, can a case of "recurrence" be recognized if there is no preexistent schema available to signal a second (or third, etc.) case of the same (or similar) thing? Schema theory, as it stands, cannot account for this process which is required by a comprehensive theory of learning. Further difficulties which Rumelhart fails to recognize are (1) how can a configuration be recognized as a configuration if there is no schema for it? and (2) what process(es) is involved in forming a "configuration" and how is this process related to the processes associated with schemas?

Similarly, van Dijk (1977:30) notes that ". . .it cannot be denied that we know many 'loose facts' that are not systematically related to our general world knowledge."[8] Though van Dijk's point is not precisely the same as Rumelhart's, it does provide and "empirical" basis for the induction model: We do, in fact, already possess in memory "loose facts," so the formation of the schemas based on the recurrence of such facts should not be too surprising. All that is needed is a matching, evaluation, and construction "mechanism" much like what is already required by the theory. Of course these two matching procedures are not identical but they are variations on the common theme of the recognition of resemblance.[9] Knowledge, then, is not totally conditioned by any limited set of schemas. This, I suggest, should not finally be considered a weakness in the theory-- though in the theory's present form it certainly is an area needing further development--but the recognition that learning and creativity are human activities of a subject with allegiances deeper (or higher, if you prefer, the particular metaphor here is not crucial) than schemas as currently conceived. Nonetheless, these creative activities do occur in the framework of a desire and an effort for the kind of coherence reflected in schemas. Several related problems arise in conjunction with this preceeding difficulty.

The third weakness of schema theories, which is related to the difficulty of schema induction, is the problem of understand "the new." This problem is posed most pointedly by a consideration of metaphor.

I think Ortony is right when he says,

---

would have been better to say something like "pre-schematic configurations" or simply "configuration." If, on the other hand, "configuration of schemata" means a new grouping of "existing [i.e. old] schemata" for which there is no "existing schemata," the unclarity is compounded by the unarticulated distinction between "configuration" and "schema" as well as the unarticulated distinction between the process of configuring and the process of schema induction. See the text following this note for further comment.

[8] "Loose facts" means facts which do not fit easily into any existent schema(s). The problem to be pointed out in what follows is that this is a weakness for the current conception of schemas. A reinterpretation of "schema" would also bring a reinterpretation of "loose facts." Such a reinterpretation will be offered in chapter 7.

[9] The notion of "resemblance" is examined further in chapter 7, section 2.

Any theory that claims to account for the nature of human language comprehension has to be able to account for nonliteral as well as literal uses of language . . . . (1980:359; the substitution of "conventional" for "literal" would not effect Ortony's point).

Metaphor is one of these "nonliteral" uses of language. "Metaphor" says Ortony (1980: 359), "is more than a linguistic and psychological curiosity." Rather, it is closely linked with the learning of the "new." Again quoting Ortony, "It is also a means of conveying and acquiring new knowledge and of seeing things in new ways" (Ortony 1980:361; emphases added). And again,

Metaphors, then, can be a way of knowing and a way of coming to a new understanding. They are wide in scope, extending from the highest pinnacles of scientific endeavor to the most lowly explanations in the classroom or introductory texts. In other words, metaphors are an important ingredient in learning and understanding (Ortony 1980:361f; emphasis added).

In short, the implication seems to be that metaphors are credited with creating schemas.

It is not necessary here to dwell on the difficulty which metaphoric comprehension poses for schema theory--the point has been made in the previous comments. Further, theorists within schema theory recognize this fact. Ortony (1980:361) writing on metaphor and schema theory, says

This is not the place to attempt a detailed well-worked-out account of the processing and structural aspects of metaphoric comprehension in schema theory, nor do I think that such an account is yet possible . . . .

Similarly, Spiro (1980:271) notes that

We know next to nothing about the processes of conceptual change . . . . Perhaps metaphor, with its capability of describing something new in terms of what is already known plays an important role . . . . Unfortunately, it is probably the case that psychology will have to undergo its own "conceptual change" if an understanding of that essential learning phenomenon is ever to ensue.

Clearly, then, metaphor presents an outstanding difficulty for schema theory. The fact is, however, that the understanding of metaphors for

113

which there are no preexisting schemas is a common (and much cherished) occurrence. To find a schema-theoretic account of metaphor, then, must be a most significant priority for schema theorists. What hope can we find for such an account?

Ortony (1980:360) suggests that the concept of "a context-sensitive spreading activation mechanism" (cf. also Ortony 1977) might well serve to screen out the inappropriate predicates which a simple conjunction of schemas would allow.[10] This "mechanism" proposes that within schemas there are pointers and pathways to other schemas with which they are characteristically associated. A certain instantiation of a schema activates other schemas and this effect spreads like a chain reaction. The spreading is controlled by the particular context which instantiates the schemas in unique ways (Haberlandt and Bingham 1982:36ff). The general criticism which is often voiced against schema theories--that they are so general as to be able to explain anything in an ad hoc manner--is perhaps at its best here. As Carpenter and Just (1977:240) point out, the "spreading activation mechanism" is not specific enough to account for the variable control actually observed in schema selection.

It can certainly be acknowledged that two schema-like systems (cf. footnote #10) are conjoined in metaphor, and that not all characteristics of each schema are usually in focus (cf. e.g. Ricoeur 1981a:169ff; 1975a). But beyond this rather obvious fact, it is not clear that "spreading activation" really answers the "How" question. It simply states the question in another form. Further, it misses the main point that in many metaphors the associations between the schemas involved are anything but characteristic.

Another approach to salvaging a schema-theoretic approach to metaphor is to posit a "metaphor meta-schema" which controls or guides metaphoric comprehension. It would, for instance, alert one to the possible occurrence of a metaphor when, for example, the semantic "distance" between the two (or more) schemas in question exceeded a certain "amount" or when the "goodness of fit" was beyond the range of acceptability, etc. It would then activate special procedures by which to "make sense" of this anomaly. Though this well might be a fruitful line of inquiry, when all is said and done, I imagine that several problems would remain. One would still be the *how* of these procedures. Another would be the origin of the meta-schema: Did it come from a meta-meta-schema? If so, we are caught in an infinite regress with no final explanation of origin. Or did it originate the same way all other schemas do--by repeated experience? If so, there is still no explanation for the "spark" which initiates the distinction between mere repetition and (new) meaning. It is the latter which is especially pertinent to a consideration of the newness of new metaphors, i.e. metaphors for which there are no preexistent schemas

---

[10] In the traditional language of metaphor theory, the two terms so conjoined are called the "topic" and "vehicle" or "frame" and "focus." Cf. chapter 7.2 for a further discussion of metaphor theories and schema theories.

new metaphors, i.e. metaphors for which there are no preexistent schemas and for which, therefore, prior experience, even repeated prior experience, cannot provide an adequate account (e.g. "Time is a beggar," "Virginity is the enamel of the soul," etc.). Thus there seems to be no final explanation for the constructive activity of the comprehender by which a coherent world (in which the anomaly of that metaphor makes sense) is made. The process of comprehension, then, is one of creative construction for which there are guidelines,[11] but no final explanations. In short, ". . . the comprehender is a far more active participate than thought by psycholinguists of the 1960's under the influence of Chomsky and Katz (Spiro 1980:245).

This completes our attempt to salvage an account of metaphor within the schema-theoretic framework. The attempts have been failures, but as such are still helpful. A weakness in schema theories has been confirmed, and the importance of openness to dialogue with other disciplines has been established. This dialogue is picked up in the following chapters. The fourth weakness of schema theory, though, has yet to be discussed.

The fourth weakness is similar to and related to the third. This point is made provocatively by Morgan and Sellner (1980:190):

> The impression one gets from story schema literature is usually that a good story is one that fits well with some story schema, as if the enjoyment and judgment of stories were derived from trying to fit events into schemata. But this misses the point entirely. The essence of a story is the imaginary experience it evokes in the reader or hearer. People enjoy stories via the experiences that they derive from understanding the story, not through the sensual pleasures of fitting information structures into an abstract schema.

This is not to deny the role of schemas in understanding, as Morgan and Sellner go on to affirm. Their point, though, is that not all understanding, and especially the most important part as far as story comprehension is concerned, can be accounted for on the basis of story schema theories of understanding. This crucial aspect is the imaginary experience and the associated pleasure or enjoyment. The importance of the construction of a coherent world in which some otherwise anomalous expressions

---

[11] "Recipe," says R.C. Anderson and Shifrin (1980:373); "skeleton," "blueprint," says Spiro (1980:245) and (1979:2). Quite likely these terms reflect the overly mechanistic orientation of these researchers. The terms are overly "pre-set." Note also Ortony's use of "mechanism," which is conceived of as highly automatic on analogy with the endocrine system (cf. Iran-Nejad and Ortony 1982). This discussion is picked up in chapter 7.2

aren't was discussed earlier with regard to metaphor. The notion of enjoyment, though, raises a further question for schema theories.

Spiro (1980:272) notes that concepts and schemas cannot only be decomposed and analyzed, but are also *"experiences,* and as such they have textual, gestalt-like properties that can only be felt." He goes on to note, quite rightly, that "Work in the schema-theoretic tradition has focused on the structure of knowledge that must be analyzed, rather than on the texture that must be felt" (Spiro 1980:273). The enjoyment or pleasure which Morgan and Sellner write about is, no doubt, such an experience. The inference from Morgan and Sellner, which Spiro confirms, is that schema theory does not account for this aspect of understanding. A further implication is that understanding cannot be fully accounted for on the basis of current schema theory: Both the imaginary and affective domains of understanding escape an adequate account. This point will also be picked up in chapters 6 and 7 in dialogue with phenomenological theories of reading.[12]

Finally, and in anticipation of this future dialogue, a very brief note regarding the role of fitness in schema theory. There is not doubt that this notion is central to the concept of schemas. What is of further interest, however, is that fitness has also been a key *aesthetic* concept in many theories. Further still, resemblance--which in the context of schema theory could be paraphrased as the judgment regarding the acceptability or goodness of fit--is a key notion in the theory of metaphor, an especially aesthetic use of language. The hypothesis, then, is that the functioning of understanding via schemas is more "artistic" and less "analytical," even in its present form, than the prejudice and predisposition for science of most schema theorists might allow. There are, then, already avenues into schema theory which not only invite dialogue, but also allow reinterpretation and modification of schemas in their current conception (both avenues are pursued in chapters 6 and 7). Because of this openness of schema theory to dialogue and change, together with its strengths noted earlier, schema theory is judged to be a very valuable theory whose contribution must be incorporated into any comprehensive theory of comprehension.

5.3   Summaries in reading comprehension

Before entering into an analysis and discussion of theories of discourse comprehension which rely heavily on the role of summarization as a test for and an indication of comprehension, I further introduce this approach.

---

[12] It is interesting to note that the role of "affect" is picked up by Spiro (1980:270f) as closely related to "summarizing" (as discussed below, section 2.2). These "summarizing affects" of Spiro are discussed further in chapter 7, section 5.4

The main proponents of this view are van Dijk and Kintsch. The processing stages of comprehension in this model extend from sensory input to behavioral language use ("speech acts") in "response" to the text. Intermediate to these extremes are stages of word identification, syntactic analysis yielding linguistic structure, semantic analysis yielding conceptual or propositional content, and pragmatic analysis yielding the topic of discourse. These stages are interactive and recursive (Kintsch 1977:34).

The two "stages" which are of special interest here are the semantic and the pragmatic stages. They both are reductive. The first reduces phrases and sentences to propositions; the second further reduces this propositional microstructure to the propositional macrostructure. It is not clear how the first reduction is accomplished. The assumption, though, is that the reader naturally transforms such discourse fragments as

Gazing at the body in astonishment, ...

to propositions such as [where the Judge is gazing]

1. GAZE, JUDGE, BODY

2. MANNER: IN, 1, ASTONISHMENT (Kintsch 1977:36)

The exact form of the memory fragment which records such propositions is not a part of the theory. The crucial point is that the "raw discourse data" is simplified, transformed, and stored. The macro-rules, listed and developed in what is to follow, then operate on the propositional microstructure to produce the macrostructure. Says van Dijk (1977:7),

Macro-structures are assumed to be semantic structures of discourse whose meaning and reference is defined in terms of their constituents' meanings. . . .the meaning of macro-structures is a function of the meaning and reference of the constituent propositions. . . .

Given a discourse such as

Harry Duke watched them come in from his corner at the end of the bar. He looked at Clare curiously, then he put his glass down slowly on the polished counter. She was standing in the doorway with Peter just behind her and he saw her face turned at an angle and at the same time he saw the strange thing about her. As he looked at her he felt a thickness in his throat. (van Dijk 1977:23),

the first macro-level would be something like

HARRY DUKE LOOKS AT CLARE(van Dijk 1977:26).

The rules which accomplish this reduction are:

      1.   GENERALIZATION which, obviously, generalizes propositions and sequences of propositions to a "super-concept" (van Dijk 1977:9ff)

      2.   DELETION which "deletes full propositions" which are 'irrelevant' " (van Dijk 1977:11)

      3.   INTEGRATION which deletes information which "has been integrated into another proposition of the discourse" (van Dijk 1977:12)

      4.   CONSTRUCTION which is

> perhaps most characteristic of all macro-rules. It organizes micro-information by combining sequences of propositions which function as one unit at some macro-level; it reduces information without simply deleting it; and it introduces information at the macro-level that is "new" in the sense of not being part of the text base or entailed by individual propositions of the text base" (van Dijk 1977:15).

Kintsch and van Dijk 1975 examined the role of macro-structures in story comprehension, and concluded that, in fact, macro-structures are formed in comprehension.

If the notion of macro-structure seems vague and undefined, this can be taken as a fundamental weakness of the theory. Say Morgan and Sellner (1980:193),

> Van Dijk's work is vulnerable to many technical and theoretical criticisms . . . , especially (despite prolific use of fancy notations) the criticism that it is so vague as to have little content.

I will continue now with several critical comments regarding this theory.

First, it is not clear that Kintsch and van Dijk 1975, and Kintsch 1977 differ significantly from the schema theories previously mentioned. Note, for example, that Kintsch 1977, in commenting on Kintsch and van Dijk 1975, while explaining why "Scrambling the order of paragraphs in a well-structured story affects comprehension remarkably little," says

> The reason for this, I suggest, is that comprehending such a story involves filling in waiting slots in a fixed story schema according to certain well known rules and strategies (Kintsch 1977:50).

That summaries conform to schemas, and therefore that schemas are significant in summarization indeed follows. However, that summaries are indicative of macro-structures--which van Dijk, as noted, distinguishes from schemas--remains an unconfirmed hypothesis. Similarly, the relation between macro-structure processing and comprehension, and between summaries and comprehension are not established by the evidence cited. Nothing more than a summary schema, which may indeed vary according to genre, is needed to account for the experimental results. Consequently, this theory shares many strengths with schema theories, but it is not at all clear how van Dijk and Kintsch have improved upon schema theory, or that their treatment does not in fact obscure the issues.

Second, summarization by means of the macro-rules reduces the information in the text. For van Dijk and Kintsch, "the meaning of the whole seems to be less than the meaning of the parts" (Morgan and Sellner 1980:194). In short, a summary is an impoverished version of the discourse. Though van Dijk states that "the meaning or reference of a sequence as a whole is preserved" (1977:8), he does assume that information is in fact lost (1977:27f). Here the whole is not even equal to the sum of its parts; rather it is less than the parts. Consequently, van Dijk's claim that meaning is preserved is difficult to believe.

Thirdly, and closely related to the preceding point, Huggins and Adams point out that "decomposing complex sentences into simple sentences may *change meaning*" (1980:90). Their point is that "complex ideas and relationships cannot always be expressed in syntactically simple sentences alone" (1980:90). The two reductive processes which were noted earlier as essential to the van Dijk model of macro-structure formation are in fact such decomposing processes. The conclusion is that such processes cannot be relied upon to conserve meaning.

Fourth, Enkvist's research (1981) highlights a similar problem. The ordering of a text, i.e. the order of the intrasentential components and of the sentences, can turn a text into a semiotic system which itself has iconic significance. Much of this semiotic information is destroyed by the propositional analyses employed by both van Dijk and Kintsch. Again it is difficult to assume with them that meaning has been preserved by their procedures.

Fifth, Chafe has challenged the assumption that knowledge is stored as propositions, stating ". . . knowledge is not stored propositionally at all" (1977:54). Further, Ortony 1977 claims that comprehension is not only prior to, but distinct from memory representation, and thus memory representation (e.g. summarization) is not a reliable guide to comprehension per se.[13]

---

[13] This, though, is not an undisputed view (cf. Bransford 1974).

119

Sixth, though van Dijk recognizes that there are individual differences in comprehension (van Dijk 1977:30), and that the reader must construct macro-structures from topics not themselves expressed in the passage, he seems to assume that all readers operate in basically the same way and thus construct basically the same macro-structures. The constraints which cause this agreement, though, are not merely the conventionality of the schemas employed, since, again, macro-structures differ from schemas precisely in not being "conventional and general" (van Dijk 1977:22). Indeed, the macro-rules are general (van Dijk 1977:22), but their application is dependent on both the particular discourse and the particular reader. The assumption of the Kintsch and van Dijk experiment (1975), though, is that subjects can decide which summaries are good, which "poorer," and which "equivalent" (Kintsch 1977:49f), and that such decisions can serve as the basis of whether or not comprehension has occurred. If, in fact, individual differences in the use of macro-rules are allowed, then the equivalence of propositional units in the summaries is no text for comprehension, unless comprehension is simply a democratic process--i.e. comprehension occurs when there is agreement with the majority.[14] Such a view, I trust, is not seriously entertained. Nonetheless, this tendency to standardize comprehension reaches an extreme in Miller and Kintsch 1981 where comprehension is equated with agreeing with summaries as propositionalized by the researchers (cf. Miller and Kintsch 1981:217).[15]

Seventh, and closely related to the preceding point, both van Dijk and Kintsch give the impression that the macro-rule applications are almost mechanical. However, at many points in the application of the theory, the intuition of the analyst is crucial. This is seen in the prominence granted to a particular frame (van Dijk 1977:23), in the level of relevance of a frame selected (van Dijk 1977:24), in the decision as to what is "irrelevant and thus deletable" (van Dijk 1977:24), and in the selection of the topic of a discourse which, in fact, governs the construction of the macro-structures.[16]

---

[14] Rumelhart's view of schemas as operative in the summarization process (Rumelhart 1977b:277-297), together with the recognition that schemas vary from person to person (in detail, in structure, and in ways of interrelating with other schemas--in short, that no two people live in strictly identical worlds), confirms the expectation that summaries will also differ.

[15] The situation presented by Miller and Kintsch is the clearest case of an identification of summarization and comprehension. The situation with the others discussed above is admittedly not as clear, and thus my inclusion of van Dijk, for example, in this categorical judgment may be unfair. My main point, however, is that there is at least the tendency in all those discussed to make this identification, a tendency which is clear in at least the one case cited.

[16] Miller and Kintsch 1980 do, in fact, recognize this problem, and yet, in the words of Meyer 1983, "They hope to solve this problem by yet unspecified macro-components for

120

Just how crucial this latter point is can be documented from the history of literary criticism. The conclusion of a study of this history seems to be that the topic of a text is determined by the critic's interpretive prereading of the text (cf. Fish 1980).

Van Dijk though does recognize a significant role for frames (his term for schemas; van Dijk 1977:18-27) and the importance of "notions such as importance and relevance" (van Dijk 1977:8). Says he, ". . . the macro-interpretations defines the most important or essential object or event denoted by a sequence of propositions" (van Dijk 1977:8). Both of these areas do involve subjective judgment on the part of the reader. Macro-structures, however, are ". . . assumed to be semantic structures of discourse whose meaning and reference is defined in terms of their constituents' meaning" (van Dijk 1977:7). That is, macro-structures are linguistic structures which seem, from van Dijk's perspective, to inhere in the text. The difficulties of this view were discussed in section 5.1 of the preceding chapter.

Finally, though there is a recognition that interpretation of discourse units depends on other units, the direction of interpretation is only from the smaller or equal units to the larger. Van Dijk says, ". . . interpretations of larger units depend on the interpretation of smaller units" (van Dijk 1977:5) and, ". . . each macro-proposition must be interpreted with respect to other macro-propositions" (van Dijk 1977:7). Further, interpretation is relative to "other, *mostly previous*, sentences of the discourse" (van Dijk 1977:5); emphasis added). Later (chapter 6) I will argue for the classic "hermeneutic circle," but it is worth noting here that this "circle" acknowledges a reciprocal relation between the whole and the parts: The whole is known from the parts, and yet the parts are seen in the light of the whole.[17]

It should be acknowledged that van Dijk does recognize aspects of discourse which "cannot be defined in terms of individual sentences (or their underlying propositions)" (van Dijk 1977:3), and that "macro-structures also contribute to 'local' coherence at the micro-level of connections between propositions in composite sentences and successive

---

their model." Though Meyer wants to avoid this problem, it seems that she has simply replaced "intuition" with "trained intuition" (Meyer 1983:33-35).

[17] As a result of van Dijk's commitment to a "noncircular" plan of interpretation, he declares sentences "ungrammatical" when he cannot imagine a situation in which they might hold. The immediate-local incompatibility of such sentences as

"The old woman was buried in her native village. She is
dying of virulent pneumonia" (van Dijk 1972:82),

result in their "ungrammaticality" (van Dijk 1972:83) or incoherence (van Dijk 1977b). Such a judgment, though, reflects more the anthropological ignorance of the interpreter, or perhaps the lack of imagination, than linguistic incompatibility.

sentences" (van Dijk 1977:4). These are all excellent principles. There has been, though, no theoretical or practical account of how this occurs.

In summary, the van Dijk-Kintsch approach to comprehension suffers from two main faults. First, summarization is not a reliable equivalent for comprehension for two reasons. As Morgan and Sellner (1980:195) have said,

> Summarization or abstracting has to do with interpreting the world, and the world can be observed directly or vicariously through narrative. Summarization is not a linguistic operation performed on texts to recover content. Summarization may be a mark of understanding but it is not itself either understanding or what it is that is understood.

Further, the macro-rule summarization procedures reduce information, potentially change meaning, and disrupt the semiotic system of the text, all of which affect the meaning of the text, and thus affect comprehension, which is assumed to be "of meaning." Second, as intimated in the Morgan and Sellner quote above, there is much involved in comprehension which is not strictly linguistic. Though the van Dijk and Kintsch model acknowledges subjective and pragmatic factors, it labors under a commitment to a text-based mode. Points 5-7 above speak to this concern.

Finally, let me note what remains of value in this approach. First, summaries, though not in themselves comprehension, can be a mark of comprehension, and in themselves are and important and legitimate topic of study. This model may well have much to contribute to such a study. Second, the inclusion of behavioral language use as a stage of comprehension is a significant point which few make explicit. No doubt, though, much more grounding and exploration of this inclusion is required for a satisfactory treatment. And third, others have also noted that some means of organizing knowledge other than frames/schemas is needed (e.g. cf. Lytinen and Shank 1982:97-101). Van Dijk's macro-structures could be a contribution here, though is its present form, I find the macro-structure concept too vague to be useful.

5.4   Conclusions

In conclusion then, the most valuable and promising contribution from recent "discourse research" (which draws from many fields) to an understanding of discourse comprehension is schema theory. The basic problem with schema theory, though, is this: If understanding an experience is fitting its components into the slots of a schema (as it is for schema theories), how do we understand understanding: What are the components of the experience and what is the schema into which they fit? Schema theory, with its predisposition to empirical evidence, is unequipped to answer such a reflexive question. But clearly such an answer is required by a desire for a securely grounded theory. To meet this challenge for "grounding" we will turn in the following chapter to the philosophical reflection on understanding of the phenomenologists.

This need, though, is not only theoretic. We saw when examining the weaknesses of schema theory several places where understanding itself "escaped" the schema theoretic account: learning theory, metaphor, imaginative experience, and affective experience. There may indeed be others, for once a perspective is adopted which fails to account for such basic concerns, much else is likely to elude the researcher. Nonetheless, there is much of practical and theoretical value to schema theory (as noted in section 2.1). These valuable insights we will want to retain in our own development toward a comprehensive theory of understanding. These contributions of schema theory can be summarized by saying that understanding in terms of schemas is a necessary, but not a sufficient condition of understanding in the broadest sense.[18]

---

[18] Though I say "necessary," I do not mean to imply that understanding in terms of schemas is necessarily prior to that "aspect" of understanding which is not accounted for by schema theory. My predisposition, yet to be validated, is that, in fact, it is not. The impression of such precedence (i.e. what is "necessary" also necessarily precedes--in logical and/or temporal priority--that which is required for a "sufficient" account) can come simply from the linear order of the words "necessary and sufficient" (i.e. the "iconic" value of the phrase). My point here is that such a precedence is *not* necessarily the case.

CHAPTER 6

PHENOMENOLOGICAL THEORIES OF COMPREHENSION

Lovett, having surveyed various theories of reading comprehension (much as we have in the preceding chapters) states:

> Nowhere is our ignorance more blatant, however, than in the area of semantic processing. Consideration of the models just reviewed [in her case, those of Gough, Kolers, Rumelhart, and LaBerge and Samuels] illustrates this point all too clearly (1981:11).

And then, a bit later:

> In retrospect, it is not surprising that reading theorists have been sometimes vague, sometimes flippant, and sometimes negligent in their treatment of the comprehension process. It seems clear that a theory of reading comprehension must await further developments in our general understanding of language comprehension (Lovett 1981:18).

Though I find Lovett's conclusions essentially accurate (if a bit harsh), I am more hopeful. Admittedly this hope does not spring from these reading theories. Rather, the philosophical theories of comprehension which we are about to discuss do offer what Lovett looks for, "further developments in our general understanding of language comprehension." The hopeful note is that this philosophy seems to me compatible with much of what the reading theorists have discovered while at the same time offering "further developments" in foundations, as well as in detail.

The phenomenologists we are considering (cf. chapter 2 for the detailed introduction), follow (more or less) the fundamental shift which occurred in philosophy with the work of Martin Heidegger. This shift is seen as "an attempt to dig beneath the epistemological enterprise itself, in order to uncover its properly ontological conditions" (Ricoeur 1981a:53). In brief, this is a shift from epistemology to ontology.[1]

---

[1] In laymen's terms this means that no longer is the primary question "how do we know?" (epistemology; from *episteme*, knowledge), but instead, "what is the mode of being of that being (i.e. man) who exists only in understanding?" (ontology; from *ontos*, being).

Actually this definition of ontology is dominated by the interpretation introduced by Heidegger and followed by Ricoeur. More "neutrally" (i.e. traditionally), ontology is

The significance of this shift for our dialogue with the reading theorists should be immediately obvious: All the reading theorists are concerned with questions of epistemology.[2] To substantiate this claim, consider the following: Schema theory is "basically a theory about knowledge," a schema being "a data structure" (Rumelhart 1980:34), which contains "our conventional *knowledge* of the world" (van Dijk 1977:18; emphasis added). In short, schemas *are* our knowledge" (Rumelhart 1980:41). For Smith, "comprehension is the condition of having cognitive questions answered" (1975:34) in accordance with the *theory* of the world *in our head*. For Goodman (and many others) the top-down contribution of prior *knowledge* is the area of special interest to be reckoned with in reading theory. For Carpenter and Just, "the psychological processes of integrating information" (1977:217) are the final basis of "text-based" discourse processes. And for Meyer, "knowledge of logical relationship" (1983:35) is basic. The list could, of course, go on and on. But the point is the same: Reading theories have been fundamentally epistemological not ontological. This, however, is only what is to be expected from cognitive psychologists and psycholinguists, etc. Furthermore, to claim that there is a more fundamental dimension to comprehension is not to either deny, disparage, or void the obviously significant work which has been done by these researchers. Rather it is to reflect upon and orient this work within a larger framework which we anticipate will have productive consequences in each discipline concerned with reading. In what follows, this larger framework of ontology is presented in terms of a phenomenological understanding of understanding.

6.1   Preliminary orientation to "phenomenological understanding"

> It is the service of Martin Heidegger in *Being and Time* to have opened up the ontological character of understanding in a way that moves radically beyond the older conception of it within the subject-object schema. According to Heidegger, understanding is not some faculty among others that man possesses; understanding is his fundamental mode of existing in the world (Palmer 1969:227).

Essential to this reformulation of the conception of understanding is the break with the subject-object schema which dominated both the

---

simply the study of being: i.e. what there is, how what "is" is, and whether all that "is" is in the same sense and degree. The shift to an ontological interpretation of understanding is, however, a shift with which I concur. Furthermore, such a shift connects quite nicely with the orientation and emphasis of the reading theorists for whom comprehension is a central category, thus opening not only a fresh dialogue, but also the possibility of a radical reevaluation of reading theories.

[2] There are, though, glimpses of the need for "something more," which we will take note of at appropriate points throughout the discussion.

126

rationalistic and the empiricistic traditions which provide the philosophic backgrounds for the reading theorists. Man, for Heidegger, and for those who follow him, is <u>not</u> first of all "a subject [e.g. a reader] for which there is an object [e.g. a text], but is rather a being within being" (Ricoeur 1981a:54). This "embedding" in being is the fundamental starting point for understanding understanding.

Consequently, "the question of understanding is wholly severed from the problem of communication with others" (Ricoeur 1981a:55), the context so often assumed by the reading theorists (e.g. Meyer 1984:3; 1981:9; Bruce 1977:33; Clark 1977:244). Rather,

> Understanding, in its primordial sense, is implicated in the relation with my situation, in the fundamental understanding of my position within being (Ricoeur 1981a:55).

In fact, Ricoeur says, understanding is "a structure of being-in-the-world" (Ricoeur 1981a:142). As Palmer puts it:

> Understanding is then the medium by which the world comes to stand before a man; understanding is the medium of ontological disclosure.
>
> Understanding is not a tool for something else . . . but rather the medium in which and through which one exists (1969:228).

The reading theorists have, it seems, become increasingly aware of this role of "the world" in reading comprehension. All the talk about the necessary role of "prior knowledge" and the importance of interaction is, I think, the reflection of this fundamental structure of man's being into the epistemological domain. The reading theorists, though, have been bound by their methodology to "tune into" the cognitive repercussions only, and have minimized, if not eliminated, the deeper dimensions of the situation in their theoretical writings.

Before considering this fundamental ontological structure in greater detail, three implications of this "more comprehensive conception of understanding" (Palmer 1969:227) for language and reading will be drawn.

First, inasmuch as "inhabiting a world" (Ricoeur 1981a:56) is the fundamental condition which renders understanding possible,

> . . . the theory of understanding must be preceded by the recognition of entrenchment which anchors the whole linguistic system, including books and texts, in something which is not primordially a phenomenon of articulation in discourse (Ricoeur 1981a:56).

127

This means that the most fundamental ground of comprehension is pre- and/or hyper-linguistic (Ricoeur 1975a:31; 1978a:234; 1981a:56, 117-119, 243f; Reagan 1979:xviii). Consequently, models of comprehension which ground understanding in discourse are bound to fall short of understanding reading comprehension.

Second, in commenting on Heidegger's exposition of feelings like fear and anguish, Ricoeur points out that the affective domain is most revelatory of this "link to a reality more fundamental than the subject-object relation" (1981a:56). This is especially interesting in light of Athey's recent comment:

> It would be accurate to say, however, that recent work related to reading has emphasized the cognitive rather than the affective domain (1982:210f).

She goes on to indicate where she sees the affective as active in reading,[3] and approaches--but does not reach--the fundamental ontological/phenomenological perspective when she says:

> While we could legitimately conclude . . . that affective factors intrude into almost every aspect of metacognitive monitoring, it would be equally plausible to say that metacognitive monitoring is, in essence, an affective activity (1982:212).

Certainly, though, with Athey, we can conclude that the affective domain deserves much more attention and a more respected place in reading research, theory and practice.[5]

Third, a new conception of the objectivity of language is offered with this broader conception of comprehension. Because understanding is "the medium by which a situation or matter is disclosed as it is" (Palmer 1969:228), or in short, since "understanding . . . [is] the organ of ontological disclosure" (Palmer 1969:229), something other than human subjectivity is expressed by and in language. Palmer terms this "other" aspect "the being

---

[3] For example, in the assessment of the task, in the estimation of success, in the identification of strategies, and in continuous monitoring, all of which receive a deeper interpretation in the light of the ontological grounding to be developed in what follows.

[4] Her own interpretation of the relation between the affective and the cognitive follows Piaget whose famous aphorism relates the two as the two banks of the same river, which is the individual's stream of consciousness (Athey 1982:212). Ricoeur's use of the affective would extend the metaphor to include the riverbed and even the "mouth" of the river within the affective domain.

[5] I attend to this issue in more detail in chapter 7, section 5.4.

of the situation" (1969:229), and Ricoeur "a new mode of being" (1981a:192).⁶ Consequently, "to understand a text, we shall say, is not to find a lifeless sense which is contained therein, but to unfold the possibility of being indicated by the text" (Ricoeur 1981a:56).⁷ This is a difficult notion, and we will return to it in chapter 7. Before doing so, however, this phenomenological perspective must be presented in greater detail.

6.2   The hermeneutical circle

More than any other reading theorist, Goodman has recognized that reading is an interaction between parts and the whole. As he puts it "we only 'know' the parts when we've created meaning for the whole" (Goodman 1979:659); and yet, the whole is only given a part at a time. This is a restatement of the classical hermeneutical circle which Ricoeur summarizes as follows: "The presupposition of a certain whole precedes the discernment of a determinate arrangement of parts; and it is by constructing the details that we build up the whole" (1981a:175).

Before plunging more deeply into an exposition of this circular structure, it will be helpful to the dialogue we are developing to note that the philosophical recognition of the hermeneutical circle confirms one point of view on four much debated issues in reading theory. This philosophical recognition, though, also further grounds, as well as fundamentally reorients, the discussion of these issues. First, a consideration of this confirmation.

In agreement with Goodman, Ricoeur and Iser recognize that due to this "circle," reading is tentative and involves a "dialectic between guessing and validating" (Ricoeur 1981a:175), which Ricoeur hints is functional at every level of reading.⁸ For Goodman, remember, reading is "a psycholinguistic guessing game" (Goodman 1976a:498). Ricoeur, however, develops this point at the textual level of interpretation to conclude that reading functions with "procedures of validation [that] have more affinity with a logic of probability than with a logic of empirical verification" (1981a:175; cf. also Iser 1978:230). Consequently, "one construction can be said to be more probable than another, but not more truthful" (Ricoeur 1981a:175). Implicit in this development are the notions of (1) the text as

⁶ Cf. chapter 7, sections 3 and 4.

⁷ Inasmuch as the theme of disclosure is acknowledged, we as readers do not ask all the questions, nor control the answers, and therefore reading cannot be properly conceived of as purely top-down. It is even highly doubtful whether the alternative notions of bottom-up processing, nor the combined conception of the interaction account for the phenomenon of reading. More later on this point; cf. especially chapter 9.

⁸ Ricoeur (1981a:175): "This dialectic between guessing and validating is the realization at the textual level of the micro-dialectic at work in the resolution of the local enigmas of a text."

polysemous, (2) reading as construction (cf. point 2 below), and (3) criteria for evaluation of possible readings (cf. point 3 below, and chapter 8).

Second, it is sufficient here to simply note that both Ricoeur and Iser confirm the interaction view that reading is construction. As Iser (1978:163) puts it:

> As a structure of comprehension it [i.e. consistency-building; cf. chapter 2] depends on the reader and not on the work, and as such it is inextricably bound up with subjective factors, and above all, the habitual orientations of the reader.

Third, both Iser and Ricoeur understand reading to be interactive. Iser says, "Such a [textual] meaning must clearly be the product of an interaction between the textual signals and the reader's acts of comprehension" (1978:9). Having stressed the top-down aspect of interaction in the last point, here I stress the "bottom-up" processes. As Ricoeur (1981a:175) points out, though more than one reading can be given to a text, more than one construction "imposed," "the construction rests upon 'clues' contained in the text itself," and the "more probable [interpretation] is that which . . . takes account of the greatest number of facts furnished by the text . . . ." Consequently Ricoeur speaks of "the moment of the hermeneutical circle between the understanding initiated by the reader and the proposals of meaning offered by the text" (1981a:108), terms reminiscent of the interactive theories of reading.

Finally, Ricoeur and Iser concur with those theorists who recognize that coherence or consistency is the primary operative principle in the construction of meaning (e.g. Trabasso, Secco, Van Den Broek 1984). Here Ricoeur speaks of finding the better (if not the best) "convergence between the features [of the text] which it [the construction] takes into account" (1981a:176). And for Iser, consistency-building is the basis of the reader's involvement in the text (cf. 1978:118ff).

Though there are (at least) these four substantive agreements between Ricoeur and Iser on the one hand, and some reading theorists on the other, on the implications of what is called "the hermeneutical circle," there are profound differences as well. These are again best expressed in terms of the distinction between epistemology and ontology. The circle which Goodman recognizes is epistemological, and if left there may well "appear as a vicious circle" (Ricoeur 1981a:57). How can we know the whole which is necessary for a proper understanding of the parts when the whole can only be constructed from the parts? However,

> The function of a fundamental ontology is to disclose the structure which appears as a circle on the methodological plane. It is this structure that Heidegger calls *pre-understanding*. But it would be entirely mistaken if we continued to describe *pre-*

understanding in terms of the theory of knowledge, that is, in the categories of subject and object (Ricoeur 1981a:57).

To reconnect with our earlier exposition (cf. chapter 3) of reading theory in terms of the subject-object relation,

> It has been noted many times that . . . the subject and object are mutually implicated. The subject itself enters into the knowledge of the object; and in turn, the former is determined, in its most subjective character, by the hold which the object has upon it, even before the subject comes to know the object. Thus stated in the terminology of subject and object, the hermeneutical circle cannot but appear as a vicious circle (Ricoeur 1981a:57).

The point here, though, is that

> All objectifying knowledge . . . is preceded by a relation of *belonging* upon which we can never entirely reflect. Before any critical distance, we belong to a history, to a class, to a nation, to a culture, to one or several traditions . . . . this belonging . . . precedes and supports us . . . (Ricoeur 1981a:243).

This "belonging" is ". . . the very structure of a being [i.e. man] which is never in the sovereign position of a subject capable of distancing itself from the totality of its conditionings" (Ricoeur 1981a:243). Thus expounded, the reader is "always already" in possession in an anticipatory, preliminary way of a meaning of the whole which is necessary if the circle is not to be vicious. And again, this "structure of anticipation" (Ricoeur 1981a:58), this "always already" given pre-understanding is fundamentally ontological: It is the fundamental structure of our being.

   Four particular implications follow with regard to reading theory. First, these ontological insights imply the clear necessity of the top-down point of view, at least on first reading. The reader *always already* contributes to the construction of the meaning of a text. This notion of understanding is that it is "essentially a *projection*" (Ricoeur 1981a:56): ". . . it is the projection of our ownmost possibilities at the very heart of the situations in which we find ourselves" (Ricoeur 1981a:142). There is, however, a problem with a pure "projective" approach to reading: We always find ourselves already situated, and thus, as already quoted, "never in the sovereign position of a subject capable of distancing itself from the totality of its conditionings" (Ricoeur 1981a:243). As Ricoeur puts it elsewhere, the projection of which we speak is "a within a prior *being-thrown*" (1981a:56). Indeed, this is a more dialectical and paradoxical way

131

of speaking (Ricoeur 1981a:56), and we shall have to reckon with this more fully later (cf. chapters 7-9). Preliminarily I suspect that the "old wine skins" of the top-down, bottom-up terminology will not hold this "new wine."

Second, a no less reorienting implication follows from this fundamental ontology with regard to the communication situation often assumed as basic to reading. Just as a new conception of the subjectivity of the reader is implied in the preceding point, so too, with it comes a new conception of the role of intersubjectivity in the hermeneutical circle. Says Ricoeur (1981a:178):

> But I believe that the hermeneutical circle is not
> correctly understood when it is presented . . . as a
> circle between subjectivities, that of the reader
> and that of the author . . . .

This, though, is exactly what many, including Goodman (e.g. 1976b:472) assume. The reason such a view is found to be inadequate is implicit in the starting point of the fundamental ontology, man's being-in-the-world.[9] To reemphasize this important point:

> The most fundamental condition of the
> hermeneutical circle lies in the structure of pre-
> understanding which relates all explication to the
> understanding which precedes and supports it
> (Ricoeur 1981a:108).

Consequently, (and third,) because man's being-in-the-world is recognized as fundamental, the end point of reading is "the coming to language of a world and not the recognition of another person" (Ricoeur 1981a:178).[10] Before turning to a fuller exposition of this "world," a fourth and final contrast to certain reading theorists is drawn.

In the last chapter we looked at the role that summarization plays in the work of many researchers. The following comments apply not only to those theories, but also to those which rely on the reports of reading subjects to determine the degree of comprehension attained (and such an approach tends to typify research on reading comprehension).

First Ricoeur:

---

[9] This is Heidegger's term for what Ricoeur, following Gadamer (Ricoeur 1981a:106), calls "belonging."

[10] This is not to deny that the three-fold reference of discourse--to a world, a "speaker," and an "audience"--is fully operative in reading. It is, however, to prioritize the reference to the world as the basis upon which the other two references are restored in reading.

132

> The circle is between my mode of being--*beyond the knowledge which I may have of it*--and the mode of being opened up and disclosed by the text as the world of the work (1981a:178; emphasis added).

The significant point for our purposes here is contained in Ricouer's parenthetical remark (emphasized in the above quotation): "beyond the knowledge which I may have of it." For an ontological conception of understanding, using the reader's report as the only basis of comprehension could be most unreliable indeed, since comprehension is, to a most significant extent, "beyond his knowledge."

This situation is clarified by Iser's report of the involvement or entanglement which occurs in reading:

> While we are caught up in a text, we do not at first know what is happening to us. This is why we often feel the need to talk about books we have read--not in order to gain some distance from them so much as to find out just what it is that we were entangled in (Iser 1978:131).

Thus to ask a reader what he has been "entangled" in, i.e. what he has comprehended in the ontological sense, is likely to evoke the kind of searching, exploratory talk which may not be able to give expression to the "entanglement" for quite some time, if at all. And more so is this the case, the more significant the literature being read.[11]

6.3   The world

Because "being-in-the-world" is conceived of as the fundamental status of man, and because comprehension in reading is finally a matter of appropriating "the proposal of a mode of being-in-the-world, which the text discloses" (Ricoeur 1981a:192), the notion of the "world," and especially "the world of the work" calls for further explication. For reading theory this is a particularly happy development, for it is perhaps here more than anywhere else that the phenomenologists and the reading theorists come the closest together. We will develop this point at length in chapter 7.

---

[11] Several related problems face the experimenter during "in-the-lab" research on this dimension of reading comprehension: (1) The "lab" conditions may often hinder or impede both this kind of reading and the reporting of it (cf. Bloome 1983; Bloome and Green 1982), and (2) literature of such significance as to readily reveal this dimension of comprehension is typically not used in such experiments, as the research reports attest. This is not to say, however, that such reading is the exception or that it is unusual or rare. Rather such entanglement in reading is the coveted experience of all lovers of books and reading. These difficulties, though, we hope will be received not simply as a focus on shortcomings, but as a guide, a stimulus, even a challenge to further research.

Here, though, I remind the reader, first, that schemas (as previously introduced) are (cognitive) scenarios of the world, and second, that Frank Smith has recently shifted his thinking in the direction of "the world." Smith 1983 suggests that the prevailing metaphor for reading (and all language research) be changed from "the information-processing" model, which includes "communication as a metaphor for language", to "the creation of worlds . . . [as] a more productive and appropriate metaphor for language, literacy, and learning" (Smith 1983:119). Here his language is quite similar to that of Ricoeur. Says Smith (1983:119),

> . . . language--especially written language--is a particularly efficacious . . . medium by which these worlds [the "new worlds" or "possibilities in the world" (1983:119)] can be manifested, manipulated, and some times shared;

and Ricoeur, the text gives "the revelation of new modes of being--or, if you prefer Wittgenstein to Heidegger, new 'forms of life' " (1981a:192). With this introduction to the promise of a fruitful dialogue, we turn to a consideration of what Ricoeur means by the "world."

The "world" in the Heideggerian tradition is recognized as the most fundamental correlate of man's being. It is, though, more than simply a correlate, for Heidegger himself is eager (throughout *Being and Time*) to emphasize that "The compound expression 'Being-in-the-world' indicates in the very way we have coined it, that it stands for a *unitary* phenomena" (1962:78; section 12). This unity, though, ". . . does not prevent it from having several constitutive items in its structure" (Heidegger 1962:78), and Heidegger deals with the three constituents (the world, the entity, and being-in) in separate chapters.[12]

The first experience of the world is as environment which is there "ready-at-hand" for us to use. Here the function of things as available to me and as seen in the light of my concern is basic. However,

---

[12] Sections 14-24 of *Being and Time* deal with the "The worldhood of the world," our concern here.

In everything ready-to-hand the world is always "there." Whenever we encounter anything, the world has already been previously discovered, though not thematically . . . . The world is that in terms of which the ready-to-hand is ready-to-hand (Heidegger 1962:114).

Thus Ricoeur refers to this dimension as other than

. . . the level of manipulable objects, but [as] the level that Husserl designated by the expression *Lebenswelt* [life-world] and Heidegger by the expression "being-in-the-world" (1981a:141).

Again, this is the level of fundamental belonging which is prior to and mutually inclusive of "the allegedly autonomous subject and the allegedly adverse object" (Ricoeur 1981a:105). In short, the concern is "with the 'world' in an ontological, rather than cosmological sense" (Ricoeur 1981a:207f).

Here we pick up a theme from chapters 2 and 4: The power of written texts (and of meaning in general) to refer to this ontological dimension. This is the significant contribution of Ricoeur to the notion of comprehension in reading which must now be developed.[13]

Recall (from chapters 2 and 4) that it is precisely because the reading situation breaks with the face-to-face situation of conversation that its power of reference is more available for ontological disclosure. Because literature ". . . speaks of things, events, states of affairs and characters which are evoked but which are not there, . . . [its] reference is no longer ostensive" (Ricoeur 1981a:177) as in a dialogue in which a common situation is shared, a situation which can be referred to ostensively, by pointing to it.[14] What, then, Ricoeur asks, is literature about? He replies:

I do not hesitate to say: about a world, which is the world of the work. Far from saying that the text is without a world, I shall say that only now does man have a world and not merely a situation . . . (Ricoeur 1981a:177).

Notice here the prominent role which texts and reading play in this "redefinition" of the "world." It is "only now" that man has a world, and "For us, the world is the totality of references opened up *by texts*" (Ricoeur

---

[13] Frank Smith 1983 is also awakening to this power of writing.

[14] Says Ricoeur, "If we cannot point to the thing about which we speak, at least we can situate it in relation to the unique spatio-temporal network which is shared by the interlocutors" (1981a:141).

1981a:177; emphasis added). The suspension of the referential function of ordinary discourse--what Ricoeur calls language's "first order referential function" (Ricoeur 1981a:112), or ostensive reference (Ricoeur 1981a:141),

> . . . releases a second order reference, where the world is manifested no longer as the totality of manipulable objects but as the horizon of our life and our projects, in short as *Lebenswelt* [lifeworld], as being-in-the-world (Ricoeur 1981a:112).[15]

This "second order" referential dimension,[16] however, attains "its full development only with works of fiction and poetry" (Ricoeur 1981a:112; cf. Heidegger 1971a,b).

What more, though, does Ricoeur say about this peculiarly literary notion of the world which, it appears, is his exposition and development of the Heideggerean notion of the "world"?[17] Four points follow.

First,

> . . . in a civilisation of writing, the world itself is no longer what can be shown in speaking but is reduced to a kind of "aura" which written works unfold (Ricoeur 1981a:149).

> Thus we speak of the "world" of Greece, not to indicate what the situations were for those who experienced them, but to designate the non-situational references which outlast the effacement of the first and which then offer themselves as possible modes of being, as possible symbolic dimensions of our being-in-the-world (Ricoeur 1981a:177).

Though he speaks of an "aura," elsewhere Ricoeur distinguishes his sense of this term from what might commonly be associated with such a term:

> . . . the *Lebenswelt* is not [to be] confused with some sort of ineffable immediacy and is not [to be] identified with the vital and emotional

---

[15] This exclusive emphasis on texts by Ricoeur will be challenged in chapter 8.

[16] Both Heidegger and Ricoeur recognize this "second order referential dimension" as implicit in the very structure of man's being and language (Ricoeur 1981a:112; Heidegger 1962:114-122).

[17] For this theme in Heidegger, cf. 1962, section 34.

be] identified with the vital and emotional envelope of human experience, but rather is [to be] construed as designating the reservoir of meaning, the surplus of sense in living experience . . . (Ricoeur 1981a:119).

The "world," then, is fundamentally a "reservoir of meaning," but meaning as understood with reference to its ontological dimension. Ricoeur clarifies this distinction between the world (in the situational, able-to-be-pointed-to sense) and the world of the text--a distinction he correlates with spoken/written language use--in terms of differing orders of reference. This leads to the second point.

Second, reference is the "key" (Ricoeur 1981a:149, 168) to the notion of the "world"; in particular, the second order reference. This second order reference, though, is a "power" to project (Ricoeur 1981a:192) a world by means of "emergent meanings in our language" (Ricoeur 1981a:181). Further, the reference to the world which is fulfilled by the task of reading (Ricoeur 1981a:148), reinstitutes the references to the "speaker" (i.e. the author) and "audience" (i.e. the reader) which the text as text disrupted (Ricoeur 1981a:149, 168; cf. chapter 2). An interpersonal relation *like* that of dialogue is restored, though also reoriented, with the release of the reference of the world of the work by reading. We have already seen how this is understood with regard to the author (cf. "authorial intention," chapter 4); we will discuss the restoration of the "audience" in section 5 below (and both will be discussed further in chapters 7, 8, and 9). The important point here, though, is that "What gives rise to *understanding* is that which points towards a possible world, by means of the non-ostensive references of the text" (Ricoeur 1981a:177; emphasis added). Or, in short, non-ostensive reference is the key to reading comprehension.

Third, "disclosure" is the significant correlate to the "world" in reading and the key to understanding "non-ostensive reference":

Texts speak of possible worlds and of possible ways of orientating [sic] oneself in these worlds. In this way, disclosure plays the equivalent role for written texts as ostensive reference plays in spoken language (Ricoeur 1981a:177).

Alternative expressions for this "disclosure" are "manifestation" (Ricoeur 1981a:193), "revelation" (Ricoeur 1981a:192), and "projection" (Ricoeur 1981a:192). Further, Ricoeur understands that the theme of manifestation is the necessary consequence of the shift from epistemology to ontology and highlights the dethronement of the "finite capacities of understanding of a present reader" (Ricoeur 1981a:192). Instead of imposing meaning on the text, the reader receives "a new mode of being from the text" (Ricoeur 1981a:192; cf. section 5 below).

137

Fourth, the central notion of the "world" in the phenomenological notion of reading comprehension orients reading in terms of "the structure of experience" (Ricoeur 1981a:118). As Iser puts it, "Reading has the same structure as experience . . ." (1978:132). For both Ricoeur (1981a:185) and Iser (1978:129) this means that the meaning of the text must be actualized, that ". . . the interpretation becomes an event" (Ricoeur 1981a:185). Iser 1978 has described this process more than anyone else, and the implications of his description are profound for reading research.

First of all, there are fundamental indeterminacies in the text which are "essential conditions for communication" (Iser 1978:182). There are gaps or blanks which stimulate "the reader into filling the blanks with projections" (Iser 1978:168) and thus to become involved or entangled in the text. Though Iser speaks of the blanks as "a self-regulating *structure* in communication" (1978:194; emphasis added), this structure functions differently, and thus appears differently (and consequently, as different[18]) for every reader.[19] The reason is simple: ". . . each textual segment does not carry its own determinacy within itself, but will gain this in relation to other segments" (Iser 1978:195); but which "other segments" is a matter of individual interaction with the text. In short, ". . . texts always take place on the level of their reader's abilities" (Iser 1978:207).

Consequently, because ". . . the formulated text means something that has not been formulated" (Iser 1978:130), efforts to achieve an agreed upon text grammar will always be frustrated. In brief, the ". . . structure that regulates but does not formulate the connection," and therefore the meaning, is "unseen," and as unseen will always be to some extent indeterminate (Iser 1978:196).

Second, the blanks in the text function to disrupt "good continuation" in reading.

> Impeded image-building compels us to give up images we have formed for ourselves, so that we are maneuvered into a position outside our own products and thus led to produce images which, with our habitual way of thinking, we could not have conceived (Iser 1978:188).

---

[18] Whether this "unseen structure" is, in fact the same structure or a different structure for each reader remains an open question. In short, is this structure one, or many, or perhaps both?

[19] To hold that the structure is strictly different for *every* reader is, surely, to overstate and oversimplify the situation. Certainly some readers arrive at very similar results from their reading, and perhaps in some cases, identical results.

Consequently, "miscues" (as Goodman calls them) ought to be considered a normal part of reading (as Goodman does), and our definition of fluency ought to reflect this.[20]

Third, negation--the other basic structure of indeterminacy in the text--functions even more radically to disrupt the role of the familiar in reading. Remembering that schemas are structures of conventional knowledge--in short, of the familiar--current reading theory is offered a fundamental challenge. Says Iser,

> The various types of negation invoke familiar or determinate elements only to cancel them out. What is canceled, however, remains in view, and this brings about modifications in the reader's attitude toward what is familiar or determinate--in other words, he is guided to adopt a position *in* relation to the text (1978:169).

The blanks and negations, then, "arise out of the text" (Iser 1978:170) and structure the constitutive activity of the reader. And this controls the process of interaction (Iser 1978:170), provoking the reader into a synthesizing activity (Iser 1978:119). Current reading research, however, is (seemingly) wholly unaware of these structures "of the text" which interact directly with the "conventional knowledge" schemas of schema theory. The very problem with schema theories which we identified in the last chapter--the lack of an account of how new schemas are formed--returns in this new context. Here the problem can be clarified in the context of Iser's thought.

The problem is this: "The more 'present' the text is to us [i.e. by means of the 'entanglement' guided by blanks and negation], the more our habitual selves [i.e. the familiar schemas] . . . recede into the 'past' " (Iser 1978:131). This entanglement, however, does not cause our habitual criteria to disappear, but rather ". . . to interact with the as yet unfamiliar presence of the text" (Iser 1978:132). In short, "The old conditions the form of the new, and the new selectively restructures the old" (Iser 1978: 132).

Stated in this way, we see that (1) the role of schemas (and we might as well add, of all forms of conventional knowledge) is *not* dispensable, and (2) the problem of "the new"--which a consideration of the "world of the text" highlights--is not a peripheral, but a central challenge to reading theory. The development of the dialogue on this point is temporarily postponed (cf. Chapter 7, section 3) until after completing the presentation of two more basic points in the

---

[20] Notice that this is nowhere reflected in the current research on fluency as summarized by Marshall 1981; cf. chapter 1, footnote 11).

phenomenological theory of comprehension, points which bear directly on that dialogue.

6.4   Distanciation

As the astute reader has no doubt recognized, our treatment of Ricoeur's theory of comprehension is, at present, incomplete. Inasmuch as comprehension is of meanings, and meaning is, for Ricoeur, a dialectic of sense and reference, we have left the dialectic standing on one leg. We have yet to consider the role of sense.

Those who have read Ricoeur closely may quibble with my introducing the role of sense in comprehension *after* the role of reference. And the quibble is justified. Does not Ricoeur speak explicitly of reference following sense? Yes, he does:

> To understand a text is to follow its movement from sense to reference, from what it says, to what it talks about (Ricoeur 1981a:218).

> The speaker refers to something on the basis of, or through, the ideal structure of the sense (Ricoeur 1976:20).

Does he not also speak of the objectivity of meaning (i.e. the sense) necessitated by distanciation as the necessary condition and mediation of understanding? Yes he does:

> . . . the objectification of meaning is a necessary mediation between writer and reader (Ricoeur 1981a:185).

> . . . distanciation is the condition of understanding (Ricoeur 1981a:144).

Finally, does not Ricoeur speak of the interpretive process as composed of stages occurring in a linear fashion? Again, yes:

> . . . we regard structural analysis as a stage--and a necessary one--between a naive and a critical interpretation . . . (Ricoeur 1981a:161);

> . . . explanation and understanding are two different stages of a unique *hermeneutical arc* (Ricoeur 1981a:218; cf. also 164, 143);

> Understanding is entirely *mediated* by the whole of explanatory procedures which precede it and accompany it (Ricoeur 1981a:220).

These ways of speaking, though, run headlong into various problems, which introduce my quibble with Ricoeur, and with it my reasons for treating reference before sense. A discussion of these problems will also introduce the role of sense in reading comprehension.

The first point: Ricoeur's "stage" language does not give adequate credit to what Ricoeur clearly states elsewhere: Distanciation is "itself a moment of belonging" (Ricoeur 1981a:111, 245); all objectifications and explanations are preceded and supported by one's "being-in-the-world" (Ricoeur 1981a:119); there is no sovereign reading subject who can view meaning from outside his situation; etc.

But second, this is just another way of saying what Ricoeur also says so clearly: Reading is a dialectic which itself reflects the dialectic of sense and reference in meaning (Ricoeur 1981a:152, 164, 143f). And dialectic is not a linear phenomenon! However, inasmuch as reference in language has reference to the *Lebenswelt* it gains a prior significance due to the "always already" (i.e. prior) grounding of the reading subject in ther "world." Thus reference does have, in a pre-linguistic sense, precedence over sense.

Third, Ricoeur himself backs off from the implications of a strong linear emphasis. Such an emphasis would admit (1) the "other as a spiritual entity" (Ricoeur 1981a:177), (2) "an intersubjective relation of mutual understanding" (Ricoeur 1981a:182), and (3) the "historical" (Ricoeur 1981a:184) only *after* the mediation of the ideality of sense (cf. chapter 4). However, in each of these three cases, Ricoeur inserts a degree of relativism: The act of understanding is less [an intersubjective, historical relation to the other], than a relation to "the world of the work." (cf. Ricoeur 1981a:177, 182, 184). Thus what Ricoeur wants to postpone to the last stage by means of the "stage model" of reading--i.e. the other, the historical--is not postponed absolutely, but only relatively. That is, for Ricoeur, the staging is only a matter of differences of emphasis (cf. Ricoeur 1981a:177), not of "air-tight," absolutely distinct stages.[21]

Finally, Ricoeur, while linking (depth) semantics to the role of reference (Ricoeur 1981a:217) and its relation to the "world" (Ricoeur 1981a:202), and sense to "structural analysis" (Ricoeur 1981a:217) and semiotics (Ricoeur 1981a:219), goes on to assert in the strongest terms that semiotics is dependent on semantics:

> If language were not fundamentally referential, would or could it be meaningful? How could we know that a sign stands for something, if it did not receive its directions towards something for which

---

[21] The difficulties of not subordinating the psychological and historical aspects of meaning to "ideality" (other than the inconsistencies noted above) have already been rehearsed in our critique of alternative conceptions of meaning.

it stands from its use in discourse? Finally, semiotics appears as a mere abstraction of semantics. And the semiotic definition of the sign as an inner difference between signifier and signified presupposes its semantic definition as reference to the thing for which it stands (Ricoeur 1976:21; similarly, 1975a:217).

Without such a prioritizing, semiotics becomes, he says, "an absurd game of errant signifiers" (Ricoeur 1981a:202), "a sterile game, a divisive algebra" (Ricoeur 1981a:217). Thus reference itself is prioritized with regard to sense. How, though, can semiotics be the necessary mediation on the way to semantics (as in the "stage model"), and still be "a mere abstraction of semantics"?

It seems to me that we have run into a problem of consistency-building (as Iser calls it) in our reading of Ricoeur. For our purposes, this is an important point to pursue, for the "explanatory stage" of reading in Ricoeur's scheme is quite close to what the reading specialists generally term decoding.[22] Thus, to pursue this issue will lead us deeper into our dialogue.

By "explanation" Ricoeur means the construal of "the immanent pattern of discourse" (Ricoeur 1981a:171). The basis of explanation is the objectivity of the text which derives from its being ". . . produced as a work displaying structure and form" (Ricoeur 1981a:92). This structure is defined in a typically structuralist manner as the "interplay of oppositions and their combinations within an inventory of discrete units" (Ricoeur 1981a:153); and yet Ricoeur admits a broader range of explanatory procedures than just the structuralist (cf. e.g. Ricoeur 1974:27-96).

However, even within the structuralist model an important clue to the relation between Ricoeur's "explanation" and the reading researcher's decoding is given. Literature, says Ricoeur, is "an *analogon* of *la langue*" (1981a:216), the system of codes of language of which the phonological structure is the model. The point is that the explanatory moment of reading is a matter of *decoding* discourse. It must be granted that, on the one hand, Ricoeur's focus of concern has been at the sentence level and above, and therefore he does not speak of decoding as is usual for the bottom-up theorists (i.e. primarily as letter and word recognition). But, on the other hand, his use of "explanation" is not disharmonious with the bottom-up sense of decoding. Especially is this the case since (1) Ricoeur uses phonology as the model; (2) this phonological model uses difference as the key to the structure of codes, much as Smith uses distinctive features; and (3) (as quoted in section 2 above), Ricoeur considers the "macro-dialectic" of reading which he studies at the text level, to be the same process which also functions at the "micro" level, which reasonably includes

---

[22] To be substantiated in what follows.

142

"decoding skills" (cf. Ricoeur 1981a:175). There is then a significant congruence of thought between Ricoeur and the reading specialists around the notions of explanation and decoding.[23]

Ricoeur's position, however, does seem curious in the context of the bottom-up, top-down debates. On the one hand, he highlights points usually (and strongly) emphasized by the top-down and interactive theorists. And yet, on the other hand, he shares concerns with the bottom-up theorists, especially his emphasis on the necessary mediation of the decoding processes. Ricoeur also shares with the bottom-up theorists the emphasis on the stage-model of processing which stresses linearity. This, however, is the most discredited aspect of the bottom-up theories (cf. chapter 1), and a most problematic aspect of Ricoeur's own theory. Why does he hold to such a view? Five reasons can be advanced.

First, Ricoeur desires to distance himself from the Romantic tradition of interpretation for which to understand was to divine an alien consciousness through psychological or spiritual intuition. Says Ricoeur, "This route is no longer open to us, once we take distanciation by writing and objectification by structure seriously" (1981a:140). That is, meaning is necessarily mediated by the encoded text and the requisite decoding procedures; there is no direct access to authorial intention.

Second, and closely related to the preceding point, ". . . Ricoeur is struggling to reduce the arbitrariness of the hermeneutic concept of appropriation" (Hoy 1978:88). Though it is true that many constructions can be put on a text, ". . . one construction can be said to be more probable than another" (Ricoeur 1981a:175) on the basis of " 'clues' contained in the text itself" (Ricoeur 1981a:175). The more probable is that interpretation which accounts for "the greatest number of facts furnished by the text" (Ricoeur 1981a:175), and (here is the unique role of the explanatory procedures) ". . . offers a qualitatively better *convergence* between features which it takes into account" (Ricoeur 1981a:176; emphasis added). "Convergence" here is taken as an account of the "interplay of oppositions and their combinations," a recognition of "the immanent pattern of discourse," also termed a "network," and an "architecture" (Ricoeur 1981a:175). Thus, due to the limited field of possibilities (Ricoeur

---

[23] Included in Ricoeur's explanatory procedures is the "decoding" of the illusions imposed by psychological and sociological forces beyond the conscious control of the reader. This "decoding of life situations" is much akin to the concerns of Paulo Freire and will be the major topic of chapter 8.

Further, this congruence between Ricoeur's explanatory procedures and the decoding of the reading specialists offers a possible solution to various debates in reading theory regarding the interrelations between features, letters, and whole words in word identification/recognition. The hypothesis generated by this congruence would be formulated in terms of the whole-part-whole dialectic of the hermeneutic circle as applied to the "micro-processes" of reading. It would of course be subject to empirical testing.

1981a:213) which a text is, interpretation is reduced in arbitrariness by the explanatory procedures which must reckon with what is in fact there in the text.[24]

Third, Ricoeur recognizes in the experience of reading a moment which seems to exclude the input of the reader.   Illustrating from the creation account of Genesis, Ricoeur comments:

> What is interesting here is that interpretation,
> *before* being an act of the exegete, is the act of the
> text (Ricoeur 1981a:162; emphasis added).

This is a recognition of "the work of the text upon itself" (Iser 1978:164), and reading as ". . . the recovery of that which is at work, in labour, within the text" (Ricoeur 1981a:164). The conclusion is that ". . . interpretation [we can substitute "reading"] is interpretation *by* language before being interpretation [reading] *of* language" (Ricoeur 1981a:163). This, then, is the objective, or as it can now be called, the "intra-textual concept of interpretation [reading]" (Ricoeur 1981a:162) for which Ricoeur claims a long history (found even in Aristotle). Here language acts on things (Ricoeur 1981a:162). Here reading is decidedly "text-driven," and is so at every level of discourse processing. And as Ricoeur points out, this action of the text precedes the appropriation by a reader, thus the "stage model" follows.

Fourth, meaning itself attests to a phenomenological objectivity, termed "ideality," which serves as the   pole of meaningful experience. Since comprehension is "of meaning," then comprehension also must reflect some evidence of this objectivity.

Fifth, and to make explicit what is implicit in the two preceding points, for both Ricoeur and Iser, distanciation is a "basic prerequisite for comprehension" (Iser 1978:189; cf. Ricoeur 1981a:144). If there is to be comprehension, the comprehender must experience "at least two positions related to and influencing one another" (Iser 1978:197). Previously we have seen this in terms of the old and the new which are called into play by the blanks and negations which structure the reading process. Here we are focusing on the distance or the difference which is required for comprehension. Ricoeur finds this distanciation to be fundamental for the constitution of the text as text. In particular, it is fundamental to "the sense of the text" which is conceived of as structured by language as langue, and by literature as on every level the analogue of *langue*.

---

[24] The notion of what a fact in fact is, is of course part of the problem in disputes regarding the "proper," or best interpretation/reading of a text. Though Ricoeur is very aware of this, he goes on to insist that reading is not dominated by the subjective perspectives of the reader. The existence of this "objective" moment of reading is the concern of point three which follows.

This, though, is only "the condition of understanding" (Ricoeur 1981a:144) which itself must condition the subject so that ". . . we watch what we are producing, and . . . watch ourselves while we are producing it" (Iser 1978:189). This "strange, halfway position" (Iser 1978:134) of the reader as "split" (Iser 1978:156) becomes the topic of the next section. The point here, however, is that the inducement of subjective distance, or the reader's distance from himself, in establishing the condition for the subjective apprehension of meaning, also establishes a two stage process: First, the assembly (Iser 1978:152), or the construction (Ricoeur 1981a:92f; 174; etc.) of meaning (as sense); and second, the apprehension of what has been assembled (Iser 1978:152), or as Ricoeur calls it, the appropriation of the meaning.

For these five reasons then, it is difficult to avoid the linearity of the process of comprehension. It is, however, just as difficult to avoid the circularity. Ricoeur's solution is to illustrate this "linear-circularity" with the figure of the arch (as in the arch of a bridge; cf. 1981a:164). The arch reflects linearity (Hoy 1978:90), but also reflects a modification of the traditional (hermeneutical) circle. The arch is grounded in the soil of lived experience at both "ends."[25] In between is the necessary mediation of the objective, explanatory procedures which abstract away from the lived ground. The arch, then, clearly illustrates that the circle is not vicious, and the way out of this "cage" (Ricoeur 1981a:213) is to acknowledge, on the one hand, that the ontological structure of anticipation is basic to man's being (as discussed in sections 1 and 2), and on the other, to admit procedures of validation and falsification which acknowledge the objectivity of the text, its sense (Ricoeur 1981a:213). What the figure of the arch does not adequately convey is the dialectical and paradoxical character of the interaction between the subjective and the objective, the reader and the text. In other words, the sense of a "full circle," together with the attendant complexities of distinguishing "end" from "beginning", seems to be missing.[26]

---

[25] Hoy (1978:90) misses this fact, assuming that the first grounding is "an objective explication."

[26] If a "back-and-forth" picture were to be adequate to Ricoeur's descriptions, then the final grounding of one passage along the arch must be taken as the beginning of a new passage; in other words, what was appropriation or critical understanding becomes belonging or naive understanding for the next "cycle" (in quotes because the notion of a connected circle is not clearly indicated by this latter reading of the arch). This, however, is not implausible.

However, perhaps Ricoeur assumes some "subterranean connection" between the braces of the arch, thus "joining" the circle in a way which even highlights its mysteriousness. This is not an implausible suggestion, given Ricoeur's extensive work on Freud and the unconscious (cf. Ricoeur 1970; 1974:97-208, especially 99-120). To my knowledge, though, Ricoeur does not make such a "connection" explicit in his work.

6.5   Appropriation

Appropriation is placed by Ricoeur as the final stage, the culmination of the hermeneutical-reading process (Ricoeur 1981a:23, 154, 182). As already stated, this process is presented under the figure of the arch, grounded first in both the "fullness of language" (Ricoeur 1978a:37) and the pre- and/or hyper-linguistic soil of belongingness (Ricoeur 1975a:31; 1978a:234; 1981a:56, 117-19, 243f; Reagan 1979:xviii). This is the pre-understanding, the giveness and certainty of the first naivete (Ricoeur 1976:44) "which precedes and supports us" (Ricoeur 1981a:119, 243). Though this belonging is "bound up" with (Ricoeur 1981a:19), correlated with (Ricoeur 1981a:113, 143, 183), and mediated by (Ricoeur 1981a:158, 220) another moment of distanciation--that is, "communication in and through distance" (Ricoeur 1981a:131)--such distanciation is "itself a moment of belonging" (Ricoeur 1981a:111, 243, 245). Moreover, appropriation is itself the return to the understanding and naivete which the initial belongingness prefigured. No doubt belongingness is transformed by the mediation which distanciation effects--it is characterized no longer by pre-understanding but self-understanding (Ricoeur 1976:94f; 1981a:193); it is not the first pre-critical naivete, but a second, post-critical naivete (Ricoeur 1967:356)--but appropriation is indeed still a belongingness, a "making one's own." Thus is distanciation not only "a moment of belonging," but also "within the interior of appropriation" (Ricoeur 1981a:113). In this way the two poles of the hermeneutic arch display their similarity, and the whole hermeneutical-reading process its unity.

As Iser says, "The constitution of meaning . . . gains its full significance when something *happens* to the reader" (1978:152). This "happening" is what Ricoeur calls "appropriation." As expected, it is here that subjectivity is reintroduced as a major category in the comprehension process, and thus where we might expect the most productive dialogue with the top-down theories of reading. And yet, the prior mediation of distanciation necessitates "a new theory of subjectivity" (Ricoeur 1981a:182).

To review briefly, we noted previously that the key to the hermeneutical circle is the notion of reference and especially the "upheaval in the relation between the text and its world" (Ricoeur 1981a:149; cf. 168). More particularly the key is the connection between the three directions of reference, the reference to an extralinguistic reality, to its own speaker, and to the one to whom the discourse is addressed. All three references are disrupted by the text as text, while the task of reading is "precisely to fulfil the reference" (Ricoeur 1981a:148). Ricoeur's argument, following Heidegger, is that the reference to the "world," as ontologically understood, is the primary reference, the restoration of which precedes--logically and in weight of significance, though not necessarily temporally--the restoration of the subjectivities of author and reader. It is not at all clear that either Iser or Poulet shares this Heideggerian perspective. For these latter two authors (and especially Poulet, though in a modified sense), the subjectivities of the reader play a more prominent role throughout the reading process. This disagreement will become a point for further discussion in chapter 7, but first a thorough presentation of Ricoeur's notion of appropriation is required.

The key to Ricoeur's notion of appropriation is that it is "the counterpart of a concept of distanciation which is linked to any objective and objectifying study of a text" (Ricoeur 1981a:183). Appropriation is, in fact, "a dialectical concept" (Ricoeur 1981a:185), and thus is thoroughly conditioned by distance: "Appropriation is quite the contrary of contemporaneousness and congeniality: it is understanding at and through distance" (Ricoeur 1981a:143). And yet appropriation does not acknowledge the final victory of distance. It struggles against distance-- cultural, temporal, even "the estrangement from meaning itself" (Ricoeur 1981a:159)--and succeeds: "Interpretation brings together, equalizes, renders contemporary and similar" (Ricoeur 1981a:185; cf. also 159; 1976:92).

Though such "bringing together" is the goal, it is attainable only to the extent that appropriation ". . . responds to the sense, . . . is mediated by all the structural objectifications of the text" (Ricoeur 1981a:143; cf. also 184f, 192); in a word, it is "at and through distance." Here the positive point is the responsive quality. Though it may take an effort to reconstruct the "network of interactions which constitute the context as actual and unique"--in short, the "meaning of the text" (Ricoeur 1981a:174)--Ricoeur sees this as the humble task of responding, not initiating nor projecting. Though there may be work involved in this construction, the work is first of all the work *of* language, *by* language (Ricoeur 1981a:162f). The dynamic quality of meaning which is finally imparted to the reader as the goal of the hermeneutic appropriation is first of all the dynamism of the text itself. As a "network of interactions," the text ". . . directs our attention towards the semantic event which is produced at the point of intersection between several semantic fields" (Ricoeur 1981a:174). This is the formation of the "system of sense," the "decisive moment of explanation" (Ricoeur 1981a:174). Notice the language of dynamism: "directs," "event," "produced." The dynamic quality of appropriation will be recognized later when the disclosure of the world is the topic--and recognized as the "key," the "cornerstone" (Ricoeur 1981a:191; cf. also 161-164; 1976:93) of hermeneutics.[27] Before developing this point further, the responsive character of appropriation calls for further clarification.

Responsiveness implies or entails receptivity which is in fact its presupposition--we respond only to what we in some sense receive. Pressing the response of the subject back to this prior level further amplifies Ricoeur's point that the subjectivity of the reader is subordinate to the text itself. Far from dominating the hermeneutical process by imposing "our finite capacity of understanding," the reader instead must expose himself "to the text and receive from it" (Ricoeur 1981a:143). So

---

[27] Cf. chapter 7.

radical is this receptivity that it is even conceived of as a "letting-go," an "allowing itself to be carried off toward" (Ricoeur 1981a:191). Here the contribution of the ego is almost nil.[28]

The correlate of this often emphasized receptivity of the subject (Ricoeur 1981a:94, 143, 182, 190, 192; 1976:94) is the giving of the text: The subject receives what the text gives. Just as in previous works Ricoeur stressed that the "symbol gives rise to thought" (1967:348f; 1970:37ff; 1974:299f), now it is the text which gives rise to reflection (Ricoeur 1981a:19).

Two questions, though, remain: What does the text give? and, How does it give? Two main variants are given as answers to the first question. The text ". . . *gives* the subject new capacities for knowing himself" (Ricoeur 1981a:192; cf. also 1976:94); and even more radically, the text ". . . gives a *self* to the *ego*" (Ricoeur 1981a:193; 1976:95), where "ego" is taken as "the egoistic and narcissistic" self which precedes this process, and is dispossessed en route (Ricoeur 1976:94).[29]

For Ricoeur, this culmination of reflection in self-understanding is the goal sought in hermeneutics. To have been given not only a new capacity of knowing the self, but also a new self signals the completion of the process. The event character of discourse, suspended by writing, is restored by fulfilling the intention of the text in a speech-like event (Ricoeur 1981a:159, 185). The missing element of discourse as "addressed to someone" is restored as the meaning is thus actualized in self-understanding (Ricoeur 1981a:182, 185; 1976:92).

The final question of our consideration of Ricoeur's concept of appropriation remains--How does the text give this capacity of knowing and this self? Here we return to a previous allusion to the dynamism of meaning as the "cornerstone" of hermeneutics. This "cornerstone" is "the link between appropriation and revelation" (Ricoeur 1981a:191) or "disclosure" (Ricoeur 1976:93).

---

[28] The "ego" must in some sense cooperate in this process, through, e.g., a sort of secondary intention of focus of attention on text-meaning. Ricoeur terms this "secondary intention" an exposing of oneself (1981a:94, 143), an offering of oneself (1981a:177), a handing over (1981a:187), a letting go, or an allowing (1981a:191). I call this intention "secondary" because this "disappropriation" of the ego is affected by the text. It is, though, still an intention of the reading subject. Says Ricoeur, ". . . the ego divests itself of itself" (1981a:191); "This process of dispossession is the work of the sort of universality and atemporality implied by the explanatory procedures" (1981a:192), procedures which, though motivated by the work of the text on itself, do not occur without the reader.

[29] Perhaps Ricoeur takes this giving one step deeper by designating that which is given as life itself (cf. Ricoeur 1975a:43).

The text gives because its meaning is dynamic (Ricoeur 1976:92), because it carries us (Ricoeur 1981a:191), because the word has power to disclose a world variously expressed as a "new mode of being" or "new forms of life" (Ricoeur 1976:94; 1981a:192). This is what the text gives; this is what the reader appropriates. The "How" question though is still not answered. Here I mention the point I develop in chapters 7 and 9: The mode of giving and receiving is that of play--"play reveals" (Ricoeur 1981a:187)--and the active "faculty" is the imagination.

The preceding account of comprehension from the perspective of philosophical phenomenology has already introduced various points of contact with the reading theorists. The following chapter is devoted to pursuing that dialogue.

CHAPTER 7

A FURTHER DIALOGUE ON ISSUES OF COMPREHENSION

Five major topics are picked up from chapters 5 and 6, and further developed here. These topics are: the world and schemas; resemblance; the old and the new; disclosure and the source of the new; and the reader as subject. My purpose is to bring the reading specialists and the philosophers into closer "dialogue" on these topics, thus expanding the horizons of understanding, and (hopefully) clearing the way for further research.

7.1 The world of the text and schemas

The "world of the text" is termed "the matter of the text" (e.g. Ricoeur 1981a:111f, 144) by Ricoeur. This is what the text is about and it is contrasted with the reference of ordinary speech (e.g. Ricoeur 1976:19, 88, 92; 1981a:202) which refers to "circumstantial reality" (Ricoeur 1981a:149). Iser's terms are different. He refers to that which the text is about as an "aesthetic object" (1978:98), the "imaginary object" (1978:148), "the transcendental viewpoint" (1978:98), and the meaning of the text (1978:150f). For both, however, the "object" in question is that to which the text refers (e.g. Ricoeur 1976a:19-23; Iser 1978:147); in short, we are concerned here with reference, but in a somewhat specialized sense.

Our concern in this section will be to consider this "world." The process of constructing the "world" is what Iser calls "image-building," and the constitution of the "world" is that of an image. In Chapter 4 we considered the make-up of this "image" as "at one moment . . . pictorial, and at another . . . semantic" (Iser 1978:147). My task now is to expound this notion of image and its role in comprehension; later (sections 4 and 5) more attention is given to image-building.

Both Iser (1978:136f) and Ricoeur (1965; 1975a:189) operate in the Kantian tradition in which

> The image . . . is itself a *metaxu* or middle term
> between the brute presence where the object is
> experienced and the thought where it becomes
> idea, [thus allowing] the object to appear, to be
> present as represented (Dufrenne 1973:345).

Here, in a nutshell, is the characterization of "image" as akin to and partaking of aspects of both the sensory, empirical object and the mental concept or meaning, while also being distinct from both. As Iser says, ". . . it transcends the sensory, but is not yet fully conceptualized" (1978:136). With this "image" we see the possibility of a further explication of the mode of interaction between the text as a sensory, empirical object and the reader as the necessarily active participant in the generation of meaning.

The above quote from Dufrenne also highlights the role of the image in presenting, or allowing the object to appear, a point which will finally reconnect these considerations of the image with what we discussed earlier as the *disclosure* or *revelation* of the world.[1] But first, a further characterization of the *metaxu* character of the image and the significance of this character for reading comprehension.

Following Kant, Ricoeur conceives of the imagination as

> . . . productively present within perception. Far from being merely "heir of the perceived," it presides at the birth of perceptual objects. Thanks to this Kantian turn, mediating imagination shifts to the transcendental dimension of object-constitutions [cf. Ricoeur 1965:27f, 57-71] (Schaldenbrand 1979:62).[2]

Consequently, imaging is more than reproductive "picturing." Positively, ". . . [imaging] can now be understood through the [Kantian] *schema*, i.e., a moving figuration, an organizing and 'wholing' movement" (Schaldenbrand 1979:62; more will be said about the "Kantian schema" below). With the "wholing" function of the imagination, we see the philosophical grounding of what becomes "consistency-building" in Iser (cf. chapter 2 for the details), and both the "world" and the text (as "work") as a totality in Ricoeur.

There is, though, another equally significant outcome of this conception of the schema. By the exercising of its "wholing" function, the imagination discloses a most fundamental characteristic: "It relates to the nongiven or to the absent, endowing it with presence" (Iser 1978:137). The reason for this is simple: Every perspective taken on even an empirical object is finite and incomplete; thus any "wholing" of the object sketches in what is not given and endows it with presence. Thus the imagination is productive in that it "makes" something out of what is not given; and what it "makes" is a way for the concept which transcends the giveness of the sensory perspectives. This "way" is the "image." The imagination, however, also partakes of the sensory givenness of perception, imputing as it were, the presence of sensory givenness to the totalizing construct which it produces. Thus the image is endowed with a quasi-sensory presence.

Five implications for reading will be drawn from these two points. First, the imagination is especially suited to reading, and in fact is required, since with a text, the relation to the given of circumstantial, ordinary reality

---

[1] This point is the topic of section 4 below.

[2] "Transcendental" in this Kantian tradition is understood as "the condition for the possibility," in this case the condition for the possibility for the constitution of an object as object.

has been disrupted and distanced. The text presents a world as not given, or absent. Hence we see the wisdom of the phenomenological highlighting of the imagination in reading: the imagination is that which brings near (i.e. endows with presence) the distant (i.e. the absent), while simultaneously removing us to it.

Second, given that the constitution of a text as text--that is, its inherent distanciations (cf. chapter 2)--and the imagination's unique suitability to both "connect with" and overcome this distanciation, we ought not be surprised to find that within the text, the non-given or unformulated structures play as significant a role as that which is formulated. In brief, the role of the imagination is to mediate between the given and the non-given. Here we are speaking specifically of what Iser calls blanks, ". . . the unseen joints of the text . . . [which] trigger acts of ideation on the reader's part" (Iser 1978:183), automatically mobilizing the imagination (Iser 1978:186).[3]

Third, with regard to that other kind of blank which Iser terms negation, the absence to which the imagination relates is the negation (Iser 1978:216) or invalidation (Iser 1978:217) of "selected norms" (Iser 1978:213) of judgment or "meaning" (Iser 1978:217). However, the challenge presented in reading is the same as with the blank: The formation of new meaning (Iser 1978:186f; 217).[4] The particular significance of the negation, however, is that it highlights (1) that a clash or conflict is integral to reading (as does Goodman's notion of "miscues," though in a milder form), and (2) that reading involves the creation or construction of new meaning in the face of the negation of the old, expected, or familiar. Ricoeur uses the comprehension of metaphor as the paradigm case to clarify this situation (1981a:165-181; 1975a), going so far as to hypothesize that the creation of new meaning from the clash at the "literal" level of metaphor is the same process which generates all categories of meaning in the first place (1975a:197).[5] Later in this chapter I will examine this relation of the new and the old in the generation of meaning in more detail; here the point is that the role of negativity or absence at the heart of the imagination's function in reading is essential to the production of meaning.

---

[3] Note that for Iser too this process of the imagination in reading is a process of uniting perspectives which of themselves are not connected; i.e. this is akin to the Kantian productive imagination.

[4] The precise distinction between blanks and negation which Iser 1978 seems to intend (cf. 212f), is not at all clear: Negation is termed a blank (Iser 1978:212, 217); both operate by negation (Iser 1978:186f); and both are involved in acquiring a new "sense of discernment" (Iser 1978:187; cf. 216).

[5] This must remain a hypothesis, Ricoeur insists, since ". . . we have no direct access whatsoever to any such origin . . ." (1975a:197).

Fourth, the ". . . structure of the blank organizes [the reader's] participation [in the text]" (Iser 1978:203). Because the text is so essentially unformulated, it cannot serve alone as the basis of meaning. The reader must fill in the blanks in the text (Iser 1978:203) impelled by his own desire to "make sense" of the text. Thus comprehension is promoted and conditioned by the blanks and negations which are the "bread and butter" of understanding. As Palmer says,

> Negativity and disillusionment are integral to experience,[6] for there seems to be within the nature of man's historical existence a moment of negativity which is revealed in the nature of experience (1969:196).

Ricoeur's contribution is to focus on the imagination (as the interplay of identity and difference) as the leading edge of the operation of understanding; while Iser develops the same point in terms of "image-building" (cf. chapter 2.2).

Fifth, and finally, the imagination is first of all semantic rather than pictorial. That is, its formation of "wholeness" from the non-given precedes in logical priority any presentation or picturing of that "wholeness." Quite simply, the absent or the non-given, which is essential to the construction of the "wholeness," precedes and conditions the operation of the imagination, and cannot itself be pictured. In short, the absent cannot be pictured! The reason this productive formation of wholeness is termed "semantic" is that (1) its operation is akin to the naming function of the noun (and the verb; cf. Ricoeur 1965:41-52), whereby the noun names the whole beyond any finite perspective,[7] and (2) the imagination is operative in the production of meaning, as both sense and reference. Both points are further developed in the following paragraphs.[8] The point here, though, is that for Ricoeur, ". . . the imaginary is anchored in a semantic theory" (Ricoeur 1975a:208) which is first of all, "a theory of verbal meaning" (Ricoeur 1975a:208), and thus eludes psychologism. The basis of this semantic theory is, however, a notion of schema, which Ricoeur develops as the means by which to integrate the non-verbal, psychological aspects of the image with this semantic base. Before attempting to expound this reconnection with the

---

[6] And finally, understanding is defined by Palmer in terms of experience; cf. Palmer 1969:231f.

[7] This is what Schaldenbrand terms (the beginning of) Ricoeur's linguistic turn given to the conception of the Kantian schema (Schaldenbrand 1979:62).

[8] This development is especially important for it is the (philosophical) means by which a theory of the imagination and its central role in the generation of meaning escapes the critique of the picture-theory of meaning offered in chapter 4 with regard to the schema theories of the reading specialists.

psychological--to which is associated the power of the text to present or set before the eyes a world--more will be said about Ricoeur's notion of the schema.

7.1.1 Ricoeur's concept of the schema

The "schema," for Ricoeur, is understood as a linguistic variation on the Kantian conception of the schema of the transcendental imagination. For Kant, the schema is "a method for constructing images" (Ricoeur 1975a:189), "the matrix of the category" (Ricoeur 1975a:199) by which the relatedness of terms which are otherwise far apart are grasped as of one type.   Kant defines the schema as a "representation of a universal procedure [i.e. a "rule," Bennett 1966:141] of imagination in providing an image for a concept" (Kant 1956:182, [B 179]). Its purpose is to provide the means of applying any concept to its instances. Ricoeur develops this idea in stages.

First, in *Fallible Man* (1965) both the noun and the verb (as used in discourse) display the schematizing function of mediating and uniting the universal and the particular. The noun, for instance, unites a total, even infinite sense--the name--with "the never completed interplay of [finite] perspectives" (Schaldenbrand 1979:62). Taken together, the noun and the verb (the identifying and predicating functions discussed in chapter 4.1) are constitutive of discourse (cf. chapter 4.1). This is the initial linguistic turn Ricoeur gives to the Kantian schema, and it relates the function of the schema to the *semantic* naming.

In his later work on metaphor (e.g. 1975a; 1978b; 1981a:165ff; in which the understanding of metaphor is taken as paradigmatic for all text interpretation), Ricoeur develops the idea of the [Kantian] schema in terms of the metaphor as the paradigm for meaning production. Within this paradigm, the schema is "the place where the figurative meaning emerges in the interplay of identity and difference" (Ricoeur 1975a:199). With metaphor "the facts pertaining to one category [are presented] in the terms appropriate to another" (Ricoeur 1978b:146). But this is the function of the Kantian schema in the application of categories to instances in time (Kant 1956 A137 = B176ff; Bennett 1966:141ff; Strawson 1966:29ff, 88). The important development in Ricoeur, though, is that "In order that a metaphor obtains, one must continue to identify the previous incompatibility *through* the new compatibility" (Ricoeur 1978b:146).   In short, both identity (i.e. compatibility) and difference (i.e. incompatibility) must be maintained in metaphoric insight, and the "producing mechanism"--the imagination--is expounded in terms of the interplay of identity and difference.[9]   Here the "predicative assimilation" (Ricoeur 1978b:146) accomplished in metaphor restructures *semantic* fields first of all by bringing semantically near what was semantically remote.   But this

---

[9] Ricoeur's characterization of this "method" as "the interplay of identity and difference" is also highly significant, and is the topic of chapter 9.

155

"assimilation" ". . . consists precisely in *making* similar" (Ricoeur 1978b:146), and thus Ricoeur claims kinship with "the tradition of Kant's productive imagination and schematism" (Ricoeur 1978b:147).

The significant point here is that a schema ". . . before being the gathering-point of faded perceptions, . . . is the matrix of the new semantic pertinence that is born out of the dismantling of semantic networks caused by the shock of contradiction" (Ricoeur 1975a:199). In this regard, the schema for Ricoeur (as for Kant), is "a method for constructing images" (Ricoeur 1975a:189), images which are first of all emergent meanings. As Butts (1969:300) puts it, "the schemata . . . [are] semantic rules," whose operation is the source of the emergence of meaning.[10] With regard to the reading of a text this "figurative meaning" of metaphor can be taken as the emergence of meaning--both sense and reference--through the interplay of the various textual perspectives of which Iser speaks (e.g. Iser 1978:184; cf. Ricoeur 1981a:165ff, especially 166-176; also chapter 2.2). As various (different, even conflicting) perspectives are presented, the reader must occupy the perspective which solves the enigma of the different perspectives. This viewpoint, remember, is not formulated by the text, but must be constructed. This is the function of image-building which finds a perspective from which the different perspectives can be viewed as compatible. From Ricoeur's perspective, this image-building is first of all the construction of meaning as sense and it operates at the level of the text in a manner akin to the making sense of a metaphoric attribution. The construction involved is "the means by which all the words [at the sentence level of metaphor; perspectives or themes at the text level] taken together make sense" (Ricoeur 1981a:174). The "sense" at the textual level, is a whole about which Ricoeur is quite vague. Presumably, this whole is a meaning in the ideal sense, which, nonetheless, may be architecturally complex (Ricoeur 1981a:175). Iser is more explicit, calling this meaning an "aesthetic object" which bears the nature of a "code" (Iser 1978:92).[11]

However, equally significant for Ricoeur is that the image, though first of all an emergent *verbal* meaning, is also quasi-sensory and non-verbal. The imagination, remember, endows the absent with presence, and thus is responsible for putting *the object* before our eyes. As Bachelard puts it, the image ". . . becomes a new being in our language" (1964:xix). In this regard, sense becomes iconic, language becomes a verbal sculpture constructed from "a wave of evoked or aroused images [in the pictoral sense]" (Ricoeur 1975a:210) which surround words as an aura (Ricoeur 1975a:211, 214). Far from being mere associationism, ". . . iconicity

---

[10] Butts (1969:294) quotes Kant to this effect: "The schemata of the pure concepts of understanding are thus the true and sole conditions under which these concepts obtain relation to objects, and so possess *significance*" (Kant 1956, A146 = B185).

[11] This is the first aspect in which the aesthetic object is like the ideality of sense (recall Ricoeur's association of *langue* with sense). The second is that it is a system of internal reference only (Iser 1978:96).

involves meaning controlling imagery [in the pictoral sense]" (Ricoeur 1975a:211), and as such, the picture theory of meaning is avoided. Rather, Ricoeur claims that ". . . the notion of *schematism of metaphoric attribution* does not violate the boundaries of semantic theory, that is, of a theory of *verbal* meaning" (Ricoeur 1975a:208). And yet, it ". . . constitutes the point on the frontier of semantics and psychology where the imaginary is anchored in a semantic theory of meaning" (Ricoeur 1975a:208), "the borderline between a semantics of productive imagination and a psychology of reproductive imagination" (Ricoeur 1978b:149).

Presented in this manner--first semantics, then the iconic--the false impression may be left that a temporal sequence is involved. This is not the case.

> The place and role of productive imagination is. . . in the insight . . . [which] is both a thinking and a seeing . . . . But this thinking is a seeing, to the extent that the insight consists of the instantaneous grasping of the combinatory possibilities . . . (Ricoeur 1978b:145f).

In fact, that which appears as depiction is that on which the new semantic connection is read (Ricoeur 1978b:148f). And yet, the verbal meaning is recognized as generating the images to which it is bound.

> Imaging or imagining, thus is the concrete milieu in which and through which we see similarities. To imagine, then, is not to have a mental picture of something but to display relations in a depicting mode (Ricoeur 1978b:148).

Consequently, at the heart of reading is a process which is (1) complex, involving meaning and images (and as considered in section 5 below, feeling), (2) grounded first of all in semantics, (3) essentially "imaginary," and (4) ordered, with images being generated by and bound to verbal meaning.

This, then, is a sketch of the philosophical formulation of the schema which answers the needs of an adequate theory of meaning, while at the same time inviting the engrafting of psychology (and psycholinguistics). Because this grafting is of special interest to our dialogue in reading theories, we will return to it in the next sections. But first three final points will be made with regard to Ricoeur's conception of the schema.

First, this functioning of the imagination in the generation of meaning is

157

. . . not yet a *conceptual* gain, to the extent that
the semantic innovation is not separable from the
[interplay of identity and difference]. We might
say then that the semantic shock produces a
conceptual need, but not as yet any knowledge by
means of concepts (Ricoeur 1975a:296).

Only a rough outline (Ricouer 1975a:297) is constituted. Here again we
rejoin our earlier consideration of the pre-epistemological prestructuring of
the understanding to view, as it were, the first workings of the ontological
status of man in the epistemological realm. The point of contact is the
imagination, the theory of which Ricoeur admits ". . . is still in infancy"
(Ricoeur 1978b:156).

Second, Ricoeur's idea of the schema reflects in its own way, the
dialectic of sense and reference discussed earlier, a consideration of which
returns us to the notion of the "world." The emergence of meaning is first
of all meaning as sense, which the imagination accomplishes by means of
the schematization of the predicative assimilation. And yet, the schema as
image shows perhaps more clearly than before ". . . that every gain in
meaning is at one and the same time a gain in sense and a gain in
reference" (Ricoeur 1975a:297). In short, the emergent meaning is assured
(by the quasi-sensory character bestowed by the schema) of being *presented*
as that to which reference can be and is made. Interestingly, though, this
reference is the second-order reference which results from the failure of
sense to refer ostensively to circumstantial reality. Thus the image reveals
its negativity, its first-order failure to refer (Ricoeur 1978b:149f;
1975a:230f). This however, is only the "other side" of the positive
reference prepared by the imagination's endowment of presence to the
ideal sense as constituted by predicative assimilation, or as Iser calls it,
image-building. Consequently, as pointed out most clearly by Iser 1978, the
"world" to which reference is thus made is itself an "image." The
significant points resulting from this fact are that (1) the "world" is, in part,
a construct of the reader, (2) in which the reader is drawn away from the
"real world" because, (3) the subject-object division is eliminated, and yet
(4) to a significant extent, the reader is passive in image-building. These
points will be discussed in the sections to follow.

Third, some comparison between Ricoeur's and Iser's notion of
schema and that of the reading specialists is called for, especially since
some of the key reading specialist schema-theoreticians hark back to Kant
(Rumelhart and Ortony 1977; Rumelhart 1980). For instance:

It is interesting to note, however, that in his
Critique of Pure Reason, Kant (1787) utilizes a
notion of schemata that in many ways appears to
be more similar to ours than is even Bartlett's
[1932]" (Rumelhart and Ortony 1977:100f).

158

There are, though, the following three difficulties with this comparison.

First, as noted by Rumelhart himself (1980:33; Rumelhart and Ortony 1977:101, n. 2), the schema for Kant is a *rule* of the *productive* imagination. While there does seem to be the needed development in schema theory from an almost exclusive emphasis on schemas as data *structures* (e.g. Rumelhart and Ortony 1977:101) to a recognition of their active, procedural (e.g. Rumelhart 1980:38ff), and functional (Iran-Nejad 1980; Iran-Nejad and Ortony 1982) nature, and thus more of an agreement with Kant's notion of the schema as *rule*, the emphasis on the *productive* role has not yet been adequately developed. This lack is highlighted, as already noted, by a consideration of new meaning (as in metaphor). Even "schema induction" (Rumelhart 1980:54; cf. chapter 5), the proposed explanation for the generation of new schemas, has difficulties. First, the formation of a schema from the repetition of patterns ". . . is not a natural part of a schema-based system" (Rumelhart 1980:54). It presupposes the recognition of sameness in different contexts of occurrence, but such a recognition is not based on a pregiven schema since the point is precisely that there is no pregiven schema in this case. Second, even schema induction and some "mechanism" of recognition cannot account for the new meaning of metaphor or text as reported by Ricoeur and Iser, since in these cases there is no repetition: the event is unique to the particular metaphor or text. Thus it would seem that some such notion as Ricoeur's imagination (as the interplay of identity and difference) as underlying schemas is required, and with it a different (though very similar!) notion of the schema--the schema as image (in the primordial sense of the place of interplay of identity and difference). Rumelhart (1980:57) comes close to this sense when he says, noting the role of schemas in problem solving, "It is as if the schema already contains all of the reasoning mechanism ordinarily required in the use of the schemata." By this he intimates a deeper process at work within the schema, but does almost nothing to explicate such a process.

The second difficulty the reading specialists encounter with the comparison of their notion of the schema with Kant's, is that for them the schema is the representation of the general situation, more akin to Kant's concept than his schema. Kant's schema is the proposed means of relating the particular instance to the general, what the psychologists call matching. With regard to this "matching," there is a "making similar" of what cannot be judged to be similar based on any other independent criteria (this is further discussed in the next section). Rumelhart does acknowledge that the schemas must be conceived of as ". . . capable of evaluating the quality of their own fit to the available data" (Rumelhart 1980:39). But "evaluating" "goodness of fit" (Rumelhart 1980:41), and producing or creating that fit in the first place are processes needing to be both distinguished and related.[12]

Third, superficially, it sounds as if Iser's talk of "filling in the blanks" of a text is similar to the filling of the slots of the schemas. There are though, radical differences: (1) the process Iser notes often negates the familiar, i.e. the schemas of the reading theorists (cf. section 3 below); (2) the schema-theoretic account is not sufficiently precise in its conception of the schema to avoid the critique of the picture-theory of meaning, while Iser's account does avoid this critique (cf. earlier in this section); and (3) the blanks which Iser notes shift throughout reading, guided by the interaction of text and reader (1978:203), while the slots of the schemas are relatively fixed by convention. In short, Iser's blanks are different from and operate at a level more fundamental than the cognitive structures of the reading researchers. Iser's blanks, though conditioned by particular texts, are akin to the fundamental "difference" which Ricoeur posits as always at play in and with the imagination.

These three problems with identifying the schemas of schema theories with the Kantian schema (and/or Ricoeur's development of that notion) all are variations on the difficulty of schema theories to account for the new. This point recurs in the section to follow.

This section has sought to further clarify the constitution of the "world" by consideration of the schema as developed by Ricoeur. We have also touched on the active process of constituting the world. The following sections of this chapter further develop this notion of the active process of construction, culminating in the treatment given in section 5.3.

7.2 Resemblance

Ricoeur's treatment of metaphor opens further possibilities for dialogue with the schema theorists on a point in schema theory we recognized previously as both weak and promising: the characterization and role of "matching" or "correspondence." Matching, remember, is the means by which the slots of schemas are filled, thus producing comprehension. But what, we asked, constitutes a match? The terminology varies (e.g. a fit, a correspondence, a match), but the idea, vague though we found it to be, remains the same: There is a resemblance between the waiting slots and aspects of the experience which is to be understood. The reason that Ricoeur's treatment of metaphor is helpful here is that (1) "resemblance" has played an important role in the history of metaphor theory and thus has been much discussed, and (2) Ricoeur offers a substantial advance to this very notion. I will deal with these two points in order.

---

[12] Rumelhart does indeed note that schemas do have a causative contribution to make in perception (1980:47) and interpretation (1980:49ff), but this recognition has not been thoroughly integrated into his notion of the schema itself (for the above reasons).

In classical rhetoric, metaphor was the rhetorical figure in which a figurative word is substituted for an absent literal word on the basis of resemblance.

> Indeed, resemblance first of all motivates the borrowing [of the figurative for the literal]; next it is the positive side of the process whose negative side is deviation; further, it is the internal link within the sphere of substitution; finally, it guides the paraphrase that annuls the trope by restoring the proper meaning (Ricoeur 1975a:173f).

In short, ". . . resemblance is the foundation of the substitution" (Ricoeur 1975a:174). There is in this view the notion that metaphor does not produce any semantic innovation. The same meaning could have been expressed otherwise, and an exhaustive paraphrase can be given; the metaphor simply dresses up the old or naked idea in the fancy new clothes of imagistic language (Ricoeur 1975a:46). Further, the "new clothes" are not radically new, but drawn from the wardrobe of the system of common associations, relatively well established and recognized resemblances. Thus with regard to meaning, ". . . substitution plus restitution equals zero" (Ricoeur 1976:49).

Opposed to this substitution theory of metaphor is the tension or interactive theory. In this latter theory, the sentence and not the word is the linguistic unit of interest, and predication, not substitution, is the relevant operation. Here it is recognized that for many metaphors (in particular, the most interesting), two interpretations of the (metaphoric) sentence are opposed to one another. At the literal (i.e. commonplace) level of interpretation there is no apparent kinship or resemblance which can serve as "the reason" for the (odd) predication. The clash, inconsistency, absurdity, or misunderstanding (Ricoeur 1976:50f) occurring with regard to the first interpretation ". . . causes a new, hitherto unnoticed relation of meaning to spring up between the terms that previous systems of classification had ignored or not allowed" (Ricoeur 1976:51). Here resemblance is more the result than the cause of the metaphoric meaning (Ricoeur 1975a:191).

> Metaphor therefore is more like the resolution of an enigma than a simple association based on resemblance; it is constituted by the resolution of a semantic dissonance (Ricoeur 1976:52).

The distinction between these two theories--the substitution and the interaction--can be focused by the differing responses to the question, From where do we draw the meaning of a metaphor? The substitution theory answers, from the substitution of the proper word (or paraphrase) for the figurative word. The interaction theory answers, ". . . the new, emergent meaning is not drawn from anywhere, at least not from anywhere in language (the [predicated] property is an implication of things, not of words)" (Ricoeur 1981a:174).[13] The objection of the interaction theories to the substitution theories is that they ". . . continue to bind the creative process of metaphor to a non-creative aspect of language" (Ricoeur 1981a:173).

7.2.1 Schema theories and metaphor theories

How do schema theories relate to these two theories of metaphor? Because of its strong dependence on established knowledge (i.e. "the schema"), and its emphasis on the matching (or "substituting") of the given experience to the pregiven slots of the pregiven schema, the schema theories reflect the biases of the substitution theory of metaphor. The difficulty of schema theories in accounting for metaphor (as noted above and in chapter 5) further supports this conclusion.

Such a correlating of schema theories with the substitution theory of metaphor cannot, however, stand by itself when the full range of schema theories is considered. As already noted, several schema theorists speak of the "creation" of meaning (e.g. Spiro), and even emphasize, as does Ricoeur, that "a construction on the side of the reader" (Ricoeur 1981a:174) is necessary to this creative process.

Further, problem-solving is also used by schema theorists to explore the process of understanding (e.g. Spiro 1980:261; Rumelhart 1980:57; Collins et al. 1977), a process which also breaks with the crucial role of matching-resemblance.

Finally, the work of Iran-Nejad and Ortony on a functional concept of schemas comes closer to the philosophical notion of schema as a rule for producing meaning as presented in the last section than the more traditional structural conception. Here the schemas are "phenomenally transient functional patterns" (Iran-Nejad 1980:1), "domain specific relational cluster[s]" (Iran-Nejad 1980:3). Rather than being structural constructs, the central concept of this approach is "the schema-of-the-moment" (Iran-Nejad and Ortony 1982) which is explicated in terms of "the light-constellation analogy." In this metaphor, cognition is a question of "lighting up" the proper constellation of lights (pattern, color, intensity, etc.) within a room full of lights. The schema, then, is the lit-up pattern. In summary, it is argued ". . . that people do not function by selecting templates [structural, stored schemas], rather they function by creating and recreating transient cognition patterns" (Iran-Nejad and Ortony 1982:7).

Iran-Nejad (1980:16) gives the following four advantages of the "schema-of-the-moment" conception as expounded by the light-constellation analogy:

---

[13] Ricoeur does point out that the interaction theories of Black and Beardsley do not give adequate attention to this point; cf. Ricoeur 1978b:145ff; 1981a:172ff.

First, it clearly illustrates how an infinite number of unique functional patterns could be generated based on a limited number of structural elements. Secondly, there is no need for an independent storage mechanism. Thirdly, for each functional pattern, the unique functional characteristic of the whole is clearly greater than (or rather different from) that of the individual component parts: the shade of color generated by a given subset cluster will be different from that generated by individual lights. And, most importantly, there will be no need for an independent structural pattern corresponding to each distinguishable functional pattern.

There are, though, difficulties remaining with this account. First, how is it determined which lights go on? The explanation proposed is based on an analogy with the endocrine system (Iran-Nejad and Ortony 1982). This is, however, a highly "mechanistic" system--the reactions are produced automatically (except for pathological malfunction)--and runs head-on into the role of the reader in making meaning. It does, though, capture the "passive" sense of reading noted throughout this chapter. Second, and closely related to the above point, a strong a priori "pre-established harmony" (a "system" of lights available to be lit up) is implied in this account, but no theoretical attention is paid to it. Third, some "recognition device" or "mechanism" of reflective awareness is still needed by this account, by which "this" situation is judged to be like "that" one, since there is obviously some relation of recognition operative in reading (cf. the "old," familiar, etc. in Smith, Iser, schema theory, etc.). But if there is some such recognized connection between the new and the old, then there is also some sort of abiding structure--that to which the new is "compared." Finally, when is any particular light constellation acceptable as adequate (for comprehension or whatever), and what is the basis of that judgment of adequacy? No account is presently available in this theory. It would seem again that if some standard of judgment is implied, then the notion of structure cannot be dispensed with entirely. Consequently, I conclude that both structure and function are required for a full account of reading (cf. Smith and Miller 1980, who concur with this conclusion). The relation to the "schema" of Ricoeur, especially as it has been modified by a consideration of metaphor where the *creation* of meaning is the issue, should be obvious.

Consequently, here too (as with the notions of "meaning" and "schema") schema theories are inbetween a somewhat discredited view and the innovations which are bringing new insights and better accounts of well-studied problems. To recognize this fact from an interdisciplinary perspective is very valuable, for it opens schema theory not only to critique, but most importantly, to growth and improvement as well. Ricoeur's work on the notion of resemblance in metaphor has much to offer to schema theories, particularly with regard to the role of matching. That work seems

163

to provide the best exposition of what schema theories should mean by "matching." Ricoeur's work on resemblance, therefore, will now be my focus of concern.

7.2.2 Ricoeur on resemblance

Though the role of resemblance in metaphor is often rejected by the interactive theorists, Riceour argues that ". . . resemblance is of even greater necessity in a tension [i.e. interaction] theory than in a substitution theory" (1975a:193). The basis of this argument is that metaphor establishes a semantic proximity of previously distant meanings.[13] The predicative structure of metaphor (which is evident when metaphor is taken as a sentence level, rather than a word level, phenomenon) establishes a generic relatedness which, says Ricoeur, points in a preconceptual fashion to the idea of family resemblance (Ricoeur 1975a:194f). The key, though, is that the resemblance is "properly semantic" (1975a:194), rather than semiotic in character. That is, "Resemblance ultimately is nothing else than this rapprochement [cf. section 1] which reveals a generic kinship between heterogeneous ideas" (Ricoeur 1978b:145). Because that kinship had not been previously revealed, substitution based on the given semiotic system (i.e. *la langue*) cannot account for it. Because the kinship is "between . . . ideas," (Ricoeur 1978b:145) the process establishing it is properly semantic.[14]

Further, Ricoeur points out that both intuition and construction are involved in metaphoric attribution, and thus in the notion of resemblance. In fact, there is no intuitive bringing together of the disparate without the "discursive moment" which chooses and organizes the appropriate meanings while constructing the solution to the metaphoric enigma. The comprehension of a metaphor (and by extension, of a text) is "at once the 'gift of genius' [i.e. intuitive insight] and the skill of the geometer, who sees the point [by construction] in the 'ratio of proportions' " (Ricoeur 1975a:195). Thus resemblance is not simply the result of the metaphor; it is both cause and result. Consequently, resemblance is not confined to a substitution theory (of either metaphor or schemas) in which all the slots and fillers are pregiven, simply waiting to be matched. Rather, resemblance is also essential to the emergence of the new. Metaphoric

---

[13] An interesting sidelight is noted by Caillois (1968:148): ". . . the thesis, consistently maintained by Surrealism, affirms, we recall, that a poetic image will be all the more effective as the terms it joins increase in distance from one another."

[14] This, then, relates directly to the constitution of the schema as discussed in the last section. The "images" (in the pictorial sense), though semiotic (in the sense of (1) being relatively established and given, (2) operating by "non-referential interplay" (Ricoeur 1975a:225) as do signs considered semiotically, and (3) functioning to abolish reference) are bound to the semantic pertinence which is the metaphor. These two structures (semiotic and semantic), though closely related, must be distinguished.

meaning results from construction which itself is guided by that interplay of identity and difference which is resemblance.

"Resemblance," however, is redefined in the process. Rather than being a simple matching of pregiven slots and fillers (which appears to be simple only because of its theoretical obscurity; cf. chapter 5, 6), ". . . resemblance can be construed as the site of the clash between sameness and difference . . ." (Ricoeur 1975a:196). That is, the interplay of identity and difference which seems required by a full account of metaphoric (and by analogy, textual) comprehension is taken as the heart of the human imagination, which itself is the heart of human comprehension.

Ricoeur frankly acknowledges, though, that this process is paradoxical (1975a:196). The "intuitive" is a matter of discovery or revelation, while "construction" is a matter of invention or creation. And these two poles have traditionally been taken as opposites! It is Ricoeur's and Iser's contention, however, that this contradiction is just seeming, not actual.

Iser presents this paradox in terms of the role of "passive synthesis" in image-building. In fact, Iser's discussion of the role of images in reading is under the chapter title "Passive syntheses in the reading process" (1978:135). "The act of image-building," says Iser, ". . . is . . . consecutive in the sense that it depends to a large extent on the time dimension of the reading process" (Iser 1978:148). As we read, various facets of a situation and/or a character, etc. are presented sequentially in time, and the reader must synthesize these facets into a totality which is implied by the text (Iser 1978:146). The process of synthesizing this totality, though, is

> . . . passive to the extent that neither assessment
> nor predication makes itself explicit in the link-up
> of facets--not least, because this takes place below
> the threshold of consciousness (Iser 1978:139).[16]

This is one side of the paradox--the construction is guided by the textual structures, yet proceeds to a significant extent subconsciously. Thus the meaning is discovered, rather than invented. And yet, because the totality which is (to be) synthesized is "not formulated" in the text (Iser 1978:146), but ". . . has to be assembled" (Iser 1978:147),

> It is the reader who must conceive the totality
> which the aspects [of the text] prestructure, and it
> is in his mind that the text coheres (Iser 1978:147).

The interesting result is that the subject-object division which is essential to perception is eliminated, and the image is produced as a *sui generis* object. It is not an empirical object for it has been produced by the reader; nor is it (yet) the conceptualized meaning of a represented object, for as Ricoeur makes clear, the image is caught in the instability of the interplay of identity and difference. Consequently, ". . . we are actually in its [the image's] presence and it is in ours" (Iser 1978:139).[15]

Two further consequences result from this abolition of the subject-object relation in reading. First, ". . . the reader himself, in constituting the meaning, is also constituted. And herein lies the full significance of the so-called passive synthesis" (Iser 1978:150; cf. section 5 below). Second, when putting the book down, a kind of awakening occurs due to the reinstitution of the subject-object division which occurs automatically with the reinstitution of perception. Thus ". . . the real world appears [all the more] observable" (Iser 1978:140; cf. chapter 8). As noted in the documentation given with the references above, these topics are discussed further in what follows.

This paradox of (metaphoric) comprehension (i.e. intuition and construction) is reflected in the top-down/bottom-up debate in reading, though significantly, the intuition-construction formulation cuts across these categories of the reading specialists. Intuition highlights the reader's contribution (top-down), and yet by its character attests to a source which cannot be accounted for on the basis of individual subjectivity alone: An intuition is as much given (bottom-up?) as self-generated. Similarly, though "construction" is often used by the interactive theorists as (almost) synonymous with "creation" to describe the reader's input, it also highlights that the "material" from which a construction is made is, in part, given by the text. Further, the term "construction" implies that the construction itself is conditioned and guided by this material. Such a process could as well be termed "data-driven" in the bottom-up sense as "concept-driven." It appears that the simple bottom-up/top-down dichotomy will not do for capturing the full process of reading (cf. section 4 for further discussion).

At a more fundamental level, though, this paradox is just another form of that paradox which is the structure of our being: a projection (i.e. intuition, creation) within a prior being thrown (i.e. a recognition and construction of what is already given). The danger to which theorists on both sides of the debate tend to succumb is to resolve the tension of this paradox in favor of one side or the other. Ricoeur counsels us instead to live this paradox, and finally to ground this solution in a tensive theory of truth and being (1975a:257-313). Finally this vision of reality recognizes that in the play of resemblance (Ricoeur 1975a:309), language itself (as other than man) addresses man (Ricoeur 1975a:311), and that the dialectic of identity and difference (or using broader terms, the dialectic of

---

[15] Iser 1978 points out that this is why we are so often disappointed with a film presentation of a text we have read: The film presents the object to us already made (and, no doubt, differing from our own version of the object), but excludes us from its production, and thus from being mutually present with it. It is present to us, but we are not present to it, at least not in the same way as if we had produced it ourselves.

belonging and distanciation) is "the most primordial, most hidden dialectic" (Ricoeur 1975a:313). I return to this point briefly in section 4 below, and in greater detail in chapter 9. But first, a further consideration of the relation between the old and the new in reading.

7.3   The old and the new

The point of weakness of schema theories which continues to recur in these discussions is the inadequacy of the schema--which is conventional knowledge--to account for "the new," whether new information or new experience. This difficulty is readily recognized by some (e.g. Ortony, Spiro), but usually only with regard to what are seen as exceptional cases, like metaphor. Our considerations of matching and resemblance, though, indicate that the problem of "the new" is also a real problem in ordinary experience. Inasmuch as two experiences are rarely (if ever) identical, there is rarely (if ever) a case of "schema-filling" which does not involve "the new." Bartlett (1932:202) speaks similarly:

> When I make a stroke [in a game, e.g. golf; Bartlett is developing an illustration here of a "general situation"] I do not, as a matter of fact, produce something absolutely new, and I never merely repeat something old.[16]

Our consideration of the schema as the place of interaction between identity *and* difference has prepared us to incorporate the relation of the new to the old at the heart of all experience.

Though we postulate, on philosophical grounds, the necessary mediation of the imagination--as the interacting of identity and difference-- it remains true that this account has been displayed most readily in the reading of works of art. This is, however, more likely the result of the expectations of newness by aestheticians (where the presentation of the new is so often purposively sought) rather than due to any absolutely unique character of literary art. This claim is supported by the following two lines of reasoning. First of all, it remains doubtful whether there is any absolutely unique character of literary art (cf. e.g. Fish 1980:97ff, 268ff). And second, there are several common experiences in the literature of the schema theorists waiting, as it were, for reinterpretation along the lines of aesthetic experience. Spiro 1980, for instance, notes five problem areas in current schema theory which call for future research, each of which I relate directly to the problem of the new and the old.

---

[16] It is true that Piaget and others distinguish between *assimilation*, in which new information is incorporated into old structures without altering those structures, and accommodation in which conceptual change does occur. It is this latter category which is especially problematic.

First, simple schema availability is not enough to account for comprehension since even when prior knowledge is available it must be accessed and used appropriately; and often it is not (Spiro 1980:259ff). Though the schemas may be conceived of as "capable of evaluating the quality of their own fit to the available data" (Rumelhart 1980:39), Spiro's point is that there is a missing link here between the schema itself and the "data." I propose considering this a problem of the relation between the old (schemas) and the new situation.

Second, the variations of efficiency of top-down processing noted in the research (cf. Spiro 1980:265ff) imply difficulties for schema theories which relate directly to the relation of the new to the old. For example, (1) how schemas are selected with the various degrees of automaticity observed: there seem to be subconscious processes operating which relate the new to the old (Spiro 1980:266); (2) the "getting lost in reading" experience seems to relate to a level of efficiency "deeper" than the information-processing capacity, a level related to "affect," which itself is discussed in terms of the new and the old of imagination (cf. section 5 below); and (3) the demands of the cognitive economy of representation (there don't seem to be schemas for every different situation encountered since all situations differ) implies a "mechanism" of some sort for building schemas ". . . to fit the needs of the subtly changing variety of situations that they must help inform" (Spiro 1980:268), i.e. relating the ever new and the old.

Third, individual stylistic differences are recognized as playing a significant role in comprehension (Spiro 1980:262f). Evidently, the schema as a conventionalized structure shared by many is not an adequate account. *Difference* must also be incorporated into the "application" of schemas by individuals in reading. Spiro is currently ascribing this difference to individual style. Such an ascription, however, does not inquire into what it is about schemas which allow (and perhaps even encourage) such different applications by different individuals. We are suggesting that difference is already an integral "constituent" of the structure of the schema.[17]

Fourth, the question of learning is by definition a matter of "the new." Here Spiro is most frank: "We know next to nothing about the processes of conceptual change" (1980:271), even looking hopefully to metaphor for further insight (1980:271).

Fifth, the question of the affective domain in relation to schemas is posed by Spiro as ". . . an appropriate place to start looking for an answer

---

[17] Spiro's main emphasis with regard to individual differences has to do with the degree of top-down versus bottom-up emphasis in the style. Given, however, that schemas are to be filled by "data" from the text, indicating input from both the old ("the top") and the new ("the bottom"), and that the difference which (I posit) "resides" in the schema is an indeterminate openness (the "potentially new") which is to be filled by the reading, I think that Spiro's emphasis and my own are closely related.

to that most important question of conceptual change . . ." (1980:274). In section 5.4 the role of affect is presented as conceived after the pattern of the imagination, and thus as directly related to the relations of identity and difference, belonging and distanciation, and the old and the new.

Earlier (cf. chapter 6.3) we have already said a good deal about the relation between the old and the new. A bit more will be said here, but the "bottom line" question of the origin of "the new" remains unanswered from this perspective. It will, however, be addressed directly in the next section.

The important point with regard to the relation of the old and the new to be underlined here is that there is in reading comprehension an essential moment of negativity (as in all understanding). As Palmer (1969:234) notes with regard to understanding in general:

> It is but partially true that one can understand only within one's own horizon and through it. If this were so, no significant alteration of horizons could occur. Rather, in true experience there is a partial negation of one's own horizon, and through this a more encompassing understanding emerges.[18]

Similarly, Gadamer (1975:318): ". . . experience [which is the fundamental category of reading too; Iser 1978:22, 132] is primarily an experience of negation." And both Iser and Ricoeur recognize this process as operative in reading, Iser in terms of "negation," and Ricoeur in terms of the metaphoric "clash" as paradigmatic for textual understanding.

---

[18] Merleau-Ponty, another phenomenologist, also recognizes this communication of something new through variations on the old:

> ". . . the book would not interest me so much if it only told me about things I already know. It makes use of everything I have contributed in order to carry me beyond it. With the aid of the signs agreed upon by the author and myself because we speak the same language, the book makes me believe that we had already shared a common stock of well-worn and readily available significations. The author has come to dwell in my world. Then, imperceptibly, he varies the ordinary meaning of the signs, and like a whirlwind they sweep me along toward the other meaning with which I am going to connect" (1973:11f).

Merleau-Ponty's "variation," though, encompasses, but does not make explicit, both a use of the old (the "agreed upon" conventions, the ordinary) and a break with it (the "other meaning" which entails a negation of the "agreed upon").

For Iser, the role of negativity is highlighted by the fact that the familiar or habitual dispositions are quite inadequate to account for what occurs in reading (e.g. 1978:35, 67, 229). Negativity, in fact, is the operation of deforming (Iser 1978:229), invalidating (Iser 1978:217), or suspending the validity of existing norms (Iser 1978:70). This activity of negation thus ". . . tends to be on or just beyond the fringes of the particular thought system prevalent at the time" (Iser 1978:73). Similarly, for Ricoeur, it is the suspension (e.g. 1981a:149) or abolition (e.g. 1981a:111, 141, 148, 186f) of the first order, "ordinary" reference which is the necessary background out of which new meaning emerges. In short, negation is the very factor which seems especially designed to frustrate any purely schema-theoretic (in its present form) account of reading comprehension.[19]

However, rather than trying to do without negation, the phenomenological account has integrated negation into the very heart of the reader's constitution, both ontologically (cf. chapter 6, section 3), and epistemologically (cf. chapter 7, section 2).

If reading, however, can place the reader "beyond the fringes of the prevalent thought system," i.e. beyond all schemas conceived of as conventional knowledge, where does "the new" come from, and how is the reader affected in the process? These are the topics of our final two sections.

7.4 Disclosure and the source of the new

The answer of our three phenomenologists--Ricoeur, Iser, and Poulet--to the question of the origin of the new (which is operative to varying degrees in all acts of comprehension) differs. As noted in chapter 2, Poulet speaks of a profound and elusive "transcendence of mind," a transcendent consciousness which is like my consciousness as reader, but which is profoundly other, too. Iser calls this "Poulet's substantialist concept of consciousness" (Iser 1978:155), and rejects it as inexplicable Hegelianism (Iser 1978:154). If this "hypostatized consciousness" (Iser 1978:154) is indeed consciousness, he says, it must be consciousness of something. But of what? The only option which Poulet allows--a consciousness of itself--is rejected out of hand by Iser. This rejection, however, rests on the unsupported premise that there is not and could not be any such transcendent consciousness which presents itself in the affairs of men, in particular, in reading.

Iser's objection to Poulet is further weakened by his own (explicit) solution to the question, which nonetheless, seems inconsistent with his

---

[19] Leenhart (1980:221) comes to the same conclusion on the basis of a sociological investigation of reading. Reporting on his work, he says: ". . . reading cannot be described only as an effect of mental structures." This broader influence of "institutional power" is discussed in chapter 8.

explanations of reading elsewhere. When discussing the issue directly, Iser (1978:153-159) credits the presence of "the new" to the alien thoughts which the reader thinks. Thus far Iser is on safe ground; but when he goes on to consider these alien thoughts to be "the author's thoughts" (Iser 1978:154, 155), he subjects himself to the criticism of identifying the meaning of the text with the authorial intent (cf. chapter 4). Unfortunately, Iser "needs" the author to intervene at this point for he is concerned to explicate how it is that the reader is "split" in reading. That is, how it is that "Whenever I read, I mentally pronounce an *I* and yet the I which I pronounce is not myself" (Poulet 1969:56)? The presence of the personality of the author is, for Iser, the key to the development of the newness in the personality of the reader (Iser 1978:156f).

But this will not do, as Iser also seems to realize. The reader is not presented with a personality, but with a text (for which a personality is constructed). Clearly, for Iser, the meaning of the text must be constituted or assembled by the reader; it is not presented as pregiven or preformulated at all, let alone as personal. It is true that the text structures and conditions this assembly; and yet it is the reader who activates the assembly. Further, that which is assembled cannot be accounted for, according to Iser, in terms of the reader's "personal history of experience" (Iser 1978:152), or "his own disposition" (Iser 1978:153). Nor can the meaning of the text be accounted for on the basis of "any prevailing code" (Iser 1978:133), or "the schemata of the text" (Iser 1978:92), or "a linguistic model" (Iser 1978:32). Though the interaction of all these factors is recognized as necessary, the key to the constitution of meaning is not forthcoming in Iser's account. All these factors are involved in the activation of the reader's spontaneity (Iser 1978:158f), a spontaneity which is essential to reading comprehension (Iser 1978:158), but of which no coherent account is given. Having ruled out transcendence, Iser is left finally with the reader formulating himself (Iser 1978:158). But having disallowed the reader's "own past and conscious orientation" (Iser 1978:158), he concedes (in opposition to "the reader formulating himself") that ". . . the conditioning influence must be the alien thoughts" (Iser 1978:158). The alien thoughts, though, are not thoughts at all--but black marks on a page--until they are read and the meaning assembled by a reader. Clearly, "the reader formulating himself" is not an adequate account. Certainly the reader is active and engaged in the process, a point Iser makes very well. But finally, there is, for Iser, an *enablement* of the reader's spontaneity occurring in reading (Iser 1978:133, 158) which does not have either its source or foundation in the reader and which is at least as inexplicable as Poulet's substantialist concept of consciousness. It is just another name for the question of the origin of "the new," not an answer.

As already noted in the concluding pages of chapter 6, Ricoeur credits *the text* with a power to reveal (e.g. Ricoeur 1981a:191), and that which it reveals is "*new* modes of being" (Ricoeur 1981a:192; emphasis added). Further, and as with Iser (e.g. 1978:142), this revelatory power is linked with the formation of the reader as subject (e.g. Iser 1978:157): ". . . the revelation of new modes of being . . . *gives* the subject new capacities for knowing himself" (Ricoeur 1981a:192). Indeed, "It is the text, with its universal power of unveiling, which gives a *self* to the *ego*" (Ricoeur 1981a:193). In the next section (5) we look directly at this effect on (and in) the subject-reader; here we note that Ricoeur is explicit about the source of "the new": It is not the reader, but the text. As with Iser, Ricoeur emphasizes that the reader's control here is minimal at best. Rather, the reader's subjectivity is "placed in suspense, unrealized, potentialised" (Ricouer 1981a:144); rather than "taking possession" of the meaning, reading is finally, and primarily, a "letting-go" (Ricoeur 1981a:191).

Though Ricoeur emphasizes the power of *the text* to reveal, his fundamental phenomenological perspective on meaning must not be forgotten. Considered phenomenologically, meaning is always intentionally correlated with a subject. However, given this intentional relation, Ricoeur is reporting (phenomenologically) aspects of meaning which appear in the process of reading and are germane to our topic. These aspects are (1) meaning's transcendence, (2) meaning's dynamism, and (3) the power of meaning to reveal a world and affect the reader.

First, by meaning's transcendence is meant nothing more here than its ideality: Though constructed by a reader, it yet presents itself as obtaining independently. This independence is further accentuated in the following points, in which another sense of transcendence begins to emerge.

Second, meaning itself appears as dynamic. Language acts on language in that reading is the act *of* the text *before* being the act of the reader (Ricoeur 1981a:162f). This is what Iser (1978:120) terms "the interconnection between the textual signs prior to the stimulation of the individual reader's disposition." In short, the autocorrelation of textual signs. This notion is quite other than the subjective, top-down process by which the reader acts *on* the text (Ricoeur 1981a:162).

This dynamism of meaning is manifest at several levels. First, the formation of "sense" is the action of autocorrelation noted above. Second, the movement from sense to reference is conceived of as motivated by the nature of meaning itself. Says Ricoeur, ". . . the question of reference is always opened by that of sense" (1975a:217). It is true that the question of sense and reference does not even arise except for language as used by a subject (whether speaker, writer, listener, or reader), and thus the argument can be leveled that this movement from sense to reference is not a property of meaning per se, but of the animating intention of the language user. And it is true that we can only discuss meaning as so correlated. The question, though, is whether meaning (as so necessarily correlated with a subject) appears (when considered phenomenologically, i.e. as presenting its own evidence) as inherently moving from sense to reference. Ricoeur grants, in agreement with Frege, that ". . . *we* are not satisfied with a sense, we presuppose a reference" (Ricoeur 1975a:219; emphasis added). Thus he admits that this "ontological *vehemence*" (Ricoeur 1975a:249), this "*belief*" (Ricoeur 1975a:249) that whatever we are

172

saying is somehow about that which exists, does reside in us as human subjects. However, he goes beyond this to assert that the more fundamental condition of being-in-the-world (as discussed in chapter 6) is also the basis of the presupposition of reference:

> It is because there is first something to say, because we have an experience to bring to language, that conversely, language is not only directed towards ideal meanings but also refers to what is (Ricoeur 1976:21).[20]

Consequently, the movement within meaning from sense to reference, though reflected in the intention of the language user, has its foundation in man's ontological status, and in that sense, is "animated" from a much more fundamental source. Heidegger calls this "source" Being; Ricoeur, though attentive to this terminology, prefers a more "personal" (Ricoeur 1975a:312) term, and while not yet offering a clear substitute, suggests something more active, even organic (Ricoeur 1975a:215), perhaps "life" itself (Ricoeur 1975a:303ff). Finally, it seems that the "ontological vehemence" of man as language user belongs to that which transcends man (Ricoeur 1975a:299ff). But about that transcendence, Ricoeur is as yet (philosophically) silent (except for hints here and there in his writings).[21]

The final manifestation of the dynamism of meaning is also our last aspect of meaning to be discussed: Meaning reveals a world and affects the reader. Here we need only draw together strands of previous discussions: The ontological vehemence to refer and the meaning of the "world." That to which meaning refers is, for Ricoeur, finally that ontological correlate of man's being, the "world." The "world," though, due to writing (cf. chapter 2), ". . . is no longer what can be shown in speaking but is reduced to a kind of 'aura' which written works unfold" (Ricoeur 1981a:149). This "aura," however, is none other than the images which surround words (Ricoeur 1975a:211, 214) as noted in section 1. What a text reveals is new dimensions of our being as man (i.e. being-in-the-world; Ricoeur 1981a:202), presented in "outline" (Ricoeur 1981a:202) or "sketch" (Ricoeur 1981a:300), arising out of "reality" (Ricoeur 1975a:42, 229, 257ff) understood as an active (Ricoeur 1975a:42ff; "the Real as Act," 43), lively (Ricoeur 1975a:43), even life-giving (Ricoeur 1975a:303) reservoir of meaning (Ricoeur 1981a:119). As the situation of metaphor

---

[20] This is just another application of what was presented in chapter 4 as the priority of semantics over semiotics.

[21] Ricoeur terms this "transcendence" at one point "language" (1975a:311), but says very little about it (see below). However, the unfinished volumes of his overall, life-long philosophical project ("The philosophy of the will") is projected to be a "Poetics of the will," which promises to lift the previous (methodological) bracketing of the transcendent, and explicitly integrate this aspect. Thus, by design, the role, status, and character of the transcendent is not yet well developed in Ricoeur's work.

illustrates, the "new referential field" (Ricoeur 1975a:299) which metaphor displays ".... is already in some way present in a still unarticulated manner, and . . . it exerts an attraction on the already constituted sense in order to tear it from its initial haven" (Ricoeur 1975a:299).[22] Thus meaning is not "a stable form," but is "dynamic, directional, vectoral [in] character" (Ricoeur 1975a:299). Finally, reference is to "Reality" (Ricoeur 1975a:42), and the power of meaning which Ricoeur uncovers through a study of metaphor is the power of language "to make contact with being as such" (Ricoeur 1975a:43). What metaphor reveals is "the Real as Act" (Ricoeur 1975a:43), a being which is polysemous (Ricoeur 1975a:311) and alive (Ricoeur 1975a:43), even personal (Ricoeur 1975a:312).

In conclusion, Ricoeur disallows the role of the reader as finally determinative of meaning. He credits "the text" with a "revelatory power implicit in . . . discourse" (Ricouer 1981a:191; cf. 180, 182) which transcends language itself (Ricoeur 1981a:181), and is finally grounded in "being." What the reading of a text reveals is "the Real as Act," itself active in decisive ways with respect to the reader. Before turning to a more detailed consideration of this in the next section, it will be useful to compare Ricoeur's solution to the origin of "the new" with that of Poulet and Iser.

In terms of the status of transcendence--the issue which divides Poulet and Iser most decisively--Ricoeur seems to split the difference. First, he sides with Iser in emphasizing the role of the text, rather than the reader. And yet, he does not lean on "the author's thoughts" as does Iser. Rather, he places the manifestation of *the world* by the text at the center of his concept of reading (Ricoeur 1981a:193). In doing so he draws near to that Hegelian tradition of self-presentation which Iser criticizes in Poulet. Ricoeur (1981a:193) acknowledges this, and yet claims that he sufficiently distances his position from the Hegelian to avoid the pitfalls of that tradition. First, the role given to "the world" rather than Self or Spirit (as in the Hegelian tradition), distances Ricoeur from Hegel. Says Ricoeur (1981a:178):

> What we make our own, what we appropriate for ourselves, is not an alien experience or a distant intention, but the horizon of a world towards which a work directs itself. The appropriation of the reference is no longer modelled on the fusion of consciousnesses, on empathy or sympathy. The emergence of the sense and the reference of a text in language is the coming to language of a world and not the recognition of another person.

---

[22] This is Ricoeur's phenomenological uncovering of the activity of being as meaning. Here the other sense of transcendence of language alluded to above emerges in an as yet rather obscure form.

In brief, opposed to a "fusion of consciousnesses" is a "fusion of horizons [of worlds]" (Ricoeur 1981a:177). Second, the recognition that

> . . . this self-presentation [of the world of the text returns] to the event of speech in which, *ultimately*, interpretation [reading] is accomplished signifies that philosophy mourns the loss of absolute knowledge [which the Hegelian tradition asserts] (Ricoeur 1981a:193).

While it is true that the pitfall of absolute knowledge is avoided,[23] it seems that Ricoeur does not avoid the necessary role of transcendence, as Iser might like.[24] Rather, Ricoeur even sketches aspects that transcendence manifests; e.g. active, polysemous, etc.[25] Thus, Ricoeur's thought opens toward a reuniting with Poulet's and yet the mediating role of the text and the world which it manifests both avoids certain objectionable aspects of Hegelianism and reveals further characteristics of transcendence itself.[26]

---

[23] There simply is no standpoint from which a finite being could grasp the totality (of all that is) as implied in the notion of absolute knowledge; thus all human knowledge is always perspectival, and consequently limited.

[24] On the other hand, it must be acknowledged that Iser also leans upon a notion of transcendence (of sorts). He says, for instance, with regard to the dynamic interaction of text and reader, and its character as event, "It [the fictional text] does not even have to relate to any cultural code common to itself and its reader, for its 'reality' arises out of something more basic: the nature of reality itself" (Iser 1978:67f). This "nature of reality" which is more basic than cultural codes indicates a notion of (at least) quasi-transcendence quite close to Ricoeur's "the Real as Act." Consequently, Iser's resistance to Poulet's "substantialist notion of consciousness"--granting Ricoeur's critique of Hegelianism--is even less persuasive.

[25] The expansion and clarification of this point is the topic of chapter 9, section 5. Further development toward my comments regarding transcendence also occurs in chapter 8.

[26] Palmer (1969:215ff) claims, I think rightly, that Gadamer's reliance on the Hegelian dialectic helps him to escape the all-consuming role of language in the later Heidegger. Because this tendency in Heidegger continues to be played out today, it is worth noting that Ricoeur too avoids this overemphasis on passivity. Such an overemphasis claims that understanding is only an event which happens to man. There is activity too, but in paradoxical unity with passivity. As Ricoeur puts it, defending the role of man as a language user, "Languages do not speak, people do" (1976:13). The slogan of the extreme Heideggerians, on the other hand, is "Language speaks man," rather than "Man speaks Language."

7.5   The reader as subject

7.5.1   The reader, self-understanding, and decoding

For Ricoeur, all understanding is finally self-understanding (1981a:143f, 158f, 192f), and for Iser, "The constitution of meaning . . . gains its full significance when something *happens* to the reader" (1978:152). Thus, our final topic is the effect of reading on the reader. These concluding considerations will further clarify the role of the reader in reading and will prepare us for the two chapters to follow.

No one claims that a person is a reader if he only knows certain decoding skills (by which letters on a page are more than black marks). Nor can it be claimed that the mere possession of such skills is sufficient to constitute one a reader, unless, of course, these skills are so broadly defined as to exceed their usual bottom-up formulation (cf. chapter 1) and include such factors as background knowledge of the world, inferencing skills, etc. Thus in a most fundamental way, the ability to decode a text is a necessary prerequisite for reading. These are what Ricoeur calls "the explanatory procedures"(e.g. Ricoeur 1981a:192; cf. chapter 2.1) which necessarily mediate the meaning of the text, procedures designed as it were, to meet the distanciations of the text, and overcome them.This "overcoming" is the goal of reading (Ricoeur 1981a:158); it is that constitution of meaning which is comprehension. However,

> . . . understanding the text is not an end in itself; it
> mediates the relation to himself of a subject who,
> in short circuit of immediate reflection, does not
> find the meaning of his own life (Ricoeur
> 1981a:158).

Thus, the "culmination of the understanding of a text . . . [is] self-understanding" (Ricoeur 1981a:158). The point that both Ricoeur and Iser would have us recognize is that "the constitution of the *self* is contemporaneous with the constitution of *meaning*" (Ricoeur 1981a:159; cf. Iser 1978:152).[27] And it would seem that the reading researchers have (almost) entirely ignored this point. More on that later (cf. sections 5.2 and 5.4).

---

[27] This statement of the constitution of the self needs further clarification. The point in focus here is the new self which occurs in reading and emerges together with, and dependent on, the meaning of the text. The next section (5.2) speaks to the question of the self in a more general sense. The point developed there which bears on this discussion is that there is a self which is preexistent to the emergence of the new self in reading (or elsewhere).

176

While decoding skills are traditionally associated with the bottom-up theories of reading, it must be acknowledged that they are skills which the reader as subject has been taught, and thus can also be considered part of the top-down contribution of the reader. It is true, though, that these skills are highly conventional and show a great deal of uniformity, reflecting perhaps the character of the codes which they decode: collective, systematic, compulsory (Ricoeur 1976:3). At the "lower levels" of letter, word, syntax, even discourse structure recognition, such decoding seems to proceed with a highly predictable regularity. In all cases (though with less agreement as the units of discourse become larger), such decoding is necessary to reading.Even the role of schemas (those of the reading specialists, that is) can be seen as playing a necessary part in this process, emphasizing once again that the "bottom-up" processes are also "top-down." After all, the low level recognition of letters or words (whether or not they are decoded to sound) is also (in the schema-theoretic account) a matter of matching input with already possessed schemas, in this case, the schema for the letter or word in question. And in all cases, these schemas have been learned (whether or not there is some pre-existent innate competence).

These decoding processes, however, have a definite effect on the reader. The most explicit effect which Ricoeur notes is decidedly "negative." Because the codes of the text possess the character of *la langue* as outlined earlier (e.g. anonymous, not intended, a synchronic system; cf. chapter 4), a process of alienation is begun in the reader which is furthered as meaning is constructed. As noted in chapter 2, a process and relation quite other than the dialogical situation is initiated by the reading of a text. Because meaning is ideal, the "ideality of the text remains the mediator in this process" (Ricoeur1981a:192). The "explanatory [decoding] procedures" imply a universality and atemporality which works to affect a moment of dispossession of the reading ego: a separation of itself from itself. Begun in simple decoding, continued in the construction of meaning as sense, this process of dispossession culminates in the movement from sense to reference.

> Reading is an appropriation-divestiture. How can this letting-go, this relinquishment, be incorporated into appropriation? Essentially by linking appropriation to the revelatory power of the text which we have described as its referential dimension. It is in allowing itself to be carried off towards the reference of the text that the ego divests itself of itself (Ricoeur 1981a:191).

The point is that to account for reading only in terms of the reader-- "to find only oneself in a text, to impose and rediscover oneself" (Ricoeur 1981a:191), as seems to be the case in current schema theories with their inability to account for "the new"--is narcissistic indeed and ignores the obvious gain so often experienced by readers. The phenomenologists recognize that more, in fact, is going on in reading. Before the gain is

177

appropriated, though, the "false consciousness" (to speak in Marxist terms) or the "narcissistic ego" (to use Freudian language) must be "put off." This is the function of "the texture of the text" (Ricoeur 1981a:143) which the reader must decode. The transference of discourse to "a sphere of ideality" which writing implies, carries with it a similar transfer of the reader in reading (Ricoeur 1976:91f; 1981a:144). This is the point at which the primacy of the subject in modern philosophy (i.e. Descartes, Kant, Husserl; cf. Ricoeur 1981a:190) and modern reading theory is most radically challenged. As Dufrenne (1973:555) notes with regard to the aesthetic experience,

> The spectator also alienates himself in the aesthetic object, as if to sacrifice himself for the sake of its advent and as if this were a duty which he must fulfill. Still, losing himself in this way, the spectator finds himself. He must contribute something to the aesthetic object. This does not mean that he should add to the object a commentary consisting of images or representations which will eventually lead him away from aesthetic experience. Rather, he must be himself fully by gathering himself together as a whole, without forcing the silent plenitude of the work to become explicit or extracting any representations from the treasure trove. Thus the spectator's alienation is simply the culmination of the process of attention by which he discovers that the world of the aesthetic object into which he is plunged is also *his* world. He is at home in this world. He understands the affective quality revealed by the work because he *is* that quality, just as the artist is his work.

Dufrenne's insights here--the new self, the new "at-homeness," and the new affective quality--are developed in the following sections.

7.5.2 The reader, self-understanding, and the new self

This "loss of self," though, is also the precondition of "finding oneself." Again we return to the discussions of the previous section: The "new" is given by the text. But now we say that as the new is given as a proposed world, the reader is exposed to a power which proposes "an enlarged self" (Ricoeur 1981a:143), an "imaginative variation of the ego" (Ricoeur 1981a:144), a "new capacity for knowing himself" (Ricoeur 1981a:192), a "new mode of being" (Ricoeur 1981a:192). Rather than submitting the text to "the finite capacities of understanding of a present reader" (Ricoeur 1981a:192; as with schema theory, e.g.), the "reader is . . .

broadened in his capacity to project himself by receiving a new mode of being from the text itself" (Ricoeur 1981a:192).[28]

Ricoeur's account, though, is incomplete. On the one hand, he asserts that "the revelation . . . gives the subject new capacities" (1981a:192), it "opens up its readers and thus creates its own subjective vis-a-vis ["face-to-face" situation, which is only "like" dialogue, not identical to it; cf. 1981a:159, 139]" (Ricoeur 1981a:143). On the other hand, he acknowledges that the "new" is only proposed (Ricoeur 1981a:143), and the reader is exposed to what must be received (Ricoeur 1981a:143, 192). On the one hand, there is the assumption of an "efficacious calling" by the text, a bestowal to the subject of a new capacity below the threshold of conscious control. On the other, there is only the proposal of the text to which "I offer myself" (Ricoeur 1981a:177), a "letting-go" (Ricoeur 1981a:191), an "allowing itself to be carried off towards . . ." (Ricoeur 1981a:191). Ricoeur's formulations are reminiscent of the theologians" discussions of the mysteries of grace, questions which need not detain us here, except to note that the bestowal of a "self" to the reader is imputed to a "text" which nowhere is discussed by Ricoeur in such personalistic terms. We come again to Ricoeur's unfinished explications of transcendence.

Iser's account is different. While Ricoeur speaks of the possibilities of new modes of being, Iser speaks in terms of consciousness. Presumably Ricoeur's new being is also a transformed consciousness. And yet Iser speaks primarily of a cleansed consciousness and a new ability to see clearly. While Ricoeur hints that "the Real" itself is unfolded in reading and presented as new possibilities within even ordinary everyday reality (e.g. Ricoeur 1975a:246f), Iser seems less radical, recognizing only the becoming conscious of ourselves and our experience in a fresh way (Iser 1978:128, 133f, 157f). The essential operation for Iser is image-building with its elimination of the subject-object division, the reinstitution of which, on the cessation of reading, brings an awakening by which "for a brief period at least, the real world appears observable" (Iser 1978:140). However, Iser does suggest that new knowledge can be gained while caught up in the "irreal" world of the text, and that this new knowledge can be applied, upon "awakening," to "our own world," and thus "our own world" can be "freshly understood" (1978:140).[29] "Further, he acknowledges a

---

[28] The "text" which "gives" cannot, though, be identified with the simple codes of the text. Rather, the "text" is here the origin of the new in the "obscure" sense discussed in section 4.

[29] Though the arguments for this position are developed using examples from "great literature," there is no reason to believe that the same phenomena don't occur with all reading. The profundity of the enrichment, of course, would vary with the reader and the material, but the awakening process is part of the very structure of reading, and not a function of the material being read. Consider, for example, the phenomena of browsing in a book store and even the reading of the newspaper. I find the phenomenon of distancing

179

previously unconscious "layer of his [the reader's] personality" (Iser 1978:50; "an inner world," 158) coming to consciousness in reading. It may be that the difference between Ricoeur and Iser here is simply a reflection of the previously noted difference with regard to transcendence: Iser finally rests "transcendence" within the reader; while Ricoeur acknowledges that which is radically other than the reading subject. As a consequence, Iser's approach reflects a greater emphasis on the reader's role in reading, while Ricoeur highlights the influence and importance of that which is other than the reader.

The problem of the new self in reading requires both perspectives in a more integrated manner than is presently available in either Ricoeur or Iser. Riceour's emphasis on the "ontological" activity of the text gives an account of how something new is introduced to the reader: Something other than man is active in the process. Further, this "something other" is sufficiently like man to enable and enact the kinds of changes of man actually observed in reading. Ricoeur, though, seems to have overreacted to the recognition of the bestowal of a self through reading. Such statements as "the constitution of the *self* is contemporaneous with the constitution of *meaning*" (Ricoeur 1981a:159), and ". . . the text . . . gives a self to the *ego*" (Ricoeur 1981a:193), where "*ego*" seems to be "the narcissistic ego" (Ricoeur 1981a:192) or "false consciousness" (Ricoeur 1981a:191), can give the impression that prior to the understanding of a text the reader is not a self.[32] "Understanding," indeed *true* understanding, seems to be the key to the self/ego distinction in Ricoeur. However, Ricoeur's ontological interpretation of understanding as that which always precedes and supports any act of knowing and which can itself never be totally encompassed by human knowing, works against this self/ego distinction. If understanding is the key, and if we always possess (or are prepossessed by) ontological preunderstanding, then we are "always already" selves too, at least in a preliminary form.[30]

Ricoeur, in fact, needs this "pre-self" at the heart of the ego if the ego is to allow ". . . itself to be carried off towards the reference of the text . . . [and thus] divest itself of itself" (Ricoeur 1981a:191). How else could the ego "divest itself of itself" in a thoroughgoing fashion and still the new self have anything to do with the pre-reading person? If an account of

---

from the situation around me to be quite evident in these cases too. As Barthes (1979:79) puts it: "There is no structural difference between 'cultured' reading and casual subway reading."

[30] This line of argument also implies that if there is no element of truth in the preunderstanding, then there can never be any hope of knowing that we know the truth in subsequent acts of knowing. If the preunderstanding which always supports and influences knowing were itself always and thoroughly false, then all knowing would also always be false, though not known as such since there would be no unsullied access to anything true by which to judge the false to be so.

reading is to be adequate to the continuity of the person in spite of the newness experienced, there must be a self which endures throughout "ego-divestiture." It would seem evident that we as readers have as much confidence in our continuity as we do in the newness, if not more.[31]

Iser, on the other hand, acknowledges that reading does in fact uncover previously unconscious layers of the reader's personality (Iser 1978:50). That is, the reader is developed/enriched/expanded by reading, but it is precisely the same reader who is so developed. As Iser (1978:155) says,

> Thus there occurs a kind of artificial division as the reader brings into his own foreground something which he is not. This does not mean, though, that his own orientations disappear completely. However much they may recede into the past, they still form the background against which the prevailing thoughts of the author take on thematic significance. In reading, then, there are always two levels, and despite the multifarious ways in which they may be related they can never be totally kept apart. Indeed, we *can only* bring another person's thoughts into our foreground if they are in some way related to the virtual background of our own orientations (for otherwise they would be totally incomprehensible). Thus Iser gives a more adequate account of the continuity of the reader in reading than does Ricoeur; but, as noted in section 4, a less adequate account of the discontinuity, i.e. the newness, of the reader.

Obviously, I favor elements of both Ricoeur and Iser. The desired theory, then, must acknowledge transcendence of a sort compatible with both the continuities and discontinuities experienced and observed in the reading process. Further, this transcendence must be of the sort that promotes a greater knowledge of itself along with the gains of "self-understanding" of the reader. If not, then the continuities between itself and the reader which are necessary for the bestowal of a *new self* in reading would be disrupted and such bestowal would become both ineffectual and ungrounded.

---

[31] Further, this confidence cannot be shaken by any critique of illusions, for the acceptance of any such critique depends on the recognition of a truer self. This recognition, though, involves and implies some means by which the "truer self" can be recognized as in fact a "self." Without continuity of the self, of some sort, such recognition would be strictly impossible. Without this continuity, critique itself would be totally ineffective.

7.5.3 The reader and "dwelling"

Regardless of the differences between Ricoeur and Iser on the preceding point, both acknowledge that the mode of the reader's responding to a text is finally that of "inhabiting" (Ricoeur 1981a:56; 1978b:151) or dwelling in (Iser 1978:128) the living world of the text. Since this notion has appeared nowhere in my research of the reading specialists, and since it will become an especially significant notion in the next chapter, it deserves further elaboration here.

The two phenomenologists who have developed the notion of "dwelling" more than others are Heidegger and Bachelard. Ricoeur draws on both of these thinkers (cf. e.g. Ricoeur 1970, 1974, 1975a, 1976, 1978b, 1981a). Iser, however, neither develops the notion himself, nor refers directly to the work of others on the subject. It is, then, to a brief introduction of Heidegger's and Bachelard's notion of dwelling that we now turn.[32]

In both Heidegger and Bachelard, "dwelling" is of fundamental importance because it is the fundamental mode of man's being-in-the-world.

> The way in which you are and I am, the manner
> in which we humans *are* on earth, is . . . dwelling.
> To be a human being means to be on the earth as
> a mortal. It means to dwell (Heidegger 1977:325).

This fundamental dwelling, however, is not a simple phenomenon. There are two modes to this dwelling, cultivating and constructing. Cultivating highlights man's caring for and nurturing that which is given to him as independent of him in its essential nature. Man, e.g., cultivates plant life, but man cannot make plants grow nor produce that which grows of itself. On the other hand, man can and does construct that which does not grow, buildings for example. Constructing highlights man's contribution to dwelling. Both aspects--cultivating and constructing--are integral to human dwelling.

From the perspective of a reader, these two modes of dwelling serve as the basis for the recognized processes: Cultivating highlights the "giving way to" the text, the letting oneself be driven by the shape and character of the text--the "bottom-up" processes; while constructing emphasizes the reader's active building of meaning--the top-down processes. Iser uses "image-building" to note these two activities, while Ricoeur notes both intuitive and discursive moments in the comprehension of texts. Reading,

---

[32] Since I am concerned here with an introduction only, I will only present a brief, unified notion. Both the differences between these two writers and the subtleties of each will be overlooked.

182

then, becomes an apprenticeship in dwelling, the cultivation and construction of man's truest being.

Reading is specially suited to this important task because in it the intimate relation between man and the world, man and man, and man and transcendence (the latter two as mediated by that world) is revealed. We have already noted Iser's and Poulet's recognition of the suspension of the subject-object relation in reading. Similarly, Bachelard notes, with respect to the reveries of poetic reading,

> A world takes form in our reverie, and this world is ours. This dreamed world teaches us the possibilities for expanding our being within our universe (1969:8).

But further, properly attended to, the ". . . poetic image places us at the origin of the speaking being" (Bachelard 1964:xix), and as such, at the origin of "the world of the text." Consequently, the origin of creativeness (Bachelard 1964:xx)--Iser's mobilization of spontaneity--is uncovered as this creativeness emerges in human consciousness. And this "proper mode of attending" to the image is dwelling.

Dwelling--as cultivating and constructing--further reveals the paradoxical unity of activity-passivity noted earlier. With dwelling, though, there is (for Heidegger) the revelation of an internal ordering of the poles of this paradox. As Heidegger puts it, "The fundamental character of dwelling is this sparing" (1977:327), which

> . . . consists not only in the fact that we do not harm the one whom we spare. Real sparing is something *positive* and takes place when we leave something beforehand in its own essence, when we return it specifically to its essential being ... (1977:327).

Here, "to dwell" means "to be set at peace," to safeguard "each thing in its nature" (Heidegger 1977:327). Here, the activity of constructing gives way to the more passive recognition and cultivation of "each thing in its nature."

To read in this "sparing" way is to grant the text the life it awaits, and seems to beg for (Poulet 1969:53). This is that fundamental receptivity which cultivates with respect what is given in and by the text. The bottom-up processes highlight the necessity of this fundamental receptivity.[33]

---

[33] For Bachelard 1969, calling on Jungian terminology, this is "reading in *anima*" which is essentially receptive and attentive to the life of the image. The alternative is a "reading in *animus*" which is critical reading and whose tool is the concept. This distinction is

But, as we know from both the reading specialists and the phenomenologists, this is not all there is to reading. The active participation of the reader must also be acknowledged; and acknowledged as active even in and for the sake of the passive recognition. But how are the two processes related? "In what way does building belong to dwelling?" Heidegger asks for us (1977:329). Heidegger uses the bridge as an example of a built thing to pursue his answer to this question. This is especially fortunate for us, for such a choice facilitates our transfer to reading, which Ricoeur presents under the figure of the arches of a bridge (Ricoeur 1981a:164). I will attempt the transfer of Heidegger's reflections on dwelling to reading after first presenting a summary of these reflections.

Essentially, the bridge, in Heidegger's reflections, *gathers*. The bridge gathers the banks and ". . . designedly causes them to lie across from each other" (Heidegger 1977:330) in the experience of men. The banks, though, do not remain alone, for

> With the banks, the bridge brings to the stream
> the one and other expanse of the landscape lying
> behind them. It brings stream and bank and land
> into each other's neighborhood. The bridge
> gathers the earth as landscape around the stream
> (Heidegger 1977:330).

Thus the bridge appears to guide and attend the stream on its way, unhindered by the bridge-piers which sink deep into the river bed to support the arch.

The bridge, however, not only gathers the earth around it, but opens a way for man to travel, thus gathering man and earth. Further, the arch of the bridge gathers the sky and with it "the haleness of the divinities" (Heidegger 1977:331), whether or not these "divinities" are thought of or acknowledged (Heidegger 1977:331).

Heidegger summarizes: "The bridge *gathers* to itself in *its own* way earth and sky, divinities and mortals" (Heidegger 1977:331). The bridge, then, is a location which "allows a site for the fourfold [earth, sky, divinities and mortals]" (Heidegger 1977:331), a place for the unfolding of the interrelations among the fourfold admitted and installed by the building.

But what, then, is building in the verbal (versus "nominal") sense? For Heidegger, building is a "letting dwell," a bringing forth and preserving of the fourfold (Heidegger 1977:336f). It is a responding "to the summons of the fourfold" (Heidegger 1977:337). And yet, it too is based upon that dwelling which is *"the basic character of Being* in keeping with which mortals exist" (Heidegger 1977:338): *"Only if we are capable of dwelling, only then can we build"* (Heidegger 1977:338).

---

reflected in Ricoeur's dialectic of belonging and distanciation. The (more or less) obvious correlation to "right/left brain" research will only be noted in passing here.

I do not claim that this (near) poetic language of Heidegger clarifies all that needs to be or could be said. In fact, Heidegger admits that, "Enough will have been gained if dwelling and building have become *worthy of questioning* and thus have remained *worthy of thought*" (Heidegger 1977:338). It is in that spirit that Heidegger's thoughts have been shared here. Our particular concern, though, is with how dwelling and building are worthy of further thought with respect to reading.

Already in this chapter we have noted that construction is basic to reading. Resemblance (section 2) and disclosure (section 4) have revealed the most about constructing. We have also developed at length man's status as being-in-the-world and have noted how the world of the text unfolds through the interplay of sense and reference, and with it a new being for the reader. This interplay--in which the reader participates--is that dwelling which both cultivates the unfolding of the text and builds that world which is the final reference of the text. Reading, then, prepares a dwelling place for the reader which is proposed to the reader as a new mode of being or a new way of dwelling in the world. Heidegger's conception of dwelling can help us see reading as a gathering together of the (fourfold)[34] elements involved in human life. Already we have recognized an element of transcendence--perhaps what Heidegger means by "the divinities"--at the heart of reading. Further, the bridge joins different aspects of the earth and provides commerce between men in new ways. So too reading builds bridges between men and presents new ways of relating one to another. Across the bridge of the text men and materials (the earth) are brought together--first of all, the reader and the "author." But further, all readers of the text are (at least potentially) "gathered" toward one another, for the world(s) of the text generated by the reading(s) are no doubt related due to the mediation of the common text. The common text, in fact, establishes the relatedness of its readings and its readers. In Gadamer's words, horizons are fused.

Ricoeur's notion of the hermeneutic arc further enriches the relation of dwelling and reading. The bridging which the reading accomplishes is itself an enrichment of human dwelling. The result of reading is an expansion of one's horizons with regard to what it means to be human. A growth of self-understanding is offered. New potentialities and possibilities are awakened, however faintly. The "sky," and not just the "earth," at least begins to be the limit. With such an expansion of horizons--the gathering of earth to earth, and the new possibilities opened up by such a bridging, as well as the gathering of sky to earth which expands the possibilities even further--comes a (at least incipient) critique of one's present circumstances: the ability to see "the here and now" in a fresh way, as that which does not necessarily have to be the case. This is

---

[34] Heidegger's particular "fourfold" is not very important in itself to the development to follow, either with regard to the number 4 or the content. His "fourfold" will be played with (conceptually) in what follows. It is hoped that such play might "turn up" something of significance.

accomplished by the arc in Ricoeur's scheme, and it is the topic of chapter 8. It is because reading inherently offers the possibility of critique (due to its presentation of different ways of dwelling) that dwelling is both theoretically and practically important. As we will see in the next chapter, "practical" here even means "political."

At the basis of this whole process of constructing, the play of the imagination has recurred (cf. sections 1-4): the interplay of sense and reference, identity and difference, the new and the old, etc. So fundamental has the imagination been, that perhaps the mode of "play" is at least as fundamental as that of dwelling. Seemingly, the two are mutually qualifying: man's dwelling (in the specifically human sense of living in the world and not just in an environment) is due to the constructing which is generated by the interplay of the imagination; and yet, the "image-building" of reading is itself dependent on the ontological *pre*-belonging which is itself another name for dwelling, man's fundamenal givenness as "in-the-world." Identifying the interplay of the imagination with poetics, I can conclude--with Heidegger--that "poetically man dwells" (Heidegger 1971:211ff). Moreover, if Beardsley's designation of metaphor as "a poem in miniature" (Beardsley 1958:134) is acknowledged, further confirmation is given to the prominence I have granted to metaphor throughout the preceding chapters.

This section has been playful and serves to prepare the way for upcoming conceptual clarification. In chapter 8 the issue of dwelling in the quite practical sense of the quality of life--with all the implied possibilities of sociological, anthropological, even political analyses--will be raised again. There the issue of dwelling and one's awareness of it are examined as taken to the heart of reading theory and practice by Paulo Freire. Furthermore, the notion of play is itself the major topic of chapter 9 where it serves as a central notion for reading theory.

7.5.4 The reader and the affections

The final area to be discussed here with regard to the reader as subject is the role of affect in the reading process. Already we have noted with Athey and Spiro (cf. Chapter 6) that the affections are a neglected area in reading theory. The affections have, however, been recognized by the phenomenologists as significantly involved in aesthetic experience in general, and in reading in particular. Consequently, we turn to the phenomenological account of reading to learn more about the role of the affections in this process.

First, we note that affection is *not* involved as some kind of congenial coincidence with the intention and/or affections of the author. As Ricoeur's critique of this notion makes plain,

> Thanks to distanciation by writing, appropriation
> [of meaning, i.e. comprehension; cf. Ricoeur
> 1976:92] no longer has any trace of affective

186

affinity with the intention of the author. Appropriation is quite the contrary of contemporaneousness and congeniality: it is understanding at and through distance (Ricoeur 1981a:143).

Second, it is helpful to note that F.C. Bartlett (1932), a work to which much contemporary schema theory harkens,[35] developed a concept of remembering which integrates feeling or affect at its heart. Knowledge of the past (i.e. remembering, in some sense) is, of course, central to schema theory's notion of comprehension, and thus one would expect that those contemporary theories which acknowledge a fundamental debt to Bartlett 1932 would also give a prominent place to "affect" (as he did). However, as Spiro (1980:271f) points out,

> Given the avalanche of research triggered by the revival of interest in Bartlett's (1932) thinking about constructive processes, it is remarkable that a central aspect of that thinking has been totally ignored. I refer to his concept of the "attitude" . . . . [By attitude] he meant "a general impression of the whole . . . a complex state or process which it is very hard to describe in more elementary psychological terms . . . very largely a matter of feeling or affect" (pp. 206-207).

Spiro goes on to explore, "in a speculative line" (Spiro 1980:272), what these "summary feelings" (his term so as to avoid the confusion over the contemporary use of "attitude") might be. Rather than focus on the structure of knowledge alone, he recommends considering ". . . the texture that must be felt" (Spiro 1980:273). Rather than focusing on the analytic properties of concepts, he suggests also attending to "the *experience* of having an idea" (Spiro 1980:273; emphasis added). Further, Spiro speculates that affect plays a role in how things "appear," which he identifies with the feel of how things fit (with one another in understanding) and with "images" (Spiro 1980:273). Finally, he suggests that ". . . feelings and characteristics of knowledge that enable them may be an appropriate place to start looking for the answer to that most important question of conceptual change" (Spiro 1980:274).

We will return to these thoughts of Bartlett and Spiro, but introduce them here to call attention to the similarities with the previous discussion of images and the schema (section 1). You will recall that there I presented Ricoeur's notion of the schema, in which meaning and images were interrelated. There I only hinted that feeling also played a role in

---

[35] Note, for example, the documentation given in Iran-Nejad (1980:20f) to which I add Spiro 1980.

187

this process. Now we return to those considerations with regard to the role of feeling or affection.

Remembering that Ricoeur presents the metaphorical process as paradigmatic for textual understanding in general, we look at the role of feeling in that process.[36] Ricoeur contends that ". . . feeling has a place not just in theories of metaphor which deny the cognitive import of metaphor" (1978b:153). Rather, he claims that both the imagination and feeling are "genuine components" of the process by which metaphor achieves a semantic bearing (Ricoeur 1978b:153).

Before characterizing feelings directly, Ricoeur first clears the way by distinguishing feelings from emotions. It is a "bad psychology of feeling," he says, to conceive of the affections as either

> (1) inwardly directed states of mind, . . . [or] (2) mental experiences closely tied to bodily disturbances, as is the case in fear, anger, pleasure, and pain (Ricoeur 1978b:153).

In short, emotions display "little intentionality" (Ricoeur 1978b:154) and are "under the spell of our body" (Ricoeur 1978b:153). "Genuine feelings," on the other hand, "enjoy a specific kinship with language" (Ricoeur 1978b:154). Using poetic feelings as the example, he says that "They are properly displayed by the poem as a verbal texture" (Ricoeur 1978b:154). Generally speaking, it seems that the work of Bartlett 1932 and Spiro 1980 does avoid this "bad psychology of feeling," for the emphasis of their work is, as we will see, very much in line with Ricoeur's own.[37] Athey 1982, on the other hand, is concerned with the whole affective domain, including both (what Ricoeur considers) emotion (e.g. anxiety, Athey 1982:203; emotional satisfaction, 214; excitement, 214; hate, 214; love, 215) and feeling (e.g. self-consistency, Athey 1982:216f; "beliefs, values, and attitudes (including beliefs and attitudes about the self)," 216). The important point, from Ricoeur's perspective, is that the constructive role of the imagination be acknowledged (Ricoeur 1978b:153), a point which attention to "emotion" (in Ricoeur's sense) masks. Bartlett and Spiro do indeed focus on this directly, and Athey, though acknowledging

---

[36] I draw primarily on Ricoeur's "The metaphorical process as cognition, imagination, and feeling" (1978b), though also on 1975a, 1976, and 1981a.

[37] Though the emphasis does fall on "feelings" rather than "emotions," it is not clear that Bartlett and Spiro make or are even aware of a proper distinction at this point. Note for example, Bartlett's characterization of "attitude" by "doubt, hestitation, surprise, astonishment, confidence, dislike, repulsion and so on" (1932:207), and Spiro's likening the "summary feelings" to a "gut reaction" (1980:273). In both cases, it seems that what both Bartlett and Spiro consider affection, may well fall in Ricoeur's category of "mental experience closely tied to bodily disturbances" (Ricoeur 1978b:153).

this factor as important in reading (e.g. 1982:210f) does not focus on it as especially significant to a consideration of affection.

So important is the imagination that Ricoeur (1978b:154) proposes to ". . . construe the role of feeling according to the three similar moments which provided an articulation to my theory of imagination." First, feelings ". . . accompany and complete imagination in its function of *schematization* of the new predicative congruence" (Ricoeur 1978b:154). The new congruence is " 'felt' as well as 'seen' " (Ricoeur 1978b:154). The fact that it is felt emphasizes that we are participants in the process; the fact that it is a "congruence" which is felt underlines what Spiro calls "*summary* feelings" and the "wholing" function of the imagination noted earlier (cf. section 1). This participation was already noted in the constructive aspect of the imagination. Here, though, the participation is an active being "assimilated, that is, made similar, to what is seen as similar" (Ricoeur 1978b:154). It is here that ". . . poetic feeling itself also develops an experience of reality in which invention and discovery cease being opposed and where creation and revelation coincide" (Ricoeur 1975a:246). In short, the opposition of active and passive is again presented as a paradoxical unity.

Ricoeur further points out that this effect is part of the illocutionary act performed by means of metaphors. Based upon the cognitive structure of thought and the intentional distance implied between knower and known, feeling functions to abolish that distance by making the thought our own--yet without cancelling its "objective" basis. In short, the text acts through our cognitive structures to interiorize our thoughts; an act in which we participate. Here, then, with the completion *in feeling* of the predicative acts involved in the construction of meaning (Ricoeur's "*schematization* of the new predicative congruence" noted above), is Ricoeur's basis for what Iser and Poulet recognize as the elimination of the subject-object division in the experience of reading. Ricoeur's theory, though, is more complex, for (1) he recognizes that that division is not cancelled at the cognitive level by this function of feeling, and (2) what Iser and Poulet discuss in this regard is dealt with most directly by Ricoeur in his third moment of feeling-imagination. We will return to this point there, but thus far we have discussed only the "first moment," the "self-assimilation" (Ricoeur 1978a:154) corresponding to the schematized predicative assimilation.

The second moment of feeling in relation to imagination regards its accompanying and completing imagination as "*picturing* relationships" (1978b:154). Here the iconic character of the image-building is felt.

In relation to a text, this is what Ricoeur terms "the texture of the text" (Ricoeur 1981a:143) which is disclosed by a structural analysis which is "most contrary to subjectivity" (Ricoeur 1981a:143). And yet "feeling" accompanies this structural construction to create a "mood," which is "an affective fiction" (Ricoeur 1975a:245) or "hypothesis" (Ricoeur 1975a:229). Again, feeling functions to overcome the distance of objectivity.

189

With this "second moment," Ricoeur recognizes and locates within the larger theory what Spiro notes (in "speculation") as the role of affect in how things appear. Most interesting, though, is the recognition that the "texture that must be felt" of Spiro (1980:273) is grounded by Ricoeur in the texture disclosed by the structural analysis. Here Ricoeur's theory is most radically opposed to the subjectivist basis of an approach like Spiro's which emphasizes so clearly the creative activity of the reader. With Ricoeur, the "analytic properties" of the text are not opposed to the *experience* of the text, but indeed are its basis. Again, the "dialectical 'circle' " governing Ricoeur's approach integrates and orders, rather than opposes.

Ricoeur considers the third moment of feeling-imagination the most important; that is, feeling's relations to the split structure of imagination, which itself contributes to the split reference of (especially poetic) discourse. Imagination, on the one hand, suspends direct and ordinary reference by referring to what is absent, and on the other, generates models or pictures for "reading reality in a new way" (Ricoeur 1978b:155). Ricoeur proposes that feelings, too, ". . . display a split structure which completes the split structure pertaining to the cognitive component of metaphor" (Ricoeur 1978b:155). Feelings are "negative" in that they function in reading to suspend our everyday literal emotions: When we read, we do not literally feel fear or anger" (Ricoeur 1978b:155). But, as with imagination, this "negative" side ". . . is only the reverse side of a more deeply rooted operation of feeling which is to insert us within the world in a nonobjectifying manner" (Ricoeur 1978b:155). Here is the ontological dimension of feelings:

> Because of feelings we are "attuned to" aspects of
> reality which cannot be expressed in terms of the
> objects referred to in ordinary language (Ricoeur
> 1978b:156).

Here the "mood" or "state of soul" is carried from "sense" to "reference" and is "a way of finding or sensing oneself in the midst of reality" (Ricoeur 1975a:229). This way of putting it emphasizes what Ricoeur is careful to insist upon: " . . . this attunement is nothing else than the reverberation in terms of feelings of the split reference of both verbal and imaginative structure" (1978b:156).

Here with the third moment of feeling, we can return most directly to the concern of Iser and Poulet with regard to the effect of reading on the reader. That which happens to the reader in reading is a "temporary process of self-alienation" (Iser 1978:154), a "split between subject and himself" (Iser 1978:156), "a contrapuntally structured personality in reading" (Iser 1978:156). The "split" enables the subject to be present to the text and yet it also creates a tension. It is in this context that Iser introduces "affection" as a dynamic principle which ". . . stimulates the desire to regain coherence which the subject had lost through being separated from himself" (Iser 1978:157). Here, as with Ricoeur, "affection"

190

is called upon as a second-order intentionality (Ricoeur 1978b:154) which follows the first-order intentionality of "image-building." A separation has been affected which cannot be overcome by recourse to past orientations alone, since the new experience evoked by reading must be incorporated: One of the "selves" is old, the other "new," and it is these two which must be reunited, or better, reintegrated. The process proceeds as follows: The affections mobilize the spontaneity of the subject which is shaped by the nature of the text into a particular mode of spontaneity.

> These different modes of spontaneity are the reading subject's attitudes, through which he tries to reconcile the as yet unknown experience of the present text with his own store of past experience (Iser 1978:157).

In this way, the meaning of the text, stimulated by affection, ". . . brings out what had previously been sealed within us" (Iser 1978:157). Here, in Iser's terms, is the revelation of a "new self," which itself reveals what Ricoeur calls the ontological bearing of the feelings (Ricoeur 1978b:156). It is a more profound account (in outline) of what Spiro (1980:273) terms "the *experience* of having an idea."

Iser's exposition is, however, not clear and stands in need of supplementing by something like Ricoeur's account. On the one hand, affection (of the reading subject, I assume) stimulates the subject; but on the other hand, it is the text which stimulates the reader (Iser 1978:157). The missing links are supplied by Ricoeur's first two moments. First, feeling unites the reader to the predicative congruence emerging from the imaginative interplay of identity and difference through the participation which begins to assimilate the reader. It is here that "the desire to regain coherence" is initiated and is first felt. Second, the meaning is *presented* (i.e. appears) as affective, i.e. as felt. The result is that the subject-object distinction is itself played with and that which is felt is no longer clearly either subject or object. Rather, the abolition of the distance between knower and known which feeling affects opens the reader to that which is not himself under the (playful) guise of being himself. Just what that "other" is has already been discussed in the last section.

Thus what Poulet and Iser discuss as the emergence of a new consciousness, Ricoeur discusses as the positive side of the split structure of (poetic) feeling which follows (and is clarified by) the first two moments of feeling: most significantly, the split reference of both the verbal and the imaginative structure.

How, though, does this relate to the work of Bartlett? First of all, Bartlett (1932:224) conceives of the image as ". . . one of the answers of a conscious organism to the challenge of an external environment which partially changes and in part persists . . . ." In short, as with Ricoeur, the imagination is specially adapted to relating the new and the old, or as put elsewhere, is the place of interplay between identity and difference.

191

Secondly, the schemas are, for Bartlett, "living, constantly developing" (Bartlett 1932:200), "momentary settings" (Bartlett 1932:201), "[not] a passive framework, or patchwork, but . . . an activity" (Bartlett 1932:203). This is much more in line with Iran-Nejad's and Ortony's conception of the schema as functional (cf. Iran-Nejad 1980:20ff), and Ricoeur's notion of the schema, than with the structural notion which, generally speaking, dominates schema theories.

Thirdly, regarding the relation between images and schemas:

> . . . images are a device for picking bits out of schemas, for increasing the chance of variability in the reconstruction of past stimuli and situations, for surmounting the chronology of presentation (Bartlett 1932:219).

In short, the image is the means of modifying the schema so as to meet the demands of the moment (Bartlett 1932:219). Further, the imagination itself seems to be that capacity which Bartlett so highly prizes: The capacity of an organism to turn round upon its own schemas and to construct them afresh (Bartlett 1932:206, 208, 211, 301). This indeed is what the "picking" of the imagination does (as attested in the above quote), though nowhere do I find Bartlett identifying the imagination with this reflective, constructive capacity.

Thus Bartlett's conceptions are not so distant from those of Ricoeur. The imagination as the place of interaction of identity and difference, and the schema as image in Ricoeur's ("lively") sense and as the rule for producing (quasi-sensory) images (in the pictorial sense) seems only a few steps from Bartlett's own theory, and in the same general direction.[38]

But what about "affection," what Bartlett termed "attitude"? Emerging from the organism's turning around on its own schemas is an "attitude towards the massed effects of a series of past reactions" (Bartlett 1932:208). First of all, a summarizing-wholing activity is recognized by Bartlett in that a series is taken as "the massed effect." Very significant is the fact that "attitude" emerges from this wholing, confirming the priority Ricoeur gives to the imagination, with affect as a "second-order intentionality." What Ricoeur presents as the activity of the imagination fills in the "massing" of which Bartlett gives no clear account.

Second, consider the following quote from Bartlett (1932:304f):

> In the clearest and most definitely articulated cases, there first occurs the arousal of an attitude, an orientation, an interest. Then specific detail,

---

[38] In Bartlett's theory, ". . . images have fundamentally important parts to play in mental life" (Bartlett 1932:215), a rather radical break with the psychology of his day.

either in image or in direct word form, tends to be set up. Finally, there is a construction of other detail in such a way as to provide a rational, or satisfactory setting for the attitude.

Here, after the attitude (which follows the "massing") comes first images and/or words (Ricoeur's second moment), then a "setting" for the attitude (Ricoeur's reference to a world of text; the third moment). This exhibits a most striking parallel between Ricoeur's theory and Bartlett's psychological experiments!

Third, if I am correct to notice that the imagination is the "turning," then the relation of attitude to image in Bartlett parallels that of affection and imagination in Ricoeur. The fact that the dominant member in these pairs is reversed--attitude in Bartlett and imagination in Ricoeur--is due, I think, to the sensory sense in which Bartlett regularly uses "image." This sense is secondary in Ricoeur. However, what Ricoeur comes to define as primary--the interaction of identity and difference (Ricoeur 1975a:199)-- Bartlett also recognizes as essential for images:

> A difference in present circumstances, as compared with those suitable to an automatic response, sets up in the agent a conflict of attitude or interest. The appropriate response is then temporally held up, and the image, an item from some schema, comes in to help solve the difficulty (Bartlett 1932:220).

> The most typical case for the emergence of images is where personal interests or attitudes cross and combine. Material organised by one takes on a tinge of a significance commonly dealt with by another . . . . Here is a bit of material usually dealt with by one set of interests invading and combining with a realm of significance usually organised by a different set (Bartlett 1932:221).

Several points are striking in these quotes. First, the role of difference or conflict is recognized as the usual precondition for image formation. What Bartlett recognizes as the usual precondition, Ricoeur takes to the heart of his definition of the imagination, incorporating the "images" (in the sensory sense) as a secondary phenomenon. Second, and most striking, is the similarity of Bartlett's psychological description of images in relation to schemas in ordinary remembering with Ricoeur's description of metaphor discussed earlier. If I may offer an understatement, we are thus further encouraged to heed Ricoeur's work on metaphor, and to consider it relevant to schema theory in general, and to the schema-theoretic account of reading in particular.

There are, though, two final points with regard to the work of Bartlett in relation to that of Ricoeur. They amount to inconsistencies in Bartlett's work which are cleared up by Ricoeur. First, Bartlett suggests, based on his experiments, that words flow only when meanings are developed out of images (Bartlett 1932:216). Later, though, he reports that the words which flow from images occur only when the previous flow of words has been checked (Bartlett 1932:216). He wants to conclude, however, that images are more basic than words, and that thinking, whose "prevailing instruments are words" (Bartlett 1932:225f), never supercedes the image-forming process (Bartlett 1932:225). For Ricoeur, however, ". . . the image is not a residue of impression [as it seems to be for Bartlett], but an aura surrounding speech" (Ricoeur 1975a:214). This recognizes that it is not possible to meditate in a zone that precedes language; and yet, that "The poetic image places us at the origin of speaking being" (Bachelard 1964:xix; quoted by Ricoeur 1975a:214). In short, Ricoeur ties the imagination first of all to a verbal structure. But then so does Bartlett when reporting on his experiments: The images follow the speaking, and perhaps arise from it, only to check the flow of words already in process (Bartlett 1932:216).

Though Ricoeur reverses the word-image priority, he does agree with Bartlett that constructive imagination differs from and gives rise to constructive thinking. In fact, ". . . speculative discourse [e.g. the conceptual articulation of philosophy] has its condition of in the semantic dynamism of metaphorical utterance . . ." (Ricoeur 1975a:296). This "semantic dynamism" is, remember, what generates "images," and thus precedes the images. Thus "meaning" does precede "images" as we saw in Ricoeur's conception of man's initial embeddedness in "being," understood as a reservoir of meaning active in reorganizing the referential fields (in metaphor or text) from which new meaning and images emerge. This "new meaning," though, is "not yet a *conceptual* gain" (Ricoeur 1975a:296), but only a sketch and a demand for thinking. In this sense, thinking does follow the imagination, but both rest finally at a deeper level, i.e. "being." This "deeper level" is our final point of discussion.

Attitude (i.e. affection), for Bartlett, emerges from the reflective turning around of an organism on its own schemas. This "turning around" I have tentatively associated with the imagination (though Bartlett's term is "becoming conscious," 1932:208). My point, though, is that affection is here a *result* of (i.e. it emerges from) something more primitive. And yet later on the same page Bartlett speculates that attitude is ". . . a genetically primitive characteristic possessing this function [of guiding, even determining, the constructive activity of remembering]" (Bartlett 1932:208). "Genetically primitive" conveys a sense quite other than an emergent consequence of imagination (or consciousness). It is here that I suggest rejoining Ricoeur's (and Heidegger's, whom Ricoeur follows at this point) notion of the ontological bearing of feelings. What appears then as a confusion in Bartlett, is rather a recognition of two separate stages in Ricoeur's interpretive arch. Bartlett's "genetically primitive" reflects man's initial belongingness in "being" which is registered most clearly in the feelings. Bartlett's "emergent attitude" is the "deeply rooted operation of feeling . . . to insert us within the world" (Ricoeur 1978b:155) *after* the building of a schema by imagination. Whether the task is remembering a story or an incident (Bartlett's concern), or reading a text (Ricoeur's preoccupation), the process is the same. There are, though, two "stages" in this process. Ricoeur has recognized this fact, while Bartlett evidently has not. As conceived by Ricoeur, these two stages are circularly related (in Ricoeur's modified circle, the arch), and overlapping in a dialectical unity. Without this concept of dialectical circularity, Bartlett has understandably confused what needs to be both distinguished and related.

CHAPTER 8

CRITIQUE IN READING

Whether "critique" is properly understood as part of reading per se is a matter of disagreement among reading theorists. For example, such skills as judging, evaluating, analyzing, and reasoning were considered by Fries as "uses of reading" and not part of the reading process itself. Further, Lamb states that "A case can be made for placing interpretation and reaction to what is read on the periphery of the reading process" (Lamb and Arnold 1976:12), but then goes on to insist that this "periphery" is not dispensable:

> However, the reading act cannot be said to be complete if the reader is consistently unselective, uncritical, apathetic, or antagonistic in his responses to what is read (1976:12).

On the other hand, Clymer includes both *"critical evaluation"* and *"incorporating the author's message* into one's own behavior" (quoted in Lamb and Arnold 1976:9) in the reading process itself. Similarly, Goodman 1976 includes critical reading as part of reading: *"The strategies required to read critically must be developed for all reading tasks and not just for special ones designed for instruction"* (1976:496). The issue comes before literacy specialists most forcibly in the theory and practice of Paulo Freire. Consequently, a consideration of Freire and his notion of critical consciousness will form a major portion of this chapter.

There is, however, another area of study closely related to reading theory which has also debated the role and status of critique. This area is interpretation theory, and the major participants in the debate have been Hans-Georg Gadamer and Jurgen Habermas. This latter debate helps to open the question of critique in reading to philosophical investigation, a task which Ricoeur has pursued in conjunction with the development of a comprehensive theory of reading.

Furthermore, these two approaches to the study of critique in reading--Freire's and the Gadamer-Habermas debate--are not unrelated. In fact, some commentators on Habermas's work consider Freire's work to be "a practical extension of Habermas's ideal of emancipatory communicative competence" (O'Neill 1976:9; cf. also Dickens 1983:155). Our investigation of "critique" in both Freire and Habermas will substantiate this judgment as well as extend it beyond "practical" concerns alone. Further, both Freire and Habermas readily acknowledge a most influential background in the writings of Karl Marx. An examination of this Marxist background will thus provide an important link between these two lines of inquiry and will greatly facilitate our own investigation.

I will proceed, then, as follows: first, a preliminary orientation to the problem of critique with reference to the preceding discussions of understanding-comprehension (cf. chapters 5-7); second, a presentation of the role of critique in the literacy theory of Paulo Freire; third, and by way of transition to the Gadamer-Habermas debate, Marx and Freire are compared on relevant issues relating to critique in reading; fourth, the Gadamer-Habermas debate is presented; fifth, Ricoeur's mediation of the debate is presented and discussed; and sixth, the notion of critique "surviving" the Gadamer-Habermas-Ricoeur debate is summarized in coordination with a review of similarities with Freire's "conscientization."

Admittedly, this six-part approach to the problem of critique in reading may seem overly developed. It is hoped, though, that the discussion will be thorough enough to accomplish several purposes: First, to establish critique as a central (not peripheral) and essential part of reading in a theoretically respectable manner; second, to present and examine enough of the Marxist background so that what is essential to the notion of critique might be distinguished from that which is ideological[1] "accident"; third, to provide as broad a base as possible for further investigations of the role and status of critique in reading theory and practice; and fourth, to provide a solid basis for the transition to the more practical concerns of literacy practice taken up in Part III. Perhaps some of what might be judged by some to be inessential in what follows will provide just the needed stimulus for the further research of others. This, it seems to me, is one of the benefits (and/or liabilities, depending on your point of view) of such an interdisciplinary study as I have undertaken.

8.1   A Preliminary Orientation

The problem of whether and/or how critique is located in the process of reading can be oriented with reference to our previous considerations of the relation between the old and the new in the process of understanding (cf. chapter 7, section 4.3 and 4.4). The Gadamer-Habermas debate (to be discussed in greater detail in section 4) provides a convenient orientation to this perspective. Gadamer, whose philosophical commitments are fundamentally Heideggerian, represents (roughly speaking) the philosophy of understanding presented in chapter 6: Understanding is, first of all, a mode of man's being-in-the-world which is historically and linguistically conditioned. Habermas is also fundamentally concerned with understanding: His program can be represented as guided by the question, "How is understanding (among speaking and acting subjects) possible in general?" (McCarthy 1978:60). The two, however, represent two fundamentally different perspectives on the legitimacy and authority of tradition, i.e., in our terms, "the old."

---

[1] Too often the baby--the benefits of recognizing the importance of critique--are thrown out with the (to some) objectionable ideological (i.e. Marxist) bathwater.

Gadamer's perspective is that man belongs so fundamentally to history-tradition that ". . . participation in a cultural heritage is a condition of possibility of all thought, including critical reflection" (McCarthy 1978:187). Thus "the fundamental gesture of philosophy," for Gadamer, is "an avowal of the historical conditions to which all human understanding is subsumed" (Ricoeur 1981a:63). Consequently, the concepts of authority and prejudice are rehabilitated, and, in language reminiscent of our previous discussions, are "taken as an illustration for the dependency of our *schemata* of interpretation on the tradition-context of language" (Misgeld 1976:180; emphasis added). As Gadamer (1976c:9) puts it,

> Prejudices are biases of our openness to the world. They are simply conditions whereby we experience something--whereby what we encounter says something to us.

Or, as we might put it in terms of our previous chapters, the conventional knowledge of our schemas is necessary for, and determinative of, our experience.[2]

Gadamer's thoroughgoing commitment to the effect of history on the consciousness of man interferes, according to Ricoeur, with the integration of "a critical instance into a consciousness of belonging" (Ricoeur 1981a:61). The difficulty for Gadamer is brought to a head by Habermas's insistence that what tradition contributes is not positive, but instead a systematic distortion of communication which conceals the self-legitimizing exercises of domination and violence by the ruling ideology. What is needed, then, according to Habermas, is not a reappropriation of tradition, but a critique of ideology which unmasks the pretensions of an oppressive tradition. The critical gesture, then, is fundamentally "an act of defiance" (Ricoeur 1981a:63), and the primary orientation is not to the past of tradition, but to an anticipated future "free from domination" (Habermas 1980:205). Rather than the avowal of tradition and its authority, the notion of critique offered by Habermas is a "step toward dissolving prior convictions" (Gadamer 1976c:33) in favor of the new which is being built on "the rock [of reason]" (Habermas 1980:207). The criterion of "reason" is, for Habermas, the "ideal speech situation" (ISS) which is always both presupposed and anticipated in any human encounter (Habermas 1973:257; Bleicher 1980:163; Thompson 1981:93). What this ISS is will be a major topic of discussion later, for it is the most important point of contact with Freire, and a very significant point of departure for my own reflections. For now, it is sufficient to note that Habermas's theory of critique is oriented to the future and the creation of a *new* situation as guided by the ISS.

---

[2] There are, though, differences which have been previously noted, summarized in terms of the ontological versus the epistemological perspectives. This difference will play a role in our discussions later in this chapter (cf. section 5).

The Gadamer-Habermas debate restates the longstanding differences between two major traditions in Western thought--Romanticism and the Enlightenment--and with them, facets of the old-new question which extend beyond the psychological (and thus beyond schema theories as now formulated).

> The Enlightenment had regarded tradition [the old] as a fetter upon man's freedom and defined reason by its power to uproot tradition. Romanticism reversed the priorities, celebrating mythos over logos, and pleading for the old at the expense of the new (McCarthy 1978:187).

The Gadamer-Habermas debate, however, carries the previous controversy to a more fundamental level, that of the " 'transcendental', or, if you prefer, 'logical' level" (McCarthy 1978:187; cf. also Ricoeur 1973:155ff; 1981a:63ff), and thus, for our purposes, opens up the old-new relation in reading and the notion of critique to more profound investigation.

This investigation, however, also raises other larger issues. Ricoeur (1973:155) defines these larger issues as ". . . the status of historical heritages, transmission, ['in the sense that the continuity of the generations is assured through institutions,' (Ricoeur 1973:154)], and tradition [whether a positive or a negative dependency], as the locus of the emergence of values in history." Here interests are raised which concern historians, political theorists, anthropologists, sociologists, and philosophers. In fact, the claim is proposed that ". . . the paradigm of reading . . . [especially as worked out in unique ways through this debate; cf. Ricoeur 1976; 1981a:63ff; 145ff; 197ff] provides a solution for the methodological paradox of the human sciences" (Ricoeur 1981a:209). Thus, though the implications of these discussions are many, the "paradigm of reading" will remain at the heart of our concern.

8.2 "Critique" in the Reading Theory of Paulo Freire

Critical consciousness is central to the reading theory and practice, indeed the philosophy of man and the world, of Paulo Freire.[3] Says

---

[3] Some background of the man Freire may be helpful for those not acquainted with him.

Paulo Freire was born in the northeast corner of Brazil, in the city of Recife in the year 1921. Freire's family was middle-class in a region beset by poverty. Freire completed his university studies in Recife, a privilege enjoyed by a minority. The majority, on the other hand, "lived in circumstances of grinding poverty and oppression. They were not 'heard.' They lived in what Freire terms a 'culture of silence,' condemned to passivity" (Mashayekh 1974:4). It was in this environment that Freire himself first experienced hunger during the recession of 1929-30, and through these experiences he learned to identify with the poor. It was here, too, that Freire, having determined to

Goulet, ". . . the unifying thread in his work is critical consciousness as the motor of cultural emancipation" (1973:vii). I will therefore first introduce his thought in a general sketch, and then identify the central features of critical consciousness. The application of this philosophy to education, and in particular, to adult literacy, will follow. The Marxist background of these central points will then be noted in order to clarify their significance, and to prepare for the transition to the Marxist philosophy of Jurgen Habermas and a consideration of the contributions to the role of critique in reading which come from dialogue with him.

8.2.1 An overview of Freire's philosophy

> All education practise implies a theoretical stance on the educator's part. This stance in turn implies--sometimes more, sometimes less explicitly--an interpretation of man and the world (Freire 1974:64).

Thus Freire himself is quite explicit: A sound philosophy of man and the world is necessary for a sound method of literacy.

Man's relation to the world, in Freire's view, is radically distinct from that of the animals. While animals adapt to the world through the

---

devote his life to helping the poor, worked out his educational method while earning his doctorate in the philosophy of education.

At least since 1962, Freire has been active in the application of his pedagogy, which he terms a "pedagogy of freedom." In 1962 he worked with the popular cultural movement in his hometown of Recife. Here he set up "cultural circles" to take the place of traditional classes and ". . . instituted group discussions to promote the analysis of existential situations or action itself inspired by such analysis" (Mashayekh 1974:6).

In 1963 Freire was appointed coordinator of the national literacy program. In the same year he conducted the Angicos experiment in which 300 workers became literate in about 45 days. Following the success of this experiment a nationwide literacy campaign was begun. However, the political implications of this cultural movement began to provoke concern. For example, since only those who could read and write could vote, the literacy program directly effected the number of voters. In ". . . the State of Pernambuco, the electoral roll jumped from 800,000 to 1,300,000 and the same phenomenon was to be expected in other states" (Mashayekh 1974:7). Because Freire's method encouraged the literates to communicate their concerns and expectations to their leaders, Freire was suspected of subversive activity and, following a military takeover in 1964, he was imprisoned for 75 days. After four and a half years in exile in Chile (and a successful literacy program there), he has served as visiting professor at Harvard, "[worked] with the World Counsil [sic] of Churches in Geneva, in the Directorate of Education Division" (Mashayekh, 1974:9), and presently is Head of the Educational Department at the State University of Campinas (UNICAMP), Brazil. In 1975, he won the Mohammad Reza Pahlavi literacy award, thus receiving even more attention from international educators (Bendor-Samuel 1977:11).

association of sense images, based on instinct, man's orientation to the world is based on an historical and a value dimension, both of which are lacking in animals. Man's task is to "humanize the world by transforming it" (Freire 1974:64). Humanization, Freire's "inescapable concern" (Freire 1970a:27), is defined largely in opposition to the dehumanization caused by injustice, exploitation, oppression, violence, and alienation. Man must learn that the world is not primarily "a static and closed order, a *given* reality which man must accept and to which he must adjust; rather, it is a problem to be worked on and solved" (Shaull, in Foreword to Freire 1970). The problems to be solved are, in Freire's view, primarily social, political and economic contradictions, which are solved by action against the oppressive elements of reality. Education, then, is conceived of as a process of liberation which culminates in the development of "critical consciousness" (Freire 1970a:19): ". . . the process in which men not as recipients but as knowing subjects, achieve a deepening awareness both of the sociocultural reality which shapes their lives, and of their capacity to transform that reality through action upon it" (Freire as quoted in Elias 1976:133).

8.2.2 Five key points of Freire's philosophy

Says Freire, "This is the principal finality of human existence: to become human" (quoted in Collins 1977:67). Each of the five points that follow is an elaboration on Freire's understanding of what it is to be "human."

8.2.2.1 Man

A recurrent theme explicit in about everything Freire writes (Elias 1976:38) is the extended comparison between man and animals (e.g. Freire 1969:17; 1970a:87-90; 1970b:28-32; 1970c:1/4-1/9; cf. Elias 1976:38). Elias (1976:39) sees this distinction as fundamentally dependent on scholastic philosophy and theology. We will also examine the similarities of this view to that of the early Marx.

Fundamentally, man is free to create through reflective acts while animals are not. Man is able to separate himself from his activity and "to treat not only his actions but his very self as the object of his reflection" (Freire 1970a:87). Animals, on the other hand, are ". . . unable to separate themselves from their activity and thus are unable to reflect upon it" (Freire 1970a:87). Consequently, man can participate in the making of his world. This "recreating and transforming" (Freire 1970a:88) activity distinguishes culture from nature. Assumed as closely associated with this reflective ability of man is the ability to (1) infuse the transformation of nature with significance beyond itself, (2) decide for themselves (versus being "merely stimulated," (Freire 1970a:87), and (3) take risks which are "challenges perceived upon reflection" (Freire 1970a:88). All three of these abilities are unique to man.

Further, man is clearly an historical creature, while animals are ahistorical. Animals live " 'submerged' in a world to which they can give

202

no meaning, lacking a 'tomorrow' and a 'today' because they exist in an overwhelming present" (Freire 1970a:87).[4] By reflection man locates himself " 'here' [which] signifies not merely a physical space, but also an historical space" (Freire 1970a:88), which is composed of the temporal modes of past, present, and future. A being capable of such awareness of himself and his products as located in time ". . . could no longer *be* if he were *not in the process of being* in the world with which he relates" (Freire 1970a:90). Here then is a component of Freire's view of man which (we will show) has great consequences for his literacy methods: Men are "uncompleted beings" (Freire 1970a:87) in the process of a completion in which they have an active part to play. As a result, all of reality is experienced by men as a process (Collins 1977:45). As Freire (1978:89) it,

> . . . the theory of knowledge that serves a revolutionary objective and is put into practice in education is based upon the claim that knowledge is always a process, and results from the conscious action (practice) of human beings on the objective reality which in its turn, conditions them. Thus a dynamic and contradictory unity is established between objective reality and the persons acting on it. All reality is dynamic and contradictory in this same way.

Because so many situations are characterized by an oppressor-oppressed relation in which ". . . there is no difference between them and the animals" (Freire 1978:50), the process of knowledge--or in Freire's terms, the process of conscientization--is one of struggle and *revolutionary* risk-taking.

Thus far I may have given the impression that man, for Freire, is primarily an individual. This however is *not* the case. For Freire,

> To know, which is always a process, implies a dialogical situation. There is not, strictly speaking, "I think," but "we think." It is not "I think" which constitutes "we think," but, on the contrary, it is "we think" that makes it possible for me to think (Freire quoted in Collins 1977:63).

Man, then, is decidedly social, and ". . . the principles of the revolutionary theory of action [which Freire espouses] are cooperation, unity, organization, and cultural synthesis" (Lloyd 1972:7). He states the goal of these principles in a quotation from Mario Cabral:

---

[4] How the learning of tricks, the seeming recognition by pets of their owners, etc., and thus the implied memory and historicality of animals fits with Freire's views here is beyond my competence. To support Freire's notion, though, see Lewis (1946:306) where the memory of an animal is described in terms quite different from the memory of humans.

The real objective of the new system . . . is to
create new persons, workers aware of their
historical responsibilities and of avenues of
creative, effective participation in the process of
social transformation (Freire 1978:46f).

In a word, Freire's goal is to humanize man (Freire 1970a:73).

8.2.2.2 Man and the World

Following Husserl, Freire emphasizes that consciousness is always
consciousness of something:

But since men do not exist apart from the world,
apart from reality, the movement must begin with
the men-world relationship. Accordingly, the
point of departure must always be with men in the
"here and now," which constitutes the situation
within which they are submerged, from which they
emerge, and in which they intervene (Freire
1970a:72f).

Historical man, though embedded in concrete situations, is
confronted by reality as a problem, a series of challenges (Freire 1970a:88).
Many of these challenges are, in fact, the "concrete representations of [the]
. . . ideas, values, concepts, and hopes" (Freire 1970a:91) which men have
made. Nonetheless, these representations--which he calls "themes"--are
often "obstacles which impede man's full humanization" (Freire 1970a:91).
They are "found [nowhere] except in the men-world relationship" and the
complex of these themes, which Freire says are "always interacting
dialectically with their opposites," constitute a "thematic universe" typical
of every historical epoch (Freire 1970a:91f). The themes themselves
though are not yet the problematic aspect of reality:

In the last analysis, the *themes* both contain and
are contained in *limit-situations*; the *tasks* they
imply require limit-acts. When the themes are
concealed by the limit-situations and thus are not
clearly perceived, the corresponding tasks--men's
responses in the historical action--can be neither
authentically nor critically fulfilled. In this
situation, men are unable to transcend the limit-
situations to discover that beyond these situations--
and in contradiction to them--lies an untested
feasibility (Freire 1970a:92).

The limit-situations, then, pose a challenge if not a threat to men. The
"untested feasibility" is the task presented as risk, which nonetheless
promises to transform this frontier (of the limit) from a "frontier between
being and nothingness" to a "frontier between being and being more

204

human" (Freire 1970a:93). However, in this epoch in which the fundamental theme is "domination" (Freire 1970a:93) and its opposite "liberation," limit-situations imply a necessary struggle if the oppressed are to be liberated simply because those who dominate do not want the "untested feasibility" beyond the limit (i.e. beyond the status quo) to materialize.

The themes which reveal the limit-situations of man's existence are not outside of men, but are "discovered through investigations of men's thought" (Collins 1977:52). This leads us to our next concern--the role of language in the life of man.

8.2.2.3 Man and Language

For Freire, the very essence of being human is related to language: "To exist, humanly," says Freire, ". . . is to name the world, to change it" (1970a:76).[5] The problem of oppression, then, is seen as imprisonment in a "culture of silence." Illiteracy, then, is ". . . the mark of men robbed of their words, who exist not for themselves but for another, the oppressor" (Lloyd 1972:9). This is alienation from existing humanly.[6]

But human existence cannot be "nourished by false words, but only by true words, with which men transform the world" (Freire 1970a:76). Two points are worthy of further comment. First, there is a possibility of "idle chatter" (Freire 1970a:75), and worse, "alienated and alienating rhetoric" (Freire 1970a:85): "language . . . not attuned to the concrete situation of the men they address" (Freire 1970a:85). In short, this is an age in the service of false consciousness.

> By false consciousness is meant a psychic
> condition in which the role of the self's agency
> (volition, creativity, responsibility) in the
> production and maintenance of the social world is
> obscured by interpretations of reality which

---

[5] Says Freire, men are distinct from animals because men can reflect on their situation and, as a consequence, can infuse "the world with creative presence" (Freire 1970a:88), "with [a] significance beyond itself" (Freire 1970a:87).

[6] Dialogue, communication between men by means of language, is essential to man if he is to live humanly:

"If it is in speaking their word that men, by naming the world, transform it, dialogue imposes itself as the way by which men achieve significance as men. Dialogue is thus an existential necessity" (Freire 1970a:77).

"Human existence cannot be silent. . . . Men are not built in silence, but in word" (Freire 1970a:76).

conceal or disguise these dynamics from the self (Stanley 1972:390).

Obviously, this is the situation which conscientization is designed to remedy. Second, the goal of dialogue is to change the world (Freire 1970a:76), and the means of change is naming. In fact, "Dialogue is the encounter between men, *mediated by the world*, in order to name the world" (Freire 1970a:76; emphasis added). Man in the world, and man as namer are two sides of the same man in the same situation.

Dialogue which is essential to man if he is to live humanly (Freire 1970a:76) is dependent for its existence on a profound love for the world and for men (Freire 1970a:77). It requires humility (Freire 1970a:78), intense faith in man (Freire 1970a:79), hope (Freire 1970a:80), and critical thinking (Freire 1970a:81). Dialogue is essentially a "horizontal" relation of non-domination in which a sympathetic relationship sustains the active participation of communication. With this brief characterization of dialogue, a fuller picture of what Freire understands by man is gained.

"The essence of dialogue," says Freire (1970a:75f), is *the word*. The word, however, is "more than just an instrument which makes dialogue possible" (1970a:75):

> Within the word we find two dimensions, reflection and action, in such radical interaction that if one is sacrificed--even in part--the other immediately suffers. There is no true word that is not at the same time a praxis. Thus to speak a true word is to transform the world (Freire 1970a:75).

If the word is deprived of the dimension of action, it becomes "*verbalism*, . . . an alienated and alienating 'blah' " (Freire 1970a:75f). If it is deprived of reflection, it becomes "*activism* . . . action for action's sake [which] negates true praxis and makes dialogue impossible" (Freire 1970a:76).

8.2.2.4 Man and Praxis

The basic distinction between man and animals can be drawn quite clearly in terms of praxis. Says Freire (1970a:91),

> Only men *are* praxis--the praxis which, as the reflection and action which truly transform reality, is the source of knowledge and creation. Animal activity, which occurs without praxis, is not creative; man's transforming activity is.

Because man can produce products which "do not belong [immediately] to its physical body" (Freire 1970a:90), a dimension of meaning can be given

206

to a context, thus transforming an environment into a (cultural) world. The products of man's activity which Freire has in view are not only material goods, "but also social institutions, ideas, and concepts" (Freire 1970a:91). "Through their continuing praxis, men simultaneously create history and become historical-social beings" (Freire 1970a:91). This creative participation in one's own future ("revolutionary activity," Freire 1970a:72), allows man to be a "being for himself" (Freire 1970a:90), while animals remain "beings-in-themselves" (Freire 1970a:88). Dialogue, as the speaking of the true word--"which is work, which is praxis" (Freire 1970a:76)--is the essential means by which the world is transformed. Simple "action for action's sake" (Freire 1970a:76) is not praxis; rather there must be the reflective word. And yet, "reflection and action" (Freire 1970a:75)--the two dimensions of the word--are also the two dimensions of all man's activity (Freire 1970a:119). In short, saying the (true) word is human activity *par excellence*.

8.2.2.5 Man and Conscientization

With "conscientization" we reach the heart of Freire's theory and practice:

> Simply put conscientization means "to make aware" or "awakening of consciousness" or "critical consciousness." Conscientization is a social process, taking place among men as they unite in common reflection and action upon their world. This occurs not through intellectual effort alone but through "praxis," the unity of reflection and action. Conscientization, then, does not stop at an awakening of perception but proceeds to action, which in turn provides the basis for new perception, new reflection (Lloyd 1972:4f).

> Conscientization means an awakening of the consciousness, a shift in mentality involving an accurate, realistic assessment of one's locus in nature and society; a capacity to analyze the causes and consequences of that locus; the ability to compare it with other possibilities; and finally a disposition to act in order to change the received situation. In personal and human terms, conscientization means a growing awareness of one's own worth and dignity, and for Freire an almost inevitable result of that growth is the development of forms of political participation and action which will both protect and enhance it (Boston 1973:28).

"Critical" for Freire, then, seems to involve two processes, which Smith calls "critical awareness" and "critical evaluation" (n.d.:5). In the first, ". . . the individual is able to describe what he sees" (Smith n.d.:5). This is the emergence in reflection from the situation in which one has been submerged (Freire 1970a:100), the separation in thought from one's activities and concrete situation. "Critical evaluation," though, is a further step in which "I also know I can liberate myself if I transform the concrete situation where I find myself oppressed" (Freire, quoted in Lloyd 1972:5). But transformation is not something to be done "in my head" (Freire, quoted in Lloyd 1972:5), for awareness does not create reality. "No," says Freire, "conscientization implies a critical insertion into a process, it implies a historical commitment to make changes" (Freire, quoted in Lloyd 1972:5). As Freire puts it elsewhere,

> Obviously, *conscientizacao* [the Portuguese for "conscientization"] does not stop at the level of mere subjective perception of a situation but through action prepares men for the struggle against the obstacles to their humanization (1970a:112).

In these two "stages"--awareness and evaluation leading to action-- we see the two dimensions inherent in "the word"--reflection and action. Thus, it is no surprise to find the communication process central to this critical process. Mashayekh (1974:15) provides this summary of the process:

> A. At the *intransitive awareness stage* man does not perceive the dialectic relationship which unites him with nature. He is caught in its flux and cannot emerge from it: in order to satisfy his basic needs, he gives himself up to the irrational game of magical forces, which he serves by his activity. Fatalistic, and an outsider with regards to history, he lives from day to day. The society in which he exists is not a community, but at most an aggregate of families struggling for life.
>
> B. *Naive transitive awareness* is characterized by an initial perception of problems. But his examination is not pushed to its limits: it is restricted to vague global diagnoses and solutions of a similar character.
>
> C. It is only by *critical transitive awareness* that man can free himself from his alienations. At this stage the individual examines problems without allowing himself to be blinded by passion. In his diagnosis, as well as in his search for solutions, he tries to be *critical* and proceeds rationally. And as the problems to be solved are complex and affect the collectivity as well as the individual, diagnosis

208

and solutions demand dialogue and concerted efforts, in other words, true democracy.

8.2.3 Implications for education from Freire's philosophy

There are several important implications for education which follow from Friere's philosophy of man and the world. First: all vestiges of domination must be removed from the learning situation. The changes which this implies for both the methodology of education, as well as the educational components, are summarized in the following charts, adapted from Mashayekh (1974:21).

EDUCATION

METHODOLOGY

TRADITIONAL		CONSCIENTIZATION
	For whom?	
--the isolated individual (ignorant)		--man in his environment (rich in experience)
	Why?	
--to adapt the individual to the established system of values: man of man must submit to history make history		--to make man critical of the established system of values: man must make history
	What?	
--a corpus of knowledge already organized: "ready-made packages"		--a corpus of knowledge already organized: to be discovered and organized: "tailored packages"
	How?	
--by a mechanical transfer of knowledge: use of of knowledge repetition		--by the functional discovery of knowledge: use of observation, analysis and "interiorization"

EDUCATIONAL COMPONENTS

Group

--isolated individuals: "empty vessels to be filled"	--active human beings discovering the object of their knowledge

Instructor

--sole subject possessing "knowledge"; agent of transmission of "knowledge"	--co-ordinator acting as catalyzer in the search for "knowledge"

Programme

--a uniform preconceived reflecting the "knowledge accumulated by man	--learning units conceived and prepared in accordance with the identified needs of man and his environment

Method

--monologue encouraging memorization	--dialogue inviting creation

The second implication of Freire's philosophy of man for his philosophy of education has direct relevance to literacy. Because man's relation to the world and himself "involves, above all, thought-language" (Freire 1974:64),

> Learning to read and write ought to be an opportunity for men to know what *speaking the word* really means: a human act implying reflection and action. As such it is a primordial human right and not the privilege of a few. Speaking the word is not a true act if it is not at the same time associated with the right of self-expression and world-expression, of creating and re-creating, of deciding and choosing and ultimately participating in society's historical process (Freire 1974:73).

Illiteracy, then, is a typical manifestation of the "culture of silence" which contributes to the dehumanization of its prisoners by excluding them from fuller participation in the creation of their own lives: "Teaching men to read and write is no inconsequential matter of memorizing an alienated word but a *difficult apprenticeship in naming the world*" (Friere as quoted in Stanley 1972:387).

Third, dialogue is essential to both the educational situation and all learning: Any act of knowing for man ". . . demands among teachers and students a relationship of authentic dialogue" (Freire 1974:73).

210

And since dialogue is the encounter in which the united reflection and action of the dialoguers are addressed to the world which is to be transformed and humanized, this dialogue cannot be reduced to the act of one person's "depositing" ideas in another, nor can it become a simple exchange of ideas to be "consumed" by the discussants. Nor yet is it a hostile, polemical argument between men who are committed neither to the naming of the world, nor to the search for truth, but rather to the imposition of their own truth. Because dialogue is an encounter among men who name the world, it must not be a situation where some men name on behalf of others. It is an act of creation; it must not serve as a crafty instrument for the domination of one man by another. The domination implicit in dialogue is that of the world by the dialoguers; it is conquest of the world for the liberation of men (Freire 1970a:77).

Fourth, several implications follow from the fact that man is always already in a concrete situation and confronted with limit-situations. Most importantly, education itself must be "problem-posing" (Freire 1970a:67) in which the educator creates the conditions for men (including himself) "to perceive critically *the way they exist* in the world *with which* and *in which* they find themselves" (Freire 1970a:71). Because man's consciousness is intentional man cannot be educated if that consciousness is isolated from the world (Freire 1970a:71). Consequently, knowledge is raised to the level of "logos" (Freire 1970a:68) which on the one hand is "demythologized awareness" (Stanley 1972:388), and on the other, the fulfillment of man's "ontological vocation to be more fully human" (Freire 1970a:61, quoted in Stanley 1972:388). This central role of the word-in-context underlines the fact that, for Freire, "The learning of reading and writing involves also learning to 'read' reality by means of the correct analysis of social practice" (Freire 1978:89).

Fifth, and closely related to the preceding point, there is no value-free educational theory, text or method. As Stanley puts it, "*All* words either conceal or reveal something" (1972:387). Either language is "attuned to the concrete situation" (Freire 1070a:85) or it is not. And only "true words" (Freire 1970a:76) liberate men and transform the world.

8.3 Marx and Freire Compared

It is generally accepted that Marxism is one of the main influences on Freire's thought (cf. e.g. Collins 1977:32f; Stanley 1972:388f; Boston 1973:29; Freire 1970a:11, 21; 1972:7; 1973:x). Thus, we are especially interested in this background because of its influence on Freire, as well as its effect on the notion of critique as developed by Habermas and others.

211

My strategy will be to first substantiate the similarities of Freire's central notions with the ideas of Marx. Then I will highlight the differences.

8.3.1 Similarities between Marx and Freire

8.3.1.1 Marx on Man

As with Freire, Marx's goal was to humanize humanity (Bockmuehl 1980:92) through human activity: ". . . to be radical is to go to the root of the matter. For man, however, the root is man himself . . . . *The* entire so-called history of the world is nothing but the begetting of man through human labor . . ." (Marx 1978:60, 92).

In summary of Marx's view of man, Fromm says,

> Marx was opposed to two positions: the unhistorical one that the nature of man is a substance present from the very beginning of history, and the relativistic position that man's nature has no inherent quality whatsoever and is nothing but a reflex of social conditions. But he never arrived at the full development of his own theory concerning the nature of man, transcending both the unhistorical and the relativistic positions; hence he left himself open to various and contradictory interpretations (1962:31).[7]

There are, though, two models which persist in Marx's writing, the biological and the historical.[8] Both models show striking similarity to Freire. For example, Marx says,

> The animal is immediately identical with its life-activity. It does not distinguish itself from it. It is its life-activity. Man makes his life-activity itself the object of his will and of his consciousness. He has conscious life-activity. It is not a determination with which he directly merges. Conscious life-activity directly distinguishes man from animal life-activity (1978:76).

Here man is not only distinguished from animals, but consciousness of life-activity is the distinguishing trait as it is for Freire. Further, man's life-

---

[7] Wallimann disputes this view, but the point of his disagreement is not clear; cf. Wallimann 1981:20f.

[8] Several writers make the persuasive case that there is a unity in Marx's conception of man throughout both the "early Marx" and the "later"; cf. e.g. Fromm 1961:69-79; Walliman 1981:11.

activity is "productive," produced "in freedom," with reference to the future as well as present need, and in accordance with a standard which man can consciously and freely vary (Marx 1978:76), and so distinguish himself from animals. As with Freire, the world which man inhabits and reflects upon is "a world that he has created" by conscious reflection and activity (Marx 1978:76).

According to Walliman, what the biological model lacks, Marx makes up for with the historical model:

> Thus he introduces the notion that all the aspects of human nature that cannot be derived from a comparison of human beings with animals can be understood by seeing them in an historical perspective (Walliman 1981:16).

As already noted, world history is the creation of man by man's labor. A conclusion can now be drawn: inasmuch as history displays temporal progression, man too must be conceived of as an historical process. In short, ". . . the truth of [human] being [is] historical becoming" (Walliman 1981:223); or as Freire put it, men are "uncompleted beings" (1970a:76).

In further agreement with Freire, man is decidedly a social creature. In a much quoted statement Marx says,

> It is not consciousness of men that determines their being, but, on the contrary, their social being that determines their consciousness (Marx 1978:4).

Although ". . . it is just because he is a species being that he is a conscious Being, i.e., that his own life is an object for him" (Marx 1978:76), "social being" seems even more fundamentally based on "the material productive forces of society" (Marx 1978:4), than it is on man's nature per se. Man's "essential being" (Marx 1978:76) may in fact conflict with his historical "existence" (Marx 1978:76). In fact, the determination of the most basic nature of man--biological or historical--is not made by Marx. Since man is practically embedded in the historical world, the philosopher's task is to change that world (1978:145). Thus the "theoretical" question is the practical question for Marx and the historical model gains a priority: "In its reality [human essence] is the ensemble of social relations" (Marx 1978:145).

It may be that the divergence of man's historical situation from his biological possibilities only reflects the actual situation of man in capitalist society today. Marx and Freire call this situation "alienation": the involvement of men in social-labor relations ". . . transforms the real essential powers of man and nature into what are merely abstract conceits and therefore imperfections--into tormenting chimeras" (Marx 1978:105). Not only is man estranged from the product of his labor, but as a result, man is estranged from his very self (Marx 1978:75). And as with Freire,

213

revolutionary activity is called for (Marx 1978:218f, 220; 291f; 522ff; etc.), aimed at a "new man" (Marx 1978:160), indeed a new world (Marx 1978:162). As Fromm puts it, "Marx's philosophy was, in secular, nontheistic language, a new and radical step forward in the tradition of prophetic Messianism . . ." (1961:3).

8.3.1.2 Marx on Man and the World

The priority of man's social, concrete (e.g. labor) relationships has already been noted. Man is not an abstraction, but "practical activity" (Marx 1978:155). As Marx says, "We set out from real, active men, and on the basis of their life-process we demonstrate the development of the ideological reflexes and echoes of this life-process" (1978:154). The relation of man to nature ". . . has the form of an essential interdependence" (Feenberg 1981:231):

> . . . nature is his *body*, with which he must remain
> in continuous intercourse if he is not to die. That
> man's physical and spiritual life is linked to nature
> means simply that nature is linked to itself, for
> man is a part of nature (Marx 1978:75).

Marx supports this view in a brief argument against the cosmological proof for God's existence (Marx 1978:92), arguing that such questioning of the genesis of mankind is impossible for man as existent in nature. Instead, the history of the world is wholly accounted for in terms of man's self production. This argument opens the possibility of reflection on limit situations similar to Freire's, for the question of creation is but one graphic example of how man is confronted by his concrete existence with limits to his thought.

Marx extends this argument to other concrete situations. Because man is socially determined, and because the social conditions of production become intolerable, "bitter contradictions, crises, spasms . . . explosions, cataclysms" (Marx 1978:291) result. These are the limit situations which finally are to result in the "violent overthrow" (Marx 1978:292) of the existing system, so that liberation, in which the worker participates once again in the production of the world, might result.

Thus, as Feenberg (1981:230) points out,

> Marx's argument against the cosmological proof is
> part of a larger attempt to establish the
> ontological priority of the living nature of which
> we are a part over the objective nature of the
> natural sciences in which we are only a spectator.

Feenberg goes on to relate this "limiting [of] the application of the categories to the possible experience of a finite subject" (1981:232), not only to the Kantian tradition, but especially to the existential thought of

Marcel ("secondary reflection"), and the phenomemological thinking of Heidegger (the idea of "horizon"; 230ff). The point here is two-fold. First, there are striking similarities with Freire's "limit situations"; and second,

> . . . it would be too much to say that Marx succeeds in presenting a satisfactory theory there [in the Manuscripts]. He circles around the concept of a finite horizon without achieving a clear statement of a new concept of objectivity defined in the domain of lived experience . . . (Feenberg 1981:232).

8.3.1.3 Marx on Man and Language

Marx's direct comments on language are sparse, but considered in context highly significant. "Language," he says, "is as old as consciousness, language is practical consciousness that exists also for other men, and for that reason alone it really exists for me personally as well . . ." (1978:158). The notion "practical consciousness" is, as we have seen, central for Marx. Man is not an abstraction, but is always to be considered within his practical situation. In fact, "the language of real life" is, for Marx, "the material activity and the material intercourse of men" (Marx 1978:154). Language, then, "only arises from the need, the necessity, of intercourse with other men" (Marx 1978:158), and since human intercourse is thoroughly ". . . conditioned by definite development of their productive forces" (Marx 1978:154), language is always "corresponding to these [productive forces]" (Marx 1978:154) and is "the direct efflux of their material production" (Marx 1978:154).

Given this strong determination of consciousness by the concrete practicalities of the productive forces, it is not clear how these "forces of production, the state of society and consciousness, can and must come into contradiction with one another" (Marx 1978:159). One possibility arises from Marx's rejection of a purely materialistic doctrine: "The materialistic doctrine," he says, "concerning the changing of circumstances and education forgets that circumstances are changed by men and that the educator must himself be educated" (Marx quoted in Fromm 1961:22). But as Engels notes in a famous letter (to Mehring) ten years after Marx's death, he and Marx ". . . had neglected *the manner and mode of how ideas come into being*" (quoted in Fromm 1961:22). Such a neglect leaves Marx's theory of education and change undeveloped. Freire's theory provides one response to this deficiency.

8.3.1.4 Marx on Man and Praxis

"Man, for Marx, is *homo faber--a maker*" (Lynn 1979:54). Basic to man is the "principle of movement" understood as "a drive, creative vitality, energy" (Fromm 1961:30).

Inasmuch as man is not productive, inasmuch as he is receptive and passive, he is nothing, he is dead.

Consequently, labor--what man does--is basic to Marx's theory of man. In fact, labor is "the factor which mediates between man and nature"; it is "the expression of human life and through labor man's relationship to nature is changed, hence through labor man changes himself" (Fromm 1961:16).

Against this background, Marx's view of praxis comes into focus.[9] As stated by a modern Marxist, praxis is "conscious, goal-oriented social activity in which man realizes the *optimal* potentialies of his being, and which is therefore an end in itself" (Markovic, quoted in Lyon 1979:62). However, in the climate of alienation, praxis must be "revolutionising practice" (Marx 1978:144), and it is this latter sense which typifies the notion.

A problem, however, arises on closer inspection. Though the claim is often made that theory and practice are united in Marxist thought by praxis, it seems that Marx himself maintains a distinction. For example, Marx says "[the family] must then itself be criticized in theory *and* revolutionised in practice" (1978:144; emphasis added); "All mysteries . . . find their rational solutions in human practice *and* in the comprehension of this practice" (Marx 1978:145; emphasis added); and though the task of the philosopher is to change the world (Marx 1978:145), yet ". . . philosophy is the head of the emancipation, and the proletariat is its heart" (Marx as quoted in Lyon 1979:53). Rather than either radically separating theory and practice or uniting them in a new synthesis, "Marx merely invert[s] the [traditional] order of the two orders, making real activity the judge of thought" (Axelos 1976:50). As Marx himself puts it, "Man must prove the truth, that is, the reality and power, the this-sidedness of his thinking in practice" (1978:144).

Regardless of this philosophic judgment, a significant point remains for our purposes: theory and practice are not separated; neither Marx nor Freire advocates mere "action for action's sake." Rather, Marx advocates a materialism which includes "philosophy" and promotes the "liberation" of man from the domination of alienating labor (Marx 1978:169).

8.3.1.5 Marx on Critique

Although Marx does grant philosophy an important role in his revolutionary program, he breaks with the philosophic tradition of the West. Says he, "The philosophers have only *interpreted* the world, in various ways; the point, however, is to *change* it" (1978:145). Marx's theory

---

[9] There is, though, debate as to how praxis is related to nature and history; cf. e.g. Feenberg 1981:8ff.

of praxis is meant to be that "practical-critical activity" (Marx 1978:143) which changes the world. Here "critique" is wedded to practice. But what is this critical activity?

Marx assumes, based on his empirical studies of history and his contemporary world, that "most of what men consciously think is 'false' consciousness, is ideology and rationalization; that the true mainsprings of man's actions are unconscious to him" (Fromm 1961:20f). Marx, therefore, undertakes the "reform of consciousness" (Marx 1978:15) by means of a *"ruthless criticism of everything existing"* (Marx 1978:13). By "ruthless" he means that "The criticism must not be afraid of its own conclusions, nor of conflict with the powers that be" (Marx 1978:13); and by "reform of consciousness" he means "enabling the world to clarify its consciousness [by] *explaining* to it the meaning of its own actions" (Marx 1978:15). To do so a new kind of reflection is needed which Feenberg identifies as differing from the old at two levels.

> On the one hand, it treats many assumptions which the philosophical tradition took for granted as problems. On the other hand, it treats these assumptions as problems at the specific level of the social causes from which they arise (Feenberg 1981:23).

And consciousness, we should remember, is for Marx a social product (Marx 1978:158).

As already noted, labor can alienate man from himself, the objects of his labor, and from other men. Man himself is dehumanized, reduced to "spiritual and physical poverty" (Marx 1978:134). Such alienation is directly related to man's consciousness. It occurs when certain social conditions, in particular those of capitalism, ". . . block [man] from being aware of certain facts and experiences" and prevent "him from being aware of his true human needs, and of ideals which are rooted in them" (Fromm 1961:21). Consciousness, in its misery, becomes "unclear to itself" (Fromm 1961:15), and it becomes

> . . . the work of our time to clarify to itself (critical philosophy) the meaning of its own struggle and its own desires . . . . It is a matter of *confession*, no more. To have its sins forgiven mankind has only to declare them to be what they really are (Fromm 1961:15).

What, though, is "the meaning of its own struggle"? What are the "sins" of mankind? Here we agree with Goodman (1976:495) who said that to be critical one ". . . must develop a set of appropriate criteria to judge . . . , or at least . . . [to] help him [the reader] deal with matters such as plausibility, credibility, ulterior motives . . . ." What is the "set of appropriate criteria" for Marx? Here we return to the central aim of both

Marx and Freire--man! The standard by which to critique any concrete situation is man. Marx is clear that the aim of his system is a communism which is "the real *appropriation of the human essence by and for man.* This communism . . . equals humanism" (Marx 1978:84).

To review briefly: This humanism is defined by Marx according to two models, the biological and the historical. According to the first, some of the human qualities Marx advocates are (without trying to be exhaustive) "spontaneous activity, free activity" (Marx 1978:77), "beauty" (Marx 1978:76), "love" (Marx 1978:105), "trust" (Marx 1978:105), and whatever the opposites of "avarice" (Marx 1978:71), domination (Marx 1978:472), exploitation (Marx 1978:472), "private property" (Marx 1978:484), and alienation (Marx 1978:79) might be. According to the second model, man is historical. Thus men, though bound by false consciousness, must come to realize that "The history of all hitherto existing society is the history of class struggles" (Marx 1978:473). And further, the ends sought ". . . can be attained only by the forcible overthrow of all existing social conditions" (Marx 1978:500), accomplished by the unification of all the working people against those supporting the "existing social and political order of things" (500). Here, then, is the culmination of Marx's critical-philosophy, the philosophy which claims that the solutions to the "antinomies" of philosophy can be resolved only in history" (Feenberg 1981:5; cf. Marx 1978:144): i.e., in practical revolutionary action.

8.3.2 Differences between Marx and Freire

Four major differences between Marx and Freire will be noted. First, several authors have recognized what they term the "fundamentally anti-personal attitude of Marxist teaching" (Axelos 1976:137). Bulgakov[10] calls this attitude the "lack of attentions to the concrete, living, human person," a "theoretical disregard for the person, the elimination of that which is individual under the pretense of a sociological interpretation of history." This line of critique claims that Marx's identification of the individual with the universal is so thoroughgoing that the individual personality is completely absorbed by the community (Axelos 1976:137). People appear as "algebraic signs" (Bulgakov 1979:51) whose personality minus that which is non-individual is precisely zero (Bulgakov 1979:57). In short, man is conceived of as merely "the sum-total of social-economic relations" (Axelos 1976:137), with no inner spiritual life, and no ethical autonomy (Axelos 1976:133, 137). This interpretation is supported by such quotes from Marx as

> Only when the real, individual man . . . as an
> individual human being has become a *species*
> being in his everyday life, in his particular work,

---

[10] Solzhenitsyn [in Bulgakov (1979:5)] terms Bulgakov's work "one of the deepest analyses of the heart of Marxism."

218

and in his particular situation . . . , only then will human emancipation have been accomplished.

[The task is then] *changing* human nature, . . . transforming each individual, who in himself, is a complete and solitary whole, into a part of a greater whole . . . (quoted in Buckmuehl 1980:128f).

. . . the individual is . . . the social being (Marx 1978:86).

Man's individual and species life are not *different* (Marx 1978:86).

But the human essence is no abstraction inherent in each single individual. In its reality it is the ensemble of the social relations (1978:145).

Such a line of criticism is not, however, universally accepted. Fromm (1961:3), for example, says, "[Marx's philosophy] was aimed at the full realization of individualism, the very aim which has guided Western thinking from the Renaissance and the Reformation far into the nineteenth century."

My purpose here is not to resolve this issue of Marxist interpretation. Rather, I want to point out that this anti-personal tendency (at least) in Marx is not evident in Freire. With Freire, that tendency is countered and overcome by the combined influences of the personalism of Mournier, the existentialism of such writers (whom Freire quotes) as Sartre, Jaspers, Marcel, Camus, Buber, and Heidegger, and by traditional Catholicism (Collins 1977:29-36).

The second noticeable difference between Marx and Freire is the increased role of language, and especially of dialogue, in Freire's philosophy. By drawing upon the Genesis story of Adam's domination over nature by means of naming the world (Collins 1977:50f), Freire identifies men's linguistic abilities with "their ontological vocation to be more fully human" (Freire 1970a:61; cf. Stanley 1972:387). The "bottom line" for Freire, then, is not the socio-economic forces of material production, nor the necessity of intercourse with other men, but a God-given ability and task which precedes such concerns.

Consequently (and this is the third difference), Freire grants a larger role to the changing of consciousness through dialogue than does Marx. The deficiency regarding "the manner and mode of how ideas come into being" which Engels recognized in Marxist thought is remedied by Freire by attention to language and dialogue. For Freire, the Marxist "false consciousness" is dispelled in the first place by the true word which, spoken in dialogue, transforms the world (Freire 1970a:76).

219

Finally, because of this prominent role given to language and human communication in Freire, his philosophy does not make the same claim to empiricism and materialism as does Marx. The "themes" which Freire investigates ". . . are not things and do not exist outside men. They are discovered through investigation of men's thought" (Collins 1977:52). This is not to deny that Freire recognizes the strong hold which oppressive socio-politico-economic conditions have on the lives and minds of men. It is to assert, however, that the means of liberation are not finally grounded in materialistic forces. Rather, it is the "true word" which entails both reflection and praxis.

To summarize this difference in the language of reading theories, Freire is interactive with a primary emphasis on the top-down mode, while Marx is bottom-up in his emphasis (in terms of what is determinative for consciousness and understanding). If one wishes to argue that Marx is also interactive (and I think a good case can be made for this), then at least we must admit that his emphasis is bottom-up. This, however, introduces our next topic of discussion.

8.4 The Habermas-Gadamer Debate

Having introduced the Habermas-Gadamer debate in terms of the relation between the old and the new (section 1), discussed Freire's notion of critical consciousness in relation to reading theory (section 2), and explored the relation of Freire's thought to that of Marx (section 3), my tasks now will be (working backwards in relation to the previous sections): (1) to examine Habermas's relation to Marx, especially in regard to the five key concepts relevant to Freire's theory of reading, thus indirectly comparing Habermas and Freire in terms of general philosophical orientation (section 4.1); (2) to present Habermas's notion of critique (section 4.2); and (3) to pursue Habermas's debate with Gadamer, especially as it relates to "critique" (section 4.3). Each step will grant us greater access to the concept of critique.

8.4.1 Jurgen Habermas, orthodox Marxism, and Freire

Jurgen Habermas is perhaps the best known contemporary representative of the Frankfurt Institute for Social Research, the so-called "Frankfurt School."[11] Seeking to avoid alignment with the political factions of its founding days, the Frankfurt School returned instead to "the foundations of Marx's thought and sought to re-examine the philosophical heritage from which it arose" (Thompson 1981:75). Perhaps the major departure of the Frankfurt School from orthodox Marxism comes with regard to cultural products. While orthodox Marxism claims that cultural

---

[11] The Frankfurt Institute was founded in 1923 ". . . when the socialist movement in the Weimar Republic was sharply split between a bolshevik Communist Party and a democratic Socialist Party" (Thompson 1981:75). Other well-known luminaries in this "School" include Horkheimer, Adorno, Marcuse, Fromm, and Apel.

products are "mere epiphenomena of the economy" (Thompson 1981:75), the Frankfurt theorists

> . . . regard such products as relatively autonomous expressions of contradictions within the social whole, and they perceive within some of these expressions both the social physiognomy of the present and the critical forces which negate the existing order (Thompson 1981:75).

As a corollary of this basic difference, the Frankfurt writers emphasize the central role of enlightened self-emancipation in the revolutionary process. In short, subjective rather than objective (i.e. personal rather than impersonal) conditions of social change come to the forefront with the Frankfurt School. This basic difference of emphasis (with which Habermas agrees) shifts the Marxist foundation toward Freire's theory, influenced as it is by personalist, existentialist, and Christian influences. Habermas's own contribution brings his "Marxism" even closer to Freire's.

Habermas agrees with Marx that the task of the social sciences should be decidedly "critical," i.e. aimed at the dissolution of the oppressive and alienating relations of power and ideology. Further, Habermas agrees with Marx that the human species is fundamentally responsible for its own self-constitution; that man is essentially a social creature; and that men, though necessarily embedded in nature, have "the capacity to act freely and create the future through the use of their rationality and agency" (Shapiro 1976:147). Habermas is also committed to "set out from real, active men" (Marx 1978:154).

Habermas, however, detects a fundamental discrepancy in Marx's work. The problem centers around Marx's concept of social praxis. Marx attempts to conceive of man as fundamentally "practical activity" (Marx 1978:155). Marx seems to reduce all "the self-formative process[es] of the human species to [their] self-generation through social labor" (Thompson 1981:82). Thus he is not consistent since, on the one hand, he continues to distinguish theory from practice, while on the other, he reduces theory to practice. Though Habermas agrees with Marx that the constitution of man's relation to the world is incomplete in pure understanding, and complete only in work, he claims that the failure to adequately distinguish social labor from social interaction has prevented "Marx from providing an adequate philosophical foundation for his critical social theory" (Thompson 1981:82). Habermas's point, as for the Frankfurt School in general, is that the sphere of intersubjective communication cannot be reduced to the sphere of the sciences concerned with empirical knowledge and technical interest, and ruled by forces of production and categories of labor (Habermas 1971a). Any attempt to do so precludes the separation of diverse interests from each other--specifically the technical interests of labor from the interest in emancipation--and thus removes the basis for an adequate conception and practice of critique, which itself is primarily concerned with emancipation. Habermas locates this basis for critique and

221

emancipation in the structure of human communication (we'll look at why shortly), again a major departure from orthodox Marxism for which the active political dimension is a specific group, i.e. the proletariat. With this radical shift of emphasis to the sphere of communicative action as the basis of critique, Habermas's views can be seen as quite close to those of Freire for whom dialogue is the major category operative in conscientization.[12]

With his emphasis on human communication and language, Habermas sides with Freire in developing that which is neglected by Marx and Engels (cf. section 3.1.3). The general rubric under which Habermas develops his theory is that of "Universal Pragmatics" or "A Theory of Communicative Competence." Habermas fashions his program on the work of the generative grammarians, attempting to specify the formal features of communicative competence which are embedded in every particular utterance (cf. Dickens 1983:145-148; McCarthy 1978:272-291). The foundation for the (critical) social sciences, he argues, is in the structure of human communication. This position is a result of (1) the Frankfurt School's critique of instrumental reason,[13] culminating in Habermas's critique of positivism (Habermas 1971a) which demonstrates that the empirical-analytic sciences presuppose an "a priori of communication" (Apel 1972-3), and (2) Habermas's controversy with Gadamer which "forced" him to recognize the pervasive influence of language.

Consequently, Habermas claims that ". . . *communicative action* is a system of reference that cannot be reduced to the framework of instrumental action" (1971a:137). It will be helpful, though, to recognize that the claim of "an irreducible communicative dimension" operates as a presupposition for Habermas (Thompson 1981:80). The theoretical validity of this claim finally rests on the intuitive judgment of all human language

---

[12] Habermas claims that his distinction between social labor and social interaction (or between "forces of production" and "relations of production") is already present in Marx; but not consistently distinguished. Says Habermas (1971a:42),

> In his empirical analyses Marx comprehends the history of the species under categories of material activity and the critical abolition of ideologies, of instrumental action and revolutionary practice, of labor and reflection at once. But Marx interprets what he does in the more restricted conception of the species' self-reflection through work alone.

As Wellmer (1976:245) puts it, "Habermas explicitly introduces a categorial distinction into the theory of historical materialism which Marx, in his material analyses, had always implicitly presupposed." In short, Marx's "sensuous activity" of man is split into "man as a tool-making animal *and* man as a speaking animal" (Wellmer 1976:246).

[13] Instrumental reason is the reason which calculates means to predetermined ends without reference to an evaluation of the ends.

users regarding what is voluntary and what is coerced (White 1983:164). Thus, it rests on Habermas's project of a "*universal* pragmatics" which assumes ". . . an innate; capacity [of every human agent] to 'construct' the ideal speech situation . . . [and] to recognize what features an ideal speech situation would have" (Geuss 1981:66). The development of this point is the task appointed for section 4.2 to follow, for the notion of critique developed by Habermas is relative to and dependent on this "ideal speech situation" (Thompson 1981:94; White 1983:164; Geuss 1981:66; Bleicher 1980:163; Misgeld 1976:171; McCarthy 1978:189; Hoy 1978:123; Habermas 1971a:155). Here, though, my purpose has been to present only enough of Habermas's theory to demonstrate both similarities and differences with orthodox Marxism and to establish, in a preliminary way, the affinities between Habermas and Freire.

On four of the five topics discussed earlier with regard to Freire and Marx (cf. section 2.2 and 3.1)--man, man and the world, language, and praxis--Habermas shows clear similarities to both Freire and Marx. With regard to the four major differences between Marx and Freire (as noted in section 3.2), Habermas sides with Freire on each one: (1) the entire Frankfurt School emphasizes the individual and subjective factors more than did Marx; (2) Habermas clearly focuses on the role of language more than did Marx; (3) Habermas credits the human communicative situation with a larger role in changing consciousness than did Marx-Engels; and (4) the Marxist claim to strict empiricism and materialism is replaced by the prominent and problematic role that the "ideal speech situation" plays in Habermas's system (cf. further discussion in the next section).

We are now ready to introduce Habermas's notion of critique in greater detail and to further examine the all-important "ideal speech situation."

8.4.2 Habermas's notion of critique

"The concerns of critical theory are anchored in the writing of Kant, Hegel and Marx" (Thompson 1981:71). For this very reason, however, the "concept of critical theory is ambiguous" (Bubner 1982:42): the Kantian and the "Hegelian-Marxist" notions of critique ". . . cannot easily be reduced to one common denominator of critical reflection" (Bubner 1982:54). For Kant "critique" was the philosophical effort ". . . to elucidate the forms and categories which render . . . cognitive activity possible" (Thompson 1981:72). Reason alone was to pass judgment on the legitimacy of claims to knowledge. Kant had recognized the necessity of the synthesizing activity of the human subject if knowledge was to be more than random impressions and the human consciousness more than "a chamber of mirrors reflecting a welter of images devoid of rhyme or reason" (Bubner 1982:53). Yet this synthesizing activity remained unclear in Kant due to an overemphasis on the ideals and categories of mathematics and natural science. Hegel thus sought to clarify the status of the subject.

Hegel recognized that there was a force at work in human experience which rendered it progressive and teleologically governed. This "force" was the movement of the dialectic. The dialectic was characterized by a "power of the negative" (Hegel 1967:93) to reveal contradictions in each stage of experience, thereby giving rise to the unfolding of the next stage. Ultimately, the movement of the dialectic was conceived of as the progress of Absolute Spirit, or Self-consciousness. Marx acknowledged much value in the Hegelian perspective, yet reacted strongly against Hegel's idealism, his overemphasis on thought to the exclusion of the importance of concrete human activity. Marx maintained that the driving force of historical progress was not the dialectic of an Absolute Spirit, but ". . . the concrete sensuous activity of human beings producing goods to satisfy their basic needs" (Thompson 1981:72). The stages of history, then, were determined by the interactions of the material forces of production and social relations of production. Still, though, for Marx, there is the dialectic which functions to reveal and resolve the concrete, practical contradictions of economic and political injustice.

From Kant, Habermas gained the philosophical program of a "critique of understanding," the desire to clarify the conditions of possibility for human understanding in general. His notion of "human understanding," though, is decidedly affected by both the Hegelian emphasis on the subject and the Marxist concern for emancipation from the concrete contradictions of human life and labor. "A critical theory, then, is a reflective theory [contrary to the "objectifying" natural sciences] which gives agents a kind of knowledge inherently productive of enlightenment and emancipation" (Geuss 1981:2).[14]

From Marx, Habermas also appropriated the commitment that all human life, and in particular, philosophical discourse, is ruled by the concept of interest. Habermas insists that there are three distinguishable interests which govern all human activity.

First, there is the technical or instrumental interest. This interest governs the empirical-analytic sciences "in the sense that the signification of possible empirical statements consists in their technical exploitability" (Ricouer 1981a:80). This interest is defined by "the cognitive interest in technical control over objectified processes" (Habermas 1971a:309), and, according to the Frankfurt School, it is the dominant modern ideology.

The second sphere of interest is the sphere of intersubjective communication and understanding. This is the domain of the historical-hermeneutical sciences. The distinction between these first two interests arises from Habermas's critique of Marx alluded to in section 4.1: interest in the "forces of production" is the technical interest; interest in the "social relations of production" is the interest in communication. Habermas insists that an

---

[14] Geuss (1981:55ff) outlines the distinction between natural and critical sciences.

> . . . awareness of the distinction between instrumental and communicative action is therefore necessary in order to account for the very phenomena which Marx analysed: antagonism, domination, dissimulation, liberation (Ricoeur 1981a:81).

This is true because domination arises in the sphere of relations of production, not with the forces of production.

There is, though, a third interest which Habermas calls the interest in emancipation. This interest is proposed as the transcendental condition for the critical social sciences. The need for these sciences arises from the phenomena of ideology. Habermas, following the Marxist tradition of "ruthless criticism," recognizes that ideologies prevent ". . . the agents in the society from correctly perceiving their true situation and real interests" (Geuss 1981:3). And yet, there is always the possibility that man is able not only to recognize ideological domination and violence, but to free himself from it (at least to some extent; though Habermas's confidence in man's ability is seemingly unlimited). This possibility is accounted for by the interest in emancipation.

Because Habermas identifies emancipation as the interest which is basic to the social sciences, he is pressed (by his own thinking and by his critics) to clarify what "emancipation" means. He does this in his theory of communicative competence.[15] At the foundation of this theory is the "ideal speech situation," (ISS).

Self-consciously following in the tradition of the Enlightenment in which reason challenges the authority of tradition (cf. e.g. Habermas 1980:207f), and yet equally concerned to oppose "the tendency to define reason solely in objectivistic and instrumental terms" (McCarthy 1978:272), Habermas's task is "to articulate and ground an expanded conception of rationality" (McCarthy 1978:272). "Reason," then, is taken as "the principle of rational discourse" (Habermas 1980:207), a sense which Habermas defends as consonant with the Enlightenment conception:

> . . . it [the Enlightenment] still demanded that Reason be recognized as the principle of communication, free from force in the face of the real experience of communication distorted by force . . . (Habermas 1980:204).

---

[15] The importance of this theory for Habermas's project can hardly be overestimated:

"In short, Habermas's entire project . . . rests on the possibility of providing an account of communication that is both theoretical and normative, that goes beyond a pure hermeneutic, without being reducible to a strictly empirical-analytic science (McCarthy 1978:272)."

Rationality, consequently, is defined as the consensus which would be achieved in discourse which is carried on in ideal circumstances, i.e. "without compulsion and distortion" (Habermas 1980:205). Says Habermas,

> A critically enlightened hermeneutic that differentiates between insight and delusion incorporates the meta-hermeneutic awareness of the conditions for the possibility of systematically distorted communication. It connects the process of understanding to the principle of rational discourse, according to which truth would only be guaranteed by that *kind* of consensus which was achieved under the idealized conditions of unlimited communication free from domination and could be maintained over time (Habermas 1980:205).

Further definition of this idealized situation can be found in Habermas's work--e.g. "an unlimited community of interpreters" is required (Habermas 1980:205); there must be "a symmetrical distribution of chances to choose and to apply speech-acts" (Habermas 1971b:137; cf. also Habermas 1970a,b; Geuss 1981:65-70, 72f, 85f; McCarthy 1987:272-291)-- but that need not detain us here. Here the point is that

> The "ideal speech situation" will serve Habermas as a transcendental criterion of truth, freedom, and rationality. Beliefs that agents would agree on in the ideal speech situation are *ipso facto* "true beliefs," preferences they would agree on are "rational preferences," interests they would agree on are "real interests." The agents are "free" if their real situation is one which satisfies the conditions of the "ideal speech situation" (Geuss 1981:66).

Habermas's argument is "transcendental" since (as with Kant's transcendental philosophy) ". . . universal pragmatics aims at disclosing conditions of possibility" (McCarthy 1978:278), specifically "the possibility of reaching understanding in ordinary language communication" (McCarthy 1978:279). As mentioned earlier, Habermas follows the pattern of Chomskyian linguistics (cf. Chomsky 1965) in an effort to outline the universal core of communicative competence (McCarthy 1978:275).[16] His question is, What is necessarily required as a condition for all human agents as language users? The one condition which specifically lays the

---

16 Habermas follows the pattern, or the "inspiration," not the program of Chomskyian linguistics, since he develops a point which Chomsky chooses to ignore, i.e. *communicative* competence.

226

foundation for his critical theory is the ability to "recognize the difference between true and false statements in some general way or . . . [to] know what it means for a statement to be true" (Geuss 1981:65). More must be said, however, for the very notion of "what is true" is disputed by a theory which challenges tradition. The ISS is necessary. "The ISS," says White (1983:165), "is intended to be a theoretical reconstruction of those features of ordinary language communication which allow us to distinguish intuitively a true consensus from a false one." As Habermas (1973a:257) says, "A rational consensus can, in the final analysis, only be distinguished from a deceptive one through reference to an ideal speech situation."

Habermas's claim is that the

> . . . features of the ISS require no metaphysical foundation; rather, they are present in our use of natural language, and each speaker can impute them in discourse because of his communicative competence (White 1983:165; cf. Habermas 1970b:372).

Herein lies a distinction between Kant's project (the transcendental *deduction*) and Habermas's, and with it a major difficulty for Habermas. The a priori status which Habermas claims for the ISS is "relativized" (rather than "strong," as for Kant). That is, the ISS is a rational reconstruction which ". . . must be empirically confirmed in the normal way" (Geuss 1981:85), rather than deduced. And yet, critical theory--which is responsible for the reconstruction--also ". . . asserts of itself that it can be *definitively* confirmed or disconfirmed only . . . in the ideal speech situation" (Geuss 1981:85). The features of the ISS, then, are both known (at least implicitly)--since the ISS is assumed as always both presupposed and anticipated--and yet to be "definitively confirmed" by the actualization of the ISS. The difficulty can be stated otherwise as follows: "the only possible context for the confirmation of a critical theory [including the concept of the ISS at its basis]" (Geuss 1981:93) is the non-actual ISS. The source of our intuition about what is a true consensus is "the mastery of certain idealized features of speech situations" (White 1983:165); but how can we know what "mastery" is until the ISS is actualized? Until then there is no guarantee that even Habermas's characterization of the ISS by such terms as "free," "emancipation," "uncoerced," "without compulsion," "autonomy," etc. is a legitimate ideal. In short, perhaps the Enlightenment (and Habermas's use of the Enlightenment conceptions) is just another systematically distorted and distorting tradition.

The problem which Gadamer points out is another variation on this same theme: In order to criticize tradition, a ". . . frame of reference is to be discovered which allows us to transcend the context of tradition as such" (Misgeld 1976:181); but there is no "frame of reference" completely free of all tradition. Our considerations of Habermas's debate with Gadamer will allow us to pursue this question.

8.4.3   The Habermas-Gadamer debate

8.4.3.1 Presentation of the issues debated

Three perspectives on the issues debated by Habermas and Gadamer will be presented in what follows.

From Gadamer's perspective, the point of dispute with Habermas can be concisely stated:

> But what is really in dispute, I think, is simply whether reflection always dissolves substantial relationships or is capable of taking them up into consciousness (Gadamer 1976c:34).

Gadamer holds that ". . . reflection is not always and unavoidably a step toward dissolving prior convictions.   Authority is not always wrong" (Gadamer 1976c:32f).   To say that ". . . reason and authority are abstract antitheses" (Gadamer 1976c:33), as Habermas does, is evidence to Gadamer that Habermas is governed by a "prejudice" (Gadamer 1976c:32) which is, in fact, a "dogmatism" (Gadamer 1976c:35).   Thus: ". . . unconsciously the ultimate guiding image of emancipatory reflection in the social sciences must be an anarchistic utopia . . . the dissolution of all authority, all obedience" (Gadamer 1976c:42). This first perspective on the dispute focuses on the status and influence of tradition: Is it always negative?

McCarthy's (1978:190) summary of Gadamer's counterarguments to Habermas's position will prepare us for the second perspective on the debated issues.

"1.   Habermas attributes a false power to reflection.   As historically situated, reflection is always limited, partial, and based on taken-for-granted preconceptions and prejudgments

"2.   Habermas wants to 'get behind' language to the 'real' conditions under which it historically develops.   But language is not simply one aspect of society among others; it is a 'universal medium' of social life.   In particular labor and power are not located 'outside of' language but mediated through it

"3.   According to Habermas, the existence of systematically distorted communication requires that we go beyond hermeneutic's *verstehen* [understanding] to the critique of ideology.   But ideology is not inaccessible to hermeneutic understanding.   It appears to be such only if we set up a false opposition between understanding qua affirmation of traditional prejudice and reflection qua dissolution of traditional prejudice.   In reality understanding involves the rejection of unjustifiable prejudices as well as the recognition of justifiable authority

"4. The claims that Habermas raises on behalf of critical reflection are excessive. The critic cannot pretend to be in sole possession of the truth. His ideas of the just life are not exempt from revision and rejection in dialogue with others. Thus critical self-reflection, as well as the critique of ideological distortion, cannot be pursued in isolation from the attempt to come to an understanding with others. The ideals of reason are inherently bound up with an openness to dialogue--both actual dialogue with contemporaries and virtual dialogue with the past."

In short, Gadamer argues that the scope of hermeneutics is universal (cf. e.g. 1976b); that it is methodologically impossible to transcend the hermeneutic point of view: There simply is "no Archimedean point" (Bleicher 1980:156) outside of tradition from which tradition can be critiqued.

Habermas responds to Gadamer by attempting to establish some stable, transcendental ground from which critique might be carried on.

> Habermas's counterposition is an attempt to mitigate the radically situational character of understanding through the introduction of theoretical elements; the theories of communication and social evolution are meant to reduce the context-dependency of the basic categories and assumptions of critical theory (McCarthy 1978:193).

The second perspective, thus, focuses on the scope and extent of hermeneutics: Is it universal or not?[17]

Though Gadamer also seeks to incorporate a critical moment (cf. e.g. Gadamer 1976c:31f), he is forbidden by his formulation of "belonging" to a tradition[18] from elevating "the critical instance above the recognition of authority and above the very tradition reinterpreted" (Ricoeur 1981a:82). This, says Habermas, is really no criticism at all.

---

[17] In terms of the hermeneutic circle as introduced in chapter 6, Hoy (1978:118) states the issue between Habermas and Gadamer as follows:

"Is it possible for philosophy itself to stay within the hermeneutical circle of understanding, and within the limitation imposed by its own historical conditions, yet legitimately posit rational principles as conditions for the possible validity or truth of particular acts of understanding? Habermas continues to hold to a notion of reason demanding such transcendental principles, and Gadamer still maintains that such faith in the power of reflection alone represents an idealization that falsely attempts to break out of the hermeneutical circle."

[18] Habermas calls it Gadamer's "ontologization" of the linguisticality of "belonging."

One of his [Habermas's] basic objections to Gadamer is that criticism is impossible unless the concrete situation in which we stand can be tested against some rational principles as an ideal measure of reason (Hoy 1978:123).

Thus, closely connected to the issues of perspective on tradition-authority and the universality of the hermeneutic point of view, is the question of the standards and status of rationality without which critique has no reference point. This is the third perspective.

Thus far I have only presented the debate. What shall we make of this disagreement? I shall consider first the case against Habermas (4.3.2); then the case against Gadamer (4.3.3). Incorporated into this procedure are the arguments advanced by Ricoeur, which lay the foundation for Ricoeur's own reconstruction of the relation between critique and interpretation-reading (section 5).

8.4.3.2 The case against Habermas

Gadamer's fundamental criticism of Habermas--that no one can ever bring everything about tradition that effectively conditions consciousness under the gaze of critical reflection[19]--is widely supported by others (e.g. Dickens 1983; Geuss 1981:93f; Misgeld 1976:171, 182f; Ricoeur 1973:160ff; 1981a:95ff; Thompson 1981:66ff). As Ricoeur (1981a:97) points out:

> The interest in emancipation would be quite empty and abstract if it were not situated on the same plane as the historical-hermeneutic sciences, that is, on the plane of communicative action.

In short, ". . . this interest has no other content than the ideal of unrestricted and unconstrained communication" (Ricoeur 1981a:97), and "the only possible context for the confirmation of a critical theory" (Geuss 1981:93) is the realm of the hermeneutic sciences, i.e. in dialogue.[20]

This basic point can be further unpacked to reveal further difficulties for any non-hermeneutic critical theory. Because Habermas's critique is based upon a theoretical reconstruction of what agents in history believe

---

[19] Consider, for example, Gadamer (1976c:38): "Reflection on a given preunderstanding brings before me something that otherwise happens behind my back. Something--but not everything, for what I have called the *wirkungsgeschichtliches Bewusstsein* [consciousness of the history of effects] is inescapably more being than consciousness, and being is never fully manifest."

[20] Habermas (1980:209), in fact, grants this point: "There is no validation of depth-hermeneutical interpretation [i.e. critical theory as modelled on psychoanalysis, 208] outside of the self-reflection of all participants that is successfully achieved in dialogue."

about freedom, coercion, etc., there is no guarantee that any given reconstruction is the only one possible (Quine 1969:1ff), nor that the reconstruction itself has not changed the (initially) not clearly formulated, merely tacit beliefs by the process of "bringing certain attitudes, beliefs, behavior patterns, etc. to full consciousness" (Geuss 1981:94). Because critical theory itself requires practical validation in the (potentially infinite) realm of dialogue, there is always an element of indeterminacy at any given stage of discussion. Thus any attempt to be dogmatic is condemned to the judgment of being itself an "ideological ossification" (Gadamer 1976c:38). As pointed out at the beginning of section 4.2, "Critique is also a tradition" (Ricoeur 1981a:99).[21]

8.4.3.3 The case against Gadamer

For Gadamer (1976c:35), "Reality does not happen 'behind the back' of language; . . . reality happens precisely *within* language. And ". . . language . . . is the reservoir of tradition and the medium in and through which we exist and perceive our world" (1976c:29). Thus, in order to show that Gadamer's claim to the universality of hermeneutics is indefensible, Habermas attempts to show that it is "possible to break through the context of everyday language" (Bleicher 1980:159f).

Habermas agrees in part with Gadamer about the importance of ordinary language, but insists that language alone cannot account for human experience. Rather, ". . . the critique of ideology raises its claim from a different place than hermeneutics, namely from the place where labour, power and language are intertwined" (Ricoeur 1981a:96). As Habermas (1977:360) says,

> It makes good sense to conceive of language as a kind of metainstitution on which all social institutions are dependent; for social action is constituted only in ordinary language communication [this is Gadamer's point]. But this metainstitution of language as tradition is evidently dependent in turn on social processes . . . . Language is also a medium of domination and social power; it serves to legitimate relations of organized force. Insofar as the legitimations do not articulate the power relations whose institutionalization they make possible, insofar as these relations merely manifest themselves in the legitimations, language is *also* ideological . . . . Hermeneutic experience that encounters this dependency of the symbolic framework on actual conditions changes into critique of ideology.

---

[21] Habermas (1980:209) also grants this point: "It is, of course, true that criticism is always tied to the context of tradition which it reflects"

The nonnormative forces that infiltrate language as a metainstitution originate not only from systems of domination but also from social labor. In this instrumental sphere of action monitored by success, experiences are organized that evidently motivate linguistic interpretations and can change traditional interpretations through operational constraints. A change in the mode of production entails a restructuring of the linguistic world view. This can be studied, for instance, in the expansion of the realm of the profane in primitive societies. Of course, revolutions in the reproductive conditions of material life are for their part linguistically mediated. But a new practice is not only set in motion by a new interpretation; old patterns of interpretation are also weakened and overturned "from below" by a new practice.

In agreement with Habermas, Ricoeur (1973:162) states:

> . . . the forgetfulness of the trilogy work-power-language can always lead to a disastrous retreat into a philosophy of language which would lose its anthropological breadth. Hermeneutical philosophy must not only heed this warning, but also accept it. The very fact that linguisticality should be subordinated to historical experience and to aesthetic experience is sufficient warning that language is only the locus for the articulation of an experience which supports it, and that everything, consequently, does not arrive in language, but only comes to language. There is therefore no reason why work and power should not be taken into account in an anthropology of care [i.e. following Heidegger, as does Gadamer] where the linguistic dimension finds its privileged, yet subordinate place.

In short, the *Lebenswelt*, as discussed earlier, is, for Ricoeur and Habermas, pre- and/or hyper-linguistic (Ricoeur 1975a:31; 1978a:234; 1981a:56, 117-119, 243f; Reagan 1979:xviii).

Gadamer is certainly sensitive to this criticism. Says he,

> From the hermeneutical standpoint, rightly understood, it is absolutely absurd to regard the concrete factors of work and politics as outside the scope of hermeneutics (Gadamer 1976c:31).

232

Try as he might, though, it seems that here, as with related issues, Gadamer is unable to work out his diverse commitments and desires in a consistent system. After looking at these inconsistencies I will discuss the reason behind them.

In response to the above criticism of Habermas (and Ricoeur), Gadamer reasserts his famous aphorism: "Being that can be understood is language" (cf. 1976c:31). This, however, leads to an inconsistency in Gadamer's thought. To assert that "Being that can be understood is language" is to subordinate the historical and aesthetic experiences of being to linguisticality. Because historical and aesthetic experience partake of understanding under its ontological interpretation (as Gadamer argues in *Truth and Method* (1975)), and because being which can be understood is language, historical and aesthetic experience (as understood) are also language. However, Gadamer also says that ". . . our sensitive-spiritual existence is an aesthetic resonance chamber that resonates with the voices that are constantly reaching us, preceding all explicit aesthetic judgment" (Gadamer 1976c:8). In fact, he says, ". . . we are possessed by something and precisely by means of it we are opened up for the new, the different, the true" (Gadamer 1976c:9). But such talk of "resonance" and of being "possessed"--which precedes and makes possible linguistic understanding-- does not properly belong to the domain of linguisticality. Thus, on the one hand, aesthetic and historical experience are subordinated to linguisticality, and on the other hand, they are (pre-)determined by that which does not belong to the domain of linguisticality.

Related to the above inconsistency are two further issues, themselves closely related: the issues of the new in experience and of critique. These two further (and related) issues will reveal the reason for Gadamer's inconsistencies.

As noted in previous discussions, "the new" requires the assimilation of that which is different. Gadamer also recognizes this, associating the two as quoted above: "the new, the different" (Gadamer 1976c:9). Similarly, Hoy (1978:130) notes with regard to criticism, "Criticism implies distance, and the distance introduced by the generality of philosophical reflection makes possible the negative move essential to criticism." "Distance," "the different"--these are the stumbling blocks for Gadamer. So intent has Gadamer been on recognizing and rehabilitating the experience of belonging as "always already" determinative for aesthetic and historical experience, and thus for the human sciences, that he has been prevented "from really recognizing the critical instance [in hermeneutics-reading] and hence rendering justice to the critique of ideology" (Ricoeur 1981a:90).[22] Having emphasized belonging as opposed from the start to

---

[22] And yet, it cannot be denied that "Gadamer's hermeneutics contains . . . a series of decisive suggestions . . ." (Ricoeur 1981a:61) with regard to the inclusion of "distance," "difference," and thus, critique into a hermeneutic. Cf. also Palmer's discussion of the role of negativity in Gadamer's conception of experience (1969:194-198; 231-234). Such

difference or (in Ricoeur's term) distanciation, and battling against the alienation of distanciation (e.g. Gadamer 1975:15, 75, 145, 348ff), Gadamer is at a loss to reintegrate an adequate foundation for critique.

The fundamental conclusion to be drawn from this debate is that neither belonging nor distanciation can be overcome by the other. Further, any emphasis on one at the expense of the other leads to fundamental conceptual difficulties. In short, both belonging and distanciation must be conceived of as equally ultimate, equally foundational, and equally operative in any theory of interpretation/reading. This conclusion ought not be shocking, for it rejoins our considerations in chapter 7 where these basic terms were expressed as "identity" and "difference," and were taken as the basic and necessary "relations," the interaction of which defined the imagination.[23] The important point to be derived here is that critique, as always possible and implicitly present once the operative principle of difference is granted, is not peripheral to reading per se, but *central*.

The other basic conclusion to be proposed from the Gadamer-Habermas debate is that dialogue, or a theory of communication, is basic to a theory of reading. We have not, though, examined this conclusion directly. The reason for this is that Ricoeur challenges such a view based on his theory of the text, as we have seen in previous chapters. Thus, this latter conclusion will remain tentative until we examine Ricoeur's theory, which also proposes an integration of the critical instance into a theory of interpretation highly sympathetic to the Heideggerian-Gadamerian stance.

8.5   Ricoeur's contribution to the notion of critique

Having introduced and discussed Ricoeur's interpretation-reading theory previously (cf. chapters 2ff), I will review only briefly here. For Ricoeur, "a certain dialectic between the experience of belonging and alienating distanciation becomes the mainspring, the key to the inner life, of hermeneutics" (Ricoeur 1981a:90). Thus Ricoeur begins with *both* belonging (or "identity") and distanciation ("difference") in "dialectical relation." Belonging and distanciation, however, are *not* equally privileged. Finally, for Ricoeur, "distanciation is a moment of belonging" (1981a:111; cf. also 113). This preference is not justified by Ricoeur, except by giving expression to "the insurmountable character" of "the role of 'pre-understanding' in the apprehension of a cultural object" (Ricoeur 1981a:110). (This is basically an affirmation of Gadamer's point against Habermas.) But to affirm that "belonging" is insurmountable is not to deny that "distanciation" might also be insurmountable. This preference

---

considerations make it difficult to endorse whole-heartedly Ricoeur's reading of Gadamer. On the other hand, Habermas's debate with Gadamer, the considerations already mentioned above, and those to come, do point out at least a weakness in formulation and emphasis in Gadamer.

[23] Interestingly, Gadamer says, "It is imagination that is the decisive function of the scholar" (1976b:12); but he gives no extended treatment of the imagination as such.

also allows Ricoeur to formulate his hermeneutic arc as linear, with an essentially critical explanatory stage mediating between a naive and a critical reading (Ricoeur 1981a:161). As noted in chapter 7, there are difficulties with this construction. Another difficulty can now be noted here.

Though Ricoeur explicitly affirms the priority of belonging (e.g. 1981a:111), elsewhere in the same context (1981a:110-111) he also seems to deny this priority. Rather than belonging preceding distance,

> ... we belong to an historical tradition through a relation of distance which oscillates between remoteness and proximity. To interpret is to render near what is far (temporally, geographically, culturally, spiritually) (Ricoeur 1981a:110f).

This seems to reverse, or at least equalize, the priorities. Not to do so would be to fall prey to his own critique of Gadamer: basically, not to start with distanciation (together with belonging) is to never be able to adequately reintegrate it (Ricoeur 1981a:59-62). This same ambivalence causes further problems for Ricoeur on two other issues integrally related to the notion of critique: the question of standards in critique and the placement of subjectivity, and in particular, intersubjectivity, in the hermeneutic arc. But first some further presentation of critique in Ricoeur's scheme.

8.5.1 Further background

For Ricoeur, "Distanciation, in all its forms and figures, constitutes par excellence the critical moment in understanding" (Ricoeur 1981a:113). In chapter 2 I introduced six such distanciations which, for Ricoeur, constitute (together with the notion of work) the text qua text. These distanciations also integrate critique as a necessary part of reading (Ricoeur 1981a:139, 144); at least an incipient critique is inherent in reading. With such incipience comes the potential for full-blown critique.

To further focus his reflections, Ricoeur grounds critique in the internal dialectic of meaning itself. The culmination of reading, i.e. appropriation, is conditioned by the ". . . double distanciation which is linked to the matter of the text, as regards its sense and as regards its reference" (Ricoeur 1981a:113). These two distanciations function to highlight the two forms of critique to which Ricoeur has attended in greatest detail, the Freudian critique of the illusions of the subject, and the Marxist critique of ideologies. The explanatory procedures required by the constitution of the text qua text (I will have more to say about this shortly) dispossess the narcisstic ego of itself (Ricoeur 1981a:192, 113; cf. section 5.1 of chapter 7 for the fuller discussion). These procedures which construct an ideal sense from the structure of the text (Ricoeur 1981a:111) imply a "universality and atemporality" (Ricoeur 1981a:192) which work to accomplish this dispossession (Ricoeur 1981a:192). This distanciation, effected by the text as a structured work and the attendant necessity to reconstruct its meaning (Ricoeur 1981a:92f), is "the ruin of the *ego's* pretension to constitute itself as ultimate origin" (Ricoeur 1981a:113). Here "the primacy of subjectivity" (Ricoeur 1981a:113; and with it any "pure" top-down theory of reading) is displaced by the reader's relation to the text. Ricoeur, though, seems to go further to claim that this dispossession of the ego by the explanatory procedures both founds and constitutes the beginnings of a critique of the illusions of the subject, as e.g. in Freud (cf. Ricoeur 1970; 1975b).

The beginnings of critique accomplished by the necessities of decoding and reconstructing a written work are furthered by the movement of meaning from sense to reference. What the text presents is not only an "internal organisation" (Ricoeur 1981a:93; its "sense"), but a "mode of being," "a dimension of reality," a "mode of the possible," a mode of the "power-to-be" (Ricoeur 1981a:93), which Ricoeur calls its "reference." This "reference" is the culminating foundation for critique:

> The power of the text to open a dimension of reality implies in principle a recourse against any given reality and thereby the possibility of a critique of the real (Ricoeur 1981a:93).

And again,

> A hermeneutics of the power-to-be thus turns itself towards a critique of ideology, of which it constitutes the most fundamental possibility (Ricoeur 1981a:94).

Here the critique of the illusions of the subject and the critique of ideology coincide, for the ". . . *ego* must assume for itself the 'imaginative variations' by which it could *respond* to the 'imaginative variations' on reality that . . . [texts] engender" (Ricoeur 1981a:113f).

Ricoeur's formulation of the placement and status of critique in reading is stimulating indeed--yet finally not satisfying. This is due to his vague, if not paradoxical, formulations (e.g. distanciation is "within the interior of appropriation" (Ricoeur 1981a:113), while ". . . distanciation is the condition of understanding" (Ricoeur 1981a:144)) and to the need for further work on important issues. The first difficulty was already mentioned in the introductory remarks to this section. My task now is to pick up the related issues of standards and subjectivity, and to show that Ricoeur's silence and inconsistencies on these issues (respectively) mask important features of his basic belonging/distanciation dialectic.

8.5.2 Standards

The issue of standards in critique has already been raised with regard to Habermas. For him the ISS is the transcendental standard of freedom, truth, justice, rationality, normativity (for knowledge), normality (in social interactions and institutions), and even, reality (cf. Habermas 1970b; 1980:206; Gadamer 1976c; Bleicher 1980:158,163; Geuss 1981:31, 66; Hoy 1978:125; McCarthy 1978:189; Bubner 1982:50; Dickens 1983:145). I will return later to a further discussion of Habermas's particular choice of a standard (i.e. the ISS), but first I raise the issue of "standards" for Ricoeur.

The issue is raised as follows: Granted, the meaning of a text and a reader's understanding of it is "entirely *mediated* by the whole of explanatory procedures which precede it and accompany it" (Ricoeur 1981a:220). In short, "the construction of a network of interactions" (Ricoeur 1981a:174), which constitutes a structural analysis of the text, is necessary. This construction, however, is guided by theories. Ricoeur mentions at least four such theories--textual exegesis (Ricoeur 1981a:111), the critique of ideology (Ricoeur 1981a:111), the critique of the illusions of the subject (psychoanalysis) (Ricoeur 1981a:144), and structural analysis (Ricoeur 1981a:93, 143, 161)---but leaves the number and kind of such theories, in principle, open. Here the difficulty can be raised directly: how do we know that the world revealed by the text, and the correlated self, are not products of forces and systematic distortions introduced by the theories operative in the construction of "the network of interactions"? After all, Ricoeur does acknowledge that different constructions are possible (cf. e.g. 1981a:211ff). In short, what are the standards of critique, and what is the relation of these standards to the fundamental dialectic of belonging-distanciation? Or put another way, what constitutes the continuity of the hermeneutic arc? What is the "link" between pre-understanding, explanation, and critical understanding?

A hint of an answer is given in what Ricoeur judges to be the most basic and most important explanatory theory: structural analysis, which provides a form of explanation for the human sciences which is based in the human sciences themselves--specifically, in linguistics--rather than following the natural science model (cf. Ricoeur 1981a:152ff, 215ff). The hint begins in Ricoeur's exposition of structuralist linguistics. In that approach, the "interplay of merely distinctive entities within finite sets of such units defines the notion of structure in linguistics" (Ricoeur 1981a:216; cf. also 153). Structural analysis, consequently, ". . . bring[s] out the logic, [i.e.] the operations which relate the 'bundles of relations' among themselves" (Ricoeur 1981a:217). The important point here is that two fundamental principles are operative in such explanatory procedures. First, and readily acknowledged by Ricoeur and structuralism (also deconstructionism), is the principle of opposition or difference: ". . . units . . . are merely defined by their opposition to other units in the same system" (Ricoeur 1981a:216). The second principle is less readily acknowledged. It is this: In order for the oppositions to be meaningful, they must be "within . . . sets," "bundles," "the same system." Thus, there is also a fundamental principle of identity. (If this principle were taken together with the principle of difference, this second principle could be termed the principle of similarity; taken by itself, it could also be termed the principle of sameness.)[24] These two principles--of difference and of identity--are the same basic principles discussed in the previous chapter and identified with Ricoeur's fundamental dialectic of belonging and distanciation in this chapter. Thus the "link" between the stages of the hermeneutic arc can be located in this fundamental dialectic.[25] So fundamental are these two that I would propose them--taken together--as transcendentals (at least), conditions for the possibilities of interpretation and reading. They do not, however, in themselves, provide us with standards, since the relations of (meaningful) identity and difference are still relations subject to judgment. The standards sought, I expect, will not be provided by Ricoeur until his views on transcendence are more thoroughly worked out. I will, however, use these reflections, together with further thought on the topic of intersubjectivity, to propose a solution consistent with my reading of his current work.

8.5.3 Intersubjectivity in Ricoeur's theory of reading

Though Habermas and Gadamer both make dialogue central in their thought, Ricoeur's recognition of distanciation and the consequent central position of the text breaks with the dialogical model. Understanding must be mediated by "what seems most contrary to subjectivity, . . . what structural analysis discloses as the texture of the text" (Ricoeur 1981a:143). In short, ". . . the mediation of the text cannot be treated as an extension of the dialogical situation" (Ricoeur 1981a:91).

Though Ricoeur breaks rather effectively with the exclusive primacy of dialogue, and seeks to suppress subjectivity until the final moment of hermeneutic appropriation, this attempt succeeds only in highlighting otherwise neglected aspects of the hermeneutic process. Seven arguments support this claim that subjectivity is still integral to Ricoeur's hermeneutic arc, from start to finish.

8.5.3.1 Against Ricoeur's success in suppressing subjectivity

First, while breaking with Gadamer's conception of hermeneutics by wanting to incorporate "the critique of ideology into self-understanding"

---

[24] This principle of identity is even presupposed by the principle of difference: a system of pure difference--as often assumed by some structuralists and those borrowing this insight-- is simply nothing, which of course is no difference at all. Derrida is inconsistent at this point as we will see in the next chapter.

[25] The same two are also operative in the "assimilation" typical of the appropriation stage as discussed in the chapter 7, section 5. Thus, there is continuity throughout all the stages of the arc.

(Ricoeur 1981a:1110), Ricoeur still calls his project "a hermeneutics of communication" (Ricoeur 1981a:110). This is because

> . . . the distortions of communication [the concern of a critique of ideology] directly concern the constitution of the intersubjective network in which a common nature and common historical entities can be formed (Ricoeur 1981a:110).

Thus, for Ricoeur too, "intersubjectivity" is at the heart of that critique which is the result of the explanatory procedures which dispossess the reading subject of its primacy.

Second, while Ricoeur claims quite clearly (and seemingly decisively) "Nothing is less intersubjective or dialogical than the encounter with a text" (Ricoeur 1981a:191), and "The freeing of the written material with respect to the dialogical condition of discourse is the most significant effect of writing" (Ricoeur 1981a:139), he also affirms that ". . . the text is much more than a particular case of intersubjective communication" (Ricoeur 1981a: 131)--implying, I think, that the text is certainly *at least* that--and that one's relation to a text is more complex than the intersubjective relation of a dialogue. Rather, even the

> . . . "short" intersubjective relation [of dialogue] is intertwined, in the interior of the historical connection, with various "long" intersubjective relations, mediated by diverse social institutions, social roles and collectivities (groups, classes, nations, cultural traditions, etc.). The long intersubjective relations are sustained by an historical tradition of which dialogue in only a segment. Explication therefore extends much further than dialogue, coinciding with the broadest historical connections (Ricoeur 1981a:108).

Indeed, then, intersubjectivity is basic to the pre-understanding of belonging to a tradition, and to the "explication" (the explanatory procedures) "which precedes and supports it" (Ricoeur 1981a:108).

Third, Ricoeur is consistent in his insistence that discourse, the object of hermeneutic study, always refers to both a speaker and "another person, an interlocutor" (Ricoeur 1981a:198) by means of various devices inherent to its character as "used language" (cf. e.g. 1981a:145ff, 197ff; 1976; 1977a:65ff). Thus, again, an intersubjective situation is assumed throughout the study of discourse, even though Ricoeur argues effectively that ". . . the relation between writing and reading is no longer a particular case of the relation between speaking and hearing" (Ricoeur 1981a:139; this point will be modified slightly in point seven below).

239

Fourth, Ricoeur affirms (and modifies) both Habermas and Gadamer on the question of "consensus." To review briefly: Gadamer believes "even misunderstanding presupposes a 'deep common accord' " (Gadamer 1976b:7) which is the "comprehensive life-phenomenon that constitutes the *we* that we all are" (Gadamer 1976b:8). Habermas, on the other hand, thinks that Gadamer's account provides no basis for critique. Rather, "idealized conditions of unlimited communication free from domination" (Habermas 1980:205) must be presupposed and anticipated in every communicative action. In characteristic style, Ricoeur mediates these two views:

> Distortions can be criticised only in the name of a *consensus* which we cannot anticipate merely emptily, in the manner of a regulative idea, unless that idea is exemplified; and one of the very places of exemplification of the ideal of communication is precisely our capacity to overcome cultural distance in the interpretation of works received from the past. He who is unable to reinterpret his past may also be incapable of projecting concretely his interest in emancipation (1981a:97).

I will want to reopen this precise point of dispute between Habermas and Gadamer in the next section (5.4), but here my point is that Ricoeur affirms the intersubjectivity of a concrete ISS as essential to a critical hermeneutic.

Fifth, if Ricoeur did not admit an intersubjective context from the start, he would have the difficult problem of explaining how a subject can come to a true *self*-understanding in reference to the (impersonal, subjectless) world of the text alone, while such is not yet available at the level of the system of sense relations. Further, it seems he would fall to his own critique of Husserl's fifth *Meditation* (cf. Ricoeur 1981a:124-126; 1967:115-142). In short, this critique concludes that "If the *ego* and the *alter* ego are not coupled from the very beginning, they never will be" (Ricoeur 1981a:126).

Sixth, Ricoeur's own style of writing indicates that a written text is in fact like the dialogue situation of question and answer. Note, for instance, the frequent use of rhetorical questions and imaginary opponents as in "someone might object that . . . ."

Seventh, and finally, there is a growing body of research which supports the claim that the relations between speaking-listening, on the one hand, and writing-reading, on the other, form a continuum, rather than lending themselves to the kind of strict discontinuity Ricoeur often indicates (cf. e.g. Tannen 1978; 1980; 1982a,b,c,d; Akinnaso 1982).

The conclusion of these seven arguments is that Ricoeur cannot, and, in fact, does not suppress subjectivity until the final moment of hermeneutic appropriation. Rather, he presupposes intersubjectivity and leans on this presupposition throughout his exposition of the hermeneutic arc. In this regard, Ricoeur's use of intersubjectivity, rather than his explicitly formulated theory, confirms Habermas's conviction that an ISS (of some sort; the content of the ISS is another question) does function as at least a "quasi-transcendental" (Habermas 1970c:129).[26]

At the start of this section (5.3), I said that though Ricoeur's attempted suppression of intersubjectivity does not succeed in its stated purpose (cf. the seven arguments above), it does succeed in highlighting otherwise neglected aspects of the hermeneutic-reading process. A consideration of these neglected aspects will lead us into Ricoeur's specific contributions to the Habermas-Gadamer debate (section 5.4), and finally to our concluding comments regarding the notion of critique which results from these discussions (section 6).

8.5.4 A discussion centered around Ricoeur's contributions

Perhaps the major theoretical contribution of Ricoeur to the hermeneutic-reading process is the recognition that both belonging and distanciation are operative throughout. This means that communication is always "communication in and through distance" (Ricoeur 1981a:131). For Ricoeur, the text is "the paradigm of distanciation in communication" because ". . . it displays a fundamental characteristic of the very historicity of human experience" (Ricoeur 1981a:131), namely, that it is communication in and through distance. However, if the distanciation which the text highlights is indeed part of the fundamental structure of human existence, then one would think that it is always operative, and thus is certainly operative in speaking too. All that Ricoeur should conclude (and at times does; e.g. 1975a:321f; 1976:26; 1981a:141) is that there are features of discourse which are more clearly displayed and usually more functionally influential in writing-reading, than in speaking-listening. All the characteristics of discourse, however, are always present in all discourse, at least implicitly, and can be highlighted under different modes of expression (e.g. narrative, exposition, etc.). The research referred to in argument seven, section 5.3 substantiates this point.

A further consequence of this point can be stated as to agree with Ricoeur's usual emphasis: i.e. "The relation of writing-speaking is no longer a particular case of the relation speaking-hearing" (Ricoeur 1976:29). It must be acknowledged that both writing-reading and speaking-hearing require a common grounding. Ricoeur argues for such a common grounding in "the dialectical constitution of discourse" (1976:26), i.e. the

---

[26] "Quasi-" is used here because, as Hegel criticized Kant, transcendentals cannot be discerned "without a self-reflection on the history of the human species" (Habermas 1970c:130).

event-meaning dialectic; but section 5.3 above argues for the further grounding in the intersubjectivity of an "ideal speech situation" (ISS) of some sort. The "of some sort" must be emphasized since "speech" (as in Ideal Speech Situation--ISS) can no longer be tied as exclusively to the dialogical as the word "speech" implies. Thus a difference of emphasis between reading and listening can be maintained while still recognizing a common condition (the "ISS") as fundamental to both.

Yet further consequences follow from the basic affirmation of the fundamental belonging-distanciation dialectic. First, critique is affirmed as integral to the reading process, since wherever distanciation is operative, critique is incipiently present also. This point affirms distanciation and Habermas's perspective. Second, though critique is always possible, it can never be completed with finality; our participation in the tradition of Being can never be finally comprehended from a point outside of it. This point affirms belonging and Gadamer's perspective.

The second neglected aspect which Ricoeur highlights is the necessary mediation of the ideality of meaning, a notion which emphasizes distanciation. In the context of text interpretation this ideality is expanded to mean "the immanent structure, . . . the internal system of dependencies arising from the crossing of the 'codes' which the text employs" (Ricoeur 1981a:111). Given the polysemy of the text affirmed by Ricoeur (e.g. 1981a:212), and the compatibility of identity and difference supposed as a fundamental dialectic, the possibility of a complex structure of the sense of a text is also affirmed. This has already been alluded to in chapter 7.

There are, though, further implications of this ideality which emerge in the context of the Habermas-Gadamer debate. First, if intersubjectivity is to be affirmed as presupposed throughout the hermeneutic arc, as I argued in 5.3, then the mediation of understanding in reading theory by the ideality of sense-structure cannot introduce a discontinuity which can be used to argue decisively against this presupposition. If ideality were to break with all traces of intersubjectivity and yet continue to be accepted as a necessary mediation, there would be no recourse for the reinstitution of subjectivity. This, however, need not be taken as an argument against Ricoeur's contention that the text does break with the subjective intention of the author. Rather, it can be taken as an argument in favor of the subjectivity of ideality in a sense which is not dependent on the subjectivities of either author or reader. Perhaps Ricoeur himself leans in that direction when he argues for the "spirituality" of discourse (1981a:201f), a term which is open to much interpretive haggling, but which nonetheless is generally considered closer in connotation to subjectivity than is usually allowed by the term ideality (cf. e.g. Hegelian and Christian thought).[27]

---

[27] This is making a stronger claim than that the grasp of meaning as ideal must be subjective. Certainly the grasp is subjective. But the phenomenological evidence presented by Ricoeur, Gadamer, Iser, and Poulet is that the reader is as much grasped by

Ricoeur's notion of the bestowal of a self to the reading ego (cf. chapter 7) focuses the problem. To reiterate an argument given elsewhere, how can ideality bestow a self without implicating itself as also a "self" (in some sense)? Thus ideality not only implies subjectivity in that only an ego can grasp it; not only does it imply intersubjectivity in that it is the "object-pole" for any possible "ego-pole"; but ideality itself participates in subject-like acts. In particular "ideality" participates in (1) the bestowal of selves, (2) the communication of meaning, and (3) the giving of liveliness (if not life) to the reader. My claim in this section is that this evidence is evidence for the intersubjectivity of ideality, an intersubjectivity which cannot be reduced to the subjectivities of any number of human intentional agents.

The second implication of the role of ideality arises directly from Ricoeur's discussion of Habermas and Gadamer (Ricoeur 1973):

> To reduce an ideological process is first undoubtedly to explain it, but in such a way that the pre-understanding we have of our situation and our project becomes less opaque and more transparent. We could only completely detach the explanation of ideologies from the movement by which we clarify the preliminary understanding which we have of ourselves if a non-historical place existed, one not situated historically, from where we could consider from a distance and from on high the theater of illusions, the battle field of ideologies. Then it would be possible to explain without understanding. But this explanation would no longer have anything to do with the restoration of our competence to communicate and therefore with the emancipation of the human species (Ricoeur 1981a:163).

Ideality, however, is described by Ricoeur as "a place which is a non-place" (1981a:153), and a text as "a kind of atemporal object which has, as it were, broken its moorings with *all* historical development" (Ricoeur 1981a:185; emphasis added). And again,

> The rise to writing implies the "suspension" of the historical process, the transference of discourse to a sphere of ideality . . . (Ricoeur 1981a:185).

Thus, it seems that the "non-historical place" required for critique does exist if ideality is a genuine characteristic of meaning as Ricoeur affirms (and I argued in chapter 4).

---

the meaning as he actively grasps it. In fact, there seems to be a priority to the being grasped; but not in such a way as to void the active participation of the reader.

Ricoeur is also concerned (as quoted above, 1973:163) that such a "non-historical" explanation would break with communication and therefore emancipation. This need not be the case if ideality itself is intersubjective in character, for then the mediation by ideality is itself subject to, and perhaps even participates in, the ISS.

Ricoeur is further concerned (as quoted above) that such an explanation would break with understanding. This would only be the case if distanciation could break with belonging to Being. This need not be the case as Ricoeur himself insists. Rather, the implication is that this break would occur only if the "non-historical place" did not belong to Being. But again, Ricoeur's own "mediation" of the different "temporal" orientations of Habermas (future) and Gadamer (past), points in another direction.

Ricoeur opposes as a "deceptive antinomy" (Ricoeur 1981a:100) any effort to

> . . . oppose the interest in the reinterpretation of
> cultural heritages received from the past and the
> interest in the futuristic projections of a liberated
> humanity (Ricoeur 1981a:100).

Rather, he terms the relations between "the recollection of tradition and the anticipation of freedom" a "dialectic" (Ricoeur 1981a:100), and even suggests that

> He who is unable to reinterpret his past may also
> be incapable of projecting concretely his interest
> in emancipation (Ricoeur 1981a:97).[28]

There is, then, a deep and inherent belonging of the past and the future to one another. Ricoeur's perspective and language in explaining this is theological: ". . . eschatology is nothing without the recitation of acts of deliverance from the past", in particular, "the Exodus and the Resurrection" (1981a:100). Without developing this into an extensive theological discussion, the following thoughts are relevant here.

First, internal to the critique of Gadamer's view of interpretation is the criticism offered by Pannenberg 1967, affirmed by Habermas (1977:361), and acknowledged by Gadamer (1976c:36ff). Pannenberg's point is that though Gadamer has been "at pains to avoid [a universal concept of history]" (Pannenberg 1967:146) as the means of spanning the past horizon of the text and the present horizon of the reader, he has been unsuccessful. Gadamer insists that a bridging of horizons occurs, but he

---

[28] This same dialectic Ricoeur develops elsewhere, both in his work on Freud (e.g. Ricoeur 1970:339ff; Ricoeur 1974:160-176) and in his theological writings (e.g. Ricoeur 1974:402-424).

has not avoided the necessity of a universal concept of history.[29] This is Ricoeur's point, in part, and mine. Pannenberg states the situation nicely:

> . . . the text can only be understood in the context of the total history which binds the past to the present, and indeed not only to what currently exists, but also to the future horizon of what is presently possible, because the meaning of the present is only illuminated by the light of the future (1967:146f).

The point: the process of interpretation-reading Gadamer outlines requires the unity of past, present, and future.

Pannenberg goes further to open up this question of "the context of universal history" (Pannenberg 1967:148) in terms of "the biblical tradition" which he even affirms "forms the origin of universal-historical thinking as such" (Pannenberg 1967:151). To take the discussion forward a few steps to the relevant conclusions, a bit more must be said from the perspective of "the history of Jesus in its relationship to the Israelite-Jewish tradition" (Pannenberg 1967:151).

It is almost axiomatic to the traditions based on the text of the Bible, that God is both personal and unchanging. The textual evidence for this perspective can hardly be interpreted otherwise (e.g. Malachi 3:6; Isaiah 41:4; 48:4; Hebrews 13:8). As paradoxical as it may seem that God is both personal and thoroughly involved in the historical affairs of men, and also is represented as eternal or non-historical in his own being, this is the orthodox interpretation of both Jewish and Christian traditions. The implications for our discussion are: first, the "non-historical place" can belong to Being in a most decisive way; and second, the "non-historical" is not necessarily incompatible with the personal, nor, if the trinitarian account of God is to be believed, the interpersonal (i.e. the intersubjective). Further, following the recent developments in Reformed thinking on eschatology (e.g. Ridderbos 1962; 1975; Gaffin 1978), the anticipation of the future freedom promised to those "in Christ" is already a present reality, though not yet a fully consummated reality. Thus the presence of the Holy Spirit in the lives of those who believe in Jesus as the Christ is both the present testimony to the historical-past resurrection event and the present guarantee of the promised future fulfillment. This, in fact, is also Pannenberg's solution: " . . . the end of history can also be understood as something which is itself only *provisionally* known" (Pannenberg 1967:151); but nonetheless *known*. This is to say that to one in this tradition, Ricoeur's mediation of the past and the future is a very reasonable solution. Further, this tradition also offers such concepts as "the personal, even interpersonal, non-historical" which is involved in the

---

[29] Pannenberg's detailed arguments are found in Pannenberg 1967:146-152.

historical, and even incarnates the "ISS" historically (e.g. Colossians 2:9; cf. also Gadamer 1976c:37).[30]

This theological excursus has been offered as a development both consistent with and relevant to the more philosophical discussions regarding the hermeneutic-reading process and the notion of critique. The conclusion is that there are concepts available in the Christian tradition which offer the kind of mediation which Ricoeur seeks: a mediation

> . . . between explanation and understanding, between a critique of ideologies and the extension of communication, between the projection of freedom and the reinterpretation of the past (Ricoeur 1973:165).

Further, this mediation offers a reopening of the "theoretical solution to the fundamental antinomy" (Ricoeur 1973:165) which Ricoeur doubts exists. Finally, these Christian notions sketch the direction of my proposed development of Ricoeur's undeveloped ontology. This latter point will be further developed a bit in what follows; but the hints at an ontology scattered throughout this chapter and the previous one will not finally be collected until chapter 9.

There are three further implications from this extension of Ricoeur's contribution to the Gadamer-Habermas debate. First, some further content is offered to the standard for critique which was left rather abstract in Ricoeur, as noted in section 5.2. There only the dialectical unity of the principle of identity and difference could be affirmed as a "standard," which, because of its abstractness, amounts to hardly a standard at all.[31] Section 5.3 adds some flesh to the abstract bones of identity-difference in terms of intersubjectivity. Clearly, identity and difference are presupposed in intersubjectivity: identity because like subjectivities are in view; and difference because more than one such subjectivity is involved. With intersubjectivity there is, though, no mention of how many subjectivities are presupposed. Earlier in this section, God as triune was mentioned as a proposed solution. If that tradition were followed, then this necessary "ideal" (in Habermas's language) could be further developed. More could be said about those characteristics Habermas finds inherent in the ISS--e.g. truth, justice, freedom, goodness, etc.--though from a tradition which at the

---

[30] Ricoeur recognizes the lack of such incarnation (theoretical in this case) of the ISS as a weakness in Habermas (Ricoeur 1981a:97).

[31] "Hardly," but still a standard of sorts. The principles which Ricoeur adopts from Beardsley as constituting a "logic of validation" for interpretation--the principles of congruence and plentitude (Ricoeur 1981a:175f)--can be argued for on the basis of the principles of identity and difference. These principles do not, of course, wring out every element of subjectivity and personal difference in interpretive judgment, but they do offer guidance for the discussion of such judgments.

same time offers a critique of Habermas's Enlightenment tradition. It is not my purpose here to pursue either the development of a concrete standard resulting from a Christian reading of the ISS, or to critique Habermas's tradition. Here it is enough to notice the possibility

The second implication concerns a sticky point in the Habermas-Gadamer debate regarding the supposed consensus which Gadamer asserts always precedes and supports even misunderstandings (Gadamer 1976b:7), while Habermas denies its validity due to the reality of ideological systematic distortion (Habermas 1970c:124ff). Habermas asserts that Gadamer's "consensus" is not "deep" enough to escape the possibilities of ideologically forced distortions. And on this point I agree with Habermas: Gadamer's ontologizing of "the context-dependency of the understanding of meaning" (Habermas 1970c:124) does not reckon with the extent of the deceptiveness which, in Ricoeur's words, is sin as "an ontological dimension of existence" (Ricoeur 1974:428). That is, the powers of deception to which man is subject are at least as profound and pervasive as his linguistic tradition, which Gadamer offers as the "safe" playground for both the assimilation of tradition and emancipation from unfounded prejudice. Habermas argues instead for competencies of the species man (McCarthy 1978:277), which Ricoeur points out is an empty ideal without reinterpretations of the past. Here a seeming inconsistency in Gadamer--another form of the same overemphasis on belonging over against distanciation--rejoins both Habermas and Ricoeur.

Gadamer speaks as if the consensus which we are is bound by the particular tradition(s) and language(s) in which we participate. He does talk that way (Gadamer 1976b:7f), and Habermas takes him that way (Habermas 1980:204ff). And yet, Gadamer explicitly and forcefully asserts that ". . . there is absolutely no captivity within a language--not even within our native language" (1976b:16). The overemphasis on belonging to a tradition-language limits the openness to the new (Gadamer 1976b:15), even "the infinite realm of possible experience" (Gadamer 1976b:16) which Gadamer also affirms. I have spoken of this before as an unbalanced neglect of "the different," etc. The new point here is that what Gadamer wants to affirm as "consensus," or "the 'we' that we all are" (1976b:8) is, in fact, some tradition in which every man participates by virtue of being a man. Underlying this notion lies some conception of the species-being of man (whether Marxist, Christian, or another) which is ontological--thus grounding the ontologizing of hermeneutic belonging--and always escaping the particulars of any specific tradition. Thus far Gadamer is successful in avoiding Habermas's criticisms. What such a conception cannot escape, however, is the radical critique of this species tradition as itself subject to distorting dominations. It does, though, provide the background for another contribution from the Christian tradition.

Briefly (using admittedly problematic language to sketch a proposal whose development is again beyond this work): The species being of man was constituted in the first man, Adam. This man fell from the realm of undistorted communication and ever since, every man (excepting one) has

247

been subject to the bondage imposed by that fall. The one exception is Jesus Christ, conceived of by Paul as the second (and last) Adam (Romans 5; 1 Corinthians 15). This second Adam is a new beginning for humanity, himself embodies the "ISS," and offers participation in this radically new beginning which alone actualizes freedom from distorting influences.[32]

It is true that this Christian tradition can be viewed as just another ideology, perhaps even the worst from the Enlightenment perspective. Regardless, the Christian "solution" does provide answers to the weaknesses in Habermas's, Gadamer's, and Ricoeur's theories (cf. also Pannenberg 1967:150ff).

The third, and final, implication from Ricoeur's mediation of Gadamer and Habermas (and my extensions from Ricoeur's position) regards the question, How can Ricoeur's distanciation function within the subjectivity of the reader (cf. Iser's and Poulet's divided self in reading)? Simply to notice and describe the phenomenon does not account for it. Nor does the discernment of a transcendental ISS--which after all, for Habermas, functions as an epistemological category. To leave such a transcendental floating, as it were, is not satisfying, especially when one grants the force of the Heideggerian move to the explication of ontological grounding (cf. chapter 6). Already I have been anticipating the answer to the question above (and the dissatisfaction with the approaches of Iser, Poulet, and Habermas) in the preceding points. The transcendental ISS needs ontological grounding for itself, and hopefully, in such a way as to account for the "divided self" in reading. The anticipated answer is in line with Ricoeur's objection to Heideggerian ontology

> . . . in which the neutral is more expressive than
> the personal . . . . This ontology proceeds from a
> listening turned more attentively to the Greeks
> than to the Hebrews, more to Nietzsche than
> Kierkegaard (Ricoeur 1975a:312).

I, however--as does Ricoeur--do follow Heidegger's fundamental move. How, though, does this move look when ". . . turned more attentively to the . . . Hebrews"?

There are some absolutely crucial differences which this "Hebraic turn" necessitates--such as the fundamental distinction within Being itself between Creator-Being and creature-being (including humans), and the asymmetry of this relation within Being--which nonetheless, can not detain us here. What is acknowledged is the fundamental definition of man in correlation to Being. The theological formulation of this correlation is

---

[32] The claim here is not that Christ is a neutral ISS, but that He is fundamental to all humanity in a way that is basic to every human tradition, including of course the historic Christian traditions, which can be distinguished from and critiqued in terms of the "Christ tradition" sketched above.

quite simply that man is the image of God. Thus, with God presented as triune (and thus, intersubjective), man is defined ontologically as intersubjectively structured. The following implications will be drawn from this. First, the ISS as an epistemological condition is ontologically grounded in man's constitution as man. Second, the "divided self" in reading is a particular manifestation and exploitation of this intersubjective possibility inherent in man's being. Third, the interplay of identity and difference is absolutely fundamental to man's ontological character and thus is totally inescapable. Fourth, because all men are equally created in the image of the same God, communication between men is inherently possible, is mediated by God (as the proto-image), and is of the character of an image-image relation. Fifth, the preceding exposition of man as image in terms of the interplay of identity and difference, and Ricoeur's exposition of the poetic imagination in terms of the same interplay, elevate poetics to the position of a justified paradigm for human communication. And sixth, the reflective awareness of an ISS as presupposed and anticipated is made possible by the intersubjective constitution of man, and is inherent in the possibility of man knowing God and other men. In fact, the actuality of that knowledge is entailed in man's "definition" as image.

This now concludes my discussion of Ricoeur's contribution to the notion of critique. My remaining tasks for this chapter are (1) to relate the contributions to the notion of critique raised by the Gadamer-Habermas-Ricoeur dialogues to the thought of Freire (section 6), and (2) to summarize (as a sketch) the concept of critique in preparation for its application to reading (cf. chapter 10).

8.6   Critique: a composite and summary

In addition to the similarities between Habermas and Freire noted at the end of section 4.1, further similarities can now be noted. These are especially significant because they survive the dialogues with Gadamer and Ricoeur, and are even confirmed through their penetrating examinations of Habermas's theory. The confirmation, though, does not come without modification of the original position. The presentation of these "modified similarities" follows.

First, critique is recognized as of essential importance to the reading process; but critique must also acknowledge an insurmountable belonging to tradition.

Second, dialogue is confirmed as of central importance; but the dialogical model is modified by the uniqueness of text interpretation to a generalized presupposition of intersubjectivity which itself stands in need of further exposition.

Third, critique requires standards. The Enlightenment standards of freedom, equality, etc., however, cannot be blindly accepted as themselves beyond critique.

Fourth, the generalized model of intersubjectivity is inherently involved in these standards, even serving to define the standard required by critique. Freire calls this standard "love," a formulation which harmonizes well with my own "theological extension" of Ricoeur's thought.[33]

Fifth, both a past and a future orientation is required by critique. Freire and Habermas overly disparage the past as primarily negative in influence but rightly recognize the importance of a future orientation.

Sixth, Freire, Habermas, Gadamer, and Ricoeur all affirm that an action orientation is inherent in reading-interpretation. Both Freire and Habermas affirm the role of praxis, which asserts that critical thinking aims at the dissolution of oppressive and alienating relations guided by "the formal anticipation of genuine living" (Habermas 1970c:126; also termed "true living," "correct living"). Certainly Habermas's views are more thoroughly and rigorously philosophical, while Freire's are more practically oriented, but both agree on the point under discussion.

Further, Habermas (1977:351) comments on Gadamer:

> I find Gadamer's real achievement in the demonstration that hermeneutic understanding is linked with transcendental necessity to the articulation of an action-orienting self-understanding.

This point is worked out by Gadamer in terms of the application which understanding always is, due to the operative effectiveness of the traditions to which we belong (cf. Gadamer 1975:274ff; the concept "application" is guided by the Aristotelian *phronesis*, Gadamer 1975:278ff). As noted earlier, Habermas disagrees with Gadamer as to the means of this influence of tradition--Gadamer claiming the universality of linguisticality, while Habermas claims that ". . . language and action [i.e. labor and power] mutually interpret each other" (Habermas 1980:185). But both acknowledge the practical, action orientation which is necessarily involved in interpretation-reading. Thus critique, due to its future and action orientation, is practical.

Ricoeur also acknowledges this practical orientation as he speaks in terms of possible forms of life, and of interpretation as "a kind of obedience to [the] . . . injunction [addressed to the reader] starting from the text" (1975a:319).

Seventh, man as "transcendentally free" (i.e. as able potentially to transcend his conditions of bondage) is affirmed by all the participants in

---

[33] However, simply calling the standard "love" does not in itself say much about the actual content of the concept. That, too, must be further explicated if the standard is to be of any theoretical or practical significance.

this discussion. This condition of possible freedom is even affirmed as inherent in man's ontological constitution. Correlated with this point is the next.[34]

Eighth, man is a "cultural animal," which is to say he transcends his embeddedness in nature in a way which animals do not. And specifically, the notion of culture and cultural products present themselves as means (perhaps not sufficient means; cf. footnote 34) toward that conscientization which liberates.

Ninth, both Habermas and Freire depend on the reconstruction through dialogue of what Habermas calls "scenic understanding." Using psychoanalysis as the model, the procedure is as follows:

> Through reconstruction of the original conflictual situation, or "scene" in early childhood, the patient is given the possibility to re-symbolize those areas in his life-history that have been kept semantically empty (Bleicher 1980:160f).

"Scenic understanding," then, "is an explanatory understanding in that it can pinpoint the initial conditions that led to the systematic distortion of language" (Bleicher 1980:161). And through pinpointing these initial conditions, emancipation is offered based on the ISS which is presupposed, anticipated, and (to some greater extent than operative in the circumstances surrounding the initial conditions) actualized. For Freire, the "scenic understanding" is promoted through the use of "key words" and pictures which present "the original conflictual situation" in the present life-images of the participants in the dialogue. Here it can be reaffirmed, in terms of both the hermeneutic criticism of Habermas and our earlier (cf. chapter 4) criticism of the picture theory of meaning, that the reconstruction of this "scene" is not free from ideological prejudice. Nonetheless, our earlier (cf. chapter 7) considerations of that which is quasi-sensory in the functioning of the imagination confirm that this "scenic understanding" is unavoidable. Ricoeur's development of the concept of "world" as central to reading interlocks with and supports this conclusion.[35]

---

[34] Even if one held to the classical Reformation conception of the inability of man to affect such liberation in his own strength and the consequent need of grace, man is still "transcendentally free" in the sense that it is a possibility for man to be freed and still be man. To say that man is "transcendentally free" is simply to not comment on the means for the attainment of that freedom.

[35] Interestingly, Habermas says ". . . there are situations in which attempts at radical reformism--which try not only to preach to the converted but also to convert--are more promising than revolutionary struggle" (Habermas 1971c:37). This simply underlines the fact that a variety of speech-acts--including preaching--are "fair game" for the "dialogue-situation." The only rule imposed by the ISS is that every participant in the dialogue be given an equal chance at participation in terms of the opportunity to exercise speech-acts.

Tenth, and finally, the notion of confronting "limit situations" recurs throughout these discussions of critique. For Freire and Habermas, the specific limits confronted by critique are those imposed by the dominating social forces which hold men in bondage. The bondage itself is the limit; and the confrontation is by means of the ISS which, as it were, comes to those enslaved from the "other side" of the limit, and from within one's experiences (especially in dialogue). Thus the limit is simultaneously presented as a limit--because it is shown to possess an "other side" not yet occupied--and as a limit which can be transcended, i.e. overcome--because the "other side" (the ISS) has already been presupposed as present (in some form) in the concrete dialogical realization of the limit as limit. As Habermas (1977:360) puts it,

> Hermeneutics comes up against walls of the traditional framework from the inside, as it were. As soon as these boundaries have been experienced and recognized, cultural traditions can no longer be posed as absolute.

For Gadamer, tradition functions as a limit which always holds us in "bondage" to itself by possessing us prior to our own willing or doing. As Gadamer (1975:xvi) puts it, in terms of the main concern of his philosophy,

> My real concern was and is philosophic: not what we do or what we ought to do, but what happens to us over and above our wanting and doing.

But as Gadamer argues, this "bondage" is not necessarily an enslavement from which to be liberated; rather, it can constitute the active basis for enrichment--as Freire might say, the means to become "more human" (Freire 1970a:93). Here again, the boundaries of prejudice can always be pushed back by becoming conscious of the effectiveness of history in our lives, but they cannot ever be completely transcended.

For Ricoeur, the worlds of texts confront readers with "boundary situations" (1981a:217) which open up new dimensions and possibilities of being, as well as questions concerning the relations of these possibilities and our current situations. Consequently, through the "playful metamorphosis" of reading, ". . . reality truly becomes reality, that is, something which comprises a future horizon of undecided possibilities, something to fear or to hope for, something unsettled" (Ricoeur 1981a:187). For Ricoeur, the possibility of a new, or another, world is also "the possibility of a critique of the real" (Ricoeur 1981a:93).

It is difficult to imagine, though, that everyone could be equally "gifted" and therefore effective at such participation. Perhaps only a fuller explanation of what "equality" means is required here.

We find, then, that limit situations, and an awareness of them (the possibility of which is accounted for by the transcendental and intersubjective nature of the ISS), is essential to the notion of critique.

These ten points, then, constitute the composite notion of critique gathered from the preceding discussions. Freire, Habermas contributed to this composite (as have I), but none of the participants appears in totally unmodified form. But that simply confirms their attention to the importance and power of dialogue.

CHAPTER 9

THE ROLE OF PLAY IN READING

The preceding theoretical discussions of reading (chapters 4-8) are brought to a completion in this chapter with a discussion of play. Ricoeur recognizes play as a very integral part of his theory of reading. I have found, however, no theoretical recognition of the significance of play for reading among the reading researchers. That play is intimately related to reading will come, though, as no great revelation to instructors of reading, as we will note in the next chapter. That it has been overlooked theoretically, therefore, is even more surprising.

I begin by orienting this discussion of the role of play in reading in terms of Ricoeur's theory of reading as outlined in chapter 2. To review briefly, reading is, for Ricoeur, the dialectic between distanciation and appropriation (Ricoeur 1981a:143; 183). Says Ricoeur, "It is at the very heart of reading that explanation and interpretation [terms correlated with distanciation and appropriation respectively] are indefinitely opposed and reconciled" (1981a:164). The reader begins grounded in and belonging to his "life-world" (cf. Chapter 6), with the aim of reading being a further, though mediated, grounding.

This aim is finally manifest as the "execution" (Ricoeur 1976:81), "enactment" (Ricoeur 1981a:159), or "actualization" (Ricoeur 1981a:185) of the text; or, in line with the more traditional language of hermeneutics, "the appropriation of meaning" (Ricoeur 1981a:185). Such appropriation Ricoeur sees as the "culmination of reading in a concrete reader" (1981a:182; cf. also 164). This is "the final brace of the bridge, the anchorage of the [hermeneutic] arc in the ground of lived experience" (Ricoeur 1981a:164) once again. The figure of the arc[1] is used to depict the beginning and the ending of the reading process in lived experience, with "the objectification of meaning a necessary mediation between the writer and the reader" (Ricoeur 1981a:185).[2] What is of special interest to us now is that, for Ricoeur, " 'Play' [is] the mode of being of appropriation" (Ricoeur 1981a:185). Before focusing on the role of play in reading (section 3), I present the notion of play as understood by Ricoeur, and those he relies on (section 1), and critique and develop this notion (section 2).

---

[1] With the figure of the bridge used by Ricoeur to explain the hermeneutic *arc*, I take the liberty to equate "arc" and "arch," and to use them somewhat interchangeably.

[2] This objectification summarizes the distanciations imposed by the text which I discussed previously; cf. chapter 2.

9.1 The notion of "Play"

Ricoeur draws heavily upon Gadamer's account of play (Gadamer 1975:91-119; cf. Ricoeur 1981a:185ff) and Gadamer upon Huizinga 1950 (cf. Gadamer 1975:93ff).

The central point of the Gadamer-Ricoeur account is that "Play is not determined by the consciousness which plays; play has its own way of being" (Ricoeur 1981a:186). "Play has its own essence, independent of the consciousness of those who play" (Gadamer 1975:92). This essence is "the to-and-fro movement" (Gadamer 1975:93; cf. Ricoeur 1981a:186) which "has no goal which brings it to an end" (Gadamer 1975:93). Thus Ricoeur likens play to dance (1981a:186); Huizinga says that "all poetry is born of play" (1950:129), and "music never leaves the play-sphere" (1950:158); and Hans (1981a:4), commenting on Huizinga, says that ". . . all poetry (and all art) is born, lives and dies in play." The point is that play manifests a moment which breaks with necessity, utility, and duty as such. Rather, play is "the performance of the movement as such" (Gadamer 1975:93), as it were, for its own sake.

This "for its own sake" underlines the "primacy of the game over the players engaged in it" (Gadamer 1975:95). Gadamer says, ". . . [play's] mode of being is self-representation" (Gadamer 1975:97). The aspect of "self-" emphasizes that finally the "real subject of the game is . . . the game itself" (Gadamer 1975:95f). Consequently, "all playing is a being played" (Gadamer 1075:95). The players are therefore carried away (Ricoeur 1981a:186), "seized" (Huizinga 1950:17), lost (Gadamer 1975:92), "wholly absorbed" (Gadamer 1975:98) by their play. In fact, only in such a loss of self of the players can play fulfill its purpose (Gadamer 1975:92).

The "re-" of "self-representation" is meant to emphasize that play "renews itself in constant repetition" (Gadamer 1975:93). Through all its various manifestations and endless variations, "the game" maintains an "identity" (Gadamer 1975:108ff). As Gadamer (1975:109f) says,

> The representation has, in an indissoluble, indelible way the character of the repetition. Repetition does not mean here that something is repeated in the literal sense, i.e. can be reduced to something original. Rather, every repetition is equally an original of the work.

In short, ". . . in the representation the unity and identity of a structure emerge" (Gadamer 1975:109). This problematic "structure" of play will receive further explication later.

Finally, the "presentation" of "self-representation" emphasizes that the "being of all play is always realization, sheer fulfillment, *energeia* which has its telos with itself" (Gadamer 1975:101). This presence, though, is not the "utilitarian preoccupation where the self-presence of the subject is too

256

secure" (Ricoeur 1981a:186). Rather, the game presents itself as "a closed world" (Gadamer 1975:96), the "presentation of a world" (Ricoeur 1981a:186). The presence is, in the first place, the presence of a world, not the presence of the individual subject. The ordinary, everyday self-presence of the subject is displaced in favor of the extraordinary world of play. As Huizinga (1950:9) puts it,

> Play is distinct from "ordinary" life both as to
> locality and duration . . . . It is "played out"
> within certain limits of time and place. It contains
> its own course and meaning.

The representation, then, is "not merely repetition, but a 'bringing forth' "(Gadamer 1975:103): "In the representation of play, what is emerges" (Gadamer 1975:101). "What is," though, is not everyday reality, but transformed reality, the emergence of *the new* which is "a metamorphosis according to the truth" (Ricoeur 1981a:187). All three authors illustrate this transformation with the example of a child playing by dressing up (Huizinga 1950:13; Gadamer 1975:102; Ricoeur 1981a:187). Ricoeur (1981a:187) puts it most concisely: the "child who disguises himself as another expresses his profoundest truth." Rather than hiding behind "the dress-up," the child actually reveals himself in a deeper, more authentic way than usually accomplished in "real life."

Furthermore, play is not haphazard. In fact, "it creates order, is order" (Huizinga 1950:10). Play has rules which impose themselves on the players (Ricoeur 1981a:186), and "Any breach of the rules spoils the game" (Huizinga 1950:188). As Huizinga (1950:11) puts it:

> Indeed, as soon as the rules are transgressed the
> whole play-world collapses. The game is over.
> The umpire's whistle breaks the spell and sets
> "real" life going again.

The relation of play to seriousness also must be considered. All three authors recognize that play is "the direct opposite of seriousness" (Huizinga 1950:5; cf. also Gadamer 1975:91, and Ricoeur 1981a:186). Play shatters "the seriousness of a utilitarian preoccupation" (Ricoeur 1981a:186). However, all three also recognize that "Play has its own relations to what is serious" (Gadamer 1975:91). It is "the utmost seriousness" of absorption, a devotion that passes into rapture and, temporarily at least, completely abolishes that troublesome "only [pretending] feeling" (Huizinga 1950:8). The distinction between play and seriousness is "always fluid" (Huizinga 1950:8), not "an absolute antithesis" (Huizinga 1950:18), "a hazy borderline" (Huizinga 1950:52). Finally the game is conceived of as cutting "clean across any possible distinction between play and seriousness" (Huizinga 1950:110). And yet, "The play-concept as such is of a higher order than is seriousness" (Huizinga 1950:45). The reason for this is that "seriousness seeks to exclude play, where play can very well include seriousness" (Huizinga 1950:45).

257

As a result of this analysis, at least two authors have renamed man accordingly. Huizinga offers the term *Homo Ludens* (Man the Player) as of equal value as the more prestigious terms *Homo Sapiens* (Rational or Wise Man) or *Homo Faber* (Man the Maker).

Lanham 1976 has also recognized the duality between play and seriousness reflected in the preceding paragraph. Consequently he sees man as both *homo seriosus* (serious man) and *homo rhetoricus* (rhetorical or playful man). The rhetorical view of life, says Lanham (1976:4), "conceives reality as fundamentally dramatic, man fundamentally a role player." Here "play" is taken in the theatrical sense, a sense which both Gadamer (1975:97, 114ff) and Ricoeur (1981a:117) also exploit. And in conclusion, Lanham (1976:35) says, these two "men" represent two ways of knowing which ideally are to be held together because "*together* [they] make us human."

In conclusion and by way of summary I simply quote Huizinga's summarizing definition of play:

> Summing up the formal characteristics of play we might call it a free activity standing quite consciously outside "ordinary" life as being "not serious," but at the same time absorbing the player intensely and utterly. It is an activity connected with no material interest, and no profit can be gained by it. It proceeds within its own proper boundaries of time and space according to fixed rules and in an orderly manner. It promotes the formation of social groupings which tend to surround themselves with secrecy and to stress their difference from the common world by disguise or other means (Huizinga 1950:13).

9.9.2 Further contributions to the notion of play

Though Huizinga 1950 is widely acknowledged as both foundational and seminal for theories of play, he has also been subjected to criticism.

Caillois has criticized Huizinga's definition of play as "at the same time too broad and too narrow" (Caillois 1961:4). First of all, it is too broad because it does not adequately delineate the distinctions between play and the sacred institutions of a culture. Caillois argues that play tends to expose, publish, and somehow expend the secret and the mysterious (to the detriment of the mystery) while sacred institutions tend to preserve the sense of mystery (Caillois 1961:4; cf. also Schall 1976:16; Ehrmann 1968:31; Neale 1969:90f). This relation between play and the sacred is one particular application of the more general criticism that Huizinga has posited play as "the source of culture" (Neale 1969:91). This criticism will present itself for further discussion in section 9.3.3 where play is discussed in relation to critique in reading. There the significance of play confronts the fundamental--in particular, Marxist--category of labor, and man-as-worker.

Second, Huizinga's definition of play is "too narrow" because Huizinga has defined play as "an activity connected with no material interest, and no profit can be gained from it" (Huizinga 1955:13). In particular, Caillois argues that Huizinga's definition

> . . . excludes bets and games of chance--for example, gambling houses, casinos, racetracks, and lotteries--which, for better or worse, occupy an important part in the economy and daily life of various cultures (Caillois 1961:5).

This is a particular example of Huizinga's focus on only one characteristic of play--its competitive aspect--to the exclusion of other aspects. Caillois extends his own classification of games to include four basic types: competitive, chance, mimicry, and those which pursue vertigo (Caillois 1961:11-26). Similarly, Caillois evaluates play along a continuum which extends from *ludus* to *paidia* (Caillois 1961:27-35). *Ludus* is "allied to the taste for gratuitous difficulty" (Caillois 1961:27) and is tied to the rule-nature of games, while *paidia* is "a primary power of improvisation and joy" (Caillois 1961:27) whose

> . . . first manifestations . . . have no name and could not have any, precisely because they are not part of any order, distinctive symbolism, or clearly differentiated life that would permit a vocabulary to consecrate their autonomy with a specific term (Caillois 1961:29).

Paidia speaks of the "spontaneous manifestations of the play instinct" (Caillois 1961:28), e.g. a cat in a ball of wool, or a child laughing at a rattle. It expresses what Caillois calls an "elementary need for disturbance and tumult . . . [which] readily can become a taste for destruction . . ." (Caillois 1961:28). *Ludus*, on the other hand, is "complementary to and a refinement of *paidia*, which it disciplines and enriches" (Caillois 1961:29). *Paidia* tends to promote games of vertigo and chance, while *ludus* contains the element of competition. At the extremes, *paidia* and *ludus* exclude each other, as do games of competition and chance. Caillois' addition of *paidia* to the conception of play becomes an issue in reading-interpretation theory between Gadamer and Ricoeur on the one hand, and Derrida (and the deconstructionist school) on the other. I take up the discussion of this issue in section 3.1 with regard to meaning and play in reading.

Though Caillois' criticisms of Huizinga do establish the basic orientation to Huizinga taken by many others (cf. e.g. Miller 1970; Ehrmann 1968; Neale 1969; Schall 1976), both Huizinga and Caillois have been criticized for holding too limited a perspective on play. Both accept

. . . "reality," the "real," as a *given* component of the problem, as a referent needing no discussion, as a matter of course, neutral and objective. They define play in opposition to, on the basis of, or in relation to this so-called reality . . . . But it is legitimate to wonder by what right "reality" may be said to be first, existing prior to . . . play . . . and serving as . . . [its] standard (Ehrmann 1968:33).

And again, Hans (1981:2) says,

Although both Huizinga and Caillois argue that play is important to human culture, they offer their arguments too late; once the cleavage between the "real" world and the world of play takes place, play will always have a subsidiary role, no matter what the rhetoric might suggest . . . .

Such criticism reopens the question as to whether Huizinga's definition of play is "too broad," though from another perspective. The general criticism of Huizinga--that play is not the only activity which produces culture--will stand. The relation of play to the sacred--the basis of Caillois' judgment of Huizinga's view as "too broad"--however, will require further examination.

Pieper (1965:9), for example, argues that play is ". . . chiefly a mere *modus* of action, . . . a purely formal determination." As such, play cannot determine the meaning of human actions, which is derived (in Pieper's view) from content. Thus, if religious festivals were purely play--as Huizinga proposes--then these sacred acts would be meaningless. Pieper cannot accept that conclusion. Therefore he concludes that Huizinga's formulation of the relation between play and the sacred is faulty. But if "the sacred" is somehow to be correlated with "the real" (cf. Ehrmann 1968 and Hans 1981), and the role of play is *not* separated from "the real" (Ehrmann's and Hans' criticism of both Huizinga and Caillois), then the relation of play to the sacred must be reexamined even if Huizinga's formulation is faulty. Pieper presumes that play is "purely formal"; this premise will be questioned in section 9.5. As "purely formal," Pieper assumes that play has no inherent relation to meaning (recall his argument: if religion is play, then religion is meaningless). This premise is examined in section 9.3.1.

9.3 Play in relation to reading

I will now reconsider three topics of major importance to reading which have been previously discussed: meaning, understanding, and critique. The capstone of this theory--the promised ontology--will be presented in the final section (section 9.5).

260

9.3.1 Meaning and play

Following Ricoeur (cf. Chapter 4), meaning is conceived of as the dialectic of sense and reference: "The sense of the work is its internal organization, whereas the reference is the mode of being unfolded in front of the text" (Ricoeur 1981a:93). Play has much to do with both these aspects of meaning.

9.3.1.1 Play, and meaning as sense

In Ricoeur's view, reading necessarily involves "the *mediating* role played by structural analysis" (Ricoeur 1981a:218). Structural analysis, though, is conceived of in terms of the semiological model which also serves as the basis of the notion of sense. This is "the literary object . . . [as] a closed system of signs, analogous to the kind of closed system that phonology discovered . . ." (Ricoeur 1981a:216). Within such a system, signs refer to other signs only: The text has no outside, only an interior (Ricoeur 1981a:216).

But how is it that signs refer to signs? It is not in accordance with "the classical causal model" (Ricoeur 1981a:216), but rather in terms of "correlations." Says Ricoeur,

> Structural systems imply relations of a quite different kind, correlative rather than sequential or consecutive (1981a:219).

Here Ricoeur is in agreement with the semioticians Peirce and DeMan (cf. Ricoeur 1981a:163f) in recognizing that the process by means of which "one sign gives birth to another" is not the same kind of process by which "the object engenders the sign" (DeMan 1979:9). As Barthes (1979:76) puts it,

> The logic that governs the Text is not comprehensive . . . but metonymic; and the activity of associations, contiguities, and cross-references coincides with a liberation of symbolic energy.

I temporarily postpone treating this semiotic process directly, and only note in passing that DeMan considers this process to be "pure rhetoric," thus offering a preliminary link to "play."

Following Ricoeur's analogy between literature and *la langue* or language as system (Ricoeur 1981a:216), this structural explanation in terms of correlation has interesting consequences for reading. Reading becomes an "intra-textual concept," which "before being the act of the exegete, is the act of the text" (Ricoeur 1981a:162).³ There is a "process which is at work in the text . . . [,] the work of the text upon itself," which it is the job of the reader to recover by placing himself "within the *sense* indicated by the relation of interpretation supported by the text" (Ricoeur 1981a:164; emphasis added).

It is at the point of emphasis above (i.e. "the sense") that Ricoeur's account becomes problematic. The difficulty, for our purposes, is focused by the question, Is play at work in the text? On the one hand, Ricoeur reserves the notion of play for appropriation (Ricoeur 1981a:185ff) which is postponed (Ricoeur 1981a:164) until after the "structural analysis . . . stage" (Ricoeur 1981a:161). Further, while play is fundamentally a dynamic process (recall the "to and fro"), "to explain is to bring out the structure, that is, the internal relations of dependence which constitute *the statics* of the text . . ." (Ricoeur 1981a:162; emphasis added). Thus play seems to be granted no special role in the mediating stage of analysis. On the other hand, the text itself is conceived of as dynamic in a manner which escapes the subjectivity of the reader, just as play does. For instance, the "text seeks to place us in its meaning" (Ricoeur 1981a:161); interpretation is "the act *of* the text [first of all]" (Ricoeur 1981a:162); interpretation is "*by* language before being interpretation *of* language" (Ricoeur 1981a:163); there is a "labour . . . [at work] within the text" (Ricoeur 1981a:164). Further, the "*ideal* sense" (Ricoeur 1981a:148) of the text is understood by Ricoeur as on the one hand, orienting the reader in the direction of "the intention . . . of the text" (Ricoeur 1981a:161), and, on the other, as actually moving (or "fading," Ricoeur 1981a:148) from sense to reference (Ricoeur 1981a:218). Again, the tension is between a (more or less) static notion of sense and a (more or less) dynamic notion of sense. The picture is further clouded by Ricoeur's consistent use of the language of work rather than that of play to describe this action of the text. And yet his notion of work at this point is thoroughly consistent with his notion of play

---

³ Ricoeur's "before" here can cause confusion. Here too it is Ricoeur's "linear model" which causes the difficulty. On the one hand, that which precedes the reader is the ontological pre-understanding; but that is not "the text" nor "the act of *the text*," strictly speaking. On the other hand, in order for the text to act, the reader must act first to take up the text and begin reading it: The text does not read itself, and acts only within the reading of a reader. Thus if the "stage model" is taken seriously, then Ricouer's formulation here is false. Rather, it seems that the acting of the text is a textual mediation, or incarnation, of that Being which precedes, supports, influences, even orients the "structural explanation" which the text enacts through the intra-textual correlations. There is no reason to think that the transcendence which is evident in both the pre-understanding and the explanation "stages" is a different transcendence. Since failure to find continuity between these stages causes the problems noted earlier, and since the same type of phenomenon is evident in both stages, it is reasonable to suppose that the continuity required is provided for by the transcendence of "Being," or whatever. All that should be ascribed to Ricoeur's comments is that this transcendence must be acknowledged throughout the reading process (though in different ways at different "stages") if an adequate account of the process is to be given.

as presented earlier. Thus to our question--Is play at work in the text?--I think Ricoeur would answer, No; but as noted, not without inconsistency.

One reason for this inconsistency may stem from Ricoeur's desire to distance himself from those who hold to what he calls "the ideology of the absolute text" (Ricoeur 1981a:148f). This view claims that there is no reference of a text to a world outside of texts. In short, reference (except of signs to other signs) is obliterated (Ricoeur 1981a:148). One adherent to such an "ideology" is Derrida for whom the "free play" of signs, "infinite substitutions in the closure of a finite ensemble" (Derrida 1972:260) is all there is. Perhaps it is to avoid this conception of free play as "the [continual] disruption of presence" (Derrida 1972:263) that Ricoeur denies the notion of play to "the work" of the text. To our question--Is play at work in the text?--Derrida would likely respond, No, play is at play in the text. And in fact, following DeMan, this "ideology" would likely go even further, affirming that the text itself is constituted as text by that deconstruction which is free play (cf. DeMan 1979:17). As Barthes (1979:75) puts it, ". . . what constitutes the Text is . . . its subversive force with regard to old classifications," and ". . . the Text is always *paradoxical.*"

Consequently, all "seriousness" seems to be voided by this deconstructive ideology. The difficulty with such consistency in exalting play is not that play ought not be so exalted. Rather, as pointed out earlier, ". . . play itself contains its own . . . seriousness," and to rule it out is to void the very heart of play. As Hans (1981:10), who is otherwise most sympathetic with Derrida's views, has pointed out "Play . . . [is] restricted by its own play, by the play of the world itself, as Gadamer points out in speaking of play as a 'transformation into structure'." The same point is made by Said 1979 with regard to the reading of a text: "[Texts] . . . place restraints upon what can be done with (and to) them interpretively" (Said 1979:142). It is these "restrictions" (Hans) or "restraints" (Said) which reflect the seriousness of play. In the context of games, such restrictions are called rules.

A possible rejoinder to such criticisms might draw upon Caillois' inclusion of *paidia* and games of vertigo within game theory. These concepts seem to support Derrida's concepts. Several problems, however, arise with this conception of free play.

First, Caillois' formulation of *paidia* and *ludus* is unclear, and perhaps inconsistent. On the one hand, Caillois claims there can be "no connection between *ludus* and *ilinx* [games of vertigo]" (Caillois 1961:31). On the other hand (and only two pages later), Caillois points out that *ludus* disciplines *paidia* to give "the fundamental categories of play [including *ilinx*] their purity and excellence" (Caillois 1961:33). Further, "*ludus* is . . . [a] metamorphosis of *paidia*" (Caillois 1961:33), implying some kind of continuity. And since *paidia* and *ilinx* are so closely related (cf. Caillois 1961:23-29), presumably *ludus* and *ilinx* are not unconnected. Finally, it is not obvious that games of chance (*paidia*) do not *involve* competition (*ludus*), against "the odds" or "fate," for example. Thus Caillois' distinction between *paidia* and *ludus* is in need of clarification.

Further, Caillois claims that rules are inseparable from play, but seems to imply that this is only the case *after institutionalization.* Before that point there is that "basic freedom . . . central to play" which is *paidia*, that "primary power of improvisation and joy" (Caillois 1961:27). The purpose of this "basic freedom," this "primary power" is "to stimulate distraction and fantasy" (Caillois 1961:27), a purpose seemingly expressed in its greatest purity in games of vertigo (i.e. *ilinx*). I, though, can find no example among the many instances of *ilinx* given by Caillois 1961:23-26) which reflect the total absence of rules. In each case there are procedures to be followed and specific skills to be gained in order to achieve the desired effect (i.e. "transport"; Caillois 1961:26). Not to follow the rules (of physics, at least)--e.g. of staying on skis to a high speed, or spinning wildly, etc.--is to fail or lose at the game, which brings the game (more or less) quickly to an end. The point is that there are always restraints which must be taken seriously if any game is to succeed as play.

The same point can be made more philosophically in a manner akin to the argument against skepticism. The skeptic claims that nothing can be known with certainty. He, therefore, cannot claim any certainty for his own claim either, thus being forced to admit the opposite of his own point of view as inherently allowed by his own. Similarly, to claim that the essence of play is freedom from rules, i.e. the "free play" of Derrida-- always "being" what it is not, not being what it "is"--is to assert "No Rules" as a rule, and indeed, a very strict one. Rather than promoting pure play, it promotes pure impossibility. The alternative to rules is "not something else, but nothing at all . . . " (Schall 1976:39).[4]

But, as Hans (1981:10) pointed out, nothing--as opposed to Being--is precisely what Derrida asserts as "behind" his free play. Contrary to Derrida (and Hans), I would assert that Nothing as the "source" and "motive" of play, in and of "itself" alone, is not only pure "nonsense," but utterly inconceivable. To summarize: To attempt a conception of play without the sense of constraints is to (self-)deconstruct such a notion of play. In fact, such a "conception" is never even "constructed" in the first place. It simply isn't. To put the same point in a more personal way: As Gadamer is reputed to have said, Derrida would be very upset if we didn't take all his talk about play seriously.

It is true, however, that there is a proper sense in which the essential constraints on play are arbitrary, i.e. they didn't have to be the way they now are. Because there is this element of arbitrariness in all rules, play--though constrained--is freer than might otherwise be supposed. I will use this point to recover many of the valuable (and valid) insights of

---

[4] This argument closely parallels the argument in chapter 8 with regard to pure difference being precisely nothing, not even difference.

Derrida. To further the discussion in this direction, another conflict between Ricoeur and "the ideology of the absolute text" must be considered. It too remains within the sphere of meaning as sense. This conflict centers around the notion of structure, and is best considered, I think, in terms of the *re*-presentational character of play as introduced earlier.

Huizinga, Gadamer, and Ricoeur all are eager to point out that representation has the character of repetition (Gadamer 1975:109): There is an "identity . . . that presents itself . . . in the changing course of ages and circumstances" (Gadamer 1975:108). Precisely put, "meaning . . . [is] an ideal object which can be identified and reidentified, by different individuals in different periods, as being one and the same object" (Ricoeur 1981a:184; cf. also Gadamer 1975:105, 106, 113). This is not, however, to deny that there are variations in the presentation. Rather, "this identity . . . . presents itself . . . *differently* in the changing course of ages and circumstances" (Gadamer 1975:108; emphasis added).

Derrida (and others: e.g. DeMan 1979:76; Hans 1981:23) also wishes to highlight the differentness of presentations. From his point of view, though, there is no center to the notion of structure, or rather, "this center . . . [is] a deficiency . . . which makes possible 'free play' " (Derrida 1972:268). In this conception there is no fixedness and thus no identity of structure. The notion of structure is then better replaced by that of structuration, an ongoing process in which variation or differance rules.[5] As Derrida puts it,

> The movement of signification adds something,
> which results in the fact that there is always more,
> but this addition is a floating one because it comes
> to perform a vicarious function, to supplement a
> lack on the part of the signified (1972:260f).

As we shall see, this "surplus of meaning"[6] always evident in the "movement of signification," this openness of the "identity and continuity of the work [or text] . . . towards its future" (Gadamer 1975:107), has not been overlooked by those we are considering as espousing identity. Rather, they have taken note of the mode of being of play in which "the actual subject of play is obviously not the subjectivity of an individual who among other activities also plays, but instead the play itself" (Gadamer 1975:93). Difference is thus implicit in such a notion of openness which transcends the subjectivities of the individuals involved: essential to play is that which cannot be accounted for in terms of given individuals and their given structures, whether epistemological (e.g. schemas), psychological,

---

[5] This spelling, "*differance*," with an "a," is Derrida's, and reflects a specialized concept discussed below.

[6] This phrase is part of the subtitle of Ricoeur 1976.

sociological, etc. As an epigram (and cryptically put): Play *is* (essentially part of and dependent on) that which it is not (from the perspectives of the players and with regard to the game insofar as it is rule-governed). Put in this way, we do come quite close to Derrida's conception. The question 'Who is the actual subject of play?' is the same question raised in chapter 7, section 4.4 with regard to "the source of the new." By "new" there was meant that which is "not the subjectivity of an individual" here. That there is such an "element" involved in reading and in play is beyond dispute. The only question is, what more can be said about it? Here it can be said that "it" is free from the control of human subjectivity; and in that sense, play is therefore "free." But this is not to assert that play is therefore "unordered" or "wild" or "unruly" as implied by Caillois' *paidia* (and *ilinx*). Nor is this notion of play threatened by Derrida's deconstructive free play. Rather, "it" could be kindly, positively liberating, restorative, gracious, etc.

But even more needs to be said. In the previous point I argued that play is *also* dependent on the rules. Further, as far as the players are concerned, and almost tautologically, play is dependent on the players too: At least *for the player*, there is no play without a player. The player is the one who plays and that without which there is no play, but he is not therefore either all there is to play or play itself (in its essence).[7] Thus Gadamer (1975:105) says,

> Play is structure--this means that despite its dependence on being played it is a meaningful whole which can be repeatedly represented as such and the significance of which can be understood.

Put into the language of chapter 8, for play to be humanly meaningful, it must be "incarnated," but in a manner which also transcends individual (human) bodily existence. In short, there is a "binding nature" (Gadamer 1975:107) to that which is represented: ". . . one fails to appreciate the compelling quality of the work . . . [Gadamer is concerned here with art; we could substitute "the text"] if one regards the variations possible in the representation as free and optional" (Gadamer 1975:106). Rather, interpretation is *"both* bound *and* free" (Gadamer 1975:107; emphasis added). Any creation in the interpretive process must be and is guided by the work itself and thus is better termed *re*-creation. This is simply the interplay of the old and the new as discussed in chapter 7.

---

[7] The play of light upon the water, etc. seems to offer a counterexample to this point. However, the *observation* of such play does involve the observer in what can legitimately be called play. At this point, though, the case of the play of light without an observer stands as a counterexample. I will not, though, speak to it until section 5. In the meantime, it does support the distinction between the player and play itself.

This highly puzzling structure of the work of art, our three authors find well illustrated by festivals. As Huizinga points out, "feast and play have their main characteristics in common" (1950:22):

> Both proclaim a standstill to ordinary life. In both, mirth and joy dominate, though not necessarily--for the feast too can be serious; both are limited as to time and place; both combine strict rules with genuine freedom (Huizinga 1950:222).

Festivals are different from year to year; and yet, it is "one and the same festival that undergoes this kind of change" (Gadamer 1975:110). Thus, though "highly puzzling" and even paradoxical, this interesting combination of bound and free, is characteristic of human beings. This paradox, rather than Derrida's resolution in favor of difference alone, is accepted here as basic to the structure of meaning.

In fact, as I read Derrida's famous article, *"Differance"* (1973b), he is not consistent in his (seeming) favoritism of difference over against identity. Derrida 1973b begins by noting two senses of the (French) verb "to differ":

> On the one hand, it indicates difference or distinction, inequality, or discernibility; on the other, it expresses the interposition of delay . . . . In the one case "to differ" signifies nonidentity; in the other, it expresses the order of the *same*. Yet there must be a common . . . root within the sphere that relates the two movements of differing to one another. We provisionally give the name *differance* to this *sameness* which is not identical . . . (Derrida 1973b:129).

The remarkable point here is that identity (i.e. the same) and difference are presented as somehow belonging together, and as dependent upon the assumption of "a common . . . root" and the common signification, *"differance."*

However, from the emphasis given to difference (by Derrida and others) one would think that "the order of the *same*" had no place in Derrida's thought. No doubt the reason is rhetorical: Derrida seeks to redress the imbalance and prejudice in favor of identity in Western metaphysics. I suggest, though, that Derrida himself has laid a better foundation (with his combination of identity and difference) than even he has fully exploited (especially since he is so anti-foundational; e.g. cf. Derrida 1972:257).

Three further comments are relevant at this point. First, Derrida has associated his *differance* with "Saussure's principle of semiological difference" (Derrida 1973b:130). This principle has been picked up by the structuralists and also Ricoeur as providing a legitimate and basic conception of system; in particular, the system of language. This has been especially important for Ricoeur since it provides a rigorous basis for the human sciences, a basis which allows "explanation" to be integrated into the interpretive process without recourse to explanation as conceived of in the natural sciences. Ricoeur (1976:81) says, for instance:

> It is henceforth possible to treat texts according to the explanatory rules that linguistics successfully applied to the elementary systems of signs [i.e. phonology] which underlie the use of language.

The point here, though, is that system is defined in terms of the "interplay of *merely* distinctive entities within finite sets" (Ricoeur 1981a:216; emphasis added). This would seem to grant a fundamental legitimacy to the principle difference, indeed "mere difference." This conception of "mere difference," however, is quite suspect. First of all, Derrida's *differance* is not defined in terms of mere difference (see above), even though he does say "Within a language, within the *system* of language, there are only differences" (Derrida 1973b:140). This is a clear (and damaging) inconsistency. Second, it is also quite suspect whether Ricoeur's reliance on the Prague and Danish schools of linguistics (cf. Ricoeur 1976:81f; 1981a:216) will bear the weight he rests upon them. The point is that the Prague school did not conceive of the phoneme as a merely negative entity; in fact, "their phoneme" was dependent on "differences of meaning [i.e. including reference]" (Anderson 1974:16) and not just relations between signs. Thus the meaning of "phoneme" was dependent in its definition on (positive) extra-linguistic reality. Similarly, the Prague phoneme was also dependent on the phonetic reality, understood as a physical reality, thus further strengthening the tie to that which is "outside" of language as system. Further, the Danish school's conception of the phoneme as totally abstract cannot withstand linguistic arguments to the contrary (cf. Jakobson and Halle 1956; Postal 1968; Anderson 1974:16-18). Third, regardless of whether Saussure or other linguists meant a representation of phonological systems in terms of "pure opposition" to stand as an adequate account, such is (generally) no longer the case in linguistic studies. Consider, for example, the linguist Pike, for whom linguistic units must be defined in terms of both contrast (i.e. opposition) and variation (i.e. emic identity; cf. e.g. Pike 1982:39-65).[8] Further, the school of generative phonology, while clearly using distinctive features, also gives the phoneme a positive quality which even relates directly to what is phonetically possible. With a relation to "phonetic reality" comes an inherent relation to bodily life, which is far removed from a system of "mere differences." (Interestingly, Ricoeur refers to the generative conception of structure with approval; cf. Ricoeur 1974:89ff.)

---

[8] Pike further insists that distribution--roughly, context--be included along with contrast and variation; cf. e.g. 1982:60ff.

The point is that phonological systems are best represented in terms of both identity and difference. Thus it would seem that Ricoeur has bought into an outdated and discredited model of phonology. But fortunately, the "improved version" in fact strengthens his position, removing the problem of continuity between his stages discussed in chapter 8. Especially is this the case if Pike's insistence on "distribution" is granted as just as necessary as contrast and variation, for then context, including the life context (or *Lebenswelt*) must be acknowledged as always operative and influential.

Second, Derrida says, "*Differance* . . . precedes and sets up the opposition between passivity and activity" (Derrida 1973b:130). This is of interest since we too have noted the paradox of activity and passivity in reading. It further confirms the importance of a mediating "paradoxical" notion.

Third, *differance* is identified by Derrida with play:

> With a, *differance* more properly refers to . . . the *play* [*jeu*] of differences (Derrida 1973b:130).

> What we note as *differance* will thus be the movement of play that "produces" . . . differences . . . (Derrida 1973b:141).

Further, "*Differance* is . . . the structured and differing origin of differences" (Derrida 1973b:141). Here, then, Derrida admits (as do Gadamer and Ricoeur) that play is both structured, and open to changing presentations.

Finally, in a manner quite reminiscent of our own treatment of the old and the new in the schema, Derrida says ". . . [*differance*] dictates all the relations between usage and the formal schema, between message and the particular code . . ." (Derrida 1973b:146). I simply reiterate that both identity and difference are simultaneously operative (or "at play").

Thus it is that Derrida can be read as inconsistent (differing with himself?) in important respects (which lead to nonsense), *and* as supportive of several very important points which were developed above.

Let us now tie this discussion more directly to meaning, summarizing our findings and thus conclude this section on play in relation to meaning as sense.

That which emerges from interpretation, that which "unfolds before one" (Gadamer 1975:113) as binding and compelling is the meaning, understood in the first instance as ideal structure. As ideal, this meaning is "the same," what can be identified and reidentified from one reading to the next. As ideal--i.e. as neither a physical nor a psychical reality (cf. chapter 4)--meaning as sense contributes to that "drawing us out of ourselves"

(Schall 1976:24) so often attributed to games. Further, the formulation or construction by which this sense emerges must recognize a process at work in and by the text which escapes the control of the individual, and in such a way as to "catch the reader up," as in a game. So profoundly similar to play is this process of "correlating construction," that Gadamer (1975:92) says the mode of being of the work (in our case, the text) is play. Inherent in the emergence of the meaning of the text is the detachment of that meaning from "the representing activity" (Gadamer 1975:99) of the reader, just as with play. Thus, just as with games, the meaning of a text (as sense) is "fundamentally repeatable and hence permanent" (Gadamer 1975:99). This repeatable character, though, is paradoxical, for the representational character of play is "explicitly left open to . . . recreation" (Gadamer 1975:107). And so too with meaning: The interpretation is not differentiated from the text itself in the experience of reading (Gadamer 1975:107). The text invites recreative participation, "knowing" full well that it is only in performance that it exists at all, and that performance is itself recreation. So close is the experience of play to that of reading--as the recovery of meaning as sense--that we can conclude that play is the mode of being of meaning as sense. At least we can say that play is an excellent model for this aspect of reading. But there is more to reading, even as the recovery of meaning.

9.3.1.2 Play, and meaning as reference

Meaning is also reference as we have argued previously (cf. Chapter 4), and we must say something about play with regard to reference.

Remember that for Ricoeur, "Reading is like the execution of a musical score; it marks the realization, the enactment, of the semantic possibilities of the text" (Ricoeur 1981a:159). This enactment or "performance" (Gadamer 1975:105) is there joining of the event pole to the meaning pole of the meaning-event dialectic. On the one hand, this dialectic is basic to all discourse, and on the other, it is disrupted by the existence of the text as text. Another of the distanciations introduced by the text was the interruption of language's referential dimension--its intent to be "about something." With performance, though, both deficiencies are remedied.

> The "actualized" text finds a surrounding and an ambience; it resumes the referential movement--intercepted and suspended--towards a world and towards subjects . . . .
>
> Initially the text had only a sense, that is, internal relations or a structure; now it has a meaning, that is, a realisation in the discourse of the reading subject (Ricoeur 1981a:159).

This reconstitution of the text as meaning *and* event must, as noted above, follow "the obligating path of understanding" which is "structural analysis" (Ricoeur 1981a:138). That is, reference follows sense and is in accordance with the sense of the work. Sense, then, leads naturally to reference. The motion of play will help us explicate this movement.

Rather than being simply "a sterile game, a divisive algebra" (Ricoeur 1981a:217), the interplay of signs, by the very nature of play, not only breaks with "ordinary life" (Huizinga 1950:21), but creates its own order and "play-ground" (Huizinga 1950:10), or as Ricoeur (1981a:177) puts it, its own "world," and possible modes of being-in-the-world. To understand, then, is "to follow its movement from sense to reference . . ." (Ricoeur 1981a:218), a movement which is itself playful, and motivated by the "game" itself.

This movement is seen by many writers as necessary. Gadamer says that it is characteristic of playful nature not only to present a "closed world of play," but also to ". . . [let] down as it were, one of its walls" (1975:97). This is the notion of that openness of the work which invites participation in the construction of the meaning. In fact, Gadamer goes so far as to say that the "openness towards the spectator is part of the closedness of the play. The audience only completes what the play as such is" (Gadamer 1975:98).

Lanham (1976:31) further supports this point when he says,

> But . . . a movement toward . . . pure verbal play, activates our resources for making meaning, our impulses for purpose. I try to "make sense of" nonsense.

Ricoeur calls this impulse the "ontological vehemence" of language, its tendency to always be about something (Ricoeur 1977:255f, 299f). Thus the reader's participation is not only invited but called for by that work of language on itself which begins as sense, and "escapes" adequate explication in terms of the subjectivity of the reader.[9] The movement from sense to reference, and the formation of the "about what," displays the activity of "catching up" the reader through a participation he does not (and cannot) master. This is akin to the playing of a game, and thus both the movement from sense to reference and the formation of the reference is called playful.

Our three authors on play further note that play is not just a human activity, but is also quite observable in nature as well. For example, animals play, and also light, and waves. It would seem, then, that even the "ordinary life" of the world is no stranger to play, and thus the transition from the "pure play of signs" (if there is such) to a world need not be seen

---

[9] Again, remember that this "ontological vehemence" is ascribed to language (not just to the reader; cf. chapter 7), and as such, language participates in that transcendence.

as an incoherent leap. Such a conclusion is in line with Hans 1981 and Ehrmann 1968, as mentioned in section 2. It will be exploited in section 5.

Finally, even the very act of "enactment" necessary for reading at all brings with it what Ricoeur calls "the irrationality of the event" (1981a:137). But, says Huizinga (1950:4), "play is irrational," and thus we might well expect--given the association suggested above--that the heart of this enactment is play. Or in particular, "the *fun* of playing [which] resists all analysis, all logical interpretation" (Huizinga 1950:3) is the rationally irreducible element which motivates the reading process. Again, this is another way of saying that the heart of meaning as reference escapes man's rational control.

In the introduction to this section we reminded ourselves that the referential movement of language which was "intercepted and suspended" by the text is tri-partite. Not only a world is referred to, but also subjectivities, in particular, the reader and the author.

Because reference is tri-partite, our consideration of the role of play in meaning as reference is not complete without a reconsideration of the subjectivities of the reader and the author.[10] The preliminary reconsiderations of the reader and the author will introduce section 3.2 on comprehension and play; the further reconsiderations of the subjectivities will introduce section 3.3 on critique and play.

9.3.2 Comprehension and Play

For Heidegger, the notion of understanding was "wholly severed from the problem of communication with others" (Ricoeur 1981a:5) and became an ontological rather than an epistemological notion. Rather than starting with being-with-another, Heidegger's conception of comprehension begins with being-in-the-world. This conception, together with the notion of meaning as sense, depsychologizes the motion of reading. Reading is not the "recovering [of an intention] . . . by congenial coincidence" (Ricoeur 1981a:190) with the mind of the original author. Rather, what is presented to the reader is a world, anew dimension of meaning in language (Ricoeur 1981a:181) which projects a new "mode of being" (Ricoeur 1981a:178) as an emergent possibility. Understanding, then, before being interpersonal, is "worldly" (Ricoeur 1981a:56), a dynamic orientation within and in relation to the proposed world of the text.

---

[10] It is, however, with the reintroduction of the question of subjectivity that our "neat" division into chapters and sections breaks down most obviously. At this point in these extended discussions (which began in chapter 4), it is perhaps more helpful to "fuzz" the boundaries between topics than to maintain artificial distinctions which were (hopefully) helpful for clarification of the issues involved through the (somewhat) particularized treatment of each. Consequently, I shall "fuzz" the boundaries in what follows.

But how are worlds presented by the text? Ricoeur is to the point: "Worlds are proposed in the mode of play" (Ricoeur 1981a: 186). They are given to us as possibilities just as in play possibilities are presented in the game, and we come to understand them as in play: "In entering a game, we hand ourselves over, we abandon ourselves to the space of meaning which holds sway over the reader" (Ricoeur 1981a:187). There is indeed a personal commitment involved, but it is for Ricoeur "entirely *mediated* by the whole of explanatory procedures which precede it and accompany it" (Ricoeur 1981a:220; cf. also 1977:249). However, before becoming serious, this personal commitment is in the mode of play, a mode in which "the distinction between belief and make-believe breaks down" (Huizinga 1950:25; cf. also Gadamer 1975:93f). Possibilities are tried out as clothes are tried on to see if they fit. Here we rejoin our consideration of the "split reader" (cf. chapter 7, section 5 and chapter 8, section 5). Now the "split" is understood in terms of play. The notion of the "split reader" as evident in Ricoeur, Iser, and Poulet is precisely echoed in the students of play. For example, Fink (1968:23):

> It is necesaary [sic] at the outset to define the notion of the player more precisely and more strictly, for here we find a quite peculiar "schizophrenia," a kind of split personality that is not to be mistaken for a manifestation of mental illness. The player who participates in a game executes in the real world an action of a familiar type. Within the context of the internal meaning of play, however, he is taking over a role. Here we must distinguish between the real man who "plays" and the man created by the role within the play. The player hides his real self behind his role and is submerged in it. He lives *in* his role with a singular intensity, and yet not like the schizophrenic, who is unable to distinguish between "reality" and "illusion." The player can recall himself from his role; while playing, man retains a knowledge of his double existence, however greatly reduced this knowledge may be. Man exists in two spheres simultaneously, not for lack of concentration or out of forgetfulness, but because this double personality is essential to play (cf. also Sadler 1969:65f; Neale 1969:55ff).

And yet, though the worlds and the selves are "tried on" in a fictional mode, the reader is also played by them, and any final choice has the same quality as the classic theological sense of "the call": a claim is made upon one which is "not a question of choice" (Gadamer 1975:117; cf. also 112f). I will have more to say about this in the next section.

The subjectivity of the author is also restored by play. He appears as the creator of the world of the text (Ricoeur 1981a:189); a "playful figure" (Ricoeur 1981a:187ff). Having no access to the author directly, "The text is the very place where the author appears" (Ricoeur 1981a:149). As far as the reader as reader is concerned (i.e. not as dialogue partner with the author in a common speech situation), the author is "fictitious" (Ricoeur 1981a:188). He is any number of imaginative variations which remain a function of the (playful) presentations of the text.

Comprehension, then, is the playful restoration of a playful relation to a playful author by means of the world of the text which is presented in the mode of play.

With the ontological understanding of comprehension, together with the role of play incomprehension (as just discussed), the possibility of an ontological interpretation of play is presented. Having already suggested the necessity of a playful transcendence as "operative" throughout the comprehension process, I now simply connect that transcendence with the more common term "Being."[11] Such an effort, fortunately, finds support for several theorists of play. Three are mentioned here (more in section 5).

> The activity of play itself needs to be described, then, and my basic model for that activity derives from Heidegger's description of the hermeneutic circle. For Heidegger, the process of inter-pretation involves the paradoxical relationship between the part and the whole of that which is to be interpreted: one can only understand the whole through the parts, but one cannot begin to understand the parts without some understanding of the whole. Thus, one begins with certain prejudgments about what the whole is, confronts the parts with this set of prejudgments, and allows the sense of the whole to be continuously altered through an interaction with the parts. It is the back-and-forth movement between whole and parts that constitutes the hermeneutic circle; and that, contrary to those who characterize this as a vicious circle, is the movement that makes interpretation possible to begin with (Hans 1981:5f).

Says Fink (1968:29): "Being in its totality functions like play . . ." and ". . . play is always a confrontation with being" (Fink 1968:23); "Play is an essential element of man's ontological makeup . . ." (Fink 1968:19).

And similarly, Ehrmann (1968:33), quoted earlier as the basis of a criticism against both Huizinga and Caillois: "But it is legitimate to wonder

---

[11] It is, in fact, the element of transcendence--the always preceding and supporting, never escapable influence--which warrants the capital "B" of Being.

by what right 'reality' may be said to be *first*, existing prior to . . . play . . . and serving as . . . [its] standard." And again, with an obvious biblical allusion (to be developed later; cf. section 5), ". . . in the beginning there was play" (Ehrmann 1968:48).

All three of these authors affirm the very basic nature of play. Hans, though, is most helpful for the present task.[12] He identifies the hermeneutic circle in its ontological interpretation, as itself playful. That association is supported by the many elements which are held in common (as essential) by both play and the hermeneutic circle: neither are (fully) determined by the consciousness of the subjectivities involved; both are essentially a "to-and-fro movement"; neither can be finally subordinated to utilitarian purposes[13] alone; both are characterized by the "absorption" of the subjects involved; both involve the interplay of identity and difference, whole and parts; both present a "separate" world; both display the emergence of the new; both involve the metamorphosis of the subjects; and both necessitate rules or conventions.

I, however, wish to go beyond the identification of play with "Being" or "reality." My thesis is that included in the "whole" which is "always already" operative are the subjectivities implied by the communication situation, i.e. at least two "interlocutors." This thesis is supported most immediately in this context by a transcendental argument regarding the subjectivities of author and reader. The fact of the restoration of these subjectivities (as considered above) necessarily implies an intersubjectivity as the condition of possibility for such a restoration. That is, the communication situation cannot be excluded as fundamental to the hermeneutic situation (as done by Heidegger and Ricoeur); instead, it must be assumed from the start and throughout the process. This point was, of course, argued at greater length in chapter 8, especially sections 5.3 and 5.4.

---

[12] I am postponing a fuller treatment of the issues involved in Hans' departure from the Heideggerian-Gadamarian prejudice for Being, but mention the fact of this departure here in fairness to Hans. I will, though, simply raise the question whether a notion of "play . . . free from Being" (Hans 1981:10) makes any sense at all. If "play" in any sense "is," then it is not completely free from Being. I will propose, rather, that a different notion of Being is required, one which is not "pure presence" (cf. Hans 1981:7). Perhaps this is all Hans wants to oppose, but his alternative is not at all clear.

[13] I think this is the case even with the reading of directions for the operation of some piece of machinery, which would seem to be the best kind of counterexample. Note, for instance, (1) the difficulty often (usually? always?) experienced in making the transfer from the text to the machine, and (2) the necessity of learning to read directions for application as opposed to just reading the directions. (This highlights the "awakening" from reading developed by Iser 1978; the disjunction between the world of the text and the "ordinary world.") Though training in this activity does bring improved performance, special training is needed, and never entirely suppresses the non-utilitarian "moment" of reading.

Thus, it would seem that Ricoeur's prejudice in favor of the priority of "the world" is unfounded. Rather, it should be said that being-in-the-world--the presentation of a world--is necessary but not sufficient to a full account of the processes of interpretation-reading. But neither is being-with-another a sufficient basis of explanation. Both are needed and the relation between them must be formulated as dynamic, interactive, and tentative (i.e. as playful). Neither should be granted the status of first priority; and in fact, both are presupposed in the formation of the other. The projection of what someone (i.e. a subject) might mean, or what kind of world someone might want to present, is as formative of what world the text is taken to present, as vice versa. In fact, it is this very *interplay* which is basic to comprehension as the recovery of meaning as both sense and reference (and reference as tri-partite!). Again, play is highlighted as of central significance for the reading of meaning.

9.3.3 Critique and Play

Just as the question of how critique can be accounted for in the Heideggerian framework remains the *aporia* of Ricoeur's reading of Heidegger (Ricoeur 1981a:59), so too our treatment of comprehension on a Heideggerian base remains incomplete until critique is integrated. I have already argued in agreement with Ricoeur, Habermas, and Freire that critique must be integrated into reading as essential (Chapter 8). I do now what could not (yet) be done there: orient that discussion in terms of play.

Though "play occurs as if by itself, that is, without effort or applied intention" (Ricoeur 1981a:186), it is also "first and foremost . . . a voluntary activity" (Huizinga 1950:70). Though there is a "curious lack of decisiveness in the playing consciousness" (Gadamer 1975:93), the player must participate and cooperate if the playing is not to be spoiled. Thus there is a paradoxical relation of the player to the game and to himself which occurs in playing: not only do the players play, but the game also seems to play itself in and through the players. Consequently, the players themselves take on the character of the game, as different from their ordinary selves as the game is different from their ordinary lives. In relation to "ordinary life," the game and the players of it are fictions.

Readers also display this character of players. Inasmuch as subjectivity is subordinated to the matter of the text, "the subjectivity of the reader is no less held in suspense, no less potentialised, than the very world which the text unfolds" (Ricoeur 1981a:94). Because "fiction is a fundamental dimension of the reference of the text,[14] it is equally a fundamental dimension of the subjectivity of the reader" (Ricoeur 1981a:94). Because play is the mode of being of the world of the text, and because the person reading is a "being-in-that-world" (in the fundamental

---

[14] This is due to the distanciations of the text (cf. Chapter 2) and the resultant necessity of mediation by the objective structures of the text.

sense discussed in chapter 6), the reader is also a "playful figure" (1981a:189). In short, "in reading, I 'unrealise myself' " (Ricoeur 1981a:94).

We have already seen this "unrealisation" of the player in play. Huizinga (1950:13) called it the "absorbing [of] the player intensely and utterly", and Gadamer (1975:92), the player's losing of himself in play. Reading, then, just as playing, "introduces me to imaginative variations of the ego" (Ricoeur 1981a:94), and because of this metamorphosis in reading, "we can . . . look at ourselves" (Ricoeur 1981a:189; quoting Kayser). This playfulness of reading is the condition of integrating critique into the reading process. I turn more directly now to a consideration of play and critique.

The moment of critique begins, for Ricoeur, with that "*game* by which we exchange signs for things and signs for other signs" (1981a:116; emphasis added). Signification itself interrupts the primordial belonging (which is itself best examined as a game; cf. Gadamer 1975) with the distanciations implicit in this game of exchange. Ricoeur argues, in agreement with Husserl, that all consciousness of meaning involves distanciation from and an interruption of "lived experience":

> For all consciousness of meaning involves a moment of distanciation, a distancing from "lived experience" as purely and simply adhered to. Phenomenology begins when, not content to "live" or "relive," we interrupt lived experience in order to signify it (Ricoeur 1981a:116).

Further, this "interruption" is "easy to discern in the case of language" (Ricoeur 1981a:116).

> The linguistic sign can *stand for* something only if it is *not* the thing. In this respect, the sign possesses a specific negativity. Everything happens as if, in order to enter the symbolic universe, the speaking subject must have at his disposal an "empty space" from which the use of signs can begin. The *epoche*[15] is the virtual event, the imaginary act which inaugurates the whole game by which we exchange signs for things and signs for other signs (Ricoeur 1981a:116).

The reader, in beginning with a text, begins with an object and attention to an object which requires the same kind of "break" with lived experience as exercised in the (Husserlian) phenomenological reduction (cf.

---

[15] The epoche is the philosophical gesture of phenomenology by which the natural attitude and the relation to "lived experience" is suspended; cf. chapter 3 for a brief introduction of the phenomenological reduction(s).

Walrod 1983:9-11, together with chapters 2 and 3 above for more detailed support of this point). This is because of the very nature of a text as constituted by the distanciations discussed in chapter 2. Thus, the text as text already partakes of that "game by which we exchange signs for things. "That, however, is just the beginning, for the text still has to be decoded, and meaning reconstructed. Here, the semiotic game of exchange of signs for signs is ruled by the unique principle of semiotic correlation discussed earlier (section 3.1.1). The reader, then, is confronted with a game within a game, and reading "is always a question of entering into an alien work" (Ricoeur 1981a:190), like wanting to join a game already in progress. In order to do so there must be a "divesting [of] oneself of the earlier 'me' in order to receive, as in play, the self conferred by the work itself" (Ricoeur 1981a:190). Elsewhere, Ricoeur refers to this as an "exchange" of selves (Ricoeur 1981a:113).

This divesting power of the text seems to reside first of all in the inherent negativity of the signs as signs (Ricoeur 1981a:116); second, in the sense of the text, first as structural features akin to "explanatory rules" (Ricoeur 1981a:153), and then as "the construction of a network of interactions which constitutes the context as actual and unique" (Ricoeur 1981a:174); and finally, the movement from sense to reference which manifests "the revelatory power of the text" (which is linked directly to "its referential dimension"; Ricoeur 1981a:191). Says Ricoeur, "It is in allowing itself to be carried off towards the reference of the text that the *ego* divests itself of itself" (Ricoeur 1981a:191).

Thus it is at all three levels of the text--"its structures, its sense and its reference" (Ricoeur 1981a:144)--that play is at work to offer the reader anew world and a new way of being. This "newness" of the world and of the subject (discussed in greater detail in chapter 7, especially section 4.1, 4.3, 4.4, and 4.5) which is presented in play is the basis of that critique we looked at in greater detail in the last chapter (chapter 8, especially section 5). The point added here to those previous discussions is that the processes by which the new is presented can be accurately modelled by the concept of play.

The concept of play, however, has further contributions to make to the discussion of critique, especially as presented in chapter 8. Recall the all-inclusive statement of Marx, "The entire so-called history of the world is nothing but the begetting of man through human labor" (Marx 1978:2). Obviously, *homo faber* ("man the maker," "man the worker") is central to the Marxist schema. Just as obviously, *homo ludens* ("man the player," to borrow Huizinga's title) presents a fundamental challenge to *homo faber* as *the* fundamental category of philosophical anthropology. The situation, though, is a bit more complicated than a simple opposition might indicate. First of all, Huizinga's broad claim that *all* of culture is the result of play has been adequately criticized by Caillois: play is *one* of the major factors in the formation of culture, but so is "non-play" (cf. also Miller 1970:70). Secondly, Hans 1981 has presented a persuasive case that ". . . 'play' is the most pertinent word to use in the context of all of the productive processes, precisely because it is the only word that adequately describes the entire process" (1981:32). From this perspective,

> . . . to be alienated from one's work [the Marxist concern] would mean simply that one does not play with his work anymore, that his work is not an essential activity connecting him to his world, but instead a separable aspect of his life that has value only as part of the economic play of exchange (Hans 1981:25).

Though such an identification of play and work is arguably not the best formulation of the relationship (cf. Johnston 1983:125-137), Hans' related point stands:

> But the fact is that people still play on the job no matter how alienated they are from their labor; that even though the work itself may not be essentially playful, people work at making it playful and find ways of doing so (Hans 1981:26).

Several sociological studies in Salter 1978 support this point. Third, the earlier critique of Huizinga and Caillois as assuming a preexistent cleavage between "reality" and "play" also speaks against the Marxist conception of man and reality, and against a simple opposition between work and play.

The point here is not to explore what kind of relationship there is between work and play (Johnston 1983:128ff proposes five options). It is, rather, to stress that human labor, and categories of work, cannot serve as the only fundamental categories of human activity. Consequently, critique also cannot be founded on relations of labor alone.[16]

The general point, then, contra a (pure) Marxist conception of critique, is that play is a very human, and a very pervasive, activity which is meaningful, purposeful, and productive in such a manner that it is "not subordinate to the ultimate purpose served by . . . other human activity" (Fink 1968:21), but rather "epitomizes . . . [that] pure purposefulness in itself . . . [which is] meaningful in itself, needing no utilitarian justification . . ." (Pieper 1965:8). Our conception of critique echoes this perspective. Further, to rejoin the Marxist concern for emancipation, the claim is even made that the detachment of play (the "playground" phenomenon; Sadler

---

[16] It is worth noting that the (neo-Marxist) Frankfurt School has also found labor, by itself, to be an inadequate basis for the analysis of human activity. In particular, human relations of communication are proposed as an equally fundamental basis which contributes most directly to cultural development. Whether the Frankfurt conception is adequate to explain every aspect of human creativity is a debatable point, which is, however, beyond the scope of my current project (though an answer to this concern was sketched in chapter 8).

1969:61f) and festivity (Pieper 1965:32) is a liberation through which the player "becomes aware of, and may enter, the greater reality which gives a wider perspective on the world of everyday work, even as it supports it" (Pieper 1965:32). Barthes (1979:76) attributes this liberating activity to the "logic which governs the Text" and the reading of it (which earlier we called the "playful" semiotic relations). And again, "What constitutes a Text is . . . its subversive force with regard to old classifications . . . [; Text] always implies an experience of limits" (Barthes 1979:75). As such, reading--because it is the necessary correlate of a text--always involves limit-situations and the potential for liberation (actualized to different degrees, no doubt).

Consequently, play is shown to be of central and prominent importance, even with reference to the central concerns of Marxism--e.g. labor, production, liberation. Thus, the notion of critique is not threatened by play, but rather needs the latter notion to be fully developed.

9.4   More on Play

Three final points will be made before extending these discussions into ontological considerations: First, on the role of dialectic in Ricoeur's thought; second, a reconsideration of subjectivity and objectivity from the perspective of play; and third, a few comments on the subject (i.e. the "actor") of play.

9.4.1   Dialectic and play

Central to Ricoeur's notion of discourse is "dialectic": that of event and meaning, and within meaning, of sense and reference. Reading is conditioned by this dialectic character of discourse. It too is a "dialectic of . . . two attitudes" (Ricoeur 1981a:152), the semiotic and the semantic. As Ricoeur (1981a:164) says elsewhere, "It is at the very heart of reading that explanation [which treats various levels of semiotic systems] and interpretation [which focuses on the completion of semantic considerations] are indefinitely opposed and reconciled".

This dialectic, which always involves two players, is the "incessant conversion of one into the other" (Ricoeur 1976:116), "the mutual reference of each by means of its own peculiar features to the other" (Ricoeur 1981a:160), each finding its necessary complement in the other (Ricoeur 1981a:185). But what is this dialectic, if not play, the self-motivated to and fro of the game?[17]   From this perspective, Ricoeur's conceptions of discourse and reading are thoroughly playful.

9.4.2 Subjectivity and objectivity

Second, earlier (in chapter 3 especially) I setup the dialogue between the bottom-up and the top-down theories of reading in terms of the different emphases on the subject (the reader as "the top," the "up") and the object (the text as the "bottom," the "down"), especially as these are correlated with the philosophical traditions of empiricism and rationalism. Phenomenology was seen as a effort to mediate these two orientations, in (preliminary) sympathy with the interaction view of reading. Now this dialogue will be seen from the perspective of play, itself seen as the best model for the phenomenological description of man's interaction with the world. Says Hans (1981:x):

> Husserl was trying to overcome our static conceptions of subjects and objects by focusing on the interaction between them; the value of his work comes from the shift in orientation that allies his work with the movement of play.

Recalling the "to-and-fro" of play (conceived of as essential by Gadamer 1975), Hans (1981:x) goes on to assert that

> . . . the fundamental activity of man . . . [is] the back-and-forth movement of encounter and exchange with the world in which man is continually engaged.

In that regard, Hans (1981:x) conceives of play as fundamental to the ontological understanding of understanding as developed in the phenomenological tradition: "It [play] is a *structuring* activity, the activity out of which understanding comes. "Further, "Play is at one and the same time the location where we question our structures of understanding and the location where we develop them . . ." (Hans 1981:x). Thus, that questioning of ourselves and our relation to the world which is critique is integrated with understanding by play. In the same activity the "instrumental attitude" of the worker is superceded by the more

---

[17] As Palmer (1969:234) says, "The dialectical approach of Socrates may serve as a model for all truly dialectical questioning, for in his vacillation between knowing and not knowing, in the *playful* probing of the subject from different angles, lies the willingness to risk everything and to be instructed by the subject-matter itself. Beneath the artful shiftiness of Socrates is the serious intention to let the subject under discussion lead the way"; (emphasis added). At least playfulness is not to be excluded from dialectic.

fundamental level of *Lebenswelt,* where the subject is no longer opposed by the object, nor vice versa.[18]

Having thus recapitulated earlier discussions in terms of the subject and the object, I am again reminded of the power of the play-model to describe what has gone before.

9.4.3 The subject of play

Finally, I take up the topic of "the subject" of play: who plays? Our authors on play do not consider the players themselves as the proper subject. Says Gadamer: ". . . the actual subject of play is obviously not the subjectivity of an individual . . . , but instead the play itself" (1975:93; cf. also 92, 94, 107); Ricoeur: ". . . the subject . . . is not the player himself, but rather what 'takes place' in play" (1981a:186). And Huizinga: ". . . the whole point is the *playing*" (1950:17).

This implies that interpretation in general, and reading in particular, is *not* "top-down." This view, rather,

> . . . begins with intention: It regards reading as a truly active, centrally motivated and centrally directed process in which readers hypothesize or predict, among a certain range of meaningful likely alternatives and search and analyze among the featural information available in the print only to the extent necessary to resolve their remaining uncertainty (Smith 1983:61).

Yet Ricoeur warns that reading is ". . . [*not*] the projection of the subjectivity of the reader into the reading itself" (1981a:178). If this were so, then interpretation-reading would be "subsumed . . . to the finite capacities . . . of a present reader" (Ricoeur 1981a:192). In short, the top-down view is "the victim of errors linked to the primacy of the subject in modern philosophy" (Ricoeur 1981a:190). As we have already seen by recognizing the element of play in comprehension and critique, the top-down approach does not give an adequate account of the experience of reading. This is not to deny that the reading subject is active in the ways Smith and others recognize. It is to deny that the reading subject plays the central role ascribed in the above quote. I will return below to a discussion of these two factors--the player and play--with reference to each other.

---

[18] As Hans (1981:7) puts it:

> The activity of play does not concern itself with an instrumental attitude toward the world; there is no sense in which the player is a subject opposed to or separated from an object or objects.

Would it be fair, on the other hand, to term these "play theories" of reading as "bottom-up"? Certainly the "play theories" do recognize an active role of the text as do bottom-up theories. But there is a mismatch here too, for the "play theories" do not treat the print of the text as "stimulus" (Smith 1983:60) which merely needs decoding to sound to result in meaning. Play, then, explodes the traditional categories of reading theory.

Our original question, though, still remains: Who plays? Firm answers to this question cannot be given from the authors we are considering, even though they are not entirely silent on the subject. Says Gadamer, "The real subject of the game . . . [is] the game itself" (1975:95f). Elsewhere Gadamer ascribes a "spirit" to games (Gadamer 1975:96) and to play (Gadamer 1975:98),[19] which may or may not be distinguishable from the game itself. Consider, for example:

> We have seen that play does not have its being in
> the consciousness or the attitude of the player, but
> on the contrary draws the latter into its area and
> fills him with its spirit (Gadamer 1975:98).

But is "its spirit" to be strictly identified with "play"? It seems that either reading (i.e. either ayes or a no answer to this question) is allowed; and regardless, there is too much not said (here or elsewhere) on the subject to warrant any firm conclusions. For example, what is the ontological status of play and spirit? Such a question, however, does seem appropriate since later Gadamer refers to "the metaphysical order of being that is true for all" (Gadamer 1975:117) which is manifest by play.

Huizinga (1950:1) speaks similarly when he says, with reference to the recognition of play in (non-human) nature:

> In play there is something "at play" which
> transcends the immediate needs of life and
> imparts meaning to the action. All play means
> something. If we call the active principle that
> makes up the essence of play, "instinct," we
> explain nothing; if we call it "mind" or "will" we
> say too much. However we may regard it, the
> very fact that play has a meaning implies a non-
> materialistic quality in the nature of the thing
> itself.

Perhaps this "non-materialistic quality" is Gadamer's "spirit." But if so, we must then distinguish "spirit" from "mind" and "will"; at least if we confine ourselves to the preceding quote. The situation is further complicated

---

[19] Gadamer (1975:93) also ascribes a "spirit" to language and conversation.

when a few pages later Huizinga reintroduces "mind" to the domain of play:

> But in acknowledging play you acknowledge mind, for whatever else play is, it is not matter. Even in the animal world it bursts the bounds of the physically existent. From the point of view of a world wholly determined by the operation of blind forces, play would be altogether superfluous. Play only becomes possible, thinkable and understandable when an influx of *mind* breaks down the absolute determinism of the cosmos. The very existence of play continually confirms the supra-logical nature of the human situation (1950:3f).

On the next to the last page of his book, Huizinga suggests an answer to what this supra-logical mind might be.[20] Following Plato he says that it is only with our "eyes on God and moved by Him" (Plato, Laws 803-4; cf. also 685), only "by turning toward the ultimate" (Huizinga 1955:212) that we can go beyond the "logical thinking [which] does not go far enough" (Huizinga 1955:212) to hope to discern what play is.

Then, to further develop this line of thought, Huizinga quotes from the Book of Proverbs [21] (Wisdom is speaking):

> The Lord possessed me in the beginning of his ways, before he made any thing from the beginning. I was set up from eternity, and of old before the earth was made . . . I was with him forming all things: and was delighted every day, playing before him at all times; playing in the world. And my delights were to be with the children of men (Proverbs viii, 22-3, 30-1, Douay translation as quoted in Huizinga 1950:212).

This too is no final clear answer to the question, Who plays?, but it does intimate that in the beginning there was play, that there is something divine, personal, and creative about play, and that the proper subject of play is God. Such an answer, of course, flies in the face of much contemporary effort to deconstruct the onto-theological perspective of western metaphysics. I will return to this point below.

---

[20] Hans 1981 seems to miss this probing of the transcendent by Huizinga as an answer to the question of the relation between play, nature, and mind (cf. Hans 1981:6).

[21] Several other authors on play also quote this passage from Proverbs; cf. Schall 1976:84; Rahner 1967:19; Martin 1976:22f; Miller 1970:101.

I have left a consideration of Ricoeur on the question, Who plays?, until last because of the special problem this presents for him. I call this problem Ricoeur's *aporia*.

Ricoeur has traced the history of hermeneutics in terms of unresolved problems, *aporia*s. The romantic hermeneutic of Schleiermacher and Dilthey left (natural) life and (human) meaning in conflict by subsuming textual understanding to "the laws of understanding another person who expresses himself therein" (Ricoeur 1981a:52). The fundamental ("ontological") hermeneutic of Heidegger and Gadamer does not allow the integration of critique because its starting point--a consciousness of belonging, of being-in-the-world--expressly excludes such a possibility (Ricoeur 1981a:54-61). However, as we have seen, play transcends the nature/man distinction, and is at the heart of both critique and belonging, and thus offers a solution to these two *aporia*s.

Ricoeur, however, in subordinating the subjectivity of the author to the objective structures of the text in order to overcome the romantic hermeneutic, seems to have subordinated all subjecivity as well. This can be seen from two different but closely related perspectives. Here I summarize the major arguments already discussed in chapter 8, section 5.3.1, yet with an eye toward the question of play.

"The essential structures of the text" (Ricoeur 1981a:51), which necessarily mediate appropriation (Ricoeur 1981a:143, 184f, 192), are characterized by analogy with the structuralist conception of *langue*. Ricoeur uses the structuralist model of explanatory rules in terms of the "interplay of oppositions and their combinations" among "systems of units devoid of proper meaning" (Ricoeur 1981a:153) as guiding the explanatory attitude which defines the structure of the text. The "sense" of an element then becomes "its capacity to enter in relation with other elements and with the work as a whole" (Ricoeur 1981a:156). Ricoeur's linking of this notion to the Husserlian notion of "ideality" allows him to graft the structuralist notion of *langue*, which is properly semiotic--i.e., "devoid of proper meaning" (Ricoeur 1981a:153)--to semantics, since "ideality" describes meaning proper. Both these notions taken together reinforce the "depsychologisation" (Ricoeur 1981a:152) which is affected by the mediation of the explanatory procedures.[22] Consequently, subjectivity is "lost as radical origin" (Ricoeur 1981a:113) only to be regained as the final stage of the interpretation process (Ricoeur 1981a:112f), *after* mediation by "*langue*-ideality." As Ricoeur puts it, "it is the matter of the text which gives the reader his dimension of subjectivity" (Ricoeur 1981a:94). The difficulty for Ricoeur is how to account for the fact that a subjectless, impersonal ideality bestows subjectivity on a reader. This is Ricoeur's *aporia*.

---

[22] *Langue* is universal, atemporal, anonymous, and not intended (Ricoeur 1976:3); the ideality of meaning is neither a mundane, physical nor a psychic, mental reality (Ricoeur 1981a:152, 184).

285

The same difficulty is seen in Ricoeur's conception of play. Contrary to Gadamer, Ricoeur says, "play is something other than the activity of a subject. The to and fro of play occurs as if by itself, that is, without effort or applied intention" (Ricoeur 1981a:186). While Gadamer restricts the lack of subjectivity to that of the players, he does imply some transcendent subject as we have already seen. Ricoeur does not; at least not clearly. Ricoeur, following Heidegger, does speak of Being bestowing the "I am" of the subject by and from language (1974:234f). But when approaching Heidegger in this way, Ricoeur's hesitations are as equally evident as his affirmations (cf. e.g. 1977:309ff). And besides, how Being per se (i.e. "Being" in and of itself which is not usually considered subjective) can *give* a self to an *ego* and not affirm its own subjectivity is the same difficulty we encountered above.

Poulet (1969:68) has, I think, expressed well the current dilemma with regard to our question:

> One may ask oneself: What is this subject left standing in isolation after all examination of a literary work? Is it the individual genius of the artist, visibly present in his work, yet having an invisible life independent of the work? Or is it, as Valery thinks, an anonymous and abstract consciousness presiding in its aloofness, over the operations of all more concrete consciousness? Whatever it may be, I am constrained to acknowledge that all subjective activity present in a literary work is not entirely explained by its relationship with forms and objects within the work. There is in the work a mental activity, forsaking all forms, a subject which reveals itself to itself (and to me) in its transcendence over all which is reflected in it. At this point, no object can any longer express it, no structure can any longer define it; it is exposed in its ineffability and in its fundamental indeterminacy.

Obviously, there remains important work to be done in clarifying who it is that plays: "important" because of the pervasive activity of "play" throughout the reading process; "work to be done" because of the evident lack of clarity in these current authors. I pursued this direction already in chapter 8, section 5.4. I continue this pursuit in the final section below.

9.5   Toward an ontology

As indicated from the earlier discussion, Derrida is opposed to traditional ontology. Since his line of thinking may be the strongest contemporary challenge to my purpose in this section, it is with a few comments "to Derrida" that I begin this section.

9.5.1 "To Derrida"

Derrida's objection to ontology is not total; rather, he rejects the ontology of pure presence, i.e. Being conceived of as presence (e.g. Derrida 1973b:153). It is true that the history of Western metaphysics has been dominated by this notion. And it is true that Derrida has successfully challenged this tradition. However, as argued earlier, though Derrida has argued admirably for difference as equally ultimate with identity, he has not been able to argue for the priority of difference over identity. Nor is it clear that he wants to do so, for *differance* entails both. On this point, Derrida and Ricoeur are in agreement: Both identity and difference are equally fundamental. Thus ontology as pure presence (i.e. identity) is no longer possible. But that does not mean that ontology per se is impossible.

Another problematic notion, however, has just been used: "fundamental." Derrida is opposed to this notion too because it (generally) belongs to the same tradition of "presence ontology." Says he, ". . . it is necessary to forego . . . the absolute requirement that we go back to the source, to the center, to the founding basis, to the principle, and so on" (Derrida 1972:257; similarly Barthes 1979:76; Hans 1981:23). The point is simply that if there is an "origin," it is a "nonsimple 'origin' " (Derrida 1973b:141), a system without an end or center (Barthes 1979:76), a system "not capable of being centered" (Hans 1981:23). But this is not to deconstruct all ideas of the center, just some of them--in particular, those which do not give full "place" to difference and "free play."

Karl Barth (1959:61f), on the other hand, argues that "Beautiful playing presupposes a childlike knowledge of *the center* of all things-- including the knowledge of their beginning and their end." Further,

> . . . this center is rather a splendid annulment of balance, a *turn* in the strength of which the light rises and the shadow winks but does not disappear; happiness outdistances sorrow without extinguishing it and the "Yes" rings stronger than the still-existing "No" (Barth 1959:76).

In short, both "Yes" and "No," i.e. both identity and difference[23] are entailed by play (cf. also Martin 1976:18).

Nor is Barth alone in this affirmation. Rahner 1967, Pieper 1965, Sadler 1969, Schall 1976, Martin 1976, Miller 1970, Neale 1969, Johnston 1983, Lewis 1955, Berger 1970, Ong 1967, Caillois 1959, Huizinga 1955, and Cox 1969 all affirm notions of play akin to Barth's. But merely citing references does not prove the point. It does, however, add weight to the importance of keeping the question open.

---

[23] Here I am associating the principle of "no" with that of discontinuity and difference, and the principle of "yes" with that of continuity and identity.

As Derrida (1972:256) acknowledges, what is needed to "refute" his idea of free play, i.e. of play without a presence-center, is "a theological idea." And, as may be recognized from the above list of references, many theologians think that they are providing just that idea. Derrida (1972:256) does not refute the possibility of such "a theological idea." He only doubts that such an idea, which takes account of *"differance,"* has been successfully formulated.

Consequently, to assert the impossibility of ontology after Derrida, as many followers of Derrida seem to do, is simply that: an act of assertion of an unproven (personal) preference which even (in some cases) claims support from the fact that it is unproven. Certainly such an assertion is to be allowed in the forum of ideas, but it is only honest to recognize this speech act for what it is while allowing its force. We should not be intimidated, though, or worse, allow ourselves to be terrorized by such acts. They are but claims, and (even) Habermas (who has no "personal preference" for "a theological idea") insists that all participants in the forum be allowed the same opportunities to exercise speech acts.

It is true that finally everyone's position, rests on presuppositions which are otherwise unprovable. But this does not mean that every position is equally defensible. It does mean (at least) that every position must be accompanied by some degree of uncertainty and by genuine humility. But can we say more about the standards for judging between positions? This was a question taken up in chapter 8. Granting that the question of standards is of a piece with one's fundamental assertions and methodology, let me offer the following. As much as possible, an interpretation-explanation should arise out of and be consistent with the data or experience under consideration (as experienced and reported by any who desire to participate in the considerations). The best position, then, is the one which accounts for the most details of the greatest number of experiences in a manner satisfying to those who care to consider the issue. At the same time, the best position is the one which can be sustained with the least violence to the freedom of inquiry of others. The best position can "take on" all comers, and invites further participation, even challenge. The best position is also "fecund"; it is enriching to the most other areas of research, and generative of insights which "solve" problems in other areas without losing its specific benefit by being too general. For example, Miller (1970:17-94) points out that the notion of play is increasingly of interest and of academic import to anthropology, ethnology, sociology, economics, psychology, literary criticism, philosophy, mathematics, and theology. Bateson (1978:10) concurs: ". . . the whole notion of play and its complexities is . . . *absolutely* central for any scientific discussion of human behavior." If these claims can be sustained, then an explanation in terms of play is "fecund."

Before proceeding toward ontology I reiterate that this study has been interdisciplinary. The strength of this approach is that through the dialogue of various disciplines, different aspects or characteristics of "Being" have been disclosed. Thus, from the start, these characteristics

288

have fecundity in that they offer a "solution" to a variety of problems which can be tested in a variety of disciplines. In this regard, then, the characteristics of "Being" pointed to by the preceding discussions are proposed as necessary "pieces" of a unified ontology. The "pieces" are all the more necessary because their need has been confirmed by the different demands of the different disciplines (and methodologies) involved.

With this introduction, I am ready to review the characteristics of "Being" which have emerged from the preceding discussions.

9.5.2 A review of characteristics of "Being"

Already in chapter 7, I began to take note of various characteristics of "Being" which emerged from our study of the process of understanding. The focus of the study at that point (chapter 7, section 4.4) was the source of the new which was disclosed in comprehension. There the issue of transcendence was discussed, especially as Poulet and Ricoeur and Iser differed. I argued in favor of a conception of transcendence agreeable with the character of meaning as ideal. That is, transcendence, though related to the subjectivity of the reader, *obtains independently*. Further, this independence testifies to a freedom with respect to human subjectivity. So, first of all, this transcendence "is" in some sense which is not the same as the sense in which things in the world "are" (just as meaning "is" in a sense different from the being of things). All I am concluding here, though, is that this transcendence "is" in a sense *like* the being of the ideality of meaning. I am not claiming that the being of transcendence is of an identical sort as that of meaning; nor am I claiming that it is not. Rather, transcendence is more like meaning in its being than like things. But I am claiming that this transcendence "is"--i.e. "it" *exists*--in a meaningful sense. Thus, we at least have something to talk about which is properly ontological.

Further, the dynamism of meaning was taken to indicate that "Being" is itself active. Ricoeur preferred the term *lively*, even with the sense of *life-giving*, due to the experience of the bestowal of meaning and liveliness to the reader. Thus "Being" is *creative*, generative of new meaning; and *gracious*, since "it" gives to the reader. Correlated with this experience is the sense of a surplus or abundance of meaning which a text generates. As with metaphors, texts were seen as polysemous. Consequently, "Being" too was seen as a *reservoir of meaning*, and itself *polysemous*. Thus, we can say immediately that "Being" is not "simple," not "pure undifferentiated presence." Rather, "Being" is *complex*, even structured in some "*multi-leveled*," interactive way (analogous to syntactical structure in relational grammar theory).

Our studies of the role and characteristics of the imagination further support the complex nature of "Being." Both "*identity*" *and* "*difference*" must find "a home" in "Being." Ricoeur called this the *tensiveness* of "Being." Further, "Being" must be like the self of the reader in such a way that "it" can bestow a (new) self to the reader. Ricoeur preferred a more *personal* sense to "Being" (than Heidegger). Our studies of the affections support this preference (cf. chapter 7). But still "it" must have a world*ly* aspect, in the atmospheric, capable-of-being-dwelt-in sense.

Our studies in chapter 8 added further characteristics to "Being." The importance of both identity and difference was confirmed once again. Transcendence was seen as not just personal or subjective, but *intersubjective* (cf. the ISS). Further, "Being" is not only related to history, but also *transhistorical*, even *eternal*; and yet, not in a manner opposed to its incarnation in history.

Chapter 9 adds the interesting and provocative characteristic of *playfulness* to "Being." Further, this playfulness is seen especially in language. Thus "Being" is intimately related to language.

Though these qualities of "Being" have arisen (mostly) from the study of the experience of reading, the application to a more general ontology is supported by (1) the diverse disciplines which have contributed to these studies, and (2) the basis of these studies in the philosophical ontology of Heidegger, which is already a general ontology.

Though Ricoeur (1974:19) doubts whether a unified ontology is possible, I do not. The "trick" will be to present such a unification of the preceding characteristics. But first, I present further steps in that direction which are encouraged by our studies of play.

9.5.3 A few more steps

Many authors on play note the "purposelessness" of play, i.e its freedom from "an instrumental attitude" (Hans 1981:7). Thus, play is considered activity for its own sake (cf. Pieper 1965:7; Neale 1969:24). This "purposelessness," though, seems to tend to its opposite, or perhaps to a realm of human experience which escapes definition in terms of purpose. Pieper (1965:8), for example, asks (rhetorically), "Does not play epitomize that pure purposefulness in itself, we might ask?" Caillois (1961:27) notes "a basic freedom . . . central to play" which, though dependent on rules for its human enactment, seems nonetheless to escape rules in its essential conception. The rules, in fact, because they are in an essential sense arbitrary, serve as signs "that things which exist for their own sakes are the highest things" (Schall 1976:34). Similarly, Fink (1968:21) says,

> It is frequently said that play is "purposeless" or "undirected" activity. This is not the case . . . .
> But the *immanent* purpose of play is not subordinate to the ultimate purpose served by all other human activity.

And Bateson (1978:14), "They say play has no purpose, but really its purposes are of a paradigmatic order."

Here, then, with the transcendence of purposefulness--when purpose is conceived of in terms of the ultimate purpose served by all other human activity (Fink 1968:21)--we approach the step toward ontology which many authors on play take. I too will follow this step which I present in terms of festivity. This step, however, itself "plays with" the line of demarcation between play and "all other human activity."

Already we have used festivals to illustrate the unique time and space of play. There are other similarities which have caused others to place these two activities--festivals and play--in a common category: for example, "the dialectic of *yes* and *no*" (Martin 1976:18) between the identity and difference of the festival and everyday life. Further, and the most important point here, the role of transcendence in both. As with purpose in play, Pieper (1965:7) notes with respect to festivals, "To celebrate a festival means to do something which is in no way tied to other goals, which has been removed from all 'so that' and 'in order to'." Festivity and play both enter into the realm of "pure purposefulness," "activity meaningful in itself" (Pieper 1965:8). And, with a keen eye to that which is "new," or at least not everyday, Pieper (1965:32) notes:

> Festivity . . . is a liberation. Through it the celebrant becomes aware of, and may enter, the greater reality which gives a wider perspective on the world of everyday work, even as it supports it.

Martin (1976:17) too, though critical of Pieper in other regards, notes, "He [*homo festivus*] is in search of higher stages of life and consciousness . . ."

Clearly, such language recalls the concerns of the critical theorists (cf. chapter 8), as well as the formulations of Ricoeur (new and possible modes of being-in-the-world) and Gada-mer (the fusion of horizons). All these echoes tie these considerations of festivity (and play) that much closer to reading per se.

The important steps, for my purposes, which Pieper and Martin take are (1) to isolate the element of "the realm of activity that is meaningful in itself" (Pieper 1965:7), and (2) to develop this element in a distinctly religious direction.

Pieper (1965:30) says quite forthrightly, "Thus, when a festival goes as it should, men receive something that it is not in human power to give." He also affirms that "Secular as well as religious festivals have their roots in the ritual of worship," and even that "A festival without gods is a non-concept, is inconceivable" (1965:26f). Interestingly, the same thought is expressed by others with regard to play. Based on empirical studies, Miller (1970:103) says, "For Greek, then, as for Jew, Christian, Chinese, and Indian, the origin of ideas about play is in religion." Similarly, Rahner (1967:8f) says that the unique characteristics of play ". . . only become possible when man's mind is open to God, when in the shaping of his life he has in some measure anticipated eternity." And these unique characteristics are freedom, activity for its own sake, spontaneity, and pure realization (Rahner 1967:ix). The point is that a consideration of play and festivity lead us to develop an ontology in the direction of a theology.

This direction is further supported by the comment regarding "eternity" just quoted from Rahner. With this concern we return to (1) the notion of time and universal history as discussed in chapter 8, and (2) the "same-different" structure of festivals, play, and meaning (as especially noted in the interpretive-reading process). Again, the sketched out "onto-theology" of chapter 8, section 5.4 affirms both of these points. An "eternity" (i.e a non-temporal) seems to be required. As Pieper (1965:31f) says,

> A true festival does not take place "here" at all. It occurs only apparently here and now . . . *not in time*, but beyond time[;] . . . not in this eon nor on earth (emphasis added).

And yet, though "beyond time," festivals (and play) are also related to the everyday:

> *Homo festivus* remains faithful to the earth as something that can be finitely transcended. He is in search of higher stages of life and consciousness without omitting, repressing, or disdaining the basis. Therefore he doesn't fall into nonfreedom or euphoria; he does not underestimate the objective dangers and social threats and he does not overestimate the increase of festive freedom (Martin 1976:17).

And again,

> Fests [and play] make one painfully aware of the limitations, armor-plating, and ritualizations of everyday life. It is precisely this--and not aesthetic higher spirits--which forces people to integrate the good experiences of fest into everyday life, and that means to contradict the unsuccessful everyday life not only in an extraordinary, festive way but also in an ordinary, everyday way. The new alertness enables and demands the concrete *no* to subsanity, the opposition and action to greater sanity (Martin 1976:17).

Thus ". . . the consciousness of everyday life and the experience of fest belong constitutively together" (Martin 1976:16). This claim is related to the claim that the "stages" of Ricoeur's arc "belong constitutively together"; that the worlds of literature (written or oral) which serve as the basis of critique are really possible modes of being in this world too. Martin

(1976:16) goes on to claim that there exists ". . . a reality principle" which transcends all these different worlds, a "reality principle which is enlarged and opened and not simply screened out [by fest and play]" (Martin 1976:16). Granting this claim (which I do), together with the requirements that this principle be (1) "eternal" (i.e. at least "omnitemporal"), (2) omnispatial (in that it rules over every alternative world, whether "on earth" or not), (3) able to bestow "something that it is not in human power to give" (Pieper 1965:27), and, perhaps most importantly, (4) personal, even intersubjective, these suggestions point us toward "God" in the more or less traditional sense. I know of no alternative conception which accounts for this collection of characteristics.

Schall (1976:34) draws the same lesson from his reflections on games, and in particular, the arbitrariness of the rules:

> The rules of the game, then, their rigidity, yet their unnecessity can serve to assist us in a reflection about God and creation. Indeed, it might well be argued that games and sport and play are found in creation as the finite, earthly sign that things which exist for their own sakes are the highest things.

His phraseology returns us to our initial presentation of the "pure purposefulness" of play. The point here, though, is that that which exists for its own sake is, in the highest sense, God alone--a classical conception of God.[24]

---

[24] Schall 1976 and Martin 1976 take this point a step further to point out the "incarnational" aspect of sports. Says Schall, sports "reveal the degree to which the human spirit can and does suffuse and modify the human body precisely as it exists in the material world. . . ; [in short, the] 'incarnational' aspect of sports" (Schall 1976:53; cf. similarly, Sadler 1969:79). Martin 1976 claims that ". . . the only context extensive and intensive enough to bear fest as the transformation of everyday life is the messianic presence of God's kingdom" (Meeks 1976:xii). Such a "transformation of everyday life" is, of course, central in the concerns of Freire (and myself). The necessary "link" between "fest" (and play and "worlds of the text") and everyday life is the transcendent as I have been sketching it. Martin 1976 advances this sketch in a significant way. In chapter 8 I noted the importance of the incarnation, i.e. the historical, concrete realization in human life of the ISS ("the ideal speech situation"). Also noted there (and elsewhere) was the conflicting character of "new worlds," the moment of negativity in understanding. Martin 1976 notes the pain of contrast between fest and the everyday. He sees the incarnation of the Messiah, culminating in the crucifixion, as the "sign" under which, and on the basis of which, such contrast or contradictions can be coordinated. Says he, "The cross is the final consequence of the incarnation as realization of God in the world" (Martin 1976:41). And again, "If this coordination of everyday life and festive time really happens in the sign of the cross, happiness, freedom and pain will increase at the same time" (Martin 1976:41). With this move toward a "Messianic theory of fest, play, and reading," I am in essential agreement. I will not, however, in this project, seek to work out such a theory.

9.5.4 The "promised land"

According to Ricoeur (1974:24), " . . . ontology is indeed the promised land for a philosophy that begins with language and with reflection . . . ." In this section I propose to fill in the sketch of ontology already begun.

In the last section (5.3) a few steps were taken toward ontology, religion in general, and "God" in particular. It might well be asked what all this has to do with reading. Thus I pause briefly to quote five "secular" thinkers on reading to help verify the value of this approach.

Hans 1981, while using play to characterize the productive processes (Hans 1981:32), notes first that "Reading has vast productive potential if one gives oneself over to a good book, which is as capable of affecting one's life as is anything else one may be involved with in everyday life . . ." (Hans 1981:48). Later, Hans (1981:131) notes that ". . . the play of production [can][25] generate within the 'player' a feeling that corresponds in force to what has often been characterized as a *kind of* religious *experience*" (Hans 1981:131; emphasis added).

Similarly, Palmer 1969 parallels the religious and the literary experiences, the point of parallel being the inadequacy, even the inability to control the experience conceptually. This is the issue of transcendence in reading. Says Palmer (1969:226):

> . . . the hubris of trying to be the absolute master of a religious experience is apparent; the hubris of trying to be the master in the literary encounter is less apparent but no less real.

Gadamer (1975:378-387) also ties the interpretive-reading enterprise closely to the religious paradigm. I will return to Gadamer's comparison below.

Finally, Iser (1978:156) affirms, with regard to reading,

> Cavell's statement that ". . . the demands [of following a drama, or reading] are as rigorous as those of any spiritual exercise . . . ." In particular this "exercise" has to do with a relation to time-- the past and the future, which translate just as nicely as the old and the new. Says Cavell (1969:322) about this "spiritual exercise," we must "let the past go and . . . let the future take its time; so that we not allow the past to determine

---

[25] This "can" depends on "the degree of intensity" (Hans 1981:131) which itself depends on "the person" and "his orientation" (1981:48).

294

> the meaning of what is now happening . . . and
> that we not anticipate what will come of what has
> come. Not that anything is possible . . . but that
> we do not know what is, and is not, next.

Here then, reading is likened to a "spiritual exercise" due to the relation to time which we have also seen in festivals, themselves essentially religious in nature.[26]

In each of these cases, the relation of reading to religion has only been suggested, perhaps used as a metaphor. It seems beyond dispute, however, that even these secular authors on reading give indications that point in the direction I am pursuing.[27]

With this support, then--from the studies as summarized in section 5.2, from the steps taken in section 5.3, and from the "secular" authors quoted above--I proceed to present the thesis that God as understood in the Christian tradition is himself the (imminent and always transcendent) "promised land" of ontology.

The major challenge of Derrida (et al.) to ontology will be dealt with immediately. Says Van Til (1955:25), expounding the doctrine of God,

> Using the language of the One-and-Many question
> we contend that in God the one and the many are
> equally ultimate. Unity in God is no more
> fundamental than diversity, and diversity in God is
> no more fundamental than unity. The persons of
> the Trinity are mutually exhaustive of one another.
> The Son and the Spirit are ontologically on a par
> with the Father. It is a well-known fact that all
> heresies in the history of the church have in some
> form or other taught subordinationism [i.e., in
> essence, the inequality of "the one" and "the
> many"].

---

[26] This perspective of Cavell and Iser is dominated by an overemphasis on, even a bondage to, "continuous presentness" (Cavell 1969:322; cf. Iser 1978:156). Here they are vulnerable to Derrida's deconstruction.

[27] Though not speaking in as explicitly religious terminology, Fink (1968:19, 23, 29)--using the term "Being"--as well as Ehrmann (1968:33) and Hans (1981:2)--using the term "the real"--indicate the centrality of what others consider religious. For example, both Martin (1976:16, 22f) and Pieper (1965:15, 24, 53) correlate "the real" with God. Van Til (1955:23ff) points out, though, that that there are dangers with a simple identification of reality with God.

And I might add, all "ontological heresies" too.[28] Derrida has exposed one such heresy--pure-presence ontology--but is in danger of falling into another--pure-absence "ontology."

Elsewhere Van Til (1955:12) varies his terminology to approach my own: ". . . there are three distinct persons in this unity; the diversity and the identity are equally underived"; and again ". . . in him unity and diversity are equally ultimate" (Van Til 1974:231). Finally, in a manner which confirms Ricoeur's "Hebraic turn" mentioned earlier, Van Til (1955:25) says,

> God is absolute personality and therefore absolute individuality. He exists necessarily. He has no non-being over against himself in comparison with which he defines himself; he is internally self-defined.

This, then, is the foundation, the bedrock.[29] How, though, does this doctrine of the Trinity relate to the more mundane affairs of everyday life, like reading?

We proceed with Van Til (1974:230):

> So then, though we cannot tell why the godhead should exist tri-personaly [sic], we can understand something of the fact, after we are told that God exists as a triune being, that the unity and the plurality of this world has back of it a God in whom unity and plurality are equally ultimate. Thus we may say that this world, in some of its aspects at least, shows analogy to the Trinity. This world is made by God and, therefore, to the extent that it is capable of doing so, it may be thought of as revealing God as he exists. And God exists as a triune being.

Thus we expect to find this "analogy" (in mitigated form, no doubt) of the Trinity in all aspects of the world. In fact,

> The things of the universe must be interpreted in relation to God. The object of knowledge is not interpreted truly if though brought into relation with the human mind, it is not also brought into

---

[28] I consider "ontological heresies" to be those which are internally inconsistent and/or do not account for the (philosophical) "facts."

[29] I will modify the meaning of this terminology later.

relation with the divine mind. God is the ultimate
category of interpretation (Van Til 1955:44).

And God is triune!

Based on these presuppositions, there exists not only an eternal one
and many, but a created, temporal one and many:

> All aspects being equally created, no one aspect of
> reality may be regarded as more ultimate than
> another. Thus the created *one* and many may in
> this respect be said to be *equal* to one another;
> they are equally derived and equally dependent
> upon God who sustains them both. (Van Til
> 1955:27).

(Implicit in this creative activity are the notions of God as active, life-
giving, and gracious; cf. section 5.2.)

Most especially is this the case with regard to humans, "the created
image-bearer of God" (Van Til 1974:232). We have already seen the
interplay of identity and difference at the core of human knowing. Here I
simply propose the (orthodox) doctrine of the Trinity as the ontological
foundation for this. Without going into a full-blown discussion of
epistemology on this point (cf. e.g. Van Til 1969; 1977), I summarize a
point pertinent to our previous discussion:

> Every knowledge transaction has in it somewhere
> a reference point to God. Now since God is not
> fully comprehensible to us we are bound to come
> into what seems to be contradiction in all our
> knowledge. Our knowledge is analogical and
> therefore must be paradoxical (Van Til 1955:44).

Van Til develops this point further in a manner which accounts for
another attribute of "Being." The language is similar to Heidegger's
"being-in-the-world," yet develops what Heidegger called "the worldhood
of the world" (cf. chapter 6) in different terms.

> Man cannot help but know himself at once in
> relation to his environment. The subject of
> knowledge must know itself in relation to and in
> contrast with the object of knowledge.
>
> The contention that man must know himself in
> relation to his environment is not merely a general
> consideration obtained by observation of
> experience. It is implied in the very bedrock of
> Christian-theism. This may be seen by again
> referring to our idea of God and God's relation to

the created universe. Man exists by virtue of God's existence. Man's environment precedes man. God is man's ultimate environment and this environment is completely interpretative of man who is to know himself.

In other words man's environment is not impersonal. It is, moreover, not merely personal in the sense that simultaneous with his own appearance there are also other finite persons in relation to which he knows himself to be a person. Back of this relationship of finite persons to other finite persons and to other finite but impersonal things is the absolute personality of God. Back of the question as to whether man needs other finite persons or needs a finite non-personal environment is the question of the environment of man's immediate environment. God is man's ultimate environment and this ultimate environment controls the whole of man's immediate environment as well as man himself. The whole of man's own immediate environment as well as man himself is already interpreted by God (Van Til 1955:42).

There is much in this quote worthy of further discussion, but I highlight only a few points. First, man is conceived of "in relation to his environment," but this "environment" is ultimately God. In short, the ultimate "worldhood of the world" is God.[30] Second, this ultimate environment, which precedes "other finite persons" and "a finite non-personal environment," is not only personal, but given God as triune, it is also interpersonal. Here is the basis for an ISS which is not only transcendental, but transcendent. Third, man's mode of being could be described as "dwelling," correlative to man's relation to God as environment.[31] Thus, as anticipated in chapter 7, man as image and man as dwelling are mutually defining designations. In both cases the necessary correlate is God; in each case a different aspect of that one relation is in view.[32]

---

[30] Gaffin (1978:107ff) speaks similarly, though with special reference to God the Holy Spirit.

[31] This point is not as explicit in Van Til as I have made it in chapter 7.

[32] This characteristic of "dwelling" is finally grounded in the mode of being of the persons of the trinity in relation to one another. The classical formulation of these relations is in terms of *perichoresis* (Greek), *inhabitatio* (Latin), or co-inherence (cf. Hodge 1975:461; Kelly 1958:264).

These comments bring me to a reconsideration of God as "bedrock." Without losing the aspect of the final reference point in which human knowledge rests, the bottom, as it were, falls out of this "bedrock." The "problem" is that while God is the final reference point of any knowledge transaction, and the environment in which "we live and move and have our being" (Acts 17:28), he is also infinite. Because "God is the ultimate category of interpretation" (Van Til 1955:44), and because ". . . we cannot fully understand God's plan for created things . . . [;] we cannot fully understand things" (Van Til 1955:44) either. As noted earlier, "Our knowledge is analogical and therefore must be paradoxical" (Van Til 1955:44). This means there are no final univocal formulations for us. Polysemy is inherent in all human knowledge, and finds its cause in the incomprehensibility of God. God, then, can be seen by humans as the reservoir of meaning, and himself polysemous (for us). His very "structure" (i.e. tri-unity) is complex and interactive, and this structure is reflected to some extent in all that is and in any knowledge of what is. Thus, there is always more that can be said about any topic, and because paradox is inherent in human knowledge, even seemingly opposite statements can be persuasively put forth. Thus deconstruction is a possibility inherent in human knowledge. This does not mean, however, that the diversity of interpretations which can be persuasively presented are finally and ultimately only diverse. The tri-unity of the paradigm is also a "unity": unity and diversity exist as equally ultimate and equally underived.[33]

A final aspect of "Being" warrants further attention: playfulness. Does the idea of God, especially within the Christian tradition, allow for such playfulness? Several of the authors already quoted support the association of playfulness with God.

Already, with Schall (1976:34) we have noted that play "assists us in a reflection about God," serving as "a finite, earthly sign [of] . . . the highest things." Schall goes further, though, to relate the delightful and gracious quality of play to "the superabundance of the internal life of God which is, itself, the most fascinating reality" (1976:32). Being a spectator at a sporting event, then, is "the beginning of contemplation, worship, and festivity" (Schall 1976:64).

Schall is not alone in relating the internal life of God to play. Rahner (1967:23) says the Son is termed son because in "eternal youth he eternally enacts a game before his Father." And again, ". . . the mystical play of the Logos finds a place in the inner-most being of the Triune God" (Rahner 1967:23). And finally,

---

[33] Van Til is not alone in this perspective. Schall (1976:73), whom I have already quoted on play, says, "And since creation itself reflects also its source, there remains a certain irreducible mystery to everything in creation and history."

The whole game of the Logos which he enacts upon the earth to the delight of the Father, his cosmic dance on the globe of the world, is only a playful hint of what has reposed since before the beginning of time in the divine archetypes of Eternal Wisdom, and of what will be revealed when the earthly dance has come to an end (Rahner 1967:24).

Similarly, Gadamer (1975:378-387) uses both the intra-trinitarian relations (cf. e.g. 1975:384), and the messianic incarnation (cf. e.g. 1975:385) as models for the process of thought.³⁴

There is a warning, though, against too strict an identification of play with God. It comes from the nature of both play and God. Van der Leeuw (1963:112) puts it this way:

Play is the prerequisite for those forms of existence which strive toward a communion with the others, and finally for a meeting with God.

Play is a prerequisite, a necessary condition, but not a sufficient condition. Johnston (1983:80) develops this point further:

I did not want to compromise either God's freedom or the "purpose-lessness" of play by suggesting a necessary relationship between our play and the divine encounter. Rather it is enough to suggest that in play God can, and often does, meet us and commune with us. The result is a new openness to the religious more generally, our experience of the sacred in play serving as a prolegomenon to further encounters with God.

In short, God is not bound to human play; nor does play necessarily lead to God. It is enough to say that play is *like* God in a very high sense and that the openness of play is a prerequisite to an encounter with God.

Certainly these brief comments do not exhaust the development of an ontology which answers all the needs of modern philosophy or a comprehensive theory of reading. But I trust enough has been said to warrant the conclusion that the orthodox Christian doctrine of the Trinity matches the requirements of an ontology developed from our investigations

---

³⁴ Interestingly, Gadamer also relates "unity and multiplicity" (Gadamer 1975:386) based on this divine model. Miller (1970:109-112) extends the support for the play-game model of the Christian life to include an impressive listing of church fathers: Gregory Nazianzua, Maximus Confessor, Clement of Alexandria, The Venerable Bede, Bernhardt, Jerome, and Luther.

of reading. If the Christian presuppositions, as put forth by Van Til for instance, are valid, then the further uncovering of "aspects of Being" by various disciplines should support the thesis proposed in this section. Any such further investigation, even challenge, should of course be welcomed. New insight must often come through conflict.

CHAPTER 10

THE PRACTICE OF LITERACY INSTRUCTION

The purpose of this concluding chapter is to apply the previous theoretical discussions to the practice of teaching reading. The material in print on reading methods is staggering indeed, both in quantity and quality. It would be hard to find an area of reading not touched on by someone somewhere. If one did propose such a find, it is most likely that the pertinent piece had just been overlooked. Such a situation calls for humility.

I will not, therefore, presume to present a comprehensive new method of teaching reading. Rather, I will be making spot suggestions, doing fine tuning, and suggesting some global reconsiderations with regard to methods already being (more or less) successfully employed. I will be mainly applying the insights of the earlier chapters to these established methods. Clearly, these contributions are limited by my own lack of field or classroom experience in this area, and consequently should be taken as hypotheses to be tested by experience.

Though there is no lack of methods for teaching reading, what is not so readily available--and is widely recognized as missing--is a coherent framework which is comprehensive enough to integrate and harmonize the research already so widely available. Reading instruction, though, is definitely influenced by reading theory. As Weaver (1980:131) points out:

> The most successful reading instruction is likely to
> be that which is based on a solid understanding of
> the reading process itself, and which promotes
> rather than thwarts the acquisition of good reading
> strategies.

Consequently, I am operating under the assumption that the theoretical discussions of Part II do have implications for the practice of teaching reading.

I will proceed, then, as follows: section 1 will consist of a brief review of theories of reading as summarized in definitions of reading; section 2 will consist of a discussion of these definitions of reading in light of Part II, including the proposal that a theory emerges from Part II which integrates (and goes beyond) current theories of reading; section 3 will consist of an introduction to methods of teaching reading in relation to the corresponding definitions, and a preliminary critique of these methods; section 4 will consist of a presentation and comparative critique of the Freire and Gudschinsky methods of teaching reading; and section 5 will consist of final considerations. The main reasons for focusing on Freire and Gudschinsky are given in section 4.[1]

10.1 A review of theories of reading

Recall (from chapter 1) the three major categories of reading theories: bottom-up, top-down, and interactive. These three theory-types have generated three major types of methods for teaching reading. Before introducing these methods, I review the three theory-types.

For the bottom-up theorists, "Reading means pronouncing words" (Weaver 1980:132). As Bloomfield (1961:10) put it, reading is "producing the phonemes of one's language when one sees the written marks which conventionally represent these phonemes." Bottom-up approaches focus, then, on surface-structure features of printed material.

For the top-down theorists, the essential aspect of reading is the bringing of meaning *to* the text. Reading is a matter, first of all, of predicting meaning, and secondly, a matter of sampling and selecting the print in order to confirm or disconfirm the projected prediction. That is, reading means using deep structure to interpret surface structure (Weaver 1980:132).

The interactive theories of reading attempt to take into account the weaknesses as well as the strengths of both bottom-up and top-down theories. As Goodman (1979b:660) summarizes this effort: "I believe that what the reader brings to the text is as important as what the author did in understanding the meaning a given reader constructs." For the interactive theories (as for the top-down), "Reading is not reading unless there is some degree of comprehension . . ." (Goodman 1973:26). This is also the case for the schema theories of reading: Reading comprehension is defined in terms of filling schemas ". . . in such a way as to jointly satisfy the constraints of the message and the schemata" (Durkin 1980:6).

Though there are real differences between reading theorists, these differences are usually a matter of different emphases on either bottom-up or top-up processes, rather than an outright and total exclusion from the concept of reading of something another theorist has identified as significant. Because I think this is the case, in the general discussion of these definitions in light of Part II which follows, I will consider these theories of reading in terms of either bottom-up or top-down emphases.

---

[1] In addition, both are used in *adult* literacy programs throughout the "third-world," have been tested in various cultural and linguistic settings (contrary to so much which is confined to one language group, e.g. Indo-European languages), and thus coordinate with my own interests.

10.2 A discussion of definitions of reading

The genius of the hermeneutic-phenomenological account of reading is that both top-down and bottom-up processes are integrated by the philosophical framework sketched in chapter 6. In particular, the hermeneutical circle as the interaction of the whole and its parts provides a tidy harmonization of the reading processes. The formulation of understanding as a mode of man's embeddedness in the world (and finally, in Being) which always precedes and supports any particular act of knowing provides the basis for the top-down emphasis on prediction. The "always already" preunderstanding implied in this phenomenological position means that there is always some grasp of the whole which the reader brings to the text at every stage of reading. Our studies in chapters 8 and 9, though, have cautioned us against prioritizing identity (i.e. the whole) over difference (i.e. the parts), and thus against a one-sided insistence on the role of prediction-confirmation. The "other side" is the building of the whole from the parts and this is what the bottom-up approach emphasizes.

The strong point of the bottom-up approach is its attention to the elements of the semiotic system, and to the interplay of signs within such a system. Often this interplay deals with nonsense (from the perspective of a reference dominated view of meaning), and thus is condemned by top-down approaches as not being adequately attentive to meaning. If this interplay of signs was not reconnected to reference this criticism would be valid. But equally, a view of meaning as reference to the exclusion of the interplay of signs (as sense) is also faulty. The bottom-up theories, then, tend to emphasize meaning as sense, and the top-down theories meaning as reference. In chapter 4 I argued that both are needed in dialectical interplay, and that there is a certain priority to reference. Thus, the top-down position is to be favored as the starting point, not, however, to the exclusion of the semiotic processes (more on this later).

The phenomenological emphasis on man *in the world* as the starting point for theories having to do with man (like reading theory) also confirms the importance of "schemas," "the theory of the world in the head," etc. These are typically top-down concepts, i.e. they constitute the reader's contributions to the reading process. Inasmuch as bottom-up theories do not acknowledge the essential importance of such contributions, they are faulty. Not only is this a justified criticism of bottom-up theories with respect to more global reader input, like schemas of situations in the world (e.g. a football game), but also with respect to more limited and strictly linguistic input. Bottom-up theories have typically focused on the phonological system of language, teaching grapheme-phoneme correspondences, and have given inadequate attention to syntax and semantics. Both of these latter systems of language, however, cannot be excluded from the reading process as was shown in chapter 1.

The topic of "the world" also introduces further weaknesses of the top-down approach, which have indeed included "the world" in ways bottom-up theories have not. What the top-down approach does not account for, however, is the ontological sense of "the world." Thus, it does not recognize the "mysterious aspect" of reading. We have called this variously "the source of the new," "transcendence," "Being," and "the subject of play." In short, the "top" of the top-down theorists is not "tops" enough.

A similar and related shortcoming of top-down theories is the failure to recognize the ideality of meaning, that aspect of meaning which obtains independently of the constructive activities of the reader. For the top-down theorists meaning is (instead) typically in the mind of the reader only. Interestingly, it is in the "decoding play" of the bottom-up theories that this aspect of "Being-transcendence" comes the closest to being recognized. There is, however, no theoretical recognition or status given to this aspect in bottom-up theories.

The final point to be noted here with respect to the definitions of reading given in section 1, is the (almost) total lack of any place for critique as essential to reading. As noted in chapter 8, critique is not totally ignored in reading theories; far from it! But when included, it is included as an advanced skill which must eventually be taught if a reader is to be mature as a reader. Freire, however, is the major exception to this lack of integration of critique in the theory and practice of reading.

In conclusion, then, the theory of reading developed in Part II favors a thoroughly interactive theory of reading, while identifying aspects of the reading process not accounted for in current interactive theories. Specifically, the ideality of meaning, the ontological notion of comprehension, the essentiality of critique, the role of play, and transcendence are aspects which need to be thoroughly integrated with both reading theory and practice.

10.3   Introduction to methods of teaching reading

My aim in this section is to provide a sketch of methods which have been used for teaching reading. This sketch serves as the background for a more comprehensive look at two eclectic methods in the following sections. These two methods use a combination of the other approaches presented below.

Before proceeding with this presentation, I give a summary of the conclusions with regard to "the best approach," a summary which is still true today:

1. A significant number of children have learned to read using each of the approaches studied

2. No particular approach stood out as being superior to the others

3. No approach resulted in all children learning successfully

4. The quality of teaching is of greater importance than the particular approach (Trevor 1969:34).

Weaver (1980:151) confirms several points of this summary: "Fortunately many teachers are far more effective than the approach suggested in their basal reading series." (Similarly, Pearson and Johnson 1978:vii.) A major consequence of these conclusions is that an eclectic approach to reading instruction is encouraged.[2]

10.3.1 The phonics approach

The emphasis of the phonics approach[3] is the learning of letter-sound correspondences and the ability to sound out words. The assumptions are that (1) reading means learning to pronounce words, (2) the blending of the sounds of letters in words occurs properly as sounds of letters are sequentially pronounced, and (3) the meaning of text is accessible only and automatically through the sounds. Such a bottom-up approach has obviously been challenged (cf. chapter 1), and there are clear practical weaknesses. First, most consonants cannot be pronounced without vowels, and when a student attempts such a pronunciation, the vowels employed may not relate to the word in question. Second, many orthographies do not allow a consistent sound-letter correspondence. Third, the activity of understanding is not taught due to the overattention to word recognition. Fourth, the learning process tends to be very formal, with little joy in reading.

The advantages to the phonics method are (1) the teaching of abilities to handle new words, (2) the control over the introduction of letters, and (3) the demands on the teacher are minimal compared with other methods. Whether or not the attention to, in themselves, meaningless segments of language (phonemes/graphemes) is an advantage or disadvantage depends on the overall context of teaching. Given what Ricoeur calls distanciations (as inherent in text-reading), I judge such "meaningless decoding skills" as taught by phonics to be a necessary part of reading.

---

[2] For more thorough sketches, cf. Gray 1976, Holdaway 1979, Weaver 1980.

[3] Phonics was especially popular from about 1890 to 1930. Today, when phonics is taught at all, it is used as only one component of reading instruction. The method of Dr. Frank Laubach is a modified phonics approach.

10.3.2 The sight-word approach

The sight-word approach,[4] in contrast to the phonics method, emphasizes the teaching of whole words. Only after the whole word and its meaning are grasped is the word analyzed into its parts.

Though there is a greater emphasis on meaning than with the phonics approach, new words are often "taught in isolation from a meaningful context" (Holdaway 1979:28) with a heavy emphasis on word-form recognition rather than on meaning. In short, meaning is conceived of as basically a word-level phenomenon. Further, the control of the vocabulary introduced--which can be an advantage of this approach--can lead to a "distorted and impoverished" (Holdaway 1979:28) text-book language. Finally, this approach suffers from the lack of a clear research-based understanding of "what features or details of words are significant . . . in recognizing or discriminating words" (Holdaway 1979:28).

The main advantage of this approach is the shift in emphasis within the part-whole relation to the whole as the better starting point for instruction.

10.3.3 The linguistic approach

Devised by Leonard Bloomfield (cf. chapter 1), the linguistic approach was prominent in the 1950's and continued until the early 1970's. The emphasis is on learning and internalizing "regular patterns of spelling-sound correspondence" (Weaver 1980:26) through the reading of sets of words like "Nan can fan Dan." The assumptions of this method are (1) that the early reader can infer these regular patterns (rules are not taught), (2) that most of a language is conformable to such regular patterns, and (3) that once words are pronounced (according to the patterns), the meaning takes care of itself. Certainly pattern recognition can be an important part of reading, but as noted in chapter 1, pattern recognition alone is hardly an adequate account of the full process. Furthermore, by emphasizing regular patterns, this method, like the sight meghod, leads to the use of distorted, unnatural reading materials

The preceding three methods of teaching reading are bottom-up in their emphasis and all suffer from the inadequacies of such an account. The following two approaches, however, emphasize top-down processes.

---

[4] The sight-word approach was most popular from about 1930 until the mid-1960's. In these latter years it became intertwined with phonics (Weaver 1980:25), and virtually indistinguishable from what came to be called analytic (as opposed to synthetic) phonics. This analytic/synthetic distinction has to do with whether one starts with the whole and breaks it down into its parts (analytic) or starts with the parts and builds up to the whole (synthetic).

10.3.4 The language experience approach

In reaction to unnaturalness of most reading materials, the language experience approach (LEA) develops reading materials from the experiences of the learners. The LEA is "concerned with helping beginners learn to bring their knowledge and experience to bear in getting meaning from the printed word" (Weaver 1980:26). Typically, the learner(s) and the teacher together compose a story which the teacher writes down on the board. The story is then read and reread until the learner associates the written form of the word with the spoken.

While highly motivational, LEA places a great demand on the teacher who must proceed without prepared materials. Adequate repetition of words is difficult to provide, as is adequate monitoring of progress. Without controlled vocabulary the transfer to prepared materials is far from systematic and often poorly accomplished. Finally, the LEA fails to recognize the crucial differences between spoken and written language, and the different strategies necessary for comprehension.

10.3.5 The psycholinguistic approach

Based upon the theoretical work of Kenneth Goodman and Frank Smith, the psycholinguistic approach attempts to teach the use of "nonvisual information . . . plus the fewest, most productive visual cues to get deep structure [i.e. meaning]" (Weaver 1980:133). Rather than teaching reading *skills*, specifically word pronunciation and/or identification skills, the psycholinguistic approach helps readers develop *strategies*, specifically predicting, sampling, and confirming/correcting strategies. The methods for teaching these strategies are at least as well worked out as those of any method, and, as expected, significantly different (cf. e.g. Weaver 1980:213-246; Tompkins and Webeler 1983; Blackowicz 1983; Moldofsky 1983). While other approaches usually focus on word recognition, using context as a last resort, the psycholinguistic approach teaches the use of context--syntactic, semantic, and grapho/phonic--as the first resort. While other approaches recommend the sequence "memory (for word forms)--word analysis skills--context" for identifying words, the psycholinguistic approach recommends the sequence "context--word--context," where the first "context" in this list includes the "entire store of knowledge and experience plus the preceding [textual] context" (Weaver 1980:140), and the second "context" is that which follows the word.

As noted in Part II, this "context--word--context" pattern closely parallels Ricoeur's pre-understanding--explanation--understanding arc. Thus the contribution of the psycholinguistic approach are acknowledged as very valuable. The major weaknesses of the psycholinguistic approach are its minimizing of the importance of the bottom-up decoding procedures, particularly those which decenter the reader as the sole controlling factor in reading.

As expected, the benefits of the various approaches to reading instruction are widely recognized, and several attempts have been made to collect and combine the methods, and thus the benefits. These are the eclectic approaches. Two such approaches are presented in some detail in the following section.

10.4   Two eclectic approaches

A major consequence of the preceding section is that an approach to reading instruction is needed which maintains the beneficial elements of all of the methods surveyed.   Further, these elements must not be combined in a manner which distorts the benefit of any of the elements. The two methods presented and discussed in this section--Freire's and Gudschinsky's--are both arguably eclectic, and thus make an attempt to collect and use the positive aspects of other approaches.   But they are both just as arguably inadequate as they stand.   In fact, eclectic approaches have been criticized for the presupposition that

> ... if one approach which did not make so great a
> difference was somehow insufficient, several such
> insufficient approaches--end to end, simultaneous,
> stirred and served, or presented separately in an
> inviting smorgasbord--would create a sufficiency
> (McCullough 1976:6).

And it is true that most eclectic approaches continue to focus on word identification skills rather than on meaning-getting strategies (Weaver 1980:27).   A further difficulty with eclectic approaches is their lack of "consistency and coherence" (Holdaway 1979:30), resulting from simple pragmatic considerations rather than any theoretical unity.

In what follows my aims will be (1) to see if the preceding criticisms of eclectic approaches in general are applicable to Freire's and Gudschinsky's methods, and (2) to exploit the theoretical framework emerging from Part II to improve methods which have been already proven successful in a variety of situations.

These two approaches to reading instruction are first presented (section 4.1), then critiqued, both in terms of insights from the theories of the reading researchers and with direct reference to the theoretical discussions of Part II (section 4.2).   Again, my aim is to provide general suggestions for modifications of the eclectic approach emerging from the earlier discussions, not to work out this method in detail.   I am well aware that much hard work will remain to be done, much of it experiential field work.

10.4.1 Presentation

10.4.1.1   Freire's method of teaching reading

Just as conscientization[5] is the goal of education for Freire, so too it is the key to understanding his method of teaching literacy. Says Freire (1974:86),

> Conscientization occurs simultaneously with the literacy or post-literacy process. It must be so. In our educational method, the word is not something static or disconnected from man's existential experience, but a dimension of their thought-language about the world.

The means for conscientization in literacy grew out of Freire's previous experience with the "culture circles" in Recife (cf. footnote 1, chapter 1). In these circles, Freire says,

> . . . we attempted through group debate either to clarify situations or to seek action arising from that clarification. (Freire 1976, quoted in Bendor-Samuel, 1977:15).

The setting for these discussions is the "cultural circle," not a school; the leader is a trained coordinator, not the traditional teacher; and the method is dialogue, not lecture. Says Freire, in a letter sent to the coordinators of the cultural circles in Chile:

> A cultural circle is not a school, in the traditional sense. In most schools, the teacher, convinced of his wisdom, which he considers absolute, gives classes to pupils, passive and docile, whose ignorance he also considers absolute.
>
> A cultural circle is a live and creative dialogue, in which everyone knows some things and does not know others, in which all seek, together, to know more (Freire 1971b:61f).

Two main premises underlie Freire's method. The first premise is that

> . . . it ought to be possible to select a brief list of words that would contain all the phonemes in Portuguese, so that learning this minimal linguistic universe would enable a reader to sound out any

---

[5] That is, critical consciousness; cf. chapter 8.

other words or to record any words he knew
orally (Lindvall 1980:24).

The second premise is that "adults can easily learn to read words that are
familiar and meaningful to them" (Lindvall 1980:24). In summary,

> . . . the essence of literacy through
> conscientization, in a [regular] syllabic language
> such as Portuguese, is to help man discover
> critically, the mechanisms of word composition, so
> that he himself can enter into the creative game of
> combining words (Mashayekh 1974:24).

Based upon these premises, the preparation of the teaching
materials proceeds in three stages. First, an inventory of sounds is made.
Second, key words are chosen from words previously gathered. Three
criteria are used in the selection of these words: (1) the words chosen
must contain the basic sounds of the language; (2) they must be arranged
according to phonetic difficulty; and (3) the "words included should be
resonate of the social, cultural and political context. They should provide
an emotional and mental stimulation; they should be suggestive"
(Mashayekh 1974:26).

The third phase involves the actual production of the teaching
material. First, a series of pictures are prepared, each of which represents
some situation related both to the key word and to the lives of the
participants. Second, cards are prepared which show the key word broken
into syllables, with each syllable given in a phonemic sequence of
contrasting vowels. For instance, for the key word "favela" (fa-ve-la, slum),
the following card is prepared:

fa	fe	fi	fo	fu
va	ve	vi	vo	vu
la	le	li	lo	lu

This is called a "discovery card."

Just as "conscientization" guides each stage of the preparation of
materials, so too it permeates the application of the method. "The first
task in the 'search' for 'critical consciousness' is to turn the illiterate into a
spectator of his own reality so that he will think about it" (Mashayekh
1974:31). This is accomplished by presenting pictures of the key words to
the group. Discussion of the situation represented is then stimulated by the
coordinator. After the discussion had run its course, the key word is
presented as a sight word with its meaning being tied to the preceding
discussion. Next, the word is shown without the picture. Immediately
afterwards, the same word is divided into syllables. After each "piece" can
be recognized, a family of phonemic segments based on contrasting vowels
is given for each syllable in turn (for example, the top line on the discovery

312

card above). After each of the three sequences is given separately, they are combined, shown on the discovery card, and practised, being read both horizontally and vertically to learn the discrimination of the sounds. It is called a "discovery card" because the illiterates are encouraged to combine syllables on the card to form new "words," whether meaningful or not. This process of combining is encouraged both in the group meetings and at home. Writing is also begun in the very first lesson. Each following lesson, then, proceeds in this same manner.

10.4.1.2   Gudschinsky's method of teaching reading

The Gudschinsky method as now practiced began to take its present form in the 1960's. At that time Sarah Gudschinsky had more than 18 years of experience working in literacy both in the United States and abroad.

As early as 1959, Gudschinsky summarized the principles of a literacy primer which were emerging from her wide experience with various ethnic groups:

> The essential principles of a successful primer, as demonstrated by field testing, are the gradual introduction of new elements . . . , provision for independent reading by the use of syllable or letter drill . . . , provision for understanding through the use of meaningful material . . . and provision for fluency by the use of adequate repetition (Gudschinsky 1959:9).

The goal of reading acquisition is understood by Gudschinsky to be independence, comprehension, and fluency. To reach these goals, skills are developed through letter drills, functor drills, and the reading of connected material. Lee (1982:27) summarizes:[6]

> The purpose of the letter drills is to teach 1) the immediate recognition of the letters (high frequency particles) along with their correspondence to specific sounds, 2) the positions which these letters fill within the syllables, 3) the ability to chunk the letters within syllables and 4) the ability to decode those contentives.

---

[6] Lee 1982 will be used extensively throughout this section since his is the most recent and the most thorough presentation of the Gudschinsky method. Lee 1982 is used as the textbook in the literacy classes which teach this method as taught by the Summer Institute of Linguistics [S.I.L.], the organization with which Sarah Gudschinsky worked until her death in 1975.

The purpose of the functor drills is to teach 1) the immediate recognition of high frequency functors (both function words and affixes), 2) the ability to chunk functors and contentives within words, phrases, clauses, etc., and 3) the ability to decode these.

The purpose of the connected material is 1) to give practice in the use of the skills developed in the letter and functor drills in context, 2) to give practice in independent reading including hypothesizing and testing, 3) to focus on comprehension, and 4) to develop fluency in reading.[7]

The letter drills include three aspects. First, before focusing on the visual recognition of the letter, the sound it represents is presented. Second, a key word containing the letter to be taught is introduced. This key word is to be "picturable, emotive, [and] a central part of the connected material of the lesson" (Lee 1982:28). Third, the letter being taught is learned through five focus drills: analysis, synthesis, identification, contrast, and word building.[8]

---

[7] Because S.I.L.'s work is among many preliterate cultures, preliteracy training, which precedes the letter drills, is also included. Says Lee (1982:27),

> This includes such things as a desire to learn to read, a realization of the usefulness of reading and that reading is for meaning, the ability to focus on language as made up of sounds and other chunks, the ability to contrast the types of visual differences relevant to reading and a certain amount of motor skills as a background for learning to write.

[8] By analysis is meant "starting with some larger unit and then focusing on the smaller bits which compose that unit" (Lee 1982:29). The key word is the starting point and the analysis drill focuses on the letter being taught.

Synthesis means

> . . . focusing on smaller bits within a unit. Synthesis is the complement of analysis. It is used to refer to focusing on a smaller bit as it functions within a larger unit (Lee 1982:29).

The purpose of the synthesis drill is "to focus on sample combinations of the new letter along with letters which have already been studied" (Lee 1982:30). The third focus drill is the identification drill. Its purpose is "to see the sameness of the new letter and to label it (give it a name)" (Lee 1982:30). Fourth, the contrast drill: The new letter is contrasted with previously studied letters occurring in the same position in the syllable.

The functor drills are similar to the letter drills. With the functor drills, however, the linguistic context is a sentence or a phrase. Further, the functor is not presented in isolation, but focused upon by the means of negative focus.

The reading of connected material follows the drills and is considered to be "much more important" (Lee 1982:34).[9] Lee (1982:34) summarizes:

> The reading of the connected material includes independent reading by each individual, questions to answer, phrases to find, and practice in oral reading (choral and/or individual).

At this stage, the reader is expected to use linguistic context as well as background information about the world to help in the reading process (Lee 1982:19-20, 34). Questions centered around the connected material are the primary means employed to teach such use of context and background information (Lee 1982:410-415).[10]

Finally, each literacy lesson concludes with writing drills which teach letter formation and spelling, as well as creative writing.

10.4.2 A critique of the Freire and the Gudschinsky methods

This critique of the Freire and Gudschinsky methods of teaching reading will proceed in three stages. These three stages follow (roughly) the pattern of Ricoeur's hermeneutic arc. The beginning stage reflects the initial belonging to a life-context; the decoding stage reflects Ricoeur's explanation-critique stage; and the concluding stage reflects the further grounding of the reading in life, which Ricoeur terms appropriation. This

---

The effect of this drill is to teach particular syllable positions and the expectation of certain "fillers" for them. The last focus drill is called the word building drill. This drill

> ... builds words with the new letter and previously studied letters to give the reader an opportunity to read the new letter in larger chunks and also to tie it back to meaningful units (Lee 1982:31).

Usually the key word reappears here as the first "built word." This provides an analogy for other words. In addition to returning to the word level, each built word is "followed by an illustrative sentence which emphasizes meaning and provides a means of reassuring the reader that he has properly identified the new built word" (Lee 1982:32).

[9] "The term *connected material* is used rather than *story* because other types of discourse may be used such as easy poetry" (Lee 1982:34).

[10] This use of questions, though, seems to be an addition to the Gudschinsky method by Lee, as supported by more recent research.

pattern substantiates that these eclectic approaches are more than a random smorgasbord of techniques, but manifest a unity justified by our earlier discussions.

10.4.2.1   The beginning stages of instruction

Both approaches begin very much rooted in the life-context of the learners. The ontological perspective on man as "being-in-the-world" (as developed in Part II) and various aspects of reading research support this approach. Before developing this point, though, a comparison between Freire and Gudschinsky is in order.

Freire's approach is more explicit about and more committed to the importance of beginning reading instruction with discussion centered within the life-context of the illiterate. More particularly, Freire conceives of such a beginning as essential to reading. Gudschinsky recognizes the pedagogical value of involving the students in the learning process, but seems to consider this stage as peripheral to reading per se. In other words, for Gudschinsky discussion and interaction are good pedagogical procedures in general, and a good way to start a class, even a natural way to lead into teaching reading, but only tangential to the teaching of reading. Here I expect that what has been true of reading teachers in general, is true of Gudschinsky and her method:

> Fortunately, many teachers are far more effective
> than the approach suggested in their basal reading
> series. They let intuition and experience guide
> them . . . (Weaver 1980:151).

Or as Pearson and Johnson (1978:vii) put it, ". . . good teachers have good (and sound) intuition."

There are also other differences. Freire's concern is decidedly political, with an aim to thinking critically about the status quo. Gudschinsky, however, aims for social and cultural relevance while decidedly trying to avoid the political. In somewhat simplistic terms, Freire focuses upon and emphasizes what is wrong with one's world while Gudschinsky focuses upon and emphasizes what is good and right with one's world. It must also he remembered, though, that Freire highlights man's dignity and abilities to be creatively and productively involved in change. Thus, his method must not be judged to be purely or overly negative in emphasis.[11]

---

[11] Unfortunately, further weaknesses arise when Freire's notions are examined more closely. For instance, he insists that trust is an essential ingredient of true dialogue. However, "mistrust" is "the key word to describe the attitude of the leaders of the revolution toward those with whom they must work" (Griffith 1974:102). This, not incidentally, includes the "friendly peasants" as well as the "oppressors" (Freire 1970:169). Such a blatant contradiction is surely a weakness and a cause for concern with regard to

Because Freire's method is more developed than Gudschinsky's with regard to the initial discussion, I follow him at this point in my discussion.

Freire's method encourages a thorough discussion and exploration of the issues involved, guided as much by the "matter of the text" (in this case verbal) as by the teacher. This process, I suggest, contains several crucial aspects of reading, and ought to be encouraged. For example, schemas are (as it were) called forth, opened up, and explored in their interrelations and implications. The world of the participants is activated and brought to bear in relation to a particular topic. Further, these schemas are used in the context of criticism; they are not used uncritically. Thus the participants are involved in interaction with their own schemas, and encouraged to question the validity of the models of the world with which they have operated. Thus various critical thinking skills are developed such as consistency building skills, problem solving skills, inferencing skills, self-questioning skills, and an awareness of oneself as an active learner, all of which have been shown to be important in reading (cf. e.g. Flood 1981; Singer and Dolan 1982; Trabassco 1980; Durkin 1980; R.C. Anderson, et al. 1976b; Bruce and Rubin 1981; Bobbs and Moe 1983; etc.). In short, many of these skills reflect the prediction--testing--modification strategies highlighted by the phenomenologists and psycholinguists.

With regard to Freire's method in particular, the previous comments with regard to the discrepancy between his ideal of dialogue and its

---

the goals of Freire's approach. It is, however, also cause for hope to those who find many of Freire's ideas attractive, and yet dislike his notion of political revolution. As noted in chapter 8, the importance of critique in reading need not be exclusively tied to any one ideology. A similar weakness shows up in Freire's notion of dialogue. When placed in the context of revolution it negates itself: Dialogue is not appropriate with the "oppressor." As Freire (1970:134) says,

> Dialogue between the former oppressors and the oppressed
> as antagonistic classes was not possible before the
> revolution; it continues to be impossible afterward.

Further, and perhaps worse, those who later dissent are to be punished rather than engaged in creative dialogue (Freire 1970:170). Surely this is as oppressive an atmosphere for learning and critical thinking as any learning situation Freire opposes. In such a context, the meanings of words such as "love," "truth," "humility," etc. which are used to describe dialogue, are severely distorted.

Finally, when the fuller context of revolution is included in a consideration of Freire's methods of literacy, the criticism of his approach as being utopian, i.e. as overly idealistic, is indeed valid. As Griffith 1974 points out, the recognition and cultivation of revolutionary leaders as envisioned by Freire is naive indeed. Freire makes no provision for self-appointed leaders arising with "base motives and an ability to attract followers and retain their loyalty" (Griffith 1974:103f). Here Lindvall (1980:25) is correct to note that "Coordinators can become manipulators." These particular concerns, however, need not pollute the method itself. No doubt, any method could be distorted in similar ways.

revolutionary outworking must be carefully noted. Further, though, and most important for our purpose here, the kind of coordinated discussion Freire proposes lends itself to modification by more current reading research. In fact, the results of research on the kinds of skills mentioned in the previous paragraph can serve as a concrete guide for Freire's coordinators. For example, a "teacher" alert to the schematic organization of knowledge and the role of schemas in drawing inferences can help guide others to become similarly conscious of factors influencing perception and conception. McNeil (1984:9ff), for example, gives further suggestions for using schema theory in similar ways, in particular, in constructing semantic maps of relevant notions. Though such guidance is unavoidably ideological, it need not be dominated by any particular ideology. It is here that the recognition of the dynamism of meaning, play, and transcendence works to liberate one from such dominance. It is the "matter of the text" which contributes in often unexpected ways. In other words, the imagination of the participants is activated as the consideration of new possibilities for one's world are taken seriously and explored. New schemas for the world are built through active interaction, and yet, because no one individual controls the discussion process (in the ideal), this active involvement is balanced by the passive reception of new ideas contributed by others, or generated (seemingly) from "nowhere," as in a brainstorming session. This allowance of playfulness, with ideas, with worlds, etc., is judged to be an important and beneficial aspect of this first stage.

Related to the stimulation of the imagination is Freire's conception of education as utopian. Utopian for Freire "is not to be merely idealistic or impractical . . ." (Freire 1974:84).[12] Rather, to be utopian is to have hope and the commitment that education is both possible and will make a significant difference for the better (Freire 1974:83-86). Without this openness to the future, and a communal vision of possibilities, it is doubtful whether any method of education can be successful. Freire's particular strength here is that he clearly recognizes this fact and integrates its importance at the heart of his method.

A further advantage of this discussion stage is the activating of the emotions and affections of the new readers, a weak point in most theories and practices of reading. Such activation results in high motivation. As Bendor-Samuel (1977:18) notes, "Freire majors on maximum motivation." Motivation is a long held "key" to education, and any method which promotes it is bound to be strong. The particulars of how Freire maximizes motivation are, however, of special interest. Freire uses key words which are integral to the life experience and interests of the group being taught. This is not unique to Freire, as previously noted. What is unique, though, is the attention to developing the consciousness of culture (as distinct from nature) and of the implicit freedom of man to change culture. Further, Freire focuses on the desirability of change, thus stimulating emotions and energies to act in one's own best interest,

---

[12] Griffith 1974 and Lindvall 1980 miss this point in Freire.

318

including learning to read. This method of integrating reading with what it means to be human in the given situation touches depths of emotion, energy, and motivation usually not reached by other methods.

There are even more advantages for reading in this initial-discussion period. As noted in section 3.1, Freire uses the picture to "turn the illiterate into a spectator of his own reality." The use of pictures in reading instruction is a controversial topic (cf. Schallert 1980). One of the points of controversy centers around the unnaturalness of pictures: They are not reality in the same way as one's other experience. Kolers (1973:40) illustrates:

> The error [of assuming pictures necessarily communicate as intended] is clearly revealed by recent experiences in countries in which the safety precautions to be followed in gold mines, or the details of inserting and using an intrauterine device have been conveyed for illiterate persons as a series of pictures in comic book fashion. The programs have not been especially successful, however, for the users have not known how to read the pictures; whether to read from left to right or right to left, bottom to top or top to bottom, or even why a 2-inch-high drawing having a certain shape should be called a man or a woman, nor why the reader should identify himself with this 2-inch-high drawing. Thus, literacy is required for pictorial interpretation as much as for textual interpretation.[13]

These supposed weaknesses or difficulties with pictures, though, are their strengths from another perspective. First, they require interpretation; but so does reading. And the development and exercise of interpretive skills, beginning with the recognition of the need for interpretation, is essential, especially among preliterate peoples for whom whatever is written is often considered *a priori* authoritative (Wendell 1982:9; Baker 1979). Second, the "unreal" distanciation of pictures, and of the illiterate from his own everyday reality, is judged to be an important and useful preliminary to dealing with a written text. Third, though a discussion starts with a picture it should be evident (from the discussion) that its meaning does not reside "in the picture." Further, if the coordinator is functioning as Freire outlines, it should be obvious (to anyone who cares to notice) that the

---

[13] Interestingly, Schallert (1980:521) dismisses this claim of Kolers as mostly irrevelant to the teaching of reading in the United States. She does allow that this point must be considered by some in some circumstances, such as teachers of children who may have difficulty with pictures and illustrators of textbooks, but she recognizes no relevant theoretical point. This insight of Kolers, however, illustrates how those working in preliterate cultures can contribute to the theory and practice of reading.

319

course of the discussion is guided in a manner which no one in particular controls. Of course manipulation is possible, but here as in reading, one must be trained to avoid "forced" readings, and to recognize the force of the meaning emerging from the reader-text interaction.

In these ways, and no doubt others, the preliminary-discussion stage of Freire's approach is valuable to reading instruction. Such a stage should be included and developed (in accordance with intuition and research) in any reading approach. On this point Gudschinsky stands to learn, though it must also be acknowledged that her method is readily adaptable to such development.

Finally, it is worth noting that much current research on the role of schemas in education supports the general outline of Freire's approach at this initial stage. For example, this research demonstrates the importance of the activation and interaction of schemas in a manner not customary in traditional western schools, yet central to Freire's discussion-stage (cf. Olson 1977; R.C. Anderson 1977a). Similarly, Meyer 1977 and R.C. Anderson (1977:427) point out the importance of problem recognition if schema change is to be likely. Thus Freire's problem-oriented approach is commended. However, Wyer 1977 points out that the requirement for major cognitive reorganization often generates major resistance, a factor which must be taken into account in teaching new readers. Wendell 1982 and Lee 1982, working within the Gudschinsky framework, have outlined a recommended progression from familiar to unfamiliar materials. In this regard, Gudschinsky's beginning with concepts which do not require major cognitive reorganization shows significant insight. In short, both the emphases of Habermas (Freire's concern for critique) and Gadamer (Gudschinsky's concern for the affirmation of the current world of the learners) are needed, with some priority given to the emphasis of "belonging" (as with Gadamer and Gudschinsky).

Finally, a "forthrightly dialectic method such as Socratic teaching" (R.C. Anderson 1977a:430) is put forward as a plausible candidate for effective teaching. The initial discussion-stage of these eclectic methods capitalize on this plausibility.[14]

10.4.2.2   The decoding skills

As with Ricoeur's hermeneutical arc, the literacy instruction of both Freire and Gudschinsky proceeds from the pre-understanding, embedded-

---

[14] Regardless of the strengths discussed above, there remains a major weakness in this preliminary stage. It reflects the largely literate cultural situations in which Freire has worked. People from largely pre-literate cultures, for whom writing of any sort is a novelty, need much more in the way of pre-reading exercises. It is here that the Summer Institute of Linguistics has much to offer. For a sampling of the materials available see Lee (1982:147-167), Loving (1976:97-115), Wendell (1979:111-114), Gudschinsky (1973:60-68), and Gudschinsky (1960:10-15).

in-the-world stage to the teaching of decoding skills, which Ricoeur calls, more generally, explanatory procedures. Both eclectic methods have prepared for this distancing move through using pictures as mentioned above. Freire has further involved "explanation" in the discussion stage and has practiced the "decoding" of life-situations through critical examination. Such an integration of explanation with understanding is inevitable as our critique of Ricoeur's linear-stage model of interpretation-reading has shown. Thus Freire is to be commended, at least with regard to the incorporation of the critical-distanciating moment into the pre-understanding stage. However, both Freire and Gudschinsky suffer from a lack of integration in the opposite direction. This is the general problem which Weaver (1980:27) recognizes with eclectic approaches:

> With the eclectic approach as with most of its components, instructional attention tends to focus upon the identification of words, apparently on the assumption that once words are identified, meaning will take care of itself.

That is, word-attack or phonics-like decoding procedures are all that are taught. (This claim will be modified later when the role of the story in the Gudschinsky method is considered.) And, as the psycholinguists have so effectively shown, this is definitely not all that is involved in reading, and may well be the least important aspect. It is true that the word with which the decoding skills are taught is the key word which was pictured and around which the discussion took place. Thus it is not the case that the isolated word is meaningless and out of context. It is the case, though, that at this decoding stage it is out of a written-linguistic context. Regardless of the importance (or not) of the word-attack (i.e. decoding) skills, it is undeniable that both the Freire and Gudschinsky methods fail to teach the strategies emphasized by the psycholinguists. Thus they do emphasize the word-level (and below) of reading to the (relative) neglect of the syntactic, semantic, and world-building skills. Further, even at the letter and word levels, the emphasis is on grapheme-to-sound correspondences rather than on the graphemic features other than grapheme-sound correspondences (for example, letter and word shapes). My argument here is not aimed toward an either-or alternative. I am quite willing to acknowledge the importance of what both Freire and Gudschinsky do teach. My point is that these eclectic methods need to be supplemented by the procedures developed by the psycholinguist; for example, cloze exercises[15] to nurture predictive and interpretive skills. Because there is no reading--at any level--without these skills, there is no level of reading instruction which can afford to do without tending to their development.[16]

---

[15] Cloze exercises are a variety of fill-in-the-blank exercises. They are used to nurture predictive skills based on contextual clues.

[16] There may indeed be reading exercises which emphasize the development of different skills. I am not saying that each exercise must emphasize every skill. I am saying that a

Whether the top-down, psycholinguistic procedures or the bottom-up, decoding procedures would more appropriately follow from the discussion stage, and just how the two types of procedures are to be related in the actual instruction, are issues for reading research to answer. My general inclination is that the top-down procedures allow for a smoother transition from the previous discussions since they tend to maintain a firmer grasp on meaning and deal with linguistic units intermediate in size between the discussion on the one hand, and words and letters on the other. In particular, the sentence and the phrase are used as the linguistic base for most psycholinguistic exercises. At the earliest stages of reading, though, many of the exercises would need to be administered with a lot of oral mediation.[17]

I now wish to consider the decoding instruction which Freire and Gudschinsky employ. First a comparison of the two approaches; second, a brief evaluation of the linguistic feasibility of Freire's approach; and finally, comments relating to the value of such procedures in general.

Following the introduction of the key word as a sight word tied closely to the picture and the discussion, both methods analyze the key word. Gudschinsky, however, (generally) analyzes the word down to a "letter-sound," while Freire breaks the word down only to the syllable level. Gudschinsky, however, follows this analysis to "letter" with a synthesis which builds up to the syllable level again. Both methods then present a family of sounds related to the sound(s) of the key word. For Freire, each consonant is given in a phonemic sequence which is quite similar to Gudschinsky's identification step for consonants. Here, though, Freire introduces more per lesson than Gudschinsky. His method focuses on each consonant (typically at least 2, often 3) with all the vowels of the language, while Gudschinsky focuses on only one "letter"--or at most 2--but only in well controlled linguistic environments. Gudschinsky also treats the vowels separately and gives them the full attention of a separate lesson each. However, because Freire does present the phonemic sequences for each consonant and then compares these sequences with one another in one discovery chart, he does in fact provide "identification columns" which do focus on the vowels. The discovery chart also accomplishes the same purposes as Gudschinsky's contrast step. Here the columns contrast the consonants and the rows contrast the vowels in much the same way as Gudschinsky's columns of step 4, though she arranges the contrasts in the columns only.

---

balanced reading program should develop every skill at each level of reading development, though in a manner appropriate to the particular level, and in a manner which encourages the harmonious integration of whatever skills are taught through the reading of real texts.

[17] I have no doubt, though, that there are many other sociolinguistic and anthropological factors which need to be considered, a consideration of which may well lead to different conclusions in different situations.

Following these steps which work exclusively with parts of words, both methods then proceed to build up again to words. Freire works from the discovery chart syllables and Gudschinsky works with syllables introduced in the lesson, but only those syllables and words which contain the "letter" being taught in that lesson. Both methods encourage student construction of these words, though Freire seems to emphasize this aspect more. For Freire's method, the construction of words continues as a major part of the "homework" and even nonsense "words" are encouraged. Gudschinsky allows nonsense words depending on their acceptability in the culture involved.

Overall, both methods are quite similar as "literacy methods" per se. The major differences with regard to method are (1) the amount of material introduced per lesson and (2) the rate of introduction of the material even within the lesson. In short, Freire collapses in fewer exercises what Gudschinsky separates into several. Perhaps the distinction here is that Freire's work has been within literate societies, while Gudschinsky's has been mostly in pre-literate cultures. As expected, the rate of introduction must be slower in the pre-literate situation.

Turning now to an evaluation of Freire's method. First, though Freire's methods have been successful in Chile and Brazil, these languages have highly regular syllable structures and highly regular grapheme-sound correspondences. The actual "discovery card" procedure is not so easily adapted to other languages which do not share such regularities. This weakness does not touch the heart of Freire's educational philosophy, i.e. conscientization, but it does require linguistic modifications for its implementation in a host of other languages. Second, the amount of material introduced in each lesson by Freire's method would likely be a significant overload for those of a truly pre-literate culture. Thus, given the clear similarities between Freire's and Gudschinsky's methods of teaching decoding skills, an adaption of Freire to a pre-literate culture and to not-so-regular languages would likely be quite close to Gudschinsky in format.

Finally, the mistaken impression is often given that top-down reading specialists are totally opposed to the teaching of bottom-up decoding skills. The strong polemic against conceiving of reading as primarily or essentially decoding, together with the (almost) total neglect of such bottom-up teaching in their practical writings is responsible for this impression. Remember, though, that Frank Smith explicitly recognized that decoding is one option available and used by readers when confronted by an unknown word. Other than the very real problem of different sounds being correlated to the same graphemes, the major objection to decoding is that it breaks with the contextual sense of meaning and therefore with the reader's usual strategies of making meaning. Though this is in part true, and consequently serves to justify the need for other instructional practices, our studies in Part II lead us to reevaluate the force of this argument.

First, if meaning is both sense and reference then the psycholinguistic notion of meaning as reference (rooted finally in the subject's questions or schemas) cannot be allowed to dominate the discussion of meaningfulness. Sense as the interaction (even interplay) of signs in a system which transcends the individual subject must also be given its due. This is where the bottom-up procedures are the strongest, and the most offensive to the top-down orientation. This is indeed a (moment of) reduction of meaning to an almost purely linguistic context, and thus a decontextualizing of meaning as referential. This, I argued, is essential to meaning and to the reading of a text. Written language, i.e. literature, is analogous to *langue* at this point. In fact, not only does writing decontextualize (i.e. distance itself from the psychological and sociological circumstances of the author), but reading also distances the reader from himself. This is exactly what the top-down criticism of bottom-up decoding objects to. However, not only is this distanciation from pure contextual and subjective meaning legitimate, it is necessary to a full account of meaning and therefore of reading.

Second, the reduction or depsychologization of the reader by meaning as sense is an important aspect of becoming alert to that which transcends both reader and text. We noted the unavoidability of this transcendence in chapters 6-9; and the neglect of this "element" by reading specialists, both bottom-up and top-down.

Third, the decoding exercises--as illustrated by Freire and Gudschinsky, for instance--make essential use of the principles of identity and difference (e.g. the identification and contrast boxes in Gudschinsky). We saw throughout Part II the importance, even the fundamental character, of these principles. The exercise of such human skills in the decoding practices should therefore be approved. Further, other reading skills should be examined to see what role these principles play in them, and exercises developed to promote the employment of the imagination (defined as the interplay of identity and difference) at other levels of text processing. Gibson (1975:290-293), in fact, insists that these skills are important at the basic phonological, the semantic, and the syntactic levels of reading.

Fourth, it is as much with the nonsense syllables and "words" as anywhere (if not more so) that playfulness is cultivated. Freire's method seems to encourage this, while most bottom-up practices tend to try to control it. Perhaps it is this playfulness, which escapes the reader's "meaningful" control, that the top-down approach objects to. And yet, I argued in chapter 9 that play is a fundamental notion in reading theory and practice.

These four reasons support the case for bottom-up procedures in reading. They do not, however, argue against top-down procedures. In fact, they point out the abstractness of most bottom-up procedures, and thus what well might be the relative difficulty and "unnaturalness" which so many top-down specialists have noted in the bottom-up techniques. The conclusion, once again, is that both approaches are legitimate, necessary, and, in fact, complementary.

10.4.2.3   The concluding stage of reading instruction

As noted in section 4.1, both Gudschinsky and Freire conclude their reading lessons with reading and writing exercises. Though Freire's method does build words in isolation (e.g. the "discovery card"), it is not clear that word recognition in context, and, thus, reading per se is adequately taught by Freire. In short, there seems to be no teaching of the reading of connected material. This is a serious problem since it has been noted in various studies that the recognition of words in isolation and in context are two relatively independent processes (e.g. Allington and McGill-Franzen 1980). It is possible, though, that the strong contextual motivation on reading newspapers, etc. overcame this weakness for Freire. The emphasis on writing, too, and presumably the reading of one another's texts (Freire 1974:87-91), may also have supplied this lack. Regardless, Gudschinsky is more developed at this point and I will therefore be following the pattern of her method.

As for the psycholinguists, the Gudschinsky method recognizes that the ". . . goals of reading acquisition . . . are acquired primarily from reading--reading meaningful connected material" (Lee 1982:395). This emphasis is to be commended for both the manner in which materials are prepared and for the manner of teaching their use.

With regard to literature preparation, as noted earlier, stages of difficulty are recognized, ranging from the oral literature of the people (the easiest) to material written by outsiders (the hardest) (Lee 1982:403; Wendell 1974). Second, the inclusion of a large percentage of literature for enjoyment (e.g. riddles, humor, etc.) is recommended (Lee 1982:401; Wendell 1974:10). Third, the criteria for selection of discourse-type seem well considered, with the possible exception of an insufficient reckoning with the differences between spoken and written language. Fourth, the emphasis on native-authored materials where possible is surely correct.

With regard to the uses of connected materials, four practices are recommended (Lee 1982:409-421), each of which is a strength of the method. The preparation of the reader for the material to be read prior to the reading does call forth orienting schemas and so facilitates top-down processes. Second, the use of questions which rely on material ranging from "explicit and verbatim in the text" to "implicit from information going beyond the text" (Lee 1982:410) encourages close reading as well as inferencing skills. Third, the finding of phrases encourages "seeing and grouping chunks which are bigger than a single word" (Lee 1982:419), and the integration of larger sections of discourse due to syntactic and verbal repetition. Further, the opportunity is provided for the comparison of meanings in diverse contexts. Finally, oral reading encourages the interaction of both speaking-listening and reading-writing skills in ways which can strength both. For example, oral reading can encourage the better "chunking" of linguistic units, and improve the fluency and naturalness of reading.

These many strengths of the Gudschinsky "connected material" stage are counterbalanced by the severe limitation on the letters and words available for use, especially in the early lessons. Because the introduction of letters and words is highly controlled, the stories in the early primers are frequently of the "See Dick run" type which are quite unnatural and thus more difficult to read than that which more nearly approximates more familiar discourse types. When teaching adults (especially), the material must be adult-level material. Given the limited reading abilities of the new reader, such material would likely be too complex for reading. However, if this high degree of control is maintained, I would recommend the use of many oral literature based exercises--administered orally--which teach the higher level comprehension skills such as critical thinking, interpretation, prediction, world-generation (imagination skills), etc. Though these skills are similar to those employed in the earlier, preliminary discussion, the difference is that at this stage they are exercised in the context of a given, fixed text (orally conveyed). A further option for supplementing the needed simplicity of the early material is the inclusion of LEA-type materials (cf. e.g. Reimer 1983; Nesse and Jones 1981; Stauffer 1969, 1981). As noted earlier, this would place a heavy load on the teacher.

Finally, the inclusion of the writing lesson in both Gudschinsky and Freire must be highly commended. The relation between reading and writing is no doubt most intimate, both practically and theoretically (cf. e.g. Knott 1983; Kurth 1983; Raban 1982; Furniss 1983). Theoretically, reading is both a receptive and a productive skill. Because the reader makes significant contributions, reading is the production of a text (i.e. the meaning in a world context) in interaction with a written text. Similarly, writing necessarily involves the author as first reader. Further, those who read also need and (usually) want to write.

Though the writing lesson completes the reading lesson in Gudschinsky's conception, this is not the case with Freire. Nor is this the case with the conception of reading-interpretation developed in Part II. Having begun in the ground of lived experience, reading concludes in the same ground. Freire emphasizes this through his highly politicized notion of conscientization. Surviving our critique in chapter 8 is (among other things) the recognition that action is necessarily integrated with reading-interpretation. In the less politicized concept, this action is termed the fusion of horizons at the level of *Lebenswelt*.

Freire emphasizes following through on the topics and conclusions resulting from the reading lesson in the public sphere of action. This includes becoming informed about current affairs by reading newspapers, organizing to change situations which have been determined to be unjust, mounting voter registration campaigns, etc. Approached in this manner, Freire's literacy method does integrate life-context and life activity with reading instruction in a most thoroughgoing way.

There are also other ways to accomplish integration with life-context. One approach is to focus on functional applications of reading.

326

UNESCO's "functional literacy" approach (cf. Bhola 1969, 1977), popular in the 1960's and 1970's, aimed to use literacy instruction to better the economic condition of developing nations. Though the focus on "how-to" type reading materials was the major emphasis of functional literacy, such can easily be included in other approaches as well.

Another way used by some to integrate life-context with reading is to focus on moral materials. One would expect that the use of proverbs, traditional moral materials, etc. would provide a natural bridge to application in the non-reading context.

No doubt there are other means to integrate the reading situation with life activity, and certainly the three mentioned above--the political, the functional, the moral--are to some extent inherently involved with one another. My point here is that reading and non-reading contexts are already integrated, but that attention still needs to be given to recognizing and facilitating the outworkings of this mutual involvement. As Mann 1970 points out, reading has generally been conceived of as an end in itself. It needs to be more broadly defined to include, in its fundamental conception, its application to personal and social situations.

10.5   Final considerations

Here my purpose is to emphasize the most salient points to be learned from the discussions of Part II. Most of these points have already been mentioned, if only briefly, in the preceding sections, but warrant both summarization and emphasis.

10.5.1 Meaning

Our discussion of meaning (chapter 4) provided the basis for an integration of bottom-up and top-down processes. Meaning as the dynamic interplay of sense and reference serves this very purpose. The role of reference to "a world" as integral to meaning is the theoretical basis for the significance of schemas, themselves "world-fragments." The grounding of meaning, however, was further established when we considered the ontological notion of comprehension (cf. section 5.2 below).

The notion of the ideality of meaning must also be mentioned here. Ideality effectively breaks with an exclusively subject-centered (here, reader-centered) approach to meaning. One consequence of this aspect of meaning is that textual meaning cannot be identified with either authorial intention or reader response. Another consequence is that no account of reading in terms of the reader's schemas alone can be adequate. Meaning, as it were, has its own life too. Readers, then, should be instructed so as to be made aware of this aspect of meaning: It is not only constructed, but also given as obtaining independently of the reader. The notion of a forced reading, and how to avoid it, should be communicated in literacy classes.

327

Finally, the discussion of the picture theory of meaning offers a resolution to the debate regarding the role of pictures in reading instruction: Pictures (i.e sensory or quasi-sensory images) are an inevitable part of meaning. If this is clearly recognized, together with the relation between semantic and "pictoral" meaning as sketched in chapter 7, then pictures can be used most effectively to nurture many of the skills needed in reading. The difficulty some people have in "reading" pictures should be used to develop constructive part-whole, interpretive, and interactive skills. I would even suggest purposely using ambiguous pictures to demonstrate the need for and exercise of such skills. Similarly, cross-cultural art could be used to prepare for cross-cultural reading.

10.5.2 Comprehension

Included in the sense-reference dynamic of meaning is the part-whole interactive dimension, and included in the notion of ideality is the world as other, yet necessarily bound up with the subject. Both of these inclusions find their fundamental grounding in man as the being-in-the-world whose understanding is fundamentally a questioning openness within an already existent world situation. The hermeneutical circle (ontologically grounded) was presented as the basis of the whole-part-whole dynamic observed in all reading-interpretive activities. The "always already" aspects of man's situation reflects and is reflected by the ideality of meaning.

Thus, for reading too, prediction is an inescapable activity: Not just cognitive hypotheses, but man's entire being is "always already" a prediction to be discovered, clarified, and tested, in short, lived out. Consequently, questioning and the correlated seeking of answers is fundamental to being human. The incorporation of this basic characteristic into reading theory and practice by the psycholinguists is therefore to be most highly commended. Further, it comes as no surprise that the stimulation of self-questioning during reading by a variety of techniques results in increased comprehension (cf. e.g. T.H. Anderson 1978a,b, 1980; T.H. Anderson and Armbruster 1980; Singer and Dolan 1982; Peters 1981; Cohen 1983; Gibson and Levin 1975:424-435). Continued research into helpful ways to promote such questioning should therefore be encouraged. One such line of inquiry should study the varying responses to indeterminacies in text and the development of problem-solving, inferencing skills. Much work is being done here and needs to be incorporated into reading instruction (cf. e.g. Hansen 1981; Gagne and Memory 1978).

Another aspect of comprehension uncovered in chapters 5-7 is the necessary role of the imagination understood as the interplay of identity and difference. At all levels of text processing--from feature discernment to world-building--the imagination is active. Decoding skills, cloze exercises, the reading of the same word shapes in different contexts--each of these (and other reading exercises) already employ the imagination. More, however, needs to be done at the higher levels of text processing. The use of books with alternative endings, write-your-own ending exercises (cf. e.g. Thompkins and Webeler 1983), and even "daydreaming" (cf. Bachelard 1964) all are some of the options available here. One persistent area of difficulty noted for reading theories was accounting for metaphors. I would suggest the use of novel metaphors as a concise way to exercise the imagination in reading. (I have personally found unfamiliar proverbs to be a similar challenge; cf. section 5.4 below for further suggestions.)

Further, and related to the higher levels of imaginative activity, is the recognition that human comprehension is a dwelling in a world. Thus, not only is a world constructed in reading, but a mode of being (or alternative modes) for dwelling in that world is also constructed. Such a mode has certain implications for action and behavior. Because these worlds and modes of being are imaginative, i.e. they are different from ordinary life, they need to be evaluated on other grounds. This is critique. But because there is also a certain identity between the imaginative and the ordinary, the ordinary also needs to be evaluated in light of the imaginative. In short, critique is a two-way street between the ordinary, previously experienced and that which has been constructed as different through the reading process. (Cf. the next section for further development of this point.) For example, Zimet 1983 recommends exercises detecting the social bias in books, and Huck 1969 suggests giving different accounts of the "same" event and asking for evaluation.

Finally, we noted that comprehension in its ontological sense is intimately related to the affections. Because reading plays with the subject-object relation, it uncovers the deeper ontological unity (without denying the differences) of a being-in-the-world. Pleasure in reading, the experience of transport, even alienation and its overcoming seem rooted at this level. This is, however, a relatively unexplored area in reading research and practice. Freire and Gudschinsky do tap this area in the "prereading" stage with great success, but little is done with regard to the affections through the decoding or connected material stages. The most that is done is the use of enjoyable materials or materials the readers feel strongly about. The discussions in Part II recommend this area to us for further exploration.

10.5.3 Critique

The points to follow will roughly follow the ten aspects of critique noted in chapter 8, section 6.

The first and most important point already has been reiterated: Critique is a necessary part of reading, central and not peripheral. Freire's practice has worked this point out in the greatest detail and effectiveness. Marxist ideology, however, in which much of critical theory is presented, is not essential to the notion of critique. The "Marxist" point of view, though, contributes (at least) the necessity of considering the broader social, political, etc. contexts of reading in terms of both their influence on reading and reading's influence on these broader contexts. Recent research in reading theory is increasingly alert to this interaction of reading and

329

"broader" contexts (cf. e.g. Bloome and Green 1982; Bloome 1983; Steinberg 1980; Reynolds 1981; and the research cited therein).

However, it would seem that Freire's method does not do justice to the *belonging* to the positive tradition (of Being), even as Habermas fails at this point. Gudschinsky has been much more successful at integrating "belonging" into literacy practice. Again, both "belonging" and "(critical) distanciation" are needed.

Second, dialogue is recognized as closely related to reading, but not identical. Though Freire has advanced the practice of teaching critical reading, he has not been sufficiently alert to the distinction between writing-reading and speaking-hearing. Ricoeur has noted this distinction quite clearly, but it has not yet been applied to practice. Further, dialogue is, no doubt, a part of most learning situations, but more attention must be given to the difference between dialogue and reading.

Third, because standards of evaluation are inherently involved in reading due to the implicit critique executed in reading, discussion of the idea of standards and the particular standards preferred by those learning to read should be an integrated part of reading instruction. All the participants in the debate should encourage such discussion rather than "unconscious" acceptance. Such reflection on standards is part of the conscientization process which expands one's horizons and enriches one's humanity.[18]

Fourth, because of the necessary and assumed intersubjective context of reading, more attention must be given to the intersubjective components of the learning situation. For example, how are the interpersonal relations within the learning situation (between "student" and "teacher," among "students," etc.) to be evaluated with respect to the various dimensions of the speaking-hearing, writing-reading continuum? And how do these various interpersonal relations interact with the text-reader relation? Using the terminology of wave interaction, do the interpersonal relations interfere "constructively" or "destructively"? Do various forms of interpersonal relations support and reinforce the text-reader relation more than others? Further, how do the various forms of interpersonal relations compare with and reflect the "ISS" (the "Ideal Speech Situation"; cf. chapter 8)? Do cross-cultural studies help to clarify the notion of a universal ISS? Or do such studies disprove such an assumption? Such questions need to be answered if literacy practice in various cultural settings is to benefit from these theoretical investigations of the notion of critique. It is already a benefit, though, that this theoretical

---

[18] The "values clarification" movement in secondary education (especially in Canada) is an attempt at this kind of practice. No approach, though, is itself free from values; thus these is always a "hidden agenda." The goal, therefore, is to continue to uncover and examine the hidden values through dialogue and reflection.

investigation suggests a research program which promises to benefit the practice of literacy training.

Fifth, the future orientation implies an action orientation as well; in particular, action which affects the future of the participants. Such "action" is not usually considered part of reading nor of literacy practice. To consider action integral to reading, however, may solve some of the practical problems of lack of motivation among non-literates in pre-literate cultures. Simply put, learning to read needs to be made of practical significance to people who are oriented to practical realities. Such an orientation would no doubt also affect the construction of literacy materials and programs.

Sixth, some notion of freedom is assumed along with the future orientation. Literacy practice should be liberating to those engaged in it. Such liberation should stimulate motivation, since freedom is assumed to be innately desirable as well as possible. Consequently, if the proposed theory of critical-emancipatory science is true, then motivational problems may be indicative of a faulty concept of freedom embodied in the literacy practice. Here the proposed theory opens the relations--among the literacy practice, other social and cultural structures, and the consciousness of the people--to examination and critique. Literacy practice should not be a form of domination or oppression or alienation, but emancipation as understood by the participants themselves.

Seventh, the notions of culture, cultural enrichment, and the making of cultural objects (including literature) can be naturally integrated with learning to read. In this regard, Freire has wisely recognized that the distinction between culture and nature focuses on the point which is also at the heart of man's ability to learn to read. Thus, to thematize this distinction in reading practice is a means of uncovering a very deep reservoir of the abilities required in the reading process.

Eighth, because of the central notion of "scenic understanding," pictures can by used in reading practice, but not without further recognition of the complex relation between pictures and meaning as outlined in chapter 4 and above in this chapter.

Ninth, reading should be taught with the expectation that change will occur--individually and culturally--and the proponents of literacy must accept some responsibility for bringing such change. Reading does present a limit-situation which stimulates, even requires, growth. Reading materials should be used which make the most of this benefit; yet, the proponents of literacy must also acknowledge the unavoidable ideological influence which will always be present, regardless of who designs the materials. On the other hand, our discussions of transcendence in chapters 7-9 do relieve the literacy worker of some responsibility here, since there is always some influence which escapes human intentional effort.

331

Finally, the interplay of identity and difference is recognized as fundamental to being human, as unavoidable operations in human cognition, and as necessary for the attainment of reading skills, from decoding to critique. Methods of reading which recognize and use these basic principles in a balanced way can be expected to be superior to those which do not.

The broadest issue which the notion of critique in reading faces is the relation of thinking to reading. Some have claimed that reading is quite simply a thinking process, and that critical thinking is thus a necessary part of reading which must be taught (e.g. Huck 1969; Stauffler 1969; Baker 1979; and references found therein). No doubt this is true, as the discussions of Part II (especially chapter 8) show. The most challenging implication noted here is the possibility--and if the necessary relation between reading and critical thinking is granted--even the necessity of integrating with reading instruction a relatively recent phenomenon in the area of logic, i.e. informal logic, alternately termed critical thinking. Many programs for classroom use, as well as philosophical and pedagogical reflection, are being generated. In the context established by the discussions in chapter 8, this is an exceedingly interesting and important development for reading theory and practice. But as with so much else touched on in this chapter, the outworkings are beyond this present work.

10.5.4 Play

The focus on play as a theoretical issue central to reading may have seemed surprising to some. There has been, however, much research to clarify and support the claim that play is significant for education in general, and reading in particular. For example, Palmer (1976:33) says,

> . . . the reading communication games produced highly significant improvement in general reading comprehension, and . . . this improvement was significantly greater than that achieved by the control group.

Similarly, Gentile and Hoots (1983:436):

> Recent expansion of research in the area of play and its effects on learning firmly supports the notion that concrete objects and experiences manipulated by children at play are the prerequisites to successful acquisition of more abstract skills such as learning to read . . . .

Dickerson 1982 showed how active games help teach sight words to remedial readers. Galda 1982 showed that the use of play as a follow-up activity for reading improved comprehension (i.e. remembering, understanding, and solving and analyzing questions) better than did either drawing or discussion. Harms and Lettow 1983 used semiotic word play to improve the insight derived from new and different forms. Miller and Mason 1983 used creative dramatics to improve reading. Manna 1984 showed that reading plays helped develop the connections and relations between printed and spoken language.

The use of plays (i.e. drama) introduces another area of interesting research which correlates with the discussion of chapter 9. There play was considered an aesthetic concept (as with Gadamer). Research is showing that the arts can be usefully integrated with reading. Martin, Cramond, and Safter 1982 developed creativity exercises to improve reading skills. Gemake 1984 used drawing, writing, and reading in complement to improve reading. Jalongo and Bromley 1984 used music to improve linguistic competence. Miccinati, et al. 1983 integrated the arts with reading to improve reading.

With regard to the role of play in education in general, Heitzmann 1974 gives a bibliography of 72 selected research references and 17 general references. Similarly, Kirshenblatt-Gimblatt 1976 gives a rather comprehensive survey of research on play.[19]

There is, then, no lack of the recognition of the importance of play for reading instruction. Nor is there a lack of practical materials. Mallett 1976, for example, has compiled 101 reading games in nine categories: sight-word knowledge, phonetic analysis, structural analysis, context clue usage, literal comprehension, interpretive comprehension, critical reading skills, reading in content areas, and dictionary or glossary usage.[20]

Surely such literature supports the significance of the theoretical work done in chapter 9 and both encourage the integration of play and games with reading instruction--at all levels of reading skills.

10.6 Conclusions

The result of these investigations is that, in fact, there is much that reading theory and practice have to gain from the interdisciplinary approach to the study of reading. With regard to theory, this claim has been supported from the investigation of the (widely-recognized) central concepts of reading--meaning and comprehension. Further, the role of critique in reading--at best, disputed; at worst, neglected--has been provided a sure place through substantial theoretical justification. Finally, what has been successful in reading practice, yet almost totally ignored in the theory--play--has received extended theoretical development. In addition

---

[19] However, neither of these bibliographies makes any reference to Gadamer or to the works bearing on the ontological significance of play. Along a different line of inquiry, Sherzer 1976 notes the importance of play languages (in a variety of cultures) to linguistic study.

[20] For further games for reading, cf. Kaye 1984, Lass-Kayser 1979, and Shankman 1972.

to these particulars, an integrated theory of reading has emerged, a theory which both incorporates and organizes the wide range of theories and models which have proliferated in the past decades.

With regard to the practice of teaching reading, I have scarcely begun to apply the theory developed in this present work. And yet, a theoretically motivated choice among methods has been illustrated and some significant modifications of existing methods suggested, thus illustrating that an enriched practice of teaching reading is possible through interdisciplinary dialogue.

BIBLIOGRAPHY

Adams, M. and B.C. Bruce. 1980. Background knowledge and reading comprehension. ERIC D 181 431.

Adams, M.J. 1979. Models of word recognition. Cognitive Psychology 11.2. 133-176.

Adams, M.J. 1980. Failure to comprehend and levels of processing in reading. Theoretical issues in reading comprehension: perspectives from cognitive psychology, linguistics, artificial intelligence, and education, ed. by Rand J. Spiro, Bertram C. Bruce, and William F. Brewer, 11-32. Hillsdale, N.J.: Lawrence Erlbaum Associates.

Adams, M.J. 1980. What good is orthographic redundancy? ERIC D 199 663.

Adams, M.J. and A. Collins. 1977. A schema-theoretic view of reading comprehension. ERIC D 142 971.

Adams, M.J., R.C. Anderson, and D. Durkin. 1977. Beginning reading: theory and practice. ERIC D 151 722.

Adorno, Theodor. 1976. The positivist dispute in German sociology, trans. by Glyn Adey and David Frisby. London: Heinemann.

Akinnaso, F. Niyi. 1982. The literate writes and the nonliterate chants: written language and ritual communication in sociolinguistic perspective. Linguistics and Literacy, ed. by William Frawley, 7-36. New York: Plenum Press.

Alexeiev, N.N. 1938. The Marxist anthropology and the christian conception of man. The christian understanding of man, ed. by T.E. Jessop, et. al., 83-137. London: George Allen and Unwin Ltd.

Allington, Richard and Anne McGill-Franzen. 1980. Word identification errors in isolation and in context: apples vs. oranges. The reading teacher, 795-800.

Alston, William P. 1964. Philosophy of language. Englewood Cliffs, N.J.: Prentice-Hall Inc.

Alston, William P. 1967. Meaning. The encyclopedia of philosophy, ed. by Paul Edwards, 233-241. (Vol. 5). New York: Macmillian Publishing Co., Inc. and The Free Press.

Altieri, Charles. 1983. Reading for an image of the reader: a response to Bloch, Caraher, and Mytyta. Reader 9. 38-44.

Anderson, R.C. 1977a. The notion of schemata and the educational enterprise. Schooling and the acquisition of knowledge, ed. by R.C. Anderson, R.J. Spiro, W.E. Montague, 259-288. Hillsdale, N.J.: Lawrence Erlbaum Ass.

Anderson, R.C. 1977b. Schema-directed processes in language comprehension. ERIC D 142 977.

Anderson, R.C. and J.W. Pichert. 1977. Recall of previously uncallable information following a shift in perspective. ERIC D 142 974.

Anderson, R.C. and Peter Freebody. 1983. Reading comprehension and the assessment and acquisition of word knowledge. Advances in reading/language research, ed. by Barbara A. Hutson, 231-256. (Vol. 2) Greenwich, Conn.: Jai Press Inc.

Anderson, R.C., E.T. Goetz, J.W. Pichert, and H.M. Halff. 1976a. Two faces of the conceptual peg hypothesis. ERIC D 134 930.

Anderson, R.C., J.W. Pichert, and L.L. Shirey. 1979. Effects of the reader's schema at different points in time. ERIC D 169 523. r

Anderson, R.C., J.W. Pichert, E.T. Goetz, D. L. Schallert, K.C. Stevens, and S.R. Trollip. 1976a. Instantiation of general terms. ERIC D 134 933.

Anderson, R.C., R.E. Reynolds, D.L. Schallert, and E.T. Goetz. 1976b. Frameworks for comprehending discourse. ERIC D 134 935.

Anderson, R.C., R.J. Spiro and W.E. Montague, ed. 1977. Schooling and the acquisition of knowledge. Hillsdale, N.J.: Lawrence Erlbaum Associates.

Anderson, R.C., R.J. Spiro, and M.C. Anderson. 1977. Schemata as scaffolding for the representation of information in connected discourse. ERIC D 136 236.

Anderson, Stephen R. 1974. The organization of phonology. New York: Academic Press.

Anderson, T.H. 1978a. Another look at the self-questioning study technique. ERIC D 163 441.

Anderson, T.H. 1978b. Study skills and learning strategies. ERIC D 161 000.

Anderson, T.H. 1980. Study strategies and adjunct aids. Theoretical issues in reading comprehension: perspectives from cognitive psychology, linguistics, articifical intelligence, and education, ed. by Rand J. Spiro, Bertram C. Bruce, and William F. Brewer, 483-502. Hillsdale, N.J.: Lawrence Erlbaum Associates.

Anderson, T.H. and B.B. Armbruster. 1980. Studying. ERIC D 181 427.

Andre, M.E.D.A. and Anderson, T.H. 1978. The development and evaluation of a self-questioning study technique. ERIC D 157 037.

Apel, Karl-Otto. 1972-3. Communication and the foundation of the humanities. Acta Sociologica 15-16. 7-26.

Armbruster, B.B. 1976. Learning principles from prose: a cognitive approach based on schema theory. ERIC D 134 934.

Arrington, James Michael. 1976. Linguistics in reading, ERIC D 141 769.

Asher, S.R. 1977. Sex differences in reading achievement. ERIC D 146 567.

Athey, Irene. 1982. Reading: the affective domain reconceptualized. Advances in reading/language research, ed. by Barbara A. Hutson, 203- 217. (Vol. 1) Greenwich, Conn.: Jai Press Inc.

Axelos, Kostas. 1968. Planetary interlude. Yale French Studies 41.6-1"88.

Axelos, Kostas. 1976. Alienation, praxis, and techne in the thought of Karl Marx, trans. by Ronald Brazina. Austin, Tx.: University of Texas Press.

Axelos, Kostas. 1980. Play as the system of systems. Sub-Stance 25. 20-24.

Babbs, Patricia J. 1983. Metacognition: a key for independent learning from text. The Reading Teacher 36.4. 422-426.

Bachelard, Gaston. 1964. The poetics of space, trans. by M. Jolas. Boston: Beacon Press.

Baker, L. 1979a. Do I understand or do I not understand: that is the question. ERIC D 174 948.

Baker, L. 1979b. Comprehension monitoring: identifying and coping with text confusions. ERIC D 177 525.

Baker, L. and N.L. Stein. 1978. The development of pros comprehension skills. ERIC D 159 663.

Baker, L., and R.I. Anderson. 1981. Effects of inconsistent information on text processing: evidence for comprehension monitoring. ERIC D 201 993.

Balthazar, Hans Urs von. 1965. Word and redemption. New York: Herder and Herder.

Bamberger, Richard. 1969. The joy of reading. Reading: a human right and a human problem, ed. Ralph C. Staiger and Oliver Andresen, 125-130. Newark, Delaware: International Reading Association.

Bar-Hillel, Y. 1973. On Habermas' hermeneutic philosophy of language. Synthese 26. 1-12.

Barth, Karl. 1959. Wolfgang Amadeus Mozart. Religion and culture, essays in honor of Paul Tillich, ed. by Walter Leibrecht, 61-78. New York: Harper & Brothers, Publishers.

Barthes, Roland. 1979. From work to text. Textual strategies, ed. by Josue V. Harari, 73-81. Ithaca, NY: Cornell University Press.

Bartlett, F.C. 1932. Remembering. London: Cambridge University Press.

Bateson, Gregory. 1978. Play and paradigm. West Point, N.Y.: Leisure Press, 7-16.

Bauerschimdt, Amy. 1980. The ideal orthography. Notes on Literacy. No. 32. 12-21.

Beardsley, Monroe C. 1958. Aesthetics. New York: Harcourt, Brace and World.

Beaugrande, Robert de. 1980. Text and discourse in European research. Discourse processes 3. 287-300.

Beaujour, Michel. 1968. The game of poetics. Yale French Studies 41.58-67.

Beck, Isabel L. 1977a. Comments on developmental parameters of reading comprehension. Cognition, curriculum, and comprehension, ed. by John T. Guthrie, 16-19. Newark, Del.: International Reading Association.

Beck, Isabel L. 1977b. Comprehending during the acquisition of decoding skills. Cognition, curriculum, and comprehension, ed. by John T. Guthrie, 113-156. Newark, Del.: International Reading Association.

Beck, Isabel L. 1981. Reading problems and instructional practices Reading research: advances in theory and practice, Vol. 2, ed. by G.E. Mackinnon and T. Gary Waller, 53-95. New York: Academic Press.

Becker, A. 1982. The poetics and noetics of a Javanese Poem. Spoken and written language: exploring orality and literacy, ed. by D. Tannen, 217-238. (Advances in discourse processes, IX.) Norwood, N.J.: Ablex Publishing Corporation.

Beers, Terry. 1987. Schema-theoretic models of reading: Humanizing the machine. Reading Research Quarterly 22.3. 369-377.

Bembeck, Cole and W. Hill. 1973. Cultural challenges to education. Lexington: D.C. Heath and Company.

Bendor-Samuel, Margaret. 1977. Paulo Freire: his uses of literacy in social revolution. Notes on literacy 21. 10-18.

Bennett, Jonathan. 1966. Kant's analytic. Cambridge: Cambridge University Press.

Berger, Peter L. 1970. A rumor of angels: modern society and the rediscovery of the supernatural. New York: Doubleday, Anchor Books.

Berkof, L. 1939. Systematic theology. Grand Rapids, Mich.: Eerdmans.

Berry, John. 1976. Human ecology and cognitive style. New York: John Wiley and Sons.

Bhola, H.S. 1969. Functional literacy--the concept and the programme. Paper at the Annual Study Conference, University College, Nairobi, Kenya.

Bhola, H.S. 1977. Functional literacy--the concept and the programme. Teaching reading and writing to adults, 11-28. Tehran, Iran: International Institute for Adult Literacy Methods.

Biemel, Walter. 1977. Husserl's encyclopedia Briticanica article and Heidegger's remarks thereon. Husserl: expositions and appraisals, ed. by Frederick A. Elliston and Peter McCormick, 286-303. Notre Dame: University of Notre Dame Press.

Biemiller, A.J. 1970. The development of the use of graphic and contextual information as children learn to read. Reading research quarterly 6. 75-96.

Biniakunu, D.D. 1980. Learning to read Kikongo: a primer makes a difference. The reading teacher, October. 32-36.

Bird, Graham. 1962. Kant's theory of knowledge. London: Routledge and Kegan Paul.

Blackburn, Robin, ed. 1972. Ideology in social science: reading in critical social theory. London: Fontana/Collins.

Blackowicz, Camille L.Z. 1983. Showing teachers how to develop students' predictive reading. The Reading Teacher 36.7. 680-684.

Blau, Herbert. 1980. Off the top of the head. Sub-Stance 25. 36-43.

Bleich, David. 1975. The subjective character of critical interpretation. College English 36.7.

Bleich, David. 1980. The identity of pedagogy and research in the study of response to literature. College English 42.4. 350-366.

Bleicher, Josef. 1980. Contemporary hermeneutics. London: Routledge & Kegan Paul.

Bloch, Ernest. 1968. On Karl Marx, trans. by John Maxwell. New York: Herder and Herder.

Block, E. 1983. Bleich and Iser on the reader's role. Reader 9. 1-9.

Bloom, Harold. 1975. A map of misreading. New York: Oxford University Press.

Bloome, David and Judith Green. 1982. The social contexts of reading: a multidisciplinary perspective. Comprehension and the competent reader: inter-specialty perspectives, ed. by D.F. Fisher and C.W. Peters, 309-338. New York: Praeger Publishers.

Bloome, David. 1983. Reading as a social process. Advances in reading/language research, ed. by B.A. Hutson, 165-195. (Vol. 2) Greenwich, Conn.: Jai Press.

Bloomfield, Leonard and C.L. Barnhart. 1961. Let's read: a linguistic approach. Detroit: Wayne State University Press.

Bloomfield, Leonard. 1933. Language. New York: Henry Holt and Company.

Bloomfield, Leonard. 1942. Linguistics and reading. Elementary English Review 19. 125-130, 183-186.

Bochmuehl, Klaus. 1980. The challenge of Marxism. Downers Grove, Ill.: InterVarsity Press.

Booth, Wayne. 1978a. Metaphor as rhetoric: the problem of evaluation. On metaphor, ed. by Sheldon Sacks, 47-70. Chicago: University of Chicago Press.

Booth, Wayne. 1978b. Ten literal "Theses." On metaphor, ed. by Sheldon Sacks, 165-172. Chicago: University of Chicago Press.

Booth, Wayne. 1983. A new strategy for establishing a truly democratic criticism. Daedalus 112.1. 193-214.

Bormuth, John R. 1975. Reading literacy: its definition and assessment. Toward a literate society, ed. by John B. Carroll and Jeane S. Chall, 61-100. New York: McGraw-Hill.

Bourgeois, Patrick L. 1971. Hermeneutics of symbols and philosophical reflection. Philosophy Today 15. 231-241.

Bourgeois, Patrick L. 1972. Paul Ricoeur's hermeneutical phenomenology. Philosophy Today 16. 20-27.

Bourgeois, Patrick L. 1975. Extension of Ricoeur's hermentics. The Hague: Nijhoff.

Bourgeois, Patrick L. 1979. From hermeneutics of symbols to the interpretation of texts. Studies in the philosophy of Paul Ricoeur, ed. by C.E. Reagan, 83-95. Athens: Ohio University Press.

Bransford, J.D. 1974. Bransford-McCarrell-Franks discussion. Cognition and symbolic processes, ed. by W.B. Weimer and D.S. Palermo. Hillsdale, N.J.: Lawrence Erlbaum Associates.

Brewer, William F. 1980. Literary theory, rhetoric, and stylistics: Implications for psychology. Theoretical issues in reading comprehension: perspectives from cognitive psychology, linguistics, artificial intelligence, and education, ed. by Rand J. Spiro, Bertram C. Bruce, and William F. Brewer, 221-239. Hillsdale, N.J.: Lawrence Erlbaum Associates.

Bricker, Victoria Reifler. 1976. Some Zinacanteco joking strategies. Speech play, ed. Barbara Kirshenblatt-Gimblett, 51-62. Philadelphia: University of Pennsylvania Press.

Bridge, Connie A, Peter N. Winograd, and Darliene Haley. 1983. Using predictiable materials vs. perprimers to teach beginning sight words. The Reading Teacher 36.9. 884-891.

Bright, William. 1982. Poetic structure in oral narrative. Spoken and written language: exploring orality and literacy, ed. by D. Tannen, 171-184. (Advances in discourse processes, IX.) Norwood, N.J.: Ablex Publishing Corporation.

Brislin, Richard, S. Bochner, and W. Lonner, ed. 1975. Cross- cultural perspectives on learning. New York: John Wiley & Sons.

Brooke-Rose, Christine. 1980. The readerhood of man. The reader in the text, ed. by Susan R. Suleiman and Inge Crosman, 120-148. Princeton, N.J.: Princeton University Press.

Broudy, H.S., D. Olson, E.Z. Rothkopf, H.G. Petrie, D.E. Rumelhart, R. Spiro. 1977. Open discussion on the contributions of Olson and Rothkopf. Schooling and the acquisition of knowledge, ed. by R.C. Anderson, R.J. Spiro, and W.E. Montague, 95-98. Hillsdale, N.J.: Lawrence Erlbaum Associates, Inc.

Brown, A.L. 1980. Metacognitive development and reading. Theoretical issues in reading comprehension: perspectives from cognitive psychology, linguistics, artificial intelligence, and education, ed. by Rand J. Spiro, Bertram C. Bruce, and William F. Brewer, 453-481. Hillsdale, N.J.: Lawrence Erlbaum Associates.

Brown, A.L. and J.C. Campione. 1977. Memory strategies in learning: training children to study strategically. ERIC D 136 235.

Brown, Colin. 1969. Philosophy and the christian faith. London: Inter-Varsity Press.

Brown, Gay. 1977. A transition: from Pidgin to Ngepma Kwundi. Read 12.2. 49-50.

Bruce, B.C. 1977. Plans and social actions. ERIC D 149 328.

Bruce, B.C. 1978. What makes a good story? ERIC D 158 222.

Bruce, B.C. 1980. Plans and social actions. Theoretical issues in reading comprehension: perspectives from cognitive psychology, linguistics, artificial intelligence, and education, ed. by Rand J. Spiro, Bertram C. Bruce, and William F. Brewer, 367-384. Hillsdale, N.J.: Lawrence Erlbaum Associates.

Bruce, B.C. 1981. A social interaction model of reading. Discourse processes 4. 273-311.

Bruce, B.C. 1981. Stories within stories. ERIC D 205 916.

Bruce, B.C. and A. Rubin. 1981. Strategies for controlling hypothesis formation in reading. ERIC D 201 912.

Bruns, Gerald L. 1984. The problem of figuration in antiquity. Hermeneutics, ed. by Gary Shapiro and Alan Sica, 147-164. Amherst: University of Massachusetts Press.

Bubner, Rudiger. 1982. Habermas's concept of critical theory. In Thompson and Held, 1982a. 42-56.

Buch, Marjorie J. 1973. Evaluation of Amuzgo preprimer. Notes on literacy 11. 1-7.

Bugbee, John A. 1973. The Freire approach to literacy: review and reflections.

Bugbee, John A. 1974. Reflections on Griffith, Freire and beyond. Literacy Discussion 125-132.

Bulgakov, Sergei. 1979. Karl Marx as a religious type, trans. by Luba Barna. Belmont, Mass.: Nordland Publishing Co.

Burgalassi, Silvano. 1980. Towards a theology of man as worker. Work and religion, ed. by Gregory Baum, 103-116. New York: The Seabury Press.

Butts, Robert E. 1969. Kant's schemata as semantic rules. Kant studies today, ed. by Lewis W. Beck, 290-300. LaSalle, Ill.: Open Court.

Cahn, Lorynne D. 1974 Reading and the development of intelligence. ERIC D 095 501.

Caillois, Roger. 1959. Play and the sacred. Man and the sacred, 152-162. Glencoe, Ill.: The Free Press.

Caillois, Roger. 1961. Man, play, and games. New York: The Free Press.

Cairns, Dorion. 1973. An approach to Husserlian phenomenology. Phenomenology and existentialism, ed. by Richard Zaner and Dan Ihde, 31-46. New York: G.P. Putnam's Sons.

Callinicos, Alex. 1976. Althusser's Marxism. London: Photo Press.

Cambourne, Brian. 1976-77. Getting to Goodman: An analysis of the Goodman model of reading with some suggestions for evaluation. Reading Research Quarterly 12.4. 605-636.

Canney, G. and P. Winograd. 1979. Schemata for reading and reading comprehension performance. ERIC D 169 520.

Caraher, Brian Gregory. 1983. Experience, authority and theoretical ideals: a methodological critique of some recent reader-response criticism and theory. Reader 9. 10-31.

Carey, Robert F. 1983. Theory and research in reading: insights from socio-psycholinguistics. Reader 10. 1-13.

Carpenter, Patricia A. and Marcel A. Just. 1977. Integrative processes in comprehension. Basic processes in reading: perception and comprehension, ed. by David LaBerge and S. Jay Samuels, 217-241. Hillsdale, N.J.: Lawrence Erlbaum Associates.

Carr, David. 1977. Husserl's problematic concept of the life-world. Husserl: expositions and appraisals, ed. by Frederick A. Elliston and Peter McCormick, 202-212. Notre Dame: University of Notre Dame Press.

Carroll, J.B. 1972. The case for ideographic writing. Language by ear and by eye, ed. by James F. Kavanagh and I.G. Mattingly, 103-109. Cambridge: MIT Press.

Carroll, J.B. 1977. Developmental parameters of reading comprehension. Cognition, curriculum, and comprehension, ed. by J.T. Guthrie, 1-15. Newark, Delaware: International Reading Association.

Casey, Edward S. 1977. Imagination and phenomenological method. Husserl: expositions and appraisals, ed. by Frederick A. Elliston and Peter McCormick, 54-69. Notre Dame: University of Notre Dame Press.

Cassirer, Ernst. 1946. Language and myth, trans. by Susanne K. Langer. New York: Dover Publications Inc.

Cates, Ann. 1976. How to sell books. Read 8.2. 10-13.

Chacko, Chinna. 1969. Production of reading materials. Reading: a human right and a human problem, ed. Ralph C. Staiger and Oliver Andresen, 87-92. Newark, Delaware: International Reading Association.

Chafe, W.L. 1977. Creativity in verbalization and its implications for the nature of stored knowledge. Discourse production and comprehension, ed. by R. Freedle. Norwood, N.J.: Ablex.

Chafe, W.L. 1982. Integration and involvement in speaking, writing and oral literature. Spoken and written language: exploring orality and literacy, ed. by D. Tannen, 35-53. (Advances in discourse processes, IX.) Norwood,N.J.: Ablex Publishing Corporation.

Chall, Jeanne S. 1967. Learning to read: the great debate. New York: McGraw-Hill.

Chall, Jeanne S. 1977. Reading 1967-1977: A decade of change and promise. ERIC D 146 556.

Cheska, Alyce Taylor. 1978. The study of play from five anthropological perspectives. West Point, N.Y.: Leisure Press, 17-35.

344

Chomsky, Noam. 1965. Aspects of a theory of syntax. Cambridge: MIT Press.

Chumbley, Robert. 1980. Introductory remarks toward a "Polylogue" on play. Sub-Stance 25. 7-11.

Cipollone, Anthony P. 1977. Religious language and Ricoeur's theory of metaphor. Philosophy Today 21. 458-467.

Cipollone, Anthony P. 1978. Symbol in the philosophy of Ricoeur. New Scholas 52. 149-167.

Clancy, P.M. 1982. Written and spoken style in Japanese narratives. Spoken and written language: exploring orality and literacy, ed. by D. Tannen, 55-76. (Advances in discourse processes, IX.) Norwood, N.J.: Ablex Publishing Corporation.

Clark, Gordon H. 1957. Thales to Dewey. Boston: Houghton, Miffin Co.

Clark, Herbert H. 1977. Inferences in comprehension. Basic processes in reading: perception and comprehension, ed. by David LaBerge and S. Jay Samuels, 243-263. Hillsdale, N.J.: Lawrence Erlbaum Associates.

Cohen, Ruth. 1983. Self-generated questions as an aid

Giles, Glenda. 1974. Literacy, Duna style. Read 9.2. 57-9.

Gisel, Pierre. 1977. Paul Ricoeur: discourse between speech and language. Philosophy Today 21. 446-456.

Goetz, E.T. 1982. Reading in perspective: What real cops and pretend burglars look for in a story. ERIC D 221 840.

Goetz, E.T. and B.B. Armbuster. 1980. Psychological correlates of text structure. Theoretical issues in reading comprehension: perspectives from cognitive psychology, linguistics, artificial intellegence and education, ed. by R.J. Spiro, B.C. Bruce, and W.F. Brewer, 201-220. Hillsdale, N.J.: Lawrence Erlbaum.

Golden, Joanne. 1983. If a text exists without a reader, is there meaning? Insights from literary theory for reader-text interaction. Advances in reading/language research, ed. by Barbara A. Hutson, 139-163. Greenwich, Conn.: Jai Press Inc.

Goodenough, Ward H. 1963. Cooperation in change. New York: Russell Sage Foundation.

Goodheart, Eugene. 1983. The text and the interpretive community. Daedalus 112.1. 215-231.

Goodman, Kenneth S. 1969. Analysis of oral reading miscues: applied psycholinguistics. Reading Research Quarterly 5.1. 9-30.

Goodman, Kenneth S. 1971. Decoding: from code to what? Journal of reading 14.7. 455-462, 498.

Goodman, Kenneth S. 1973a. The psycholinguistic nature of the reading process. The psycholinguistic nature of the reading process, ed. by Kenneth S. Goodman, 15-26. Detroit: Wayne State University Press.

Goodman, Kenneth S. 1973b. The 13th easy way to make learning to read difficult: a reaction to Gleitman and Rozin. Reading Research Quarterly 8.4. 484-493.

Goodman, Kenneth S. 1976-77. From the strawman to the tin woodman: A response to Mosenthal. Reading Research Quarterly 122.4. 575-585.

Goodman, Kenneth S. 1976a. Reading: a psycholinguistic guessing game. Theoretical models and processes of reading, ed. Harry Singer and Robert B. Ruddell, 497-508. Newark, Del.: International Reading Association.

Goodman, Kenneth S. 1976b. Behind the eye: what happens in reading. Theoretical models and processes of reading, ed. Harry Singer and Robert B. Ruddell, 470-496. Newark, Del.: International Reading Association..

Goodman, Kenneth S. 1976c. What we know about reading. Findings of research in miscue analysis: classroom implications, ed. by P. David Allen and Dorothy J. Watson, 57-70. Urbana, Ill.: ERIC Clearhouse on Reading and Communication Skills.

Goodman, Kenneth S. 1979. The know-more and the know-nothing movements in reading: a personal response. Language Arts 56.6. 657-663.

Goodman, Kenneth S. 1981. Letter to the editors. Reading Research Quarterly 16.3. 477-478.

Goodman, William B. 1983. Thinking about readers. Daedalus 112.1. 65-84.

Goody, J.R. 1982. Alternative paths to knowledge in oral and literate culture. Spoken and written language: exploring orality and literacy, ed. by D. Tannen, 201-215. (Advances in discourse processes, IX.) Norwood, N.J.: Ablex Publishing Corporation.

Gordon, Edmund W. 1976. Theories and practice of beginning reading: A view from the back of the bus. ERIC D 157 002.

Gough, Philip B. 1972. One second of reading. Language by ear and by eye, ed. by Kavanagh, James F. and Ignatius G. Mattingly, 331-358. Boston: MIT Press.

Gough, Philip B. 1984. Word recognition. Handbook of reading research, ed. by P. David Pearson, 225-253. New York: Longman.

Gough, Philip B. 1985. One second of reading: postscript. Theoretical models and processes of reading, ed. by Harry Singer and Robert B. Ruddell, 3rd. edition, 687-688.

Goulet, Dennis. 1971a. An ethical model for the study of values. Harvard Educational Review 41.1. 205-227.

Goulet, Dennis. 1971b. The cruel choice. New York: Athenum.

Gray, William S. 1956. The teaching of reading and writing. Paris: UNESCO.

Green, G.M. 1982. Colloquial and literary uses of inversions. Spoken and written language: exploring orality and literacy, ed. by D. Tannen, 119-153. (Advances in discourse processes, IX.) Norwood, N.J.: Ablex Publishing Corporation.

Greimas, A.J. 1980. About games. Sub-Stance 25. 31-35.

Grene, Marjorie, 1966. The knower and the known. New York: Basic Books, Inc.

Griffith, William S. 1974. Paulo Freire: utopian perspective on literacy education for revolution. Literacy Discussion 93-116.

Groff, Patrick. 1979. Goodman and his critics. Reading World 18.4. 376-383.

Gudschinsky, S.C. 1959. Recent trends in primer construction. Fundamental and Adult Education 11. 367-396.

Gudschinsky, S.C. 1960. Handbook of literacy. n.p.: Summer Institute of Linguistics.

Gudschinsky, S.C. 1969. Matrix for letter recognition: syllable or couplet. Notes on literacy: selected articles, ed. by Margaret M. Wendell, 29-31. Dallas, Tx.: The Summer Institute of Linguistics.

Gudschinsky, S.C. 1972. Notes on neutralization and orthography. Notes on literacy: selected articles, ed. by Margaret M. Wendell, 15. Dallas, Tx.: The Summer Institute of Linguistics.

Gudschinsky, S.C. 1973. A manual of literacy for preliterate peoples. Ukarumpa, PNG: Summer Institute of Linguistics.

Gudschinsky, S.C. 1974. Primer stories by indigenous authors. Notes on literacy 16. 12-13.

Gudschinsky, S.C. 1977a. Literacy. n.p.: Summer Institite of Linguistics.

Gudschinsky, S.C. 1977b. Literacy. The Summer Institute of Linguistics, ed. by Ruth M. Brend and Kenneth L. Pike, 39-56. The Hague: Mouton.

Gurwitsch, Aron. 1974. Phenomenology and the theory of science, ed. by Lester Embree. Evanston: Northwestern University Press.

Habermas, Jurgen. 1970a. On systematically distorted communication. Inquiry 13. 205-218.

Habermas, Jurgen. 1970b. Towards a theory of communicative competence. Inquiry 13. 360-375

Habermas, Jurgen. 1970c. Summation and response. Continuum 8. 123-133.

Habermas, Jurgen. 1971a. Knowledge and human interest, trans. by Jeremy J. Shapiro. Boston: Beacon Press.

Habermas, Jurgen. 1971b. Vorbereitende Bemerkungen zu einer Theorie der Kommunikativen Kompetenz. Theorie der Gesellschaft oder Sozialtechnologie--was leistest die Systemforschung, by Jurgen Habermas and Nikolai Luhmann, 101-141. Frankfurt: Suhrkamp.

Habermas, Jurgen. 1971c. Theorie und Praxis, 4th revised ed. Frankfurt: Suhrkamp.

Habermas, Jurgen. 1973a. Wahrheitstheorien. Wirklichkeit und reflexion: Walter Schulz zum 60, Gebrutstag, 219-229. Pfullingen: Neske.

Habermas, Jurgen. 1973b. Theory and practice, trans. by John Viertel. Boston: Beacon Press.

Habermas, Jurgen. 1975. A postscript to Knowledge and human interest. Philosophy of the social sciences 3. 157-189.

Habermas, Jurgen. 1977. A review of Gadamer's Truth and method. Understanding and social inquiry, ed. by Fred R. Dallmayr and Thomas A. McCarthy, 335-363.

Habermas, Jurgen. 1979. Communication and the evolution of society, trans. by Thomas McCarthy. London: Heinemann.

Habermas, Jurgen. 1980. The hermeneutic claim to universality. Contemporary hermeneutics, ed. by Joseph Bleicher, 181-211. London: Routledge & Kegan Paul.

Habermas, Jurgen. 1982. A reply to my critics. In Thompson and Held, 1982a. 219-251.

Hackett, Stuart C. 1969. Paul Ricoeur and the phenomenological movement. International Philosophical Quarterly 9. 11-39.

Halvorson, Marion. 1970. An adult literacy program: central Tanzania 1955-1968. Notes on literacy 9. 1-14.

Hamlyn, D.W. 1967. Empiricism. The encyclopedia of philosophy, Vol. 2, ed. by Paul Edwards, 499-505. New York: Collier Macmillan Publishers.

Hamlyn, D.W. 1967b. A priori and a posteriori. The encyclopedia of philosophy, Vol. 1, ed. by Paul Edwards, 140-144. New York: Collier Macmillan Publishers.

Hans, James S. 1977. Gaston Bachelard and the phenomenology of the reading consciousness. The Journal of Aesthetic and Art Criticism 35.3. 315-327.

Hans, James S. 1981. The play of the world. Amherst: The University of Massachusetts Press.

Hansen, J. and P.D. Pearson. 1980. The effects of inference training and practice on yound children's comprehension. ERIC D 186 839.

Harker, Judith O., Joellen T. Hartley, and David A. Walsh. 1982. Understanding discourse: a life-span approach. Advances in reading/language research, ed. by Barbara A. Hutson, 155-202. (Vol. 1) Greenwich, Conn.: Jai Press Inc.

Harman, D. 1971. Methodology for revolution. Review of pedagogy of the oppressed, by Paulo Freire. Saturday Review v.LIV.25. 54-55.

Harms, Jeanne McLain and Lucille J. Lettow. 1983. Poetry for children has never been better! The Reading Teacher 36.4. 376-381.

Harries, Karsten. 1978a. Metaphor and transcendence. On metaphor, ed. by Sheldon Sacks, 71-88. Chicago: University of Chicago Press.

Harries, Karsten. 1978b. The many uses of metaphor. On metaphor, ed. by Sheldon Sacks, 173-174. Chicago: University of Chicago Press.

Hawkes, Terence. 1972. Metaphor. London: Methuen & Co., Ltd.

Hayes, D.A. and R.J. Tierney. 1980. Increasing background knowledge through analogy: its effects upon comprehension and learning. ERIC D 195 953.

Heath, S.B. 1982. Protean shapes in literacy events: ever- shifting oral and literate traditions. Spoken and written language: exploring orality and literacy, ed. by D. Tannen, 91-117. (Advances in discourse processes, IX.) Norwood, N.J.: Ablex Publishing Corporation.

Hegel, G.W.F. 1967. The phenomenology of mind, trans. by J.B. Baillie. New York: Harper & Row.

Heidegger, Martin. 1962. Being and time. New York: Harper and Row.

Heidegger, Martin. 1971a. On the way to language, trans. by Peter D. Hertz. New York: Harper and Row.

Heidegger, Martin. 1971b. Poetry, language, thought, trans. by Albert Hofstadter. New York: Harper & Row.

Heidegger, Martin. 1977. Basic writings, ed. by David Farrell Krell. New York: Harper and Row, Publishers.

Heitzmann William. 1974. Educational games and simulation. Washington, D.C.: National Education Association.

Held, David. 1980. Introduction to critical theory: Horkheimer to Habermas. London: Hutchinson.

Heller, Agnes. 1982. Habermas and Marxism. In Thompson and Held, 1982a. 21-41.

Henry, Jules. 1960. An cross-cultural outline of education. Current anthropology 1.4. 267-305.

Hickman, Larry. 1977. Reply: strict meaning and reductive hermeneutics. Southwestern Journal of Philosophy 8.73-75.

Hidi, Suzanne E. and Angela Hilyard. 1983. The comparison of oral and written production in two discourse types. Discourse Processes 6. 91-105.

Hintikka, J. 1967. Cogito, ergo sum: inference or performance. Descartes: a collection of critical essays, ed. by Willis Doney, 108-139. South Bend: University of Notre Dame Press.

Hochberg, J. and V. Brooks. 1970. Reading as an intentional behavior. Theoretical models and processes of reading, ed. by H. Singer and R.B. Ruddell. Newark, Del: International Reading Association.

350

Hodge, Charles. 1975. Systematic Theology. Vol. 1. Grand Rapids, Michigan: William B. Eerdmans Publishers.

Hoetker, James. 1982. A theory of talking about theories of reading. College English 44.2. 175-181.

Hogaboam, T.W. and G.W. McConkie. 1981. The rocky road from eye fixations to comprehension. ERIC D 201 988.

Holdaway, Don. 1979. The foundations of literacy. New York: Aston Scholastic.

Holland, Norman N. 1975. 5 readers reading. New Haven: Yale University Press.

Holquist, Michael. 1968. How to play utopia: some brief notes on the distinctiveness of utopian fiction. Yale French Studies 41.106-123.

Hood, Elizabeth. 1982. Review of toward the more effective use of oral communication of the scripture in West Africa, by H. Klem. Notes on Scripture in Use 3.20-24.

Hoy, David Couzens. 1978. The critical circle. Berkely: University of California Press.

Huck, Charolette S. 1969. Teaching critical thinking through reading. Reading: a human right and a human problem, ed. Ralph C. Staiger and Oliver Andresen, 48-55. Newark, Delaware: International Reading Association.

Huggins, A.W.F. 1977. Syntactic aspects of reading comprehension. ERIC D 142 972.

Huggins, A.W.F. and M.J Adams. 1980. Syntactic aspects of reading comprehension. Theoretical issues in reading comprehension: perspectives from cognitive psychology, linguistics, artificial intelligence, and education, ed. by Rand J. Spiro, Bertram C. Bruce, and William F. Brewer, 87-112. Hillsdale, N.J.: Lawrence Erlbaum Associates.

Huizinga, John. 1955. Homo ludens: a study of the play element in cultue. Boston: Beacon Press.

Hunter, Georgia. 1974. Literature distribution...a bottleneck? Novalit 3.2. 1-4.

Hunter, Georgia. 1977. Transition primers: spanish to the idiom. Novalit 5.1. 1-7.

Husserl, Edmund. 1931. Ideas, general introduction to pure phenomenology. London: Routledge and Kegan Paul.

Husserl, Edmund. 1960. Cartesian Meditations. The Hague: Nijhoff.

Husserl, Edmund. 1964. The phenomenology of internal time consciousness. Bloomington: University Press.

Husserl, Edmund. 1973a. Experience and judgment. Evanston: Northwestern University Press.

Husserl, Edmund. 1973b. Phenomenology. Phenomenology and existentialism, ed. by Richard Zaner and Don Idhe, 46-71. New York: G.P. Putnam's Sons.

Husserl, Edmund. 1981. Husserl: shorter works, ed. by Peter McCormick and Frederick A. Elliston. Notre Dame: University of Notre Dame Press.

Ihde, Don. 1971. Hermeneutic phenomenology. Evanston: Northwestern University Press.

Illich, Ivan and Etienne Verne. 1976. Imprisoned in the global classroom. London: Writers and Readers Publishing Cooperative.

Illich, Ivan. 1971. Celebration of awareness. New York: Doubleday.

Iran-Nejad, A. 1980. The schema: a structural or a functional pattern. ERIC D 181 449.

Iran-Nejad, A. and A. Ortony. 1982. Cognition: A functional view. ERIC D 215 308.

Iran-Nejad, A., A. Ortony, and R.K. Rittenhouse. 1980. The comprehension of metaphorical uses of English by deaf children. ERIC D 193 618.

Iser, Wolfgang. 1974. The implied reader: patterns of communication in prose fiction from Bunyan to Beckett. Baltimore, Md.: Johns Hopkins University Press.

Iser, Wolfgang. 1978. The act of reading: a theory of aesthetic response. Baltimore, Md.: John Hopkins University Press.

Iser, Wolfgang. 1980a. Interaction between text and reader. The reader in the text: essays on audience and interpretation, ed. by S.R. Suleiman and I. Crossman, 106-119. Princeton, N.J.: Princeton University Press.

Iser, Wolfgang. 1980b. Texts and readers. Discourse Processes 3. 327-343.

Jakobson, Roman and Morris Halle. 1956. Fundamentals of language. The Hague: Mouton.

Jalongo, Mary Renck and Karen D'Angelo Broniley. 1984. Developing linguistic competence through song picture books. The Reading Teacher 37.9. 840-845.

Jay, Martin. 1973. The dialectical imagination: a history of the Frankfurt school and the institute of social research 1923-50. London: Heinemann.

Johnson, Barbara. 1980. The critical difference. Baltimore: The John Hopkins University Press.

Johnson, Gwendolyn D. and Lester A. Lefton. 1981. Reading comprehension: essential skills are not sufficient. Comprehension and the competent reader: inter-specialty perspectives, 116-126. New York: Praeger Publishers.

Johnston, Robert K. 1983. The christian at play. Grand Rapids: William B. Eerdmans Publishing Company.

Jones, Gareth and Gunther Kress. 1981. Classifications at work: the case of middle management. Text 1. 65-81.

Jones, Joan. 1978. Kura (Bakairi) orthography conference: growth in competence. Notes on literacy 24. 1-7.

Jones, Larry B. and Linda K. Jones. 1979. Multiple levels of information in discourse. Discourse studies in mesoamerican languages, ed. by Linda K. Jones, 3-27. Dallas: Summer Institute of Linguistics and the University of Texas at Arlington.

Jozsa, Peter. 1980. Notes for a discussion. Sub-Stance 25. 25-30.

Just, M.A. and P. Carpenter. 1980. A theory of reading: from eye fixation to comprehension. Psychological Review 87. 329-355.

Kamil, Michael L. 1977. Alternative models in reading comprehension. ERIC D 142 945.

Kane, J.H. and R.C. Anderson. 1977. Depth of processing and interference effects in the learning and remembering of sentences. ERIC D 134 942.

Kant, Immanuel. 1956. Critique of pure reason, trans. by Norman Kemp Smith. New York: Macmillan and Co Ltd. (Originally published in 1781.)

Katz, Ina and Harry Singer. 1981. The substrata-factor theory of reading: Differential development of subsystems underlying reading comprehension in the first year of instruction. ERIC D 212 985.

Kavanagh, James F. and Ignatius G. Mattingly, ed. 1972. Language by ear and by eye. Boston: MIT Press.

Kaye, Peggy. 1984. Games for reading: playful ways to help your child read. New York: Pantheon Books.

Kelly, J.N.D. 1958. Early Christian doctrine. New York: Harper & Row, Publishers.

Kelly, Michael. 1982. Modern French marxism. Baltimore: The John Hopkins University Press.

Kerr, Isabel. 1963. Evaluation of a reading readiness book. Notes on literacy 7. 4-8.

King, Ethel. 1969. Organization of reading programmes. Reading: a human right and a human problem, ed. Ralph C. Staiger and Oliver Andresen, 95-100. Newark, Delaware: International Reading Association.

Kinneavy, James L. 1971. A theory of discourse. New York: W.W. Norton.

Kintsch, Walter. 1976. Concerning the marriage of research and practice: A discussion of the papers presented at the conference in beginning reading instruction, Pittsburgh, April 1976. ERIC D 155 626.

Kintsch, Walter. 1977. On comprehending stories. Cognitive Processes in comprehension, ed. by Marcel Adam Just and Patricia A. Carpenter, 33-62. Hillsdale, N.J.: Lawrence Erlbaum Associates.

Kirshenblatt-Gimblett. 1976. Bibliographic survey of the literature on speech play and related subjects. Speech play, ed. Barbara Kirshenblatt-Gimblett, 179-223. Philadelphia: University of Pennsylvania Press.

Klima, Edward S. 1972. How alphabets might reflect language. Language by ear and by eye, ed. by James F. Kavanagh and Ignatius G. Mattingly, 57-80. Cambridge: MIT Press.

Knott, Gladys. 1983. Building bridges between receptive and productive language processes for adolescents. Advances in reading/language research, ed. by Barbara A. Hutson, 257-271. Greenwich, Conn.: Jai Press, Inc.

Kockelmans, Joseph J. 1967a. A first introduction to Husserl's phenomenology. Pittsburgh: Duquesne University Press.

Kockelmans, Joseph J. 1967b. Edmund Husserl's phenomenological psychology: a historico-critical study. (Duquesne studies, psychological series, 4) Pittsburgh: Duquesne University Press.

Kolers, P.A. 1969. Reading is only incidentally visual. Psycholinguistics and the teaching of reading, ed. Kenneth S. Goodman and James T. Fleming, 8-16. Newark, Del.: International Reading Association.

Kolers, P.A. 1973. Some modes of representation. Communication and affect: language and thought. New York: Academic Press.

Kretschmer, Joseph C. 1975. Toward a Piagetian theory of reading comprehension. Reading World 14.3. 180-187.

Kuhn, T.S. 1970. The structure of scientific revolutions. (revised ed.) Chicago: University of Chicago Press.

Kurth, Ruth J. 1983. Exploring the relationships between reading and writing in early literacy development.

Kurzweil, Edith. 1980. The age of structuralism. New York: Columbia University Press.

Kwant, Remy C. 1967. Critique: its nature and function. Pittsburg: Duquesne University Press.

Kwant, Remy C. 1969. Phenomenology of expression. Pittsburgh: Duquesne University Press.

LaBerge, David. 1972. Beyond auditory coding. Language by ear and by eye, ed. by James F. Kavanagh and Ignatius G. Mattingly, 241-248. Cambridge: MIT Press.

Lakoff, R.T. 1982. Some of my favorite writers are literate: the mingling of oral and literate strategies in written communication. Spoken and written language: exploring orality and literacy, ed. by D. Tannen, 239-260. (Advances in discourse processes, IX.) Norwood, N.J.: Ablex Publishing Corporation.

Lamb, Pose and Richard Arnold, ed. 1976. Reading: foundations and instructional strategies. Belmont, Ca.: Wadsworth Publishing Co., Inc.

Lamb, Pose. 1976. Reading: definitions, models, and beliefs. Reading foundations and instructional strategies, ed. by Pose Lamb and Richard Arnold, 2-22. Belmont, Ca.: Wadsworth Publishing Co., Inc.

Landgrebe, Ludwig. 1981. The phenomenology of Edmund Husserl. Ithaca: Cornell University Press.

Langsdorf, Lenore. 1980. Meaning and reference: an intentional approach. The Southwestern Journal of Philosophy. XI.1. 105-113.

Langsdorf, Lenore. 1981. The relevance of the Popper-Kuhn debate for the understanding of language use. Unpublished mss.

Langsdorf, Lenore. 1983. Linguistic constitution: the accomplishment of meaningfulness and the private language dispute. Human Studies 6. 77-93.

Langsdorf, Lenore. (in press). The noema as intentional entity: a critique of Follesdal. The Review of Metaphysics.

Langsdorf, Lenore and Harry Reeder. n.d. A phenomenological exploration of Popper's 'world 3'. unpublished mss. (Forthcoming in Prize essays: selected papers from the Husserl cirlce, the Heidegger conference, and the Merleau-Ponty circle, Humanities Press.)

Lanham, Richard A. 1976. The motives of eloquence. New Haven: Yale University Press.

Lapointe, Francois H. 1972. A bibliography on Paul Ricoeur. Philosophy Today 16. 28-33.

Lapointe, Francois H. 1973. A bibliography on Paul Ricoeur. Philosophy Today 17. 176-182.

Lapointe, Francois H. 1979. Ricoeur and his critics. Studies in the philosophy of Paul Ricoeur, ed. C.E. Reagan, 164-177. Athens: Ohio University Press.

Larson, M.L. and P.M. Davis. 1981. Bilingual education: an experiment in the Peruvian Amazonia. Dallas: Summer Institute of Linguistics.

Lass-Kayser, Mary Jo. 1979. Teacher's treasury of classroom reading activities. West Nyack, N.Y.: Parker Publishing Co.

Lechner, Robert. 1977a. The interpretation of Paul Ricoeur. Philosophy Today 21. 409.

Lechner, Robert. 1977b. The rule of metaphor. Philosophy Today 21. 410-411.

Lee, Ernest W. 1982. Literacy primers: the Gudschinsky method. Dallas: The Summer Institute of Linguistics.

Leech, Geoffrey. 1974. Semantics. Baltimore: Penguin Book Inc.

Lehmann, Winfred. 1975. Language and linguistics in the People's Republic of China. Austin: University of Texas Press.

356

Leibnitz, Gottfried Wilhelm. 1896. New essays concerning human understanding. New York: The Macmillan Company.

Levin, David Michael. 1970. Reason and evidence in Husserl's phenomenology. Evanston: Northwestern University Press.

Lewis, C.S. 1946. That hideous strength. New York: Macmillian Publishing Co.

Lewis, C.S. 1955. Surprised by joy. New York: Harcourt, Brace & World, Harvest Books.

Li, C.N. and S.A. Thompson. 1982. The gulf between spoken and written language: a case study in chinese. Spoken and written language: exploring orality and literacy, ed. by D. Tannen, 77-88. (Advances in discourse processes, IX.) Norwood, N.J.: Ablex Publishing Corporation.

Liberman, A.M., F.S. Cooper, D.P. Shankweiler, and M. Studdert-Kennedy. 1967. Perception of the speech code. Psychological Review 74. 431-461.

Lichtenstein, Heinz. 1972. Communication. Philosophical Phenomenology Research 32. 412-413.

Lindemann, Bernhard. 1983. Text as process: an integrated view of a science of texts. Journal of Literary Semantics 12.1. 5-41.

Lindvall, Richard. 1980. Paulo Freire: the man, the ideas, the methods. Notes on literacy 30. 22-26.

Lingenfelter, Judith and C. Gray. 1981. The importance of learning styles in literacy. Notes on literacy 36. 11-16.

Lloyd, Arthur S. 1972. Freire, conscientization and adult education. Adult education v.XXIII.1. 3-20.

Lovett, M.W. 1979. The selective encoding of sentential information in normal reading development. Child development 50. 897-900.

Lovett, M.W. 1981. Reading skill and its development: theoretical and empirical considerations. Reading research, ed. by G.E. Mackinnon and T. Gary Weaver, 1-37. (Vol. 3) New York: Academic Press.

Loving, Aretta, editor. 1976. The literacy programme. Ukarumpa, PNG: The Summer Institute of Linguistics.

Lowe, W.J. 1981. Cosmos and covenant. Semeia 19. 107-111.

Luzbetak, Louis. 1970. The church and cultures. Techny, Ill.: Divine Word Publications.

Lyon, David. 1979. Karl Marx. Downers Grove, Ill.: InterVarsity Press.

Lyons, John. 1977. Semantics. 2 Vol. London: Cambridge University Press.

Maccoby, M. 1971. Literacy for the favelas. Review of pedagogy of the oppressed and cultural action for freedom, by Paulo Freire. Science 671-673.

Madison, Gary B. 1971. Phenomenology and existentialism: Husserl and the end of idealism. Husserl: expositions and appraisals, ed. by Frederick A. Elliston and Peter McCormick, 247-268. Notre Dame: University of Notre Dame Press.

Madison, Gary B. 1977. Reflections on Paul Ricoeur's philosophy of metaphor. Philosophy Today 21. 412-423.

Maduro, Otto. 1980. Labour and religion according to Karl Marx. Work and religion, ed. by Gregory Baum, 12-20. New York: The Seabury Press.

Mallett, Jerry J. 1976. 101 Make-and-play reading games for the intermediate grades. West Nyack, N.Y.: The Center for Applied Research in Education, Inc.

Mandl, H., N.L. Stein, and T. Trabasso, ed. 1984. Learning and comprehension of text. Hillsdale, N.J.: Lawrence Erlbaum Associates.

Mandler, Jean M. 1982. Some uses and abuses of story grammars. Discourse Processes 5. 305-318.

Mann, James W. 1970. The relevance of reading to the social revolution. Reading and revolution, ed. by Dorothy M. Dietrich and Virginia H. Matthews, 1-8. Newark, Del.: International Reading Association.

Manna, Anthony L. 1984. Making language come alive through reading plays. The Reading Teacher 37.8. 712-717.

Marquardt, Willaim F. 1979. A linguist looks at reading. Linguistics and literary studies in honor of Archibald A. Hill, ed. M.A. Jazayery, E.C. Polome, and W. Winter, 335-344. (Trends in linguistics, IV.) Mouton: The Hague.

Marschank, Marc, Albert N. Katz, and Allan Paivio. 1983. Dimensions of metaphor. Journal of psycholinguistic research 12.1. 17-40.

Marshall, Nancy and Marvin D. Glock. 1978-79. Comprehension of connected discourse: A study into the relationships between the structure of text and information recalled. Reading Research Quarterly 14.1. 10-56.

Marshall, Nancy. 1981. The application of basic research to reading instruction. Comprehension and competent reader: inter-specialty perspectives, 36-50. New York: Praeger Publishers.

Martin, Charles E., Bonnie Cramond, and Tammy Safter. 1982. Developing creativity through the reading program. The Reading Teacher 35.5. 568-572.

Martin, Gerhard Marcel. 1976. Fest, the transformation fo everyday. Philadelphia: Fortress Press.

Martin, Samuel E. 1972. Nonalphabetic writing systems: some observations. Language by ear and by eye, ed. by James F. Kavanagh and Ignatius G. Mattingly, 81-102. Cambridge: MIT Press.

Marx, Karl. 1978. A Marx-Engels Reader, 2nd ed., ed. by Robert C. Tucker. New York: W.W. Norton & Co.

Mashayekh, Farideh. 1974. Freire, the man, his ideas and their implications. Literacy Discussion 1-62.

Mason, J.M. 1977a. Questioning the notion of independent processing stages in reading. Journal of Educational Psychology 69. 288-297.

Mason, J.M. 1977b. Reading readiness: a definition and skills hierarchy from preschoolers' developing conceptions of print. ERIC D 145 403.

Mason, J.M. 1981. Prereading: a developmental perspective. ERIC D 199 659.

Mason, J.M. and J.R. Kendall. 1978. Facilitating reading comprehension through text structure manipulation. ERIC D 157 041.

Mathews, Mitford M. 1966. Teaching to read. Chicago: The University of Chicago Press.

Mattingly, Ignatius G. 1972. Reading, the linguistic process, and linguistic awareness. Language by ear and by eye, ed. by James F. Kavanagh and Ignatius G. Mattingly, 133-147. Cambridge: MIT Press.

Mayers, Marvin K. 1978. The basic values. Unpublished Ms.

McCarthy, Thomas. 1973. A theory of communicative competence. Philosophy of the social sciences 3. 135-156.

McCarthy, Thomas. 1978. The critical theory of Jurgen Habermas. Cambridge, Mass.: MIT Press.

McCarthy, Thomas. 1982. Rationality and relativism: Habermas's 'Overcoming' of hermeneutics. In Thompson and Held, 1982a. 57-78.

McCormick, Peter. 1977. Phenomenology and metaphilosophy. Husserl: expositions and appraisals, ed. by Frederick A. Elliston and Peter McCormick, 350-364. Notre Dame: University of Notre Dame Press.

McDermott, R.P. 1974. Achieving school failure. Education and cultural process, ed. by G.D. Spindler, 82-118. New York: Holt, Rhinehart and Winston Inc.

McGovern, Arthur F. 1980. Marxism: an American christian perspective. Maryknoll, N.Y.: Orbis Books.

Meeks, M. Douglas. 1976. Introduction. Fest, the transformation of everyday, by Gerhard Marcel Martin, p. xi-xiv. Philadelphia: Fortress Press.

Merleau-Ponty, Maurice. 1973. The prose of the world. Evanston, Ill.: Northwestern University Press.

Merrion, Margaret Dee. 1981. Arts integration parallels between music and reading: Process, product and affective response. ERIC D 212 986.

Mervis, Carolyn B. 1980. Category structure and the development of categorization. Theoretical issues in reading comprehension: perspectives from cognitive psychology, linguistics, artificial intelligence, and education, ed. by Rand J. Spiro, Bertram C. Bruce, and William F. Brewer, 279-307. Hillsdale, N.J.: Lawrence Erlbaum Associates.

Meyer, Bonnie J.F. 1977. The structure of prose: effects on learning and memory and implications for educational practice. Schooling and the acquistion of knowledge, ed. by R.C. Anderson, R.J. Spiro, W.E. Montague, 179-200. Hillsdale, N.J.: Lawrence Erlbaum Associates.

Meyer, Bonnie J.F. 1981. Basic research on prose comprehension: a critical review. Comprehension and the competent reader: inter- specialty perspectives, ed. by D.F. Fisher and C.W. Peters, 8-35. New York: Praeger Publishers.

Meyer, Bonnie J.F. 1983a. Text structure and its use in studying comprehension across the adult life span. Advances in reading/language research, ed. by Barbara A. Hutson, 9-54. (Vol. 2) Greenwich, Comm.: Jai Press Inc.

Meyer, Bonnie J.F. 1983b. Text dimensions and cognitive processing. Learning and comprehending texts, ed. by H. Mandl, N. Stein, and T. Trabasso, 3-47. Hillsdale, N.J.: Lawrence Erlbaum.

Meyer, Bonnie J.F. 1984. Text dimensions and cognitive processing. Learning and comprehension of text, ed. by H. Mandl, N.L. Stein and T. Trabasso, 3-51. Hillsdale, N.J.: Lawrence Erlbaum Associates.

Meyer, Bonnie J.F. and G.E. Rice. 1984. The structure of text. Handbook of research in reading, ed. by P.D. Pearson. New York: Longman.

Meyer, Bonnie J.F., M.J. Harry, D.M. Brandt, and C.H. Walker. 1980. Comprehension of stories and expository text. Poetics: International review for the theory of literature 9. 203-211.

Miall, David S., ed. 1982. Metaphor: problems and perspectives. Atlantic Highlands, New Jersey: Humanities Press.

Miccinati, Jeanette Louise, Judith B. Sanford, and Gene Hepner. 1983. Teaching reading through the arts: an annotated bibliography. The Reading Teacher. 36.4. 412-417.

Miller, David L. 1970. God and games: toward a theology of play. New York: Harper & Row, Publishers.

Miller, G. Michael and George E. Mason. 1983. Dramatic improvisiation: risk-free role playing for improving reading performance. The Reading Teacher 37.2. 128-131.

Miller, James R. and Walter Kintsch. 1981. Knowledge-based aspects of prose comprehension and readability. Text 1. 215-232.

Minsky, M. 1980. A framework for representing knowledge. Frame conceptions and text understanding, ed. by Dieter Metzing, 1-25. Berlin: de Grutyer.

Misgeld, Dieter. 1976. Critical theory and hermeneutics: the debate between Habermas and Gadamer. On critical theory, ed. by John O'Neill, 164-183. New York: The SeaburyPress.

Mitchell, D.C. 1982. The process of reading. New York: John Wiley & Sons.

Mitchell, William H. 1972. Poetry: language as violence, an analysis of the symbolic process in poetry. Humanitas 8. 193-208.

Modiano, N. 1973. Education in the Chiapas highlands. New York: Holt, Rhinehart and Winston.

Moe, Alden J. 1976. Reading: current approaches, part two. Reading foundations and instructional strategies, ed. by Pose Lamb and Richard Arnold, 238-271. Belmont, Ca.: Wadsworth Publishing Co., Inc.

Mohanty, J.N. 1964. Edmund Husserl's theory of meaning. The Hague: Nijhoff.

Mohanty, J.N. 1974. On Husserl's theory of meaning. Southwestern Journal of Philosophy 5. 229-244.

Mohanty, J.N. 1977. Husserl's theory of meaning. Husserl: expositions and appraisals, ed. by Frederick A. Elliston and Peter McCormick, 18-37. Notre Dame: University of Notre Dame Press.

Mohanty, J.N. 1984. Transcendental philosophy and the hermeneutic critique of consciousness. Hermeneutics, ed. by Gary Shapiro and Alan Sica, 96-129. Amherst: University of Massachusetts Press.

Moldofsky, Penny Baum. 1983. Teaching students to determine the central story problem: a practical application of schema theory. The Reading Teacher 36.8. 740-745.

Morgan, Jerry L. and Georgia M. Green. 1980. Pragmatics and reading comprehension. Theoretical issues in reading comprehension: perspectives from cognitive psychology, linguistics, artificial intelligence, and education, ed. by Rand J. Spiro, Bertram C. Bruce, and William F. Brewer, 113-140. Hillsdale, N.J.: Lawrence Erlbaum Associates.

Morgan, Jerry L. and Manfred B. Sellner. 1980. Discourse and linguistic theory. Theoretical issues in reading comprehension: perspectives from cognitive psychology, linguistics, artificial intelligence, and education, ed. by Rand J. Spiro, Bertram C. Bruce, and William F. Brewer, 165-200. Hillsdale, N.J.: Lawrence Erlbaum Associates.

Morreal, John. 1981. Humor and aesthetic education. Journal of Aesthetic Education 15.1. 55-70.

Mosenthal, Peter. 1976-77. Bridge principles in an abridged reply to Goodman. Reading Research Quarterly 12.4. 586-603.

Mugele, Robert. 1978. The pedagogical implications of undersymbolization in orthography. Notes on literacy 24. 22-24.

Mugele, Robert. 1979. Chinantec teacher training program. Notes on literacy 28. 6-12.

Muto, Susan. 1972. Reading the symbolic text: some reflections on interpretation. Humanitas 8. 169-191.

Mytyta, Larysa. 1983. Literature lost or the politics of justification. Reader 9. 32-37.

Nash, Ronald H. 1982. The word of God and the mind of man. Grand Rapids, Michigan: Zondervan Publishing House.

Neale, Robert F. 1969. In praise of play. New York: Harper & Row.

Nelson, John O. 1967. Innate ideas. The encyclopedia of philosophy, Vol. 4, ed. by Paul Edwards, 196-198. New York: Collier Macmillan Publishers.

Nesse, D. and M.B. Jones. 1981. The language experience approach to reading. New York: Columbia University Press.

O'Neill, John. 1976. Critique and remembrance. On critical theory, ed. by John O'Neill, 1-11. New York: The Seabury Press.

Ogden, C.K. and I.A. Richards. 1938. The meaning of meaning. (5th ed.) New York: Harcourt, Brace & World Inc.

Olafson, Frederick A. 1977. Husserl's theory of intentionality in comtemporary perspective. Husserl's: expositions and appraisals, ed. by Frederick A. Elliston and Peter McCormick, 160-167. Notre Dame: University of Notre Dame Press.

Olson, D.R. 1977a. From utterance to text: the bias of language in speech and writing. Harvard Educational Review 47. 257-281.

Olson, D.R. 1977b. The languages of instruction: on the literate bias of schooling. Schooling and the acquisition of knowledge, ed. by R.C. Anderson, R.J. Spiro, and W.E. Montague, 65-89. Hillsdale, N.J.: Lawrence Erlbaum Associates, Inc.

Ong, Walter J. 1967. Preface. Man at play, by Hugo Rahner, ix-xiv. New York: Herder and Herder.

Ong, Walter J. 1975. The writer's audience is always a fiction. PMLA 90.1. 9-21.

Orasann, Judith and Sylvia Scribner. 1982. The development of verbal reasoning: pragmatic, schematic and operational aspects. Linguistics and Literacy, ed. by William Frawley, 285-313. New York: Plenum Press.

Ortony, A. 1976. Names, descriptions, and pragmatics. ERIC D 134 931.

Ortony, A. 1977 Remembering and understanding Jabberwocky and small-talk. ERIC D 137 752.

Ortony, A. 1978. Beyond literal similarity. ERIC D 166 635.

Ortony, A. 1979. Some psycholinguistic aspects of metaphor. ERIC D 165 115.

Ortony, A. 1980a. Metaphor. Theoretical issues in reading comprehension: perspectives from cognitive psychology, linguistics, artificialintelligence, and education, ed. by Rand J. Spiro, Bertram C. Bruce, and William F. Brewer, 349-365. Hillsdale, N.J.: Lawrence Erlbaum Associates.

Ortony, A. 1980b. Understanding metaphors. ERIC D 181 426.

Ortony, A., ed. 1979. Metaphor and thought. Cambridge: Cambridge University Press.

Ortony, A., D.L. Schallert, R.E. Reynolds, and S.J. Antos. 1978. Interpreting metaphors and idioms: some effects of context on comprehension. ERIC D 157 042.

Otto, Jean. 1982. The new debate in reading. The Reading Teacher 36.1. 14-18.

Palmer, Adrian S. 1976. The use of communication games in the teaching of reading. Reading: insights and approaches, ed. by Edward M. Anthony and Jack C. Richards, 26-36. Singapore: Singapore University Press.

Palmer, Richard E. 1969. Hermeneutics. Evanston: Northwestern University Press.

Palmer, Richard E. 1984. On the transcendability of hermeneutics. Hermeneutics, ed. by Gary Shapiro and Alan Sica, 84-95. Amherst: University of Massachusetts Press.

Palmer, William S. 1981. Reading theories and research: A search for similarities. English Journal 70.8. 63-66.

Pannenberg, Wolfhart. 1967. Hermeneutics and universal history, trans. by Paul J. Achtemeier. History and hermeneutics, ed. by Robert W. Funk, 122-152. New York: Harper and Row, Publishers, Inc.

Parekh, Bhikhu. 1982. Marx's theory of ideology. Baltimore: The John Hopkins University Press.

Pearson, David P. 1976. A psycholinguistic model of reading. Language Arts 53.3. 309-314.

Pearson, David P. and Dale D. Johnson. 1978. Teaching reading comprehension. New York: Holt, Rinehart and Winston.

Pearson, P.D. J. Hansen, C. Gordon. 1979. The effect of background knowledge on young children's comprehension of explicit and implicit information. ERIC D 169 521.

Pearson, P.D., and M.L. Kamil. 1978. Basic processes and instructional practices in teaching reading. ERIC D 165 118.

Pearson, P.D., T. Raphael, N. TePaske, and C. Hyser. 1979. The function of metaphor in children's recall of expository passages. ERIC D 174 950.

Pellauer, David. 1977. A response to Gary Madison's 'Reflections on Ricoeur's philosophy of metaphor'. Philosophy Today 21. 437-445.

Pellauer, David. 1979. The significance of the text in Ricoeur's hermeneutic theory. Studies in the philosophy of Paul Ricoeur, ed. by C.E. Reagan, 98-114. Athens: Ohio University Press.

Pellauer, David. 1981. Reading Ricoeur reading Job. Semeia 19. 73-83.

Pellegrini, A.D. 1982. The construction of cohesive text by preschoolers in two play contexts. Discourse Processes 5. 101-108.

Perelman, Chaim. 1965. An historical introduction to philosophical thinking, trans. by Kenneth A. Brown. New York: Random House.

Perfetti, C.A. 1976. Language comprehension and fast decoding: Some psycholinguistic prerequisites for skilled reading comprehension. Cognition, curriculum, and comprehension, ed. by J.T. Guthrie, 20-41. Newark, Delaware: International Reading Association.

Perfetti, C.A. and T. Hogaboam. 1975. The relationship between single word decoding and reading comprehension skill. Journal of Educational Psychology 67. 461-469.

Perlmutter, David M. and Carol G. Rosen. 1984. Studies in relational grammar 2. Chicago: University of Chicago Press.

Perlmutter, David M., ed. 1983. Studies in relational grammar 1. Chicago: University of Chicago Press.

Peters, Charles W. 1981. Prose comprehension research. Comprehension and the competent reader, ed. by Denis F. Fisher and Charles W. Peters, 81-106. New York: Praeger Publishers.

Philibert, Michel. 1979. The philosophic method of Paul Ricoeur. Studies in the philosophy of Paul Ricoeur, ed. by C.E. Reagan, 133-139. Athens: Ohio University Press.

Philips, S. 1970. Acquisition of rules for appropriate speech usage. Bilingualism and language contact, ed. by James Altis, 77-95. (Monograph series on language and linguistics 23.) Washington, D.C.: Georgetown University Press.

Pichert, J.W. and R.C. Anderson. 1976. Taking different perspectives on a story. ERIC D 134 936.

Pieper, Josef. 1965. In tune with the world. Chicago: Fransciscan Herald Press.

Pike, Kenneth L. 1982. Linguistic concepts. Lincoln, Nebraska: University of Nebraska Press.

Pitcher, George. 1964. The philosophy of Wittgenstein. Englewood Cliffs, N.J.: Prentice-Hall, Inc.

Platts, Mark de Bretton. 1979. Ways of meaning. London: Routledeg & Kegan Paul.

Polanyi, L. 1982. Literary complexity in everyday storytelling. Spoken and written language: exploring orality and literacy, ed. by D. Tannen, 155-170. (Advances in discourse processes, IX.) Norwood, N.J.: Ablex Publishing Corporation.

Pollard-Gott, L., M. McCloskey, and A. Todres. 1979. Subjective story structures. Discourse processes. 2. 251-281.

Pollio, Howard R., Michael S. Fabrizi, Abigail Sills, and Michael K. Smith. 1984. Need metaphoric comprehension take longer than literal comprehension. Journal of psycholinguistic research 13.2. 195-214.

Popp, Helen M. 1975. Current practices in the teaching of beginning reading. Toward a literate society, ed. John B. Carroll and Jeane S. Chall, 101-146. New York: McGraw-Hill.

Popper, K. 1977. Objective knowledge. (revised ed.) Oxford: Clarendon Press.

Post, David L. 1978. Piaget's theory of play: a review of the critical literature. West Point, N.Y.: Leisure Press, 36-41.

Postal, Paul M. 1968. Aspects of phonological theory. New York: Harper & Row.

Poulet, Georges. 1959. The interior distance, trans. by E. Coleman. Ann Arbor, Michigan: The University of Michigan Press.

Poulet, Georges. 1969. Phenomenology of reading. New Literary History 1. 53-68.

Power, David. 1977. Confession as ongoing conversion. Heythrop Journal 18L 180-190.

Powers, William. 1983. Relationships between reader-response and the research of Kenneth and Yetta Goodman. Reader 10. 28-36.

Poythress, V.S. 1981. Review of Paul Ricoeur: essays on biblical interpretation, ed. by Lewis S. Mudge. Westminster Theological Journal 2. 378-380.

Poythress, V.S. 1982. Hierarchy in discourse analysis: a revision of tagmemics. Semiotica 40.1/2. 107-137.

Pratt, Mary Louise. 1977. Toward a speech act theory of literary discourse. Bloomington, Ind.: Indiana University Press.

Prawat, Richard S. 1982. Relations between semantic memory and reading. Advancess in reading/language research, ed. by Barbara A. Hutson, 51-81. (Vol. 1) Greenwich, Conn.: Jai Press Inc.

Price, Richard and Sally Price. 1976. Secret play languages in Saramaka: linguistic disguise in a Caribbean Creole. Speech play, ed. Barbara Kirshenblatt-Gimblett, 37-50. Philadelphia: University of Pennsylvania Press.

Putnam, H. 1978. Meaning, reference and stereotypes. Meaning and translation, ed. by F. Guenthuer and M. Guenther-Reutter, 61-81. New York: New York University Press.

Quine, W.V.O. 1969. Ontological relativity and other essays. New York: Columbia University Press.

Raban, Bridie. 1982. Written language communities: writing in the context of reading. ERIC D 232 159.

Rader, M. 1982. Context in written language: the case of imaginative fiction. Spoken and written language: exploring orality and literacy, ed. by D. Tannen, 185-198. (Advances in discourse processes, IX.) Norwood, N.J.: Ablex Publishing Corporation.

Rahnema, Majid. 1974. Foreword. Literacy Discussion i-vii.

Rahner, Hugo. 1967. Man at play. New York: Herder and Herder.

Rasmussen, David M. 1971. Mythic-symbolic language and philosophical anthropology: a constructive interpretative of the thought of Paul Ricoeur. The Hague: Nijhoff.

Rasmussen, David M. 1975. The symbolism of Marx: from alienation to fetishism. Cultural Hermeneutics 3. 41-55.

Ravaux, Francoise. 1979. The return of the reader. French Review 52.5. 708-713.

Reagan, Charles E. 1968. Ricoeur's diagnostic relation. International Philosophical Quarterly 8. 586-592.

Reagan, Charles E. 1979. Psychoanalysis as hermeneutics. Studies in the philosophy of Paul Ricoeur, ed. by C.E. Reagan, 142-161. Athens: Ohio University Press.

Redeker, Gisela. 1984. On differences between spoken and written language. Discourse Processes 7. 43-55.

Reeder, Harry P. 1978. Cogito, ergo sum: inference or performance. Eidos 1.1. 30-49.

Reeder, Harry P. 1980a. 'Dialectic' and 'grounding' in Ricoeur's hermeneutic phenomenology of language: with application to the Popper-Kuhn debate. Unpublished Ms.

Reeder, Harry P. 1980b. Husserl and Wittgenstein on the "Mental picture theory of meaning". Human studies 3. 157-167.

Reeder, Harry P. 1984a. A phenomenological account of the linguistic mediation of the public and the private. Husserl Studies 1.3. 263-280.

Reeder, Harry P. 1984b. Language and experience: descriptions of living language in Husserl and Wittgenstein. Washington, D.C.: Center for Advanced Research in Phenomenology and University Press of America, Inc.

Reeder, Harry. n.d. Practical phenomenology: introductory lectures in the theory and methodd of Husserl's phenomenology. Unpublished Ms. (Forthcoming as The theory and method of Husserl's phenomenology, Washington, D.C.: University Press of America).

Reimer, Becky L. 1983. Recipes for language experience stories. The Reading Teacher 36.4. 396-401.

Remy, Jean. 1980. Work and self-awareness. Work and religion, ed. by Gregory Baum, 3-11. New York: The Seabury Press.

Resnick, L.B. 1977. Theory and practice in beginning reading instruction. ERIC D 149 292.

Resnick, L.B. 1978. Theory and practice in beginning reading instruction. Pittsburg: University of Pittsburgh, Learning Research and Development Center (LRDC Publication 1978/15).

368

Resnick, L.B. and P.A. Weaver, ed. 1979. Theory and practice of early reading. (3 Vols.) Hillsdale, N.J.: Lawrence Erlbaum Associates.

Reynolds, R.E. M.A. Taylor, M.S. Steffensen, L.L. Shirey, and R. C. Anderson. 1981. Cultural schemata and reading comprehension. ERIC D 201 991.

Ricoeur, Paul. 1965. Fallible man, trans. by C. Kelbley. Chicago: Henry Regnery Company.

Ricoeur, Paul. 1966. Freedom and nature, trans. by E.V. Kohak. Evanston: Northwestern University Press.

Ricoeur, Paul. 1967a. Husserl: an analysis of his phenomenology. Evanston: Northwestern University Press.

Ricoeur, Paul. 1967b. The symbolism of evil. Boston: Beacon Press.

Ricoeur, Paul. 1969. The religious significance of atheism. New York: Columbia University Press.

Ricoeur, Paul. 1970. Freud and philosophy, trans. by D. Savage. New Haven: Yale University Press.

Ricoeur, Paul. 1973. Ethics and culture: Habermas and Gadamer in dialogue. Philosophy Today 17. 153-165.

Ricoeur, Paul. 1974. The conflict of interpretations. Evanston: Northwestern University Press.

Ricoeur, Paul. 1975a. The rule of metaphor, trans. by R. Czerny. Toronto: University of Toronto Press.

Ricoeur, Paul. 1975b. Biblical hermeneutics. Semeia 4. 29-148.

Ricoeur, Paul. 1975c. Philosophical hermeneutics and theological hermeneutics. Studies in Religion/Sciences Religieuses 1. 14-33.

Ricoeur, Paul. 1976. Interpretation theory. Fort Worth: The Texas Christian University Press.

Ricoeur, Paul. 1978a. The philosophy of Paul Ricoeur, ed. by C.E. Reagan and David Stewart. Boston: Beacon Press.

Ricoeur, Paul. 1978b. The metaphorical process as cognition, imagination, and feeling. On metaphor, ed. by Sheldon Sacks. Chicago: University of Chicago Press.

Ricoeur, Paul. 1978c. Imagination in discourse and action. The human being in action, ed. by A.T. Tymieniecka. Boston: Reidel.

Ricoeur, Paul. 1980a. Essays on biblical interpretation, ed. by Lewis S. Mudge. Philadelphia: Fortress Press.

Ricoeur, Paul. 1980b. Narrative Time. On narrative, ed. by W.J. Mitchell. Chicago: University of Chicago Press.

Ricoeur, Paul. 1981a. Hermeneutics and the human sciences, trans. and ed. by John B. Thompson. Cambridge: Cambridge University Press.

Ricoeur, Paul. 1981b. The Bible and the imagination. The Bible as a document of the university, ed. by Hans D. Betz. Ann Arbor: Scholars Press.

Ricoeur, Paul. 1984a. Time and narrative. Vol. I. Chicago: The University of Chicago Press.

Ricoeur, Paul. 1984b. The reality of the historical past. Milwaukee: Marquette University Press.

Rosenblatt, L.M. 1978. The reader, the text, the poem. Carbondale: Southern Illinois University Press.

Rosenblatt, L.M. 1964. The poem as event. College English 26. 123-128.

Rosenshine, Barak V. 1980. Skill hierarchies in reading comprehension. Theoretical issues in reading comprehension: perspectives from cognitive psychology, linguistics, artificial intelligence, and education, ed. by Rand J. Spiro, Bertram C. Bruce, and William F. Brewer, 535-554. Hillsdale, N.J.: Lawrence Erlbaum Associates.

Rothkopf, Ernest Z. 1977. Comments on chapter 3 by Olson. Schooling and the acquisition of knowledge, ed. by R.C. Anderson, R.J. Spiro, and W.E. Montague, 91-93. Hillsdale, N.J.: Lawrence Erlbaum Associates, Inc.

Royer, James M. and Donald J. Cunningham. 1981. On the theory and measurement of reading comprehension. Contemporary educational psychology 6.3. 187-216.

Rubin, A. 1980. A theoretical taxonomy of the differences between oral and written language. Theoretical issues in reading comprehension: perspectives from cognitive psychology, linguistics, artificial intelligence, and education, ed. by Rand J. Spiro, Bertram C. Bruce, and William F. Brewer, 411-438. Hillsdale, N.J.: Lawrence Erlbaum Associates.

Rubin, A. 1980. Making stories, making sense. ERIC D 181 432.

Rubin, Joan and Bjorn Jernudd. Introduction. Can language be planned?, ed. by Joan Rubin and Bjorn Jernudd, xiii-xx. Hawaii: University Press of Hawaii.

Rumelhart, D.E. 1975. Notes on a schema for stories. Representations and understanding: studies in cognitive science, ed. by D.G. Bobrow and A.M. Collins, 211-236. New York: Academic Press.

Rumelhart, D.E. 1977a. Toward an interactive model of reading. Attention and performance VI, ed. by S. Dornic. Hillsdale, N.J.: Lawrence Erlbaum Associates.

Rumelhart, D.E. 1977b. Understanding and summarizing brief stories. Basic processes in reading: perception and comprehension, ed. by David LaBerge and S. Jay Samuels, 265-303. Hillsdale, N.J.: Lawrence Erlbaum Associates.

Rumelhart, D.E. 1980. Schemata: The building blocks of cognition. Theoretical issues in reading comprehension: perspectives from cognitive psychology, linguistics, artificial intelligence, and education, ed. by Rand J. Spiro, Bertram C. Bruce, and William F. Brewer, 33-58. Hillsdale, N.J.: Lawrence Erlbaum Associates.

Rumelhart, D.E. and A. Ortony. 1977. The representation of knowledge in memory. Schooling and the acquisition of kwowledge, ed. by R.C. Anderson, R.J. Spiro, and W.E. Montague, 99-135. Hillsdale, N.J.: Lawrence Erlbaum.

Rumelhart, D.E. and J.A. Levin. 1975. A language comprehension system. Explorations in cognition, ed. by D.A. Norman, D.E. Rumelhart and the LNR research group. San Francisco: Freeman.

Russell, Bertrand. 1948. Human knowledge: its scope and limitations. New York: Simon and Schuster.

Rystrom, Richard. 1977. Reflections of meaning. Journal of Reading Behavior 9.2. 193-200.

Sacks, Sheldon. 1979. On metaphor. Chicago: University of Chicago Press.

Sadler, William A. 1969. Creative existence: play as a pathway to personal freedom and community. Humanitas 5.57-79.

Said, Edward W. 1979. The text, the world, the critic. Textual strategies, ed. by Josue V. Harari, 161-188. Ithaca, NY: Cornell University Press.

Salter, Michael A. 1978. Play, anthropological perspectives. West Point, N.Y.: Leisure Press.

Sayers, Keith. 1976. Marketing. Read 8.2. 5-9.

Schaefer, N. 1977. The use of recorded text material for stories in Frafra primer construction. Notes on literacy 21. 1-5.

Schaldenbrand, Mary. 1979. Metaphoric imagination. Studies in the philosophy of Paul Ricoeur, ed. by C.E. Reagan, 58-81. Athens: Ohio University Press.

Schall, James. 1976. Far too easily pleased. A theology of play, contemplation, and festivity. Beverly Hill, CA.: Benziger.

Schallert, D.L. 1975. Improving memory for prose: the relationship between depth of processing and context. ERIC D 134 929.

Schallert, D.L. 1980. The role of illustrations in reading instruction. Theoretical issues in reading comprehension: perspectives from cognitive psychology, linguistics, artificial intelligence, and education, ed. by Rand J. Spiro, Bertram C. Bruce, and William F. Brewer, 503-524. Hillsdale, N.J.: Lawrence Erlbaum Associates.

Schallert, D.L. 1982. Synthesis of research related to schema theory. Reading expository material, ed. by W. Otto and S. White. New York: Academic Press.

Schallert, D.L. and G.M. Kleiman. 1979. Some reasons why teachers are easier to understand than textbooks. ERIC D 172 189.

Schallert, D.L., G.M. Kleiman, and A.D. Rubin. 1977. Analyses of differences between written and oral language. ERIC D 144 138.

Schmid, Michael. 1981. Habermas's theory of social evolution, trans. by Nicholas Saul. Habermas: critical debates, ed. by John B. Thompson and David Held. London: Macmillan.

Schwartz, R.M. 1976. Strategic processes in beginning reading. ERIC D 134 937.

Schwartz, R.M. 1979. Levels of processing: the strategic demands of reading comprehension. ERIC D 177 471.

Seebohm, Thomas M. 1977. The problem of hermeneutics in recent Anglo-American literature: part II. Philosophical rhetoric 10. 263-275.

Sensat, Julius Jr. 1979. Habermas and Marxism. (Sage library of social research 77) Beverly Hills: Sage Publications.

Seymour, J.M. 1972. Contrasts between formal and informal education among the Iban of Sarawak, Malaysia. Review of Educational Research 24. 477-91.

Shand, Jean. 1970. Couplets in Manabo. Notes on literacy: selected articles, ed. by Margaret Wendell, 32. Dallas: Summer Institute of Linguistics.

Shapiro, Gary and Alan Sica, ed. 1984. Hermeneutics. Amherst: University of Massachusetts Press.

Shapiro, Jeremy J. 1976. The slime of history: embeddedness in nature and critical theory. On critical theory, ed. by John O'Neill, 145-163. New York: The Seabury Press.

Sherzer, Joel. 1976. Play languages: implications for (socio) linguistics. Speech play, ed. Barbara Kirshenblatt-Gimblett, 19-36. Philadelphia: University of Pennsylvania Press.

Shibles, Warren, ed. 1972. Essays on metaphor. Whitewater, Wisconsin: The Language Press.

Shiff, Richard. 1978. Art and life: a metaphoric relationship. On metaphor, ed. by Sheldon Sacks, 105-120. Chicago: University of Chicago Press.

Shor, Ida. 1980. Critical thinking and everyday life. Boston: South End Press.

Siler, E.R. 1974. The effects of syntactic and semantic constraints on the oral reading performance of second and fourth graders. Reading research quarterly 9. 583-602.

Singer, Harry. 1970. Theories, models, and strategies for learning to read. ERIC D 049 006.

Singer, Harry and D. Donlan. 1982. Active-comprehension: problem-solving schema with question generation for comprehension of complex short stories. Reading Research Quarterly 17. 166-186.

Singer, Harry and Robert B. Ruddell, ed. 1976. Theoretic models and processes of reading. Newark, Del.: International Reading Association.

Smith, Eliot R. and Frederick D. Miller. 1980. Schemas in memory? Increasing the usefulness of an unconfirmable hypothesis. ERIC D 194 868.

Smith, Frank. 1975. Comprehension and learning. New York: Holt, Rinehart and Winston.

Smith, Frank. 1976. Learning to read by reading. Language Arts 53.3. 297-299, 322.

Smith, Frank. 1977a. The uses of language. Language Arts 54.6. 638-644.

Smith, Frank. 1977b. Making sense of reading--and of reading instruction. Harvard Educational Review 47.3. 386-395.

Smith, Frank. 1978. Reading without nonsense. New York: Teachers College Press.

Smith, Frank. 1979a. The language arts and the learner's mind. Language Arts 56.2. 118-125, 145.

Smith, Frank. 1979b. Conflicting appoaches to reading research and instruction. Theory and Practice of Early Reading, ed. L.B. Resnick and Phyllis A. Weaver, 31-42. (Vol. 2) Hillsdale, N.J.: Lawrence Erlbaum Associates.

Smith, Frank. 1981. Demonstration, engagement and sensitivity: the choice between people and programs. Language Arts 56.6. 634-642.

Smith, Frank. 1982. Understanding reading, 3rd ed. New York: Holt, Rinehart and Winston.

Smith, Frank. 1983. Essays into literacy. London: Exeter, Heinemann Educational Books.

Smith, Frank and Kenneth S. Goodman. 1971. On the psycholinguistic method of teaching reading. The Elementary School Journal 71.4. 177-181.

Smith, Frank and Deborah Lott Holmes. 1971. The independence of letter, word,and meaning identification in reading. Reading Research Quarterly 6.3. 394-415.

Smith, Norman Kemp. 1923. A commentary to Kant's 'Critique of pure reason,' 2nd edition. London: Macmillan and Co Ltd.

Smith, Roch C. 1982. Gaston Bachelard. Boston: Twayne Publishers.

Smith, William A. n.d. *Conscientizacao* and simulation games. Amherst, Mass.: Center for International Education.

Smith, William A. 1976. The meaning of conscientizacao: the goal of Paulo Freire's pedagogy. Amherst, Mass.: University of Massachuettes Press.

Solomon, Robert C. 1977. Husserl's concept of the noema. Husserl: expositions and appraisals, ed. by Frederick A. Elliston and Peter McCormick, 168-181. Notre Dame: University of Notre Dame Press.

Solomon, Robert C. 1979. Paul Ricoeur on passion and emotion. Studies in the philosophy of Paul Ricoeur, ed. by C.E. Reagan, 2-20. Athens: Ohio University Press.

Sosnoski, James. 1983. The role of selection strategies in literary-critical reading(s). Reader 10. 14-27.

Specht, Ernst Conrad. 1969. The foundations of Wittgenstein's late philosophy, trans. by D.E. Walford. New York: Barnes and Noble, Inc.

Spiegelberg, Herbert. 1965. The phenomenological movement. Vol. I and II. The Hague: Martinus Nijhoff.

Spindler, George D. 1974. Education and cultural process. New York: Holt, Rhinehart and Winston, Inc.

Spiro, R.J. 1979. Prior knowledge and story processing: integration, selection, and variation. ERIC D 176 235.

Spiro, R.J. 1980a. Constructive processes in prose comprehension and recall. Theoretical issues in reading comprehension: perspectives from cognitive psychology, linguistics, artificial intelligence, and education, ed. by Rand J. Spiro, Bertram C. Bruce, and William F. Brewer, 245-278. Hillsdale, N.J.: Lawrence Erlbaum Associates.

Spiro, R.J. 1980b. Schema theory and reading comprehension: new directions. ERIC D 199 661.

Spiro, R.J. and W.C. Tirre. 1979. Individual differences in schema utilization during discourse processing. ERIC D 166 651.

Spiro, Rand J., Bertram C. Bruce, and William F. Brewer, eds. 1980. Theoretical issues in reading comprehension: perspectives from cognitive psychology, linguistics, artificial intelligence, and education. Hillsdale, N.J.: Lawrence Erlbaum Associates.

Srinivasachari, G. 1969. Selection of words and structures for readers. Reading: a human right and a human problem, ed. Ralph C. Staiger and Oliver Andresen, 80-86. Newark, Delaware: International Reading Association.

Stanley, Manfred. 1972. Literacy: the crisis of the conventional wisdom. School Review 373-408.

Stauffler, Russell G. 1969. Teaching reading as a thinking process. New York: Harper & Row, Publishers.

Stauffler, Russell G. 1981. The language experience approach to the teaching of reading. New York: Harper & Row, Publishers.

Steffensen, M.S., C. Jogdeo, and R.C. Anderson. 1978. A cross-cultural perspective on reading comprehension. ERIC D 159 660.

Stein, N.L. 1978. How children understand stories: a developmental analysis. ERIC D 153 205.

Stein, N.L. 1982. What's in a story: interpreting the interpretations of story grammars. Discourse Processes 5. 319-335.

Stein, N.L., M. Policastro. 1984. The concept of a story: a comparison between children's and teacher's viewpoint. Learning and comprehension of text, ed. by H. Mandl, N.L. Stein and T. Trabasso, 113-155. Hillsdale, N.J.: Lawrence Erlbaum Associates.

Steinberg, C. and B.C. Bruce. 1980. Higher-level features in children's stories: rhetorical structure and conflict. ERIC D 198 474.

Steward, David and Algis Mickunas. 1974. Exploring phenomenology. Chicago: American Library Association.

Stewart, David. 1968. Paul Ricoeur and the phenomenological movement. Philosophy Today 12. 227-235.

Sticht, T.G., L. Beck, R. Hanke, G. Kleiman, J. James. 1974. Auding and reading: A developmental model. Alexandria, Virginia: Human Resources Research Organization.

Sticht, T.G., L.J. Beck, R.N. Hanke, G.M. Kleiman, and J.H. James. 1974. Auding and reading: a developmental model. Alexandria, Va.: Human Resources Research Organization.

Stierle, Karlheinz. 1980. The reading of fictional texts. The reader in the text, ed. by Susan R. Suleiman and Inge Crosman, 83-105. Princeton, N.J.: Princeton University Press.

Strawson, P.F. 1966a. The bounds of sense. London: Methuen and Co. LTD.

Strawson, P.F. 1966b. Review of Wittgenstein's Philosophical Investigation, ed. by George Pitcher, 22-64. Garden City, N.Y.: Doubleday and Company,Inc.

Suleiman, Susan R. 1980. Introduction: varieties of audience-oriented criticism. The reader in the text, ed. by Susan R. Suleiman and Inge Crosman, 3-45. Princeton, N.J.: Princeton University Press.

Summers, Edward G. 1979. Toward a research definition of reading. ERIC D 047 902.

Tannen, D. 1978. A cross-cultural study of oral/literate narrative style. Berkeley Linguistic Studies 4. 640-650.

Tannen, D. 1980. Spoken/written language and the oral/literate continuum. Proceedings of the sixth annual meeting of the Berkeley Linguistic Society.

Tannen, D. 1982. The myth of orality and literacy. Linguistics and Literacy, ed. by William Frawley, 37-50. New York: Plenum Press.

Tannen, D. 1982a. Oral and literate strategies in spoken and written discourse. Language 58. 1-21.

Tannen, D. 1982b. The oral/literate continuum in discourse. Spoken and written language: exploring orality and literacy, ed. by D. Tannen, 1-16. (Advances in discourse processes, IX.) Norwood, N.J.: Ablex Publishing Corporation.

Tannen, D. 1982c. Spoken and written language: exploring orality and literacy. (Advances in discourse processes, IX.) Norwood, N.J.: Ablex Publishing Corporation.

Taylor, M. and A. Ortony. 1981. Figurative devices in black language: some socio-psycholinguistic observations. ERIC D 201 989.

The national institute of education. n.d. How to use ERIC. Washington, D.C.: U.S. Department of Health, Education and Welfare.

Thevenaz, Pierre. 1962. What is phenomenology? Chicago: Quadrangle Books, Inc.

Thieman, T.J. and A.L. Brown. 1977. The effects of semantic and formal similarity on recognition memory for sentences in children. ERIC D 150 551.

Thilly, Frank. 1914. A history of philosophy. New York: Henry Holt and Company.

Thom, Rene. 1980. At the boundaries of man's power: play. Sub-Stance 25. 11-20.

Thompson, John B. 1981. Critical hermeneutics. Cambridge: Cambridge University Press.

Thompson, John B. and David Held, ed. 1981. Habermas: critical debates. London: Macmillan.

Thompson, John B. and David Held, ed. 1982a. Habermas: Critical debates. Cambridge, Mass.: The MIT Press.

Thompson, John B. and David Held. 1982b. Editor's introduction. In Thompson and Held, 1982a. 1-20.

Thralls, Charlotte. 1981. Internal and external evaluation in literary narrative. ERIC D 217 370.

Tierney, R.J. and J. Mosenthal. 1980. Discourse comprehension and production: analyzing text structure and cohesion. ERIC D 179 945.

Tierney, R.J. and P.D. Pearson. 1981. Learning to learn from text: a framework for improving classroom practice. ERIC D 205 917.

Tierney, R.J., J. Mosenthal, and R.N. Kantor. 1980. Some classroom applications of text analysis: toward improving text selection and use. ERIC D 192 251.

Tirre, W.C., L. Manelis, and K.L. Leicht. 1978. The effects of imaginal and verbal strategies on prose comprehension in adults. ERIC D 165 116.

Todorov, Tzvetan. 1980. Reading as construction. The reader in the text, ed. by Susan R. Suleiman and Inge Crosman, 67-82. Princeton, N.J.: Princeton University Press.

Tompkins, Gail E. and MaryBeth Webeler. 1983. What will happen next? Using predictable books with young children. The Reading Teacher 36.6. 498-502.

Tompkins, Jane P, ed. 1980. Reader-response criticism. Baltimore: The John Hopkins University Press.

Tough, Jean. 1983. Learning to represent meaning. Advances in reading/language research, ed. by Barbara A. Hutson, 55-81. (Vol. 2) Greenwich, Conn.: Jai Press Inc.

Trabasso, T. 1980. On the making of inferences during reading and their assessment. ERIC D 181 429.

Trabasso, T., T. Secco, P. VanDen Broek. 1984. Causal cohesion and story coherence.Learning and comprehension of text, ed. by H. Mandl, N.L. Stein and T. Trabasso, 83-111. Hillsdale, N.J.: Lawrence Erlbaum Associates.

Tracy, David. 1978. Metaphor and religion: the test case of christian texts. On metaphor, ed. by Sheldon Sacks, 89-104. Chicago: University of Chicago Press.

Trevor, Ruth. 1969. An eclectic approach to beginning reading. Reading: a human right and a human problem, ed. Ralph C. Staiger and Oliver Andresen, 34-38. Newark, Delaware: International Reading Association.

Tucker, Robert C., ed. 1978. A Marx-Engels Reader, 2nd ed. New York: W.W. Norton & Co.

Tuinman, J. Jaap. 1980. The schema schemers. Journal of Reading 23.5. 414-419.

Ullmann, Stephen. 1962. Semantics: an introduction to the science of meaning. New York: Barnes & Noble.

Vacca, Richard T. and JoAnne L. Vacca. 1983. Re-examining research on reading comprehension in content areas. Advances in reading/language research, ed. by Barbara A. Hutson, 83-106. (Vol. 2) Greenwich, Conn.: Jai Press Inc.

Van der Hoeven, Johan. 1976. Karl Marx. Amsterdam: Van Gorcum, Assen.

Van Den Hengel, John W. 1982. The home of meaning: the hermeneutics of the subject of Paul Ricoeur. Washington, D.C.: University Press of America, Inc.

Van Dijk, Teun. 1981. Semantic macro-structures and knowledge frames in discourse comprehension. Text 1. 3-32.

Van Dijk, Teun and Janos S. Petofi, ed. 1982. Text 2.

Van Peurson, Cornelius. 1977. The horizon. Husserl: expositions and appraisals, ed. by Frederick A. Elliston and Peter McCormick, 182-201. Notre Dame: University of Notre Dame Press.

Van Til, Cornelius. 1969. A survey of Christian epistemology. n.p.: den Dulk Christian Foundation.

Van Til, Cornelius. 1974. An introduction to systematic theology. Philadelphia: Presbyterian and Reformed Publishing Co.

Van Til, Cornelius. 1975. The defense of the faith. Philadelphia: Presbyterian and Reformed Publishing Co.

Van Til, Cornelius. 1977. A Christian theory of knowledge. Nutley, N.J.: Presbyterian and Reformed Publishing Co.

Vansina, Frans. 1979. Bibliography of Paul Ricoeur. Studies in the philosophy of Paul Ricoeur, ed. by C.E. Reagan, 180-194. Athens: Ohio University Press.

Vaughan, Samuel S. 1983. The community of the book. Daedalus 112.1. 85-115.

Vincent, Gilbert. 1977. Paul Ricoeur's 'Living metaphor'. Philosophy Today 21. 412-423.

Vogel, Dan. 1981. The fancy and the imagination and the teaching of literature. Journal of Aesthetic Education 15.1. 5-15.

Wallace, Stephen. 1982. Figure and ground: the interrelationships of linguistic categories. Tense-aspect: between semantics and pragmatics, ed. by Paul J. Hopper, 201-223. Philadelphia: Benjamins Publishing Co.

Walliman, Isidor. 1981. Estrangement. Westport, Conn.: Greenwood Press.

Walrod, Michael Ross. 1983. Philosophy of normative discourse and persuasion: a study of Ga'dang exhortation and argumentation. Unpublished PhD. dissertation.

Walwork, J.F. 1978. Language and people. London: Heinemann Educational Books.

Waterhouse, Roger. 1981. A Heidegger critique. New Jersey: Humanities Press.

Weaver, Constance. 1980. Psycholinguistics and reading. Cambridge, Mass.: Winthrop Publishers, Inc.

Weber, R.M. 1970. First graders' use of grammatical context in reading. Basic studies on reading, ed. by H. Levin and J.P. Williams, 147-163. New York: Basic Books.

Weber, Shierry M. 1976. Aesthetic experience and self-reflection as emancipator process. On critical theory, ed. by John O'Neill, 78-103. New York: The Seabury Press.

Weimer, W.B. and D.S. Palermo, eds. 1974. Cognition and symbolic processes. Hillsdale, N.J.: Lawrence Erlbaum Associates.

Weimer, Walter. 1979. Notes on the methodology of scientific research. Hillsdale, N.J.: Erlbaum Associates.

Weir, Ruth and Richard Venezky. 1968. English orthography: more reason than rhyme. The psycholinguistic nature of the reading process, ed. by K.S. Goodman, 187-199. Detroit: Wayne State University Press.

Weiss, Paul. 1969. Sport, a philosophic inquiry. Carbondale, Ill.: Southern Illinois University Press.

Wellmer, Albrecht. 1976. Communication and emancipation: reflections on the linguistic turn in critical theory. On critical theory, ed. by John O'Neill, 231-263. New York: The Seabury Press.

Wendell, Margaret M. 1972. Informal literacy survey. Novalit 1-2.

Wendell, Margaret M. 1974. A literature workshop, part II. Notes on Literacy 17. 6-16.

Wendell, Margaret M. 1982. Bootstrap literature: preliterate societies do it themselves. Newark, Del.: International Reading Association.

Wendell, Margaret M., compiler. 1979. Notes on literacy, selected articles, issues 1-19. Dallas: Summer Institute of Linguistics.

Westermann, Claus. 1980. Work, civilization and culture in the Bible. Work and religion, ed. by Gregory Baum, 81-91. New York: The Seabury Press.

White, Hayden. 1978. Tropics of discouse: essays in cultural criticism. Baltimore: The Johns Hopkins University Press.

White, Stephen K. 1983. Habermas on the foundations of ethics and political theory. Changing social science: critical theory and other critical perspectives, ed. by Daniel R. Sabia, Jr. and Jerald Wallulis, 157-170. Albany, N.Y.: State University of New York Press.

Whyte, Jean. 1983. Metaphor interpretation and reading ability in adults. Journal of psycholinguistic research 12.5. 457-465.

Wild, John. 1962. Preface. What is phenomenology?, by Pierre Thevenaz, 7-9. Chicago: Quadrangle Books, Inc.

Wildman, Daniel M. and Martin Kling. 1978. Semantic, syntactic, and spatial anticipation in reading. Reading Research Quarterly 14.2. 128-164.

Willard, Dallas. 1977. The paradox of logical psychologism. Husserl: expositions and appraisals, ed. by Frederick A. Elliston and Peter McCormick, 10-17. Notre Dame: University of Notre Dame Press.

Williams, Bernard. 1967. Rationalism. The encyclopedia of philosophy, Vol. 7, ed. by Paul Edwards, 69-75. New York: Collier Macmillan Publishers.

Williams, J. 1978 (August). Has the psychology of reading helped the teaching of reading? Paper presented at the meeting of the American Psychology Association. Toronto.

Wilson, Cathy Roller. 1983. Teaching reading comprehension by connecting the known to the new. The Reading Teacher 36.4. 382-390.

Wilson, Lionel. 1981. The reader's contribution in the literary experience: Interview with Louis Rosenblatt. English Quarterly 14.1. 3-12.

Winograd, Terry. 1977. A framework for understanding discourse. Cognitive processes in comprehension, ed. by Marcel Adam Just and Patricia A. Carpenter, 63-88. Hillsdale, N.J.: Lawrence Erlbaum Associates.

Wittgenstein, Ludwig. 1953. Philosophical investigations, trans. by G.E.M. Anscombe. Oxford: Basil Blackwell.

Wittgenstein, Ludwig. 1961. Tractatus logico-philosophicus, trans. by D.F. Pears and B.F. McGuinness. London: Routledge & Kegan Paul.

Wolff, Robert Paul. 1963. Kant's theory of mental activity. Cambridge: Harvard University Press.

Wood, Karen D. and Nora Robinson. 1983. Vocabulary, language and prediction: a prereadig strategy. The Reading Teacher 36.4. 392-395.

Woods, W.A. 1977. Multiple theory formation in high-level perception. ERIC D 144 020.

Woods, W.A. 1980. Multiple theory formation in speech and reading. Theoretical issues in reading comprehension: perspectives from cognitive psychology, linguistics, artificial intelligence, and education, ed. by Rand J. Spiro, Bertram C. Bruce, and William F. Brewer, 59-82. Hillsdale, N.J.: Lawrence Erlbaum Associates.

Wyer, Robert S. 1977. Attitudes, beliefs, and information acquisition. Schooling and the acquisition of knowledge, ed. by R.C. Anderson, R.J. Spiro, W.E. Montague, 259-288. Hillsdale, N.J.: Lawrence Erlbaum Associates.

Zaner, Richard M. 1979. The adventure of interpretation. Studies in the philosophy of Paul Ricoeur, ed. by C.E. Reagan, 34-56. Athens: Ohio University Press.

Zimet, Sara Goodman. 1983. Teaching children to detect social bias in books. The Reading Teacher 36.4. 418-421.

INDEX

384

Culture 111, 202, 258, 260, 278, 318, 323, 331

Dance 256

Decoding 1, 3-6, 10, 19, 26, 36, 94, 104, 142, 143, 176, 177, 236, 283, 307, 309, 315, 321-324, 329

Deconstruction 237, 263, 287, 299

Dehumanization 202

DeMan 261, 263, 265

Derrida 96, 97, 259, 263-269, 286-288, 295

Descartes 56-60, 178

Detachment 270

Determinacy 138

Dialectic 31, 34, 36, 38, 40, 41, 42, 47, 86, 99, 100, 131, 140, 141, 147, 158, 166, 167, 195, 224, 234-238, 241, 242, 246, 255, 261, 270, 280, 291, 305, 320

Dialogue 31-34, 47, 53, 55, 71, 89-100, 103, 115, 116, 126, 135, 139, 157, 160, 177, 179, 206, 210, 219, 222, 229, 230, 231, 234, 238, 240, 249, 251, 238, 239, 242, 249, 252, 274, 281, 288, 311, 317, 330

Difference 57, 64, 65, 103, 109, 110, 120, 130, 141, 142, 137, 138, 154, 156, 159-161, 168, 170, 179, 185, 194, 154, 155, 160, 165, 166, 167, 168, 169, 174, 180, 182, 186, 191-193, 200, 203, 212, 219-221, 227, 234, 237, 238, 242, 246, 248, 249, 217, 231, 233, 237, 241, 265, 267, 270, 276, 280, 281, 288, 289, 293, 298, 290, 297, 304, 305, 309, 316, 323, 324, 325, 326, 329, 330, 332

Differance 265-269, 287

Dilthey 285

Disclosure 147, 151, 185, 105, 111, 116-122, 126, 128, 142-144, 146, 148

Discourse 3, 29-34, 37-39, 83-100, 155, 177, 178, 190, 224-226, 239, 241, 242, 270, 280, 281, 325, 326

Discovery 61, 165, 209, 312, 313, 322, 323

Dispossession 36, 177, 236

Distance 32, 33, 36, 89, 143-147, 153, 174, 189, 191, 233, 235, 241, 263, 324

Distanciation 32-36, 38, 85, 140, 143-146, 153, 167, 176, 234-236, 241, 242, 248, 255, 270, 277, 307, 330

Distinctive feature 73

Distortion 199, 226, 227-229, 247, 251

Divesting 278

Domination 199, 209, 216, 218, 219, 225, 232, 240, 331

Dufrenne 152, 178

Durkin 1, 28, 75, 317

Dwelling 182-186, 298, 329

Dynamic 33, 147, 149, 172, 190, 262, 272, 276, 327, 328

Eclectic 306, 307, 310, 316, 321

Economic 16, 202, 224, 288, 327

Education 103, 201, 209, 210, 211, 215, 318, 320, 323, 333

Ego 36, 60, 63, 64, 79, 148, 177, 178, 180, 235, 243, 277

387

Foundation 57, 60-64, 107, 125, 161, 171, 173, 220, 221, 227, 230, 234, 258, 296, 297

Frankfurt 220-224

Free play 263, 288

Freedom 84, 99, 111, 213, 231, 237, 245, 246, 248, 249, 251, 264, 289, 290, 292, 318, 331

Freire 186, 197-276, 303-331

Freud 178, 235, 236

Fries 1-7, 68, 69, 104, 197

Fromm 212, 214, 215, 219

Functor 313, 315

Fundamental 65

Fusion 291, 326

Future 15, 199, 203, 207, 213, 221, 244, 245, 250, 252, 265, 318, 331

Gadamer 31, 169-200, 220, 227-235, 238, 240-244, 247, 248, 250, 252, 256-259, 263-266, 269-273, 277, 281, 283, 285, 286, 291, 294, 300, 320, 333

Game 129, 142, 256, 257, 259, 263, 264, 266, 270, 271, 273, 276, 277, 281, 283, 293, 299, 305, 332, 333

Gap 45, 47, 62, 97, 138

Genuine 250, 288

Gestalt 41, 42

God 214, 245, 246, 249, 284, 291, 293, 295, 297-300

Gods 291

Goodman 9, 12, 13, 18-26, 75, 96, 126, 129, 130, 132, 139, 153, 197, 217

Gough 1, 7, 18-20, 104, 105, 110

Grammar 103, 222, 289

Grapheme 305, 321, 323

Gudschinsky 303, 304, 310, 313, 315, 316, 320-330

Habermas 197-199, 211, 220-237, 238, 240-253, 276, 288, 294, 320, 330

Hans 328

Hebrew 245, 248, 295

Hegel 170, 174, 223, 224, 242

Heidegger 62-64, 85, 125, 128, 134, 146, 173, 182-186, 194, 219, 248, 272, 276, 285, 286, 290, 297

Hermeneutical circle 129, 130

Hermeneutics 129, 130, 132, 143, 146-148, 185, 228-234, 235, 238-241, 247, 251, 275, 285, 305, 315, 320, 328

Historical 90, 141, 198, 199, 200, 202, 203, 204, 208, 212, 213, 218, 224, 228, 233, 243, 245, 246

History 55, 76, 79, 96, 121, 144, 160, 171, 199, 200, 207, 209, 212, 213, 214, 218, 244, 245, 252, 285, 287, 290, 292, 114

Hope 72, 125, 168, 198, 204, 248, 252, 284, 318

Horizon 46, 48, 175, 185, 244, 252, 313, 326, 330

Hoy 233, 237

Light 15, 19, 45, 60, 74, 93, 94, 121, 128, 134, 162, 163, 271, 303, 304, 329

Limit-situation 204, 205, 211, 214, 253, 331

Linear 140, 141, 321

Linearity 143, 145

Literature 1, 18, 24, 40, 43, 91, 103, 108, 133, 135, 144, 167, 261, 325, 326, 331, 333

Lived-world 90

Locke 55

Logic 60, 76, 106, 126, 129, 154, 237, 272, 332

Love 188, 206

Ludus 259, 263, 264

Macro-structure 105, 106, 117-122

Manifestation 137, 173, 174, 210, 249, 256, 259, 273

Marx 178, 197, 198, 201, 202, 211-225, 235, 247, 259, 278-280, 329

Matching 8, 9, 70, 78, 79, 108-112, 159, 160-167, 177, 300

Material, reading 303, 304, 309, 312-315, 320, 323, 325-333

Materialism 216, 220, 223

Matter 6, 10, 14, 41, 51, 69, 73, 84, 90, 95, 104, 106, 110, 128, 133, 138, 141, 142, 151, 165, 167, 168, 187, 197, 210, 212, 217, 235, 260, 276, 279, 284, 285, 304

McCarthy 226, 237

Meaning 1-57, 60-114, 117, 119, 121, 122, 129-166, 170-177, 182, 186, 187, 189, 191, 194, 203, 206, 217, 235-237, 242, 243, 247, 251, 255, 257, 259, 260-276, 277, 279, 280, 282, 283, 285, 289, 291, 292, 295, 299, 304-313, 318-331

Mediate 35, 43, 88, 91, 143, 146, 147, 153, 176, 183, 216, 228, 232, 238, 240, 249, 255, 285

Metacognitive 128

Metamorphosis 252, 257, 263, 277

Metaphor 35, 73, 112-116, 123, 134, 153, 155, 156-173, 186, 188-194, 289, 295, 329

Metaphysics 267, 287

Metaxu 151

Meyer 94-96, 126, 127, 320

Mind 16, 24, 41, 42, 49-56, 59-71, 75, 76, 87, 94, 96, 165, 170, 188, 220, 272, 284, 291, 296, 297, 306

Model 1, 4, 7, 8, 9, 15, 18-31, 36, 39, 40, 53, 56, 58, 70, 73, 79-91, 104, 108, 109, 112, 117, 119, 122, 125, 128, 134, 141, 142, 144, 171, 190, 212, 213, 218, 237, 238, 249, 250, 251, 261, 269, 278, 281, 285, 300, 317, 334

Modification 16, 25, 41, 49, 50, 111, 139, 145, 249, 310, 318, 323, 334

Mohanty 81, 82, 87, 93

Monitor 232

Monitoring 128, 309

Motivation 72, 217, 309, 318, 319, 331

Music 39, 270, 333

Mysterious 105, 258

Mythos 200

Naivete 146

Naming 154, 155, 206, 211, 219

Narcissistic 36, 148, 235, 241

Narrative 122, 241

Negation 40, 47, 48, 49, 139, 144, 153, 154, 169, 170

Negativity 153, 154, 158, 169, 170, 278

Network 27, 35, 51, 86, 91, 98, 156, 237, 239, 278

New 5, 6, 9, 12, 13, 15, 16, 19, 21, 31, 32, 33, 34, 37, 38, 39, 41, 42, 43, 44, 45, 48, 49, 50, 67, 73, 74, 81, 82, 104, 106-115, 128, 129, 132, 134, 137, 139, 144, 146, 148, 151, 153, 155, 156, 157, 159-174, 177-186, 189, 190, 191, 194, 198, 199, 200, 204, 207, 214-217, 220, 232, 233, 247, 248, 252, 266, 269, 272, 275, 278, 289, 294, 300, 303, 306, 307, 308, 313, 318, 320, 325, 326, 333

Nietzsche 248

Non-ostensive 37, 137

Non-temporal 292

Nongiven 152

Nonsense 20, 269, 271, 305, 323, 324

Nonvisual 9, 13, 57

Norm 13, 21, 27, 42, 48, 55, 139, 227, 237

Norms 45, 153, 170

Noun 84, 154, 155

Object 10, 11, 16-20, 24, 29, 36, 39, 40, 42-53, 56, 59, 60, 61, 63, 64, 71, 72, 74, 77, 79-84, 86, 87, 88, 90, 94, 95, 96, 121, 127, 131, 135, 136, 140, 141, 143, 144, 145, 147, 151, 152, 156, 162, 165, 166, 170, 178, 190, 191, 202, 203, 204, 210, 212, 213, 214, 217, 221, 224, 225, 234, 239, 240, 243, 248, 255, 261, 265, 277, 281, 282, 285, 286, 287, 292, 297, 323, 324, 331, 332

Objectivity 128, 140, 142, 144, 145, 189, 215

Old 7, 42, 49, 110, 126, 139, 144, 151, 153, 161, 163, 167, 168, 169, 186, 191, 198, 200, 215, 217, 220, 232, 263, 266, 269, 280, 294

Ong 287

Onto-theological 284

Ontology 65, 99, 125, 126, 130, 132, 137, 246, 248, 260, 286-292, 294-296, 300

Openness 79, 115, 229, 247, 265, 300, 318, 328

Oral 1, 5, 6, 57, 90, 292, 312, 315, 322, 325, 326

Origin 7, 19, 20, 55, 58, 73, 86, 99, 114, 169, 170, 171, 174, 183, 194, 232, 236, 245, 249, 251, 256, 269, 272, 283, 285, 291

Ortony 75, 76, 112, 113, 114, 119, 158, 159, 162, 163, 167, 192

Ostensive 33, 38, 39, 90, 91, 135, 136, 137, 158

Outline 7, 87, 93, 98, 101, 111, 158, 177, 191, 226, 245, 255, 319, 320, 331

393

Self 18, 34, 37, 44, 50, 56, 138, 148, 166, 174, 175, 178, 180, 181, 188, 190, 191, 199, 202, 205, 206, 213, 214, 221, 229, 237, 243, 248, 249, 256, 257, 273, 280, 289, 317, 328

Self-expression 210

Self-understanding 38, 146, 148, 176, 185, 238

Semantics 82, 86, 92, 141, 142, 157, 285, 305

Semiological 35, 39, 261, 267

Semiotics 82, 92, 141, 142, 55, 57, 58, 59, 60, 61, 63, 69, 71, 80, 84-95, 99, 100, 106, 107, 109, 111, 114, 115, 118, 123, 127, 129, 133, 135, 136, 137, 140, 141, 142, 144-147

Sense 35, 38, 86-88, 154-159, 163, 165, 166, 172-174, 177, 190, 235, 236, 240-243, 262, 268-280, 300, 305, 306, 311, 327-329

Senses 55, 56

Serious 20, 70, 103, 120, 143, 257, 258, 263, 264, 267, 273, 318, 325

Sign(s) 3-8, 24, 25, 39, 40, 42-44, 47, 57, 64, 77, 81-84, 92, 93, 95, 104, 108, 112, 118, 119, 121, 122, 130, 133, 137, 141-146, 156, 158, 166, 168, 169, 172, 175, 186, 189, 191, 192, 215, 218, 249, 261, 263, 265, 267, 268, 271, 277, 278, 290, 293, 299, 305-306, 308, 309, 318, 320, 323, 324, 326, 332, 334

Significance 8, 9, 23, 32, 34, 44, 46, 47, 70, 105, 119, 126, 141, 146, 152, 153, 166, 176, 181, 193, 201, 202, 255, 258, 266, 276, 327, 331, 333

Signified 82, 92, 142, 265

Signifier 82, 92, 142

Sketch 13, 38, 65, 99, 101, 152, 157, 175, 194, 201, 246, 247, 249, 292, 294, 305, 306, 328

Slots 27, 28, 75, 76, 78, 109, 111, 118, 122, 160, 162, 164, 165

Smith 9-23, 29, 57, 58, 70-75, 79, 82, 94, 96, 103, 106, 107, 109, 110, 126, 134, 142, 163, 207, 282, 309, 323

Social 3, 45, 104, 109, 111, 202, 203, 207, 211-225, 228-232, 237, 239, 252, 258, 292, 312, 316, 329, 331

Source 1, 15, 17, 25, 29, 55, 71, 72, 73, 151, 156, 166, 171, 172, 173, 206, 227, 258, 266, 287, 289, 306

Spectator 178, 299, 312, 319

Speech act 87, 288

Spiritual 141, 143, 214, 218, 235, 294

Spiro 76, 107, 108, 109, 113, 116, 162, 167, 168, 186-191

Split 174, 190, 191, 273

Spoken 1, 10, 11, 32, 34, 88, 90, 93, 137, 247, 309, 325, 333

Spontaneous 44, 93, 100, 171, 183, 191, 292

Sport 299

Stable 56, 76, 229

Stages 4, 5, 8, 20, 21, 117, 140, 141, 155, 194, 195, 224, 238, 269, 291, 292, 312, 315, 322, 325, 329

Standards 230, 235, 236, 237, 238, 249, 250, 288, 330

Stimulus 198

Stimulus-response 57, 69

Strategies 12, 24, 25, 26, 29, 45, 118, 309, 310, 317, 321, 323

Structuralist 31, 86, 105, 109, 115-117, 121, 126, 127, 129-134, 138, 139, 140-145, 268, 285

Structure 15-17, 27, 35-40, 45, 47, 48, 52, 55, 61, 63, 72-80, 84-87, 92, 94-99, 153, 160, 163, 164-166, 168, 171, 177, 189-194, 222, 235-237, 241, 242, 249, 256, 262, 263-269, 281, 285, 289, 292, 299, 304, 309, 323, 331

Subject 8, 13, 24, 32, 35-53, 56-64, 67, 70, 71, 74-85, 87, 93, 94, 105, 106, 110-112, 120-122, 126-135, 141, 145-148, 151, 158, 165, 166, 171-186, 189-191, 198, 202, 210, 214, 221, 223, 224, 235-248, 256-258, 262, 265, 266, 270-290, 297, 306, 324, 327-329

Substitution 113, 161, 162, 164, 263

Summarize 8, 17, 21, 27, 38, 64, 77, 105, 106, 107, 109, 123, 129, 184, 198, 209, 220, 249, 264, 295, 297, 303, 304, 313, 315

Summary 15, 25, 28, 46, 70, 84, 105, 108, 119, 120, 122, 162, 184, 208, 212, 228, 258, 306, 307, 312

Supra-logical 284

Surplus 90, 137, 289

Suspension 33, 35, 38, 136, 170, 183

Symbol 1, 10, 24, 69, 136, 231, 259, 261, 277

Sympathy 174

Syntax 177, 305

Synthesis 40, 43, 45, 165, 203, 216, 314, 322

System 1-3, 11, 16, 20, 24, 35-39, 47, 56, 57, 72, 82-84, 86, 93, 95, 96, 104, 106, 111, 112, 114, 119, 122, 127, 142, 159, 161, 163, 164, 170, 177, 199, 209, 214, 218, 222, 223, 227, 228, 232, 233, 237, 240, 242, 247, 251, 261, 268, 269, 280, 287, 305, 309, 324

Tacit 72, 231

Tannen 240

Taste 259

Teacher 14, 16, 210, 307, 309, 311, 316, 317, 326

Tension 44, 107, 161, 164, 166, 190, 262

Text 1, 2, 8, 9, 10, 12-49, 52, 56, 57, 62, 64, 68, 70, 72, 74, 76, 78-80, 83, 85-195, 211, 234-252, 255, 261-266, 270-285, 289, 304, 305, 307, 308, 317-319, 324-330

Texture 116, 178, 187-190, 238

Theme 45-48, 112, 135, 137, 156, 202, 204, 205, 227

Theologian 179, 288

Theology 202, 288, 292

Time 3, 7, 12, 13, 14, 18, 19, 24, 25, 40, 42, 43, 50, 51, 60, 67, 83, 84, 89, 100, 110, 111, 117, 125, 129, 131, 133, 134, 155, 157, 158, 165, 170, 203, 210, 217, 226, 241, 257, 258, 281, 284, 288, 291, 292, 294, 295, 300, 313

399